THE
New York Mets
ENCYCLOPEDIA

PETER C. BJARKMAN

Sports Publishing Inc.
Champaign, Illinois

Director of Production: Susan M. McKinney
Senior Project Manager: Jennifer L. Polson
Interior design and layout: Michelle R. Dressen
Dustjacket layout and interior design: Kenneth J. O'Brien

ISBN: 1-58261-035-5

Printed in the United States.

SPORTS PUBLISHING INC.
www.sportspublishinginc.com

Contents

INTRODUCTION

The Miracle Mets

In the last season of the 20th century, the newly minted Arizona Diamondbacks reached baseball's postseason (as National League West Division champs) in only their second season of existence—a record for quick success and unexpected overachievement likely never to be surpassed in baseball's foreseeable future. Arizona's arrival at the top of the pecking order with 103 victories in franchise year two came considerably faster than that of the Florida Marlins (world champions in their fifth season) and the Colorado Rockies (wild-card winners in their third season), other recent expansion clubs boasting high-octane marches to respectability. But such overnight successes in Phoenix, Denver, and Miami cannot justifiably be compared with other baseball achievements during most of the century. The baseball world of the nineties, with its thin talent pools and constant roster shifts, is not measurable against a baseball scene that existed before free agency and rampant franchise expansion changed everything and tarnished many of the game's cherished milestones and traditional modes of operation. New York's beloved Mets—born during the first wave of league expansion in the early 1960s—were, for an earlier and far more stable baseball universe, unchallenged as the sport's greatest-ever expansion success story. And by all reasonable measures, they still remain so.

The New York Mets still provide one of baseball's most glamorous sagas of the modern era. In an age when dynasties such as the National League Pirates, Cardinals, and Reds and the American League Oakland A's and Baltimore Orioles still reigned supreme season after season, the lowly New Yorkers lost 100 or more and lived in the league basement for five of their first six seasons, then shocked the baseball world with nearly a 30-game turnaround and subsequent "miracle" championship in their eighth season of existence. It was an unprecedented feat at the time, and remains one of the game's most remarkable rags-to-riches stories. The Mets, who launched their existence as one of America's most consistent losers, were, at the same time, also lovable. This was especially true even before the dual "miracles" of 1969 and 1973, when New York's cherished team twice, unpredictably, sprang to the World Series in a seeming flash of the eye.

Some of baseball's most legendary moments of the past half century belong to New York's 39-year-old National League ball club. There are still no more lovable losers found anywhere in the game's annals than the players on the original Mets' team of 1962, when expansion first came to the senior circuit and left New Yorkers with a bungling, ragtag outfit that set countless new standards for epic losing and inept performance. The "miracle" pennant and world title of 1969 remains yet today the national pastime's most memorable tale of altogether unlikely success. And there are other matching tales through the years that also sound a memorable nostalgic note. There is manager Casey Stengel's stoic tomfoolery, which made an entertaining circus of daily losing. There was the dramatic rebuilding of Mets fortunes in the wake of the tragic death of original miracle worker Gil Hodges. There were the glorious half a dozen seasons of the mid-eighties that witnessed the record winning of manager Davey Johnson and the meteoric rise of pitching

phenom Dwight Gooden. And there has been the recent resurgence to prominence under manager Bobby Valentine, spiced by one of baseball's most fearsome modern-day lineups and by the short tenure of perhaps the best defensive infield in modern baseball history.

The Mets also hold their own for colorful and legendary ballplayers and managers. Tom Seaver was the first true franchise star and easily one of the most dominant pitchers of the past quarter century. Casey Stengel has no parallel in the lineage that stretches from John McGraw and Connie Mack to Sparky Anderson and Tony La Russa when it comes to baseball's most enigmatic and beloved Hall of Fame managers. Gil Hodges was one of the most idolized ballplayers in New York City in the decade before the Mets were born (the decade that also featured Mantle and Snider and Mays) and then won countless new hearts as a dedicated manager who worked true early-expansion miracles. Marvelous Marv Throneberry earned more lasting notoriety in a shorter time span and for fewer on-field accomplishments than perhaps any figure in the history of the national pastime. Slow-footed slugger Rusty Staub was a workingman's franchise hero of a most unpredictable cut when it comes to ballplaying legends. Flaky southpaw Tug McGraw not only keyed a World Series drive but coined the memorable phrases that captured an entire giddy era of New York Mets history. Dwight "Doc" Gooden was perhaps not only the most memorable tragic hero of Mets annals, but also one of the biggest talent-laced phenoms and simultaneously one of the biggest washouts of the last few decades. And in the present epoch, there is also the incomparable Mike Piazza, a big-muscled slugger who continues to thrill today's Shea Stadium partisans while on his personal road to glory as baseball's all-time best-hitting catcher.

The following pages recount the full saga of the always lovable, sometimes laughable, and often glamorous New York Mets. *The New York Mets Encyclopedia* provides the complete and exciting account of modern baseball's most popular expansion franchise. From those lovable basement-dwelling losers of 1962 and 1963 to the champion Miracle Mets of 1969 and 1973 to the year-in and year-out contenders of the 1980s and 1990s, New York's National League Mets have written some of the most exciting and colorful pages in modern major league his-

tory. This is the team that captured the hearts of New Yorkers and ball fans everywhere with their well-documented high jinks under double-talking manager Casey Stengel, then only half a dozen years later climbed straight to baseball's pinnacle under gifted yet ill-fated manager Gil Hodges. The irrepressible Stengel provided the necessary first doses of notoriety. Utility infielder Don Zimmer was the first of many to note that perhaps nobody would have paid the least notice to the earliest editions of the Mets if it had not been for the pranksterish Stengel. Hodges was responsible for the sudden dose of nobility, which soon descended upon baseball's most surprising rags-to-riches winners.

This is also the franchise that has been home to many of the game's biggest and most controversial on-field stars and celebrities of the past quarter century. Among them are such unforgettable diamond characters as self-destructive man-child Dwight Gooden; moody mound wizard David Cone, reckless renegade slugger Darryl Strawberry; limelight-loving, heavy-artillery backstop Gary Carter; gritty and determined outfielder Lenny "Nails" Dykstra; glue-fingered first sacker Keith Hernandez; and baseball's most recent high-salaried superstar, all-world catcher Mike Piazza.

Designed to overhaul and supplant all previous Mets histories, this colorful volume combines detailed and highly readable narrative history with archival photographs, rich statistical data, and intimate portraits of all the team's most memorable on-field and off-field personalities. A fast-paced opening chapter records events of the exciting 1998 and 1999 rebuilding seasons, turning-point years that brought homerun mania to big-league fans everywhere and also brought Mike Piazza, Robin Ventura, and Rickey Henderson to Shea Stadium. The events of those few upbeat and successful campaigns are painted as a vital bridge between a glorious franchise past and a hopeful franchise future poised at the threshold of a new baseball century. The full scope of the Mets' 39-season history is presented with a detailed historical overview (Chapter 2) that features a year-by-year Mets chronology and season-by-season opening-day lineups. Also provided in additional chapters are profiles of all 16 Mets field managers (Chapter 7); personal portraits (Chapter 8) of two dozen front-office personalities and beloved TV and radio broadcasters (including Ralph Kiner, Lindsey Nelson, Tim McCarver, and Bob Murphy); nostalgic looks back at unforgettable franchise moments (Chapter 4); reviews of the dozen most memorable Mets seasons (Chapter 5); and complete postseason summaries and highlights (Chapter 6). In short, this is the complete story of one of baseball's most intriguing franchises.

This book also includes capsule biographies (Chapter 3) of 100 of the top Mets players, including the 25 most memorable stars and important role players from each of the team's first four decades. Highlighted are the New York careers of notables and unforgettables such as "Marvelous Marv" Throneberry, Tom Seaver, Jerry Koosman, Al Jackson, Willie Mays, Ed Kranepool, Richie Ashburn, Duke Snider, Roger Craig, Tug McGraw, Dave Kingman, Tommie Agee, Rusty Staub, Keith Hernandez, Dwight Gooden, Gary Carter, Darryl Strawberry, Lee Mazzilli, Howard Johnson, Lenny Dykstra, David Cone, Eddie Murray, Bret Saberhagen, John Franco, John Olerud, Edgardo Alfonzo, Mike Piazza, Al Leiter, and many more who wore the blue and orange for productive full careers or perhaps only for a mere handful of swan-song seasons.

In addition to its eight narrative chapters, *The New York Mets Encyclopedia* contains a complete statistical records section, featuring career stats for all past and present Mets players, as well as all-time team and individual season and career records, plus season-by-season capsule summaries of all 39 Mets campaigns. The book thus provides a comprehensive guide to the detailed numerology that underpins the constantly evolving story of New York Mets baseball. It is hoped that this volume will hold nostalgic appeal for every Mets fan, whether his or her own attachment to the hometown team grows from the unmatched and heart-stopping miracles of the late sixties and early seventies; the heroics of Gooden, Carter, Hernandez, and Strawberry in the eighties; or the performance of the current Mets stars of the thrill-packed nineties.

As has so often been repeated in the prefatory notes of gracious authors, all books are to some extent a cooperative team effort involving many unseen collaborators, and this one is no exception to the rule. My deepest debt is to Claudia Mitroi, my editor at Sports Publishing Inc., who worked diligently to make this volume a better product. My heartfelt thanks goes to Claudia, who is responsible for the photographic record of Mets history presented here; it was she who compiled, selected, and arranged the photos that provide an important facet of this team history. Also, I am indebted to Mike Pearson, vice president of acquisitions at SPI, for standing behind the book from beginning to end. And I owe special thanks also to Mets assistant general manager and international scouting director Omar Minaya and to Mets media relations director Jay Horwitz. Jay graciously made important access to Shea Stadium and the Port St. Lucie spring training facility a possibility over the past several years. And Omar has remained not only my most vital link with the New York Mets' baseball operations, but also a valued friend and one of my most respected associates in the world of professional baseball. Finally, the usual tip of the cap to my life's partner, Ronnie Wilbur, who stood in the home dugout and cheered.

The 2000 Subway Series Season

The first season of a new millennium—the 39th of New York Mets history—was from the opening pitch a rare odyssey that opened thousands of miles from any normal major league venue and was destined to close only after considerable history was made along the way. The Mets would be featured participants in late March, when major league baseball truly turned international by staging the first ceremonial opening day of a new season not in Cincinnati or Milwaukee or Chicago, but in Tokyo, Japan. While 28 other clubs were still winding down spring training sessions in Arizona and Florida, the New York Mets and Chicago Cubs launched the new campaign with the first pair of major league games ever played outside of North America. It was indeed a historical departure for the national pastime, one that lifted the lid in grand style on a season that would wind down seven months later with another landmark event—the first one-city World Series in nearly half a century.

The Mets-Cubs two-game set in the splendid Tokyo Dome was a radical departure akin to such recent tradition-shattering events as interleague play, wild-card playoff slots, regular-season contests in Monterrey, Mexico, and a politically charged set of exhibition contests between the Baltimore Orioles and the champion national Olympic team from Cuba. Never before had the traditional opening-day pitch been thrown somewhere other than on U.S. soil—not even in Canada, where Blue Jays and Expos openers had always been carefully scheduled to follow opening-day games in older league cities. For years, openers had been restricted to the nation's capital (the regular venue for presidential first pitches) until the expansion Senators fled to Texas in 1971, and to America's most historic ballplaying city—Cincinnati. But in the never-ending search for marketing and promotion ploys, such entrenched customs were now going the way of grass fields, sunshine baseball, and a daylight-hours World Series.

Chicago's Cubs would come away victors in the historic opener. Playing a world away from friendly Wrigley Field and exchanging beer-guzzling bleacher bums for polite fans who snacked on sushi with chopsticks and washed down their repast with sake, the longtime doormat Cubs rose up and nipped the more highly touted and prosperous Mets 5-3, largely on the strength of Shane Andrews and Mark Grace homers that were the first circuit blasts of the new century. An announced sellout crowd of 55,000 included Crown Prince Naruhito and Princess Masako, who sat in their royal box throughout the entire contest and later visited with Cubs stars Grace and Sammy Sosa.

As for the game, the debut of prized left-hander Mike Hampton in a Mets uniform proved to be something of a nightmare for the New Yorkers. Fresh off a season in which he had rung up a Houston franchise-record 22 victories and had been runner-up in the NL Cy Young balloting, Hampton disappointed by walking nine Cubs in only five innings before giving way to Turk Wendell with the Cubs up 2-1. Jon Lieber hurled seven strong innings for Chicago, and the only Mets offensive noise of the day came on a two-run blast by Mike Piazza in the bottom of the eighth with the Mets already trailing 5-1. Ex-Met Rick Aguilera gained credit for a save by closing the door in the home ninth, as the Cubs ended their string of three straight opening-day losses and also defeated the Mets for the first time in six outings.

The Mets would not leave Japan without their own taste of victory, however. A rebound win on the second day of the unprecedented Asian tour came on some late-inning heroics from a player already ticketed for minor league duties at the end of the week. Brought into the game as a pinch-hitter in the top of the 11th inning of a 1-1 nail-biter, reserve outfielder Benny Agbayani slugged a game-winning grandslam. It was a dramatic win that would foreshadow the season to come for both the Mets and the AAA-bound Hawaiian native. And it stole all the thunder from another rare on-field event that occurred in the first inning when Rey Ordoñez overran an easy roller by Damon Buford, thus ending a major league–record 101 errorless games at shortstop. But Agbayani's center-field drive off rookie Danny Young was the headliner. Back on more native baseball soil half a year later, another equally clutch Agbayani homer would be destined to make even bigger headlines in New York. But there was still an entire season to be played out between two truly landmark 11th-hour Agbayani round trippers.

Back on American soil, the 2000 season soon unfolded along predictable lines. The Mets were expected to provide a stiff challenge to Atlanta in the East, and they did so from the outset, going 16-10 (.615) in the month of April and then playing near that lofty winning percent-

age for much of the remaining pennant chase. The Mets would first visit the top slot in the NL East on April 24, drop back to second two days later, and then bounce between second and third for most of the remainder of the season.

Baseball's media pundits had expected the Mets to challenge for a championship in 2000—at least a division championship—and an early April *Long Island Newsday* baseball preview supplemental section was representative of the thinking in New York when its banner headline trumpeted: "This Could Be the Year for a Big Apple Postseason." Atlanta was, of course, the overwhelming favorite to repeat as National League champion and again challenge the likely junior-circuit champions residing in Yankee Stadium. In other divisions, the St. Louis Cardinals, with slugger Mark McGwire, and the Arizona Diamondbacks, with intimidating stringbean southpaw Randy Johnson, seemed strong enough to make serious pennant runs. And there was a bulk of talent also in Los Angeles, where Davey Johnson was managing, and in the Giants' camp, where Dusty Baker's crew would be opening the luxurious new Pacific Bell Park on San Francisco Bay.

Mike Hampton was a key new element for the Mets and was expected to enhance a solid mound corps with its first true ace in years. If the Mets had a pitching weakness at the season's outset, it was that the starting rotation was only three deep—Hampton, Al Leiter, and Rick Reed—after the departures of Orel Hershiser, Masato Yoshii, and promising Dominican Octavio Dotel (sacrificed in the Hampton deal). Heavy-hitting but erratic outfielder Derek Bell was coming over from Houston alongside Hampton, but again only at the cost of 1999 surprise Roger Cedeño. Southpaw Glendon Rusch had been picked up from Kansas City in a late-season 1999 deal and would now be counted on to supplement the starting pitching. The bullpen crew, with ageless John Franco and colorful Turk Wendell as setup men, and flamethrowing Armando Benitez as closer, was the equal of any in the league. The biggest everyday lineup change would be Todd Zeile over at first in place of veteran John Olerud. Zeile—a December free-agent signing—had slugged 24 homers and knocked home 98 runs a year earlier in Texas, and thus brought another hefty bat to the Mets' slugging lineup. The general

Mike Hampton, acquired in an off-season trade with Houston, was instrumental in leading the Mets to the World Series. (AP/Wide World Photos)

take on this club (such as the ones voiced in *The Sporting News* and *USA Today Baseball Weekly*) was that winning 97 games again would be a tough order for a team that now had an aging Robin Ventura at third and a repositioned Todd Zeile at first and was still searching for two more dependable starters.

Most troublesome on the eve of the new campaign were the key absences from last year's wild-card contenders. Most significant, John Olerud was now out of the lineup with his reliable bat from the left side and his glue-fingered glove at first base. Free agency had seen to that, with Olerud opting to end his career closer to home in Seattle. Two promising youngsters— swift outfielder Roger Cedeño (acquired in '99 from Los Angeles and new owner of the club stolen-base record) and right-hander Octavio Dotel (who flashed rookie brilliance with an impressive 8-3 mark and was the club's top pitching prospect)—were the steep price paid for Mike Hampton and Derek Bell. And veteran southpaw starter Kenny Rogers had pitched his

way out of town with disappointing postseason efforts.

The summer unfolded in exciting fashion once league play was under way. A nine-game winning streak in late April (launched at the end of a road trip in Pittsburgh and carried through a home stand with Milwaukee, Chicago, LA, and finally Cincinnati) demonstrated that the Mets could likely stay close to the top slot and thus continue nipping at the Braves' heels. May was the season's only losing month, with a 13-14 ledger, but June saw a strong rebound at 16 up and 8 down. Hampton lost three straight before his first victory versus Milwaukee on April 18, but the top starter finally climbed on the winning side of the ledger on May 20 against the Arizona Diamondbacks. By that time, Hampton's southpaw teammate Al Leiter was already off to a heady 5-0 start.

A potentially crucial blow to New York's pennant hopes was an injury to Rey Ordoñez during the lengthy west coast road trip in late May. The league's flashiest shortstop suffered

Benny Agbayani is embraced by teammate Rey Ordoñez at home plate after hitting a game-winning grand slam in the 11th inning against the Chicago Cubs at the Tokyo Dome. (AP/Wide World Photos)

a non-displaced fracture of the ulna in his left arm during a second-base collision in Dodger Stadium on May 30 and immediately went on the 15-day disabled list. Veteran infielder/pinch hitter Lenny Harris was acquired three days later from Arizona for cash and left-handed pitcher Bill Pulsipher. Harris was an added piece of bench strength rather than an intended replacement for the felled Ordoñez. Thus there would now also be a frantic search for a substitute shortstop that would eventually net only Mike Bordick, who had been languishing in Baltimore. On June 21 it was announced that Ordoñez would indeed be lost for the entire year. Half of last year's stellar defensive infield was now gone, and the season was hardly two months old.

There would eventually be some significant roster adjustments in midstream. The earliest was the outright release of the disgruntled Rickey Henderson, who was cut loose on May 13 after several futile attempts to orchestrate a trade. Another involved Melvin Mora (who departed to the Orioles) and Bordick (who arrived

from Baltimore) in a crucial late-July trade designed to fill the desperate gap at shortstop that Kurt Abbott had not been able to adequately plug in the nearly two months since Ordoñez's injury. Utilityman Bubba Trammell was another important late-summer pickup when he came over from Tampa Bay on the same day as the Bordick deal. Trammell was acquired with reliever Rick White in exchange for outfield prospect Jason Tyner and right-handed pitcher Paul Wilson. And the late-season call-up of an unheralded Dominican speedster named Timo Pérez would have perhaps the most significant impact of all. Pérez is a tiny fireball outfielder who had moved from the Japanese League to Class A in the Mets' chain and on to the majors in less than a year. The unlikely left-handed-hitting prospect was destined to play a vital role in the Mets' fortunes before the season was out.

The first true season's highlight came with the renewal of the always-entertaining interleague series with the crosstown rival Yankees. From the opening pitch of the six-game home-and-home set, there would be plenty of

Timo Pérez moved from the Japanese League to the majors in less than a year. (AP/Wide World Photos)

fireworks and adequate doses of history. The rivals split the pair of June games at Yankee Stadium, with a third encounter falling victim to rain. Leiter stretched his record to 7-1 in defeating Roger Clemens 12-2, but the Yanks salvaged a split when Andy Pettitte outlasted Bobby Jones in a 13-5 affair. With a renewal of the hostilities in early July, the series shifted to Shea Stadium for a classic pitchers' duel between Leiter and Orlando Hernández, won by the Yankees' ace 2-1. One of the most unusual days of interleague play on record then transpired on Saturday, July 8, when the two clubs staged an unusual day-night doubleheader that was necessitated by the earlier rainout and that featured games in both crosstown ballparks. The evening affair in Yankee Stadium garnered most of the headlines due to a tense beanball incident involving Roger Clemens and Mike Piazza, which knocked the Mets' catcher unconscious and ignited a war of words and lingering accusations between the two rival clubs. Piazza insisted that the fastball, which dented his batting helmet, had been a vicious and uncalled-for "purpose" pitch, a charge that Clemens laughed off as ridiculous and unfounded.

From mid-season on, the Mets hung in the race for the coveted division crown or, at the very least, a repeat wild-card berth. They struggled to the top of the division with their strong spurt in late May and then spent the next two months hanging on in second or third. There were winning streaks of seven straight (all at home) in late June and 10 out of 11 during late July and early August. It was also a season that saw the nationwide baseball interest shift happily from home run heroics of the past few summers to the sport's intended staple—tense pennant races. Mark McGwire started on track for yet another season of record slugging (with over 30 dingers before midyear) but was knocked from the Cardinals' lineup with a painful knee condition by late June. Sosa carried on alone in Chicago, smacking at least 50 for the third straight year, but didn't seriously challenge any significant records. Home run numbers remained up across both leagues, yet the long ball was no longer quite such an obsession—or even an exclusive focus—either for fans or for the cheerleading media.

When September rolled around, the Mets unfortunately seemed to swoon again at the most inopportune time against their longtime nemesis, the pesky Atlanta Braves. There were crushing defeats in two mid-September series staged at Turner Field and then back at Shea. Three losses to Atlanta in the season's last two weeks seemed to squelch any remaining hope of overtaking the division top spot. But a late-September slump did not spell the end as it had in years past, as the Mets maintained plenty of distance between themselves and fading wild-card rivals Arizona and Los Angeles.

By season's end, it was the Mets' hitting that again carried the ball club. Mike Piazza owned the biggest lumber with a .324 average, 38 homers, and 113 RBIs; Edgardo Alfonzo duplicated Piazza's average and was club runner-up in homers with 25. Surprise 27-year-old rookie outfielder Jay Payton had finally shaken off several summers of injuries to hit at a .291 clip and bang 17 homers. Zeile (22) and Ventura (24) also cracked the 20 mark in home runs, and Agbayani returned from early-season duty at Norfolk to knock out 15 dingers and drive in 60 runs in only 350 official trips to the plate. The lineup proved potent even without Olerud and despite a yearlong slump by Ventura, who batted an anemic .232. Defense was not as stellar, once Ordoñez was lost, and the key shortstop duties fell to Abbott and then Bordick. The pitching was as solid as it had been in years, relying more on day-in and day-out consistency than on any one or two stellar aces to carry the full load. Although Hampton had a lower ERA (15-10, 3.14), Leiter (16-8, 3.20) actually won more games. In addition, a trio of 11-game winners—Rusch, Reed, and Bobby Jones—gave the Mets five hurlers with double-figure wins and also solved the problem of expanding the starting rotation. Benitez remained among the league's save leaders (with 41) and nearly doubled his previous year's total in this vital department. And John Franco was still an effective setup man, picking up five victories and four saves and chipping in with a 3.40 ERA.

The clincher that locked up the postseason visit came in the final week, a mere five games from the end of the season. That victory was, quite fittingly, a 6-2 Shea Stadium triumph over the Atlanta Braves. In the game that eliminated the LA Dodgers as the final wild-card challenger, Rick Reed limited the division leaders to four tame hits in eight frames. In the victorious Shea Stadium clubhouse, Mike Piazza told the press that it was just good to get the whole thing over

Mets 2000 Individual Batting Statistics

Player	BA	AB	R	H	2B	3B	HR	RBI	SB
Jorge Toca, IF	.429	7	1	3	1	0	0	4	0
Mike Piazza, C	.324	482	90	156	26	0	38	113	4
Edgardo Alfonzo, 2B	.324	544	109	176	40	2	25	94	3
Jay Payton, OF	.291	488	63	142	23	1	17	62	5
Benny Agbayani, OF	.289	350	59	101	19	1	15	60	5
Timo Pérez, OF	.286	49	11	14	4	1	1	3	1
Darryl Hamilton, OF	.276	105	20	29	4	1	1	6	2
Todd Pratt, C	.275	160	33	44	6	0	8	25	0
Todd Zeile, 1B	.268	544	67	146	36	3	22	79	3
Derek Bell, OF	.266	546	87	145	31	1	18	69	8
Melvin Mora, OF	.260	215	35	56	13	2	6	30	7
Mike Bordick, SS	.260	192	18	50	8	0	4	21	3
Lenny Harris, OF	.260	223	31	58	7	4	4	26	13
Matt Franco, OF	.239	134	9	32	4	0	2	14	0
Robin Ventura, 3B	.232	469	61	109	23	1	24	84	3
Bubba Trammell, OF	.232	56	9	13	2	0	3	12	1
Joe McEwing, IF	.222	153	20	34	14	1	2	19	3
Rickey Henderson, OF	.219	96	17	21	1	0	0	2	5
Kurt Abbott, SS	.217	157	22	34	7	1	6	12	1
David Lamb, IF	.200	5	1	1	0	0	0	0	0
Jason Tyner, OF	.195	41	3	8	2	0	0	5	1
Jon Nunnally, OF	.189	74	16	14	5	1	2	6	3
Rey Ordoñez, SS	.188	133	10	25	5	0	0	9	0
Mark Johnson, IF	.182	22	2	4	0	0	1	6	0
Mike Kinkade, IF	.000	2	0	0	0	0	0	0	0
Ryan McGuire, IF	.000	2	0	0	0	0	0	0	0
Jorge Velandia, 2B	.000	7	1	0	0	0	0	0	0
Vance Wilson, C	.000	4	0	0	0	0	0	0	0

with. After one late-season collapse in '98 and nearly another in '99, the Mets had played all season long with a monkey on their backs. On the season's last day, the club stood with 94 victories in one of its best showings in the past two decades. The final gap between New York and the Braves had been sliced to a single game. But more important, once again the Mets would be headed to a postseason party. And Bobby Valentine had once more made history. For the first time, the Mets would now enjoy back-to-back playoff appearances. And for the second straight autumn, a Subway Series seemed at least a remote possibility.

METS EARN THEIR OCTOBER SUBWAY TICKETS

If the regular season had spanned the baseball globe, so, seemingly, would the upcoming postseason. The division playoff round would open for the Mets on the West Coast in the impressive new Pacific Bell Park, a venue where the NL West–champion Giants had proven to be nearly invincible for most of the season. The

coast-to-coast five-game series with the Giants would potentially be followed by a trip into baseball's heartland in either St. Louis or Atlanta. And the prize waiting at the end of a successful postseason run might well be a showdown with the crosstown Yankees. The Mets could thus play all of the World Series—if they could only manage to get there—without ever leaving home.

But all that was perhaps idle speculation, given the immediate task at hand. The Dusty Baker–managed Giants, featuring the slugging of MVP candidates Barry Bonds and Jeff Kent, would be a tough first-round opponent. This was not the expansion Arizona Diamondbacks of a season earlier, with Randy Johnson and little else to intimidate the opposition. The Giants were viewed by many as the toughest club in baseball. They had run away from the pack early in their own division, and with 97 victories owned the best record in the majors. San Francisco's 55-26 home mark in its new ballpark was matched only by the Mets among teams in either league. But at least Bobby Valentine and crew would not have to go head-to-head immediately with the feared Braves' pitching staff of Greg Maddux, Tom Glavine, and Kevin Millwood.

Maddux and Glavine aside, the Giants gave their own early signals that the New York postseason might not be very lengthy this time

Mets 2000 Individual Pitching Statistics

Pitcher	W-L	ERA	SV	IP	H	ER	HR	BB	SO
Jerrod Riggan, RHP	0-0	0.00	0	2.0	3	0	0	0	1
Armando Benitez, RHP	4-4	2.61	41	76.0	39	22	10	38	106
Mike Hampton, LHP	15-10	3.14	0	217.2	194	76	10	99	151
Al Leiter, LHP	16-8	3.20	0	208.0	176	74	19	76	200
John Franco, LHP	5-4	3.40	4	55.2	46	21	6	26	56
Turk Wendell, RHP	8-6	3.59	1	82.2	60	33	9	41	73
Rick White, RHP	2-3	3.81	1	28.1	26	12	2	12	20
Glendon Rusch, LHP	11-11	4.01	0	190.2	196	85	18	44	157
Rick Reed, RHP	11-5	4.11	0	184.0	192	84	28	34	121
Bobby M. Jones, LHP	0-1	4.15	0	21.2	18	10	2	14	20
Bobby J. Jones, RHP	11-6	5.06	0	154.2	171	87	25	49	85
Dennis Cook, LHP	6-3	5.34	2	59.0	63	35	8	31	53
Pat Mahomes, RHP	5-3	5.46	0	94.0	96	57	15	66	76
Eric Cammack, RHP	0-0	6.30	0	10.0	7	7	1	10	9
Rich Rodriguez, LHP	0-1	7.78	0	37.0	59	32	7	15	18
Dennis Springer, RHP	0-1	8.74	0	11.1	20	11	2	5	5
Jim Mann, RHP	0-0	10.13	0	2.2	6	3	1	1	0
Grant Roberts, RHP	0-0	11.57	0	7.0	11	9	0	4	6
Bill Pulsipher, LHP	0-2	12.15	0	6.2	12	9	1	6	7
Heath Bell, RHP	0-0	36.00	0	1.0	3	4	0	3	0

around. Bonds and company jumped out to an early lead against Mike Hampton in the opener and cruised to victory behind the controlled pitching of Cuban stalwart Livan Hernández. The half-brother of Yankees ace "El Duque," Hernández scattered five harmless Mets hits over 7.2 innings, while Bonds muted his earlier postseason failures with an RBI triple and a key single, and Ellis Burks also slugged a three-run homer for the home club. The easy 5-1 victory kept the Cuban defector, who was a 1997 World Series MVP in his days with the Florida Marlins, perfect in three Octobers of postseason play.

But the Mets fought back in gallant style a single night later. The second game of the short series was, in fact, a major turning point of the entire postseason. For eight-plus innings, the New Yorkers would march relentlessly toward earning a split on the road. A two-run homer in the top of the ninth by Edgardo Alfonzo had built a seemingly safe 4-1 lead, which promised to even the series. Then in the home ninth, the usually reliable closer, Armando Benitez, almost gave it all away. A dramatic three-run homer by J.T. Snow with Bonds and Kent aboard lit a sudden fire under the Giants in the do-or-die ninth and nearly ruined a brilliant outing by ill-fated starter Al Leiter. But this was destined to be the Mets' night, and when the game moved into extra innings, a simple single by Jay Payton in the top of the tenth proved even bigger than Snow's pinch-hit circuit blast. Payton's clutch hit off Felix Rodríguez plated Darryl Hamilton, who had moments earlier stroked an equally clutch pinch-hit double. John Franco earned the first postseason save of his 16-year career with a gutsy 10th-inning performance that culminated with a strikeout of Barry Bonds with the tying run on first.

Once the series shifted cross-country to Shea Stadium, so did all the prevailing momentum. The Mets were bent on proving they had now climbed straight back into the series. A tie-breaking homer in the home 13th by Benny Agbayani was now destined to provide one of the year's most significant moments of postseason heroics. Only a single pitch into the game, Mets fans had applauded lustily at the scoreboard posting of the St. Louis Cardinals' series-clinching victory over the Atlanta Braves. More than five hours later, the exhausted throng of 56,270 exploded again when Agbayani's solo blast off Aaron Fultz sailed high over Barry Bonds and cleared the left-field wall to provide New York with a surprising 2-1 series lead. The Giants would never regain their footing in New York after Agbayani's home run dramatics. Agbayani was the surprise hero, just as he had been at the other end of the same season, more than six months earlier back in Japan.

Another early postseason surprise emerging from the talent-laden New York bench was outfielder Timo Pérez. What first seemed like a horrible break when Derek Bell was injured chasing down Barry Bonds's triple in Game 1 quickly turned into a seeming New York advantage when Pérez played flawlessly (even brilliantly at times) in right field as an emergency fill-in and also provided both speed in the leadoff slot and a surprisingly potent bat, notching three hits in Game 2 and a couple more in the final two series contests. Throughout the NL Division Series, the pint-sized outfielder seemed bent on seizing his moment in the limelight and building yet another Mets postseason legend in the process.

The final game of the series was notable for a pitching masterpiece of truly grand proportions. Righty Bobby Jones was matched against friend and fellow Fresno State alum Mark Gardner. Both veteran hurlers were effective in the early innings, although a two-out walk surrendered to Piazza and a subsequent two-run homer off the bat of Robin Ventura had buried Gardner in a first-inning 2-0 hole.

It was soon apparent nonetheless that the afternoon belonged entirely to Jones. The crafty righty enjoyed a career day of rarest proportions and in the process was as masterful as any Mets pitcher had ever been in postseason play. The end result was a true pitching gem. Only a pair of walks and a bouncing fifth-inning double over Ventura's head and down the left-field line off the bat of Jeff Kent prevented Bobby Jones from authoring the first postseason no-hitter since Don Larsen's perfect game in the same city 44 years earlier. The brilliant outing in Jones's first-ever postseason start validated the decision made by Mets manager Bobby Valentine, who had seriously considered starting Mike Hampton on only three days' rest. Valentine's gamble paid huge dividends when Jones's first shutout in three full years clinched a surprise date with St. Louis in the next round's showdown for the National League pennant.

Teammates carry Benny Agbayani after his 13th-inning home run to defeat the San Francisco Giants. (AP/Wide World Photos)

While the Mets occupied themselves by surprising the reeling Giants, a similar and perhaps even more shocking upset had been taking place in the Atlanta-St. Louis matchup. The Cardinals swept the stunned defending National League champions with convincing 7-5, 10-4, and 7-1 pastings, the last on the Braves' home field. The series was over almost before it started, with the heavily favored and pitching-rich Braves left standing on the sidelines without a single victory. This despite a nightmarish outing by young St. Louis southpaw ace Rick Ankiel in the opener. Ankiel had managed what no other pitcher had ever even approached in more than a full century of major league baseball, uncorking five wild pitches in a single inning of work.

Over in the American League, the Yankees were busy keeping up their part of a dreamed-for all-New York World Series bash. The defending world champions edged past the West Division leaders, the Oakland A's, in a tougher-than-anticipated series that went the full five games and forced the New Yorkers to fly across the country to wrap up the struggle after an unsettling 11-1 Oakland rout of Roger Clemens in Game 4 at Yankee Stadium. Now, only the AL wild-card Seattle Mariners (easy victors in three straight over the Chicago White Sox) stood in the way of the junior circuit's half of a potential Subway Series encounter.

The Cardinals were heavily favored over the Mets in NLCS play, just as the Giants had been in the opening division showdown. St. Louis had won handily all year, even without Mark McGwire, and had outpaced Central Division runner-up Cincinnati by 10 full games. The Cardinals had more than adequate pitching in the trio of Darryl Kile, former AL Cy Young winner Pat Hentgen, and 21-year-old Rick Ankiel. They had potent bats as well, including those of Will Clark (acquired in midyear from Baltimore when McGwire went down) and possible league MVP Jim Edmonds. And McGwire (relegated to pinch hitting after his September return) was always a threat for instant offense off the bench. The Cards loomed especially large after their ridiculously easy waltz through Atlanta, a team that always seemed to have the Mets' number.

If the Cardinals had surprised the faithful against the Braves, they now had more surprises in store for their loyal fans. But these would be of a far less positive nature. Another pitching gem, this time from Mike Hampton, gave the Mets an early edge. Hampton hurled seven innings of shutout baseball while his teammates built a 6-0 lead. Two unearned runs by St. Louis in the ninth were the first tallies against New York pitching since the fourth inning of Game 3 of the San Francisco series. St. Louis fans were shocked to see their team stumble badly in the first outing against the Mets. An evening later, the situation grew even more desperate for the St. Louis faithful. Jay Payton's clutch RBI single in the ninth ended a seesaw affair and closed the door again on the suddenly mortal Cardinals, this time by a 6-5 count. The biggest shock for St. Louis fans came with the opening handful of batters in Game 2, when Rick Ankiel again proved hopelessly wild. In his aborted first-inning performance, Ankiel issued three walks and uncorked two more wild pitches and several additional fastballs that unaccountably sailed high and plunked the distant backstop.

Two wins in St. Louis put the ball squarely in the Mets' court. The Central Division champs had dropped both games at home and now saw their pennant prospects—which looked so bright a week earlier in Atlanta—suddenly fading. Tony LaRussa's team would now have to

---

New York Mets 2000 Postseason Results*

NL Division Series (New York Mets 3, San Francisco Giants 1)
GIANTS 5, Mets 1 (WP-Livan Hernández, LP-Mike Hampton)
Mets 5, GIANTS 4 (10) (WP-Armando Benitez, LP-Felix Rodríguez)
METS 3, Giants 2 (13) (WP-Rick White, LP-Aaron Fultz)
METS 4, Giants 0 (WP-Bobby Jones, LP-Mark Gardner)

2000 NLCS (New York Mets 4, St. Louis Cardinals 1)
Mets 6, CARDINALS 2 (WP-Mike Hampton, LP-Darryl Kile)
Mets 6, CARDINALS 5 (WP-Turk Wendell, LP-Mike Timlin)
Cardinals 8, METS 2 (WP-Andy Benes, LP-Rick Reed)
METS 10, Cardinals 6 (WP-Glendon Rusch, LP-Darryl Kile)
METS 7, Cardinals 0 (WP-Mike Hampton, LP-Pat Hentgen)

2000 World Series (New York Yankees 4, New York Mets 1)
YANKEES 4, Mets 3 (12) (WP-Mike Stanton, LP-Turk Wendell)
YANKEES 6, Mets 5 (WP-Roger Clemens, LP-Mike Hampton)
METS 4, Yankees 2 (WP-John Franco, LP-Orlando Hernández)
Yankees 3, METS 2 (WP-Jeff Nelson, LP-Bobby Jones)
Yankees 4, METS 2 (WP-Mike Stanton, LP-Al Leiter)

*Home team indicated in all caps

Todd Zeile, who scored the winning run on Benny Agbayani's double, celebrates with Armando Benitez, who got the save, after defeating the New York Yankees 4-2 in Game 3 of the World Series on Oct. 24, 2000. (AP/Wide World Photos)

dominate in Shea Stadium, where things had always been tough for them over the years. By contrast, everything was looking surprisingly good for the Mets' pennant hopes. But the Cardinals would not go quietly. On Saturday afternoon their bats awoke early in Shea Stadium against Rick Reed. Reed surrendered eight hits and five runs in three-plus innings after being sent reeling in the first frame by a two-run Jim Edmonds double. Cardinals starter Andy Benes effectively cut off rallies by enticing a pair of timely double plays and worked eight innings of the 8-2 win. The game was effectively salted away in the first five innings, which produced all the St. Louis scoring, and the Cardinals thus cruised to their first (and what would soon prove to be their only) victory of the NLCS showdown.

In Game 4 it was the Mets' bats that did heavy damage against St. Louis starter Darryl Kile, who was pitching his second game of the series on a minimal three days' rest. New York pounded the St. Louis right-hander for a record

five doubles in the first inning and quickly sealed a game that eventually wound up as a 10-6 laugher. Mets starter Bobby Jones also showed little effectiveness in giving back five runs before being pulled in the fifth, and the victory thus fell to bullpen replacement Glendon Rusch, who hurled three middle innings. Piazza belted his second homer of the series, and phenom outfielder Timo Pérez was again a thorn in the Cardinals' side with two hits, a stolen base, and three runs scored.

The final two games of the NLCS turned as much on shoddy St. Louis defense as on the Mets' clutch pitching and opportunistic hitting. The pennant-clinching game was a 7-0 runaway that saw the Mets coast to victory aided by several key Cardinal errors in the infield, including two by the usually reliable Will Clark at first base. Pitching on 16 days' rest, Cardinals starter Pat Hentgen was blown out in the fourth after Todd Zeile's double cleared the loaded bases and staked Mike Hampton to a 6-0 lead. Edgar

Renteria's misplay of Timo Pérez's infield grounder had opened the floodgates in the fateful fourth frame. Hampton coasted with a three-hit complete-game shutout, and the Mets showed considerable restraint in victory when a fastball from reliever Dave Veres struck Jay Payton's helmet and cleared both benches.

The Mets had now finally won their fourth National League crown and their first in 14 seasons. This one—unlikely as it may have been—was not as much of a complete surprise as that true miracle back in 1969, but it was nonetheless certainly unanticipated in just about every imaginable quarter. When the Yankees shut down the AL wild-card Seattle Mariners in a closing Game 6 at Yankee Stadium, it was a thrilling conclusion, even for legions of Yankee-hating Mets fans. There would now be a long-awaited Subway Series for the first time in 44 years.

It was a baseball dream that had lingered in the minds of all New Yorkers since 1962. All was somehow right once again with the baseball universe, which nearly 50 years earlier had featured magnificent American League and National League showdowns in the Bronx, Manhattan, and Brooklyn as an almost annual rite of autumn. While the rest of the nation moaned about the dreaded New York baseball celebration, and dire predictions of a sparse nationwide television audience for the Fall Classic abounded, New Yorkers were truly delirious.

A TALE OF ONE CITY

Sixty-nine-year-old Yankee coach (and 1956 Brooklyn infielder) Don Zimmer was the last man still active in the major leagues from that last Yankees-Dodgers Fall Classic in 1956. It had been a historic Subway Series, highlighted by Don Larsen's perfect game in Game 5 and Brooklyn's only appearance as a defending world champion. New York fans were once more giddy in anticipation of another epic series.

There were many additional subplots to the 2000 Series that extended beyond the New York-versus-New York overlay. The Yankees were shooting for a rare Fall Classic three-peat, the first in several decades. They were also shooting for a 26th world championship banner to extend their dynasty status under George Steinbrenner. The Mets, for their part, were trying to capture only their third world title, a far more modest number. But the New York National Leaguers had just passed their first decade (the 1990s) in club history without a single World Series appearance. The Yankees were managed by Joe Torre, a former Mets skipper. The Mets' bench boss, by contrast, was making his first World Series visit after 12 seasons of managing contenders in Texas and New York. For Bobby Valentine, a 12-year dry spell in reaching baseball's biggest show had finally come to an end. Yankees right-hander Orlando "El Duque" Hernández was protecting a perfect postseason mark of record proportions—eight victories and no playoff or World Series defeats. And Yankees reliever Mariano Rivera was also closing in on the postseason scoreless-innings record (32) held by former Yankee great Whitey Ford. Ford's string had come exclusively in World Series play and as a starting hurler; Rivera's included plenty of ALDS and ALCS outings, and all were short stints in relief.

But more than anything else, there was the rivalry itself, and the obvious issue of bragging rights. The local press had made much of the July 8 beanball incident between Roger Clemens and Mike Piazza—and was sure to fan the fires around the pair's renewed face-off. Would Clemens be allowed to pitch at Shea Stadium, where he would not be protected by the DH rule and thus have to face potentially vengeful Mets hurlers? New York was wild with enthusiasm for this showdown Series, even if the rest of the nation might turn a deaf ear or click off their televisions sets in droves.

The Mets and Yankees were not exactly strangers. In addition to the annual off-field battles by Mets and Yankees management for the most media attention in New York, the ball clubs themselves had played numerous times over the years. Official meetings in games that counted were, of course, only a recent development linked to the 1997 inauguration of midsummer interleague play. But there had been plenty of spirited exhibition matchups in both Florida and New York through the years, including the first-ever face-off in St. Petersburg on March 22, 1962, when Casey Stengel started all his Mets regulars, and the expansion club won 4-3 on Joe Christopher's triple and Richie Ashburn's pinch single in the bottom of the ninth. The franchises had also shared 67 players (starting with Marv Throneberry in 1962 and continuing with José Vizcaino in 2000) and no fewer than four famed managers. Casey Stengel,

Yogi Berra, Dallas Green, and Joe Torre had all served as bench bosses in both Yankee Stadium and either the Polo Grounds or Shea Stadium.

The Subway Series opener at historic Yankee Stadium proved to be a marathon affair drenched with all the excitement that the pre-Series hype had outrageously promised. The game stretched for 12 innings and a Series-record four hours and 51 minutes. There were several lead changes and some seat-gripping, late-inning momentum shifts. The Mets had their chances to put the home team away but never could take full advantage. The entire Mets' offensive outburst was concentrated in the seventh when pinch-hitter Bubba Trammell singled home a pair of runs and Edgardo Alfonzo plated another with an infield tap. Two more Mets runs were lost earlier when Todd Zeile's apparent homer bounced off the top of the wall for a double and base runner Timo Pérez (who had merely trotted to second and third) was thrown out at the plate to end the inning. In the end, the game was won by an unlikely hitting hero, when ex-Met (and also ex-Dodger and ex-Giant) José Vizcaino singled home the winning tally in the third extra inning.

When the two teams returned to battle a night later, the Mets still appeared to be stunned by their opening-night fate, which had been sealed by bad base running and a string of missed offensive opportunities. And the shock of that opening Series loss was now compounded by the overpowering mound work of veteran fireballer Roger Clemens, who seemed from the outset to be on top of his game.

There was a moment of tension early in Game 2 that almost seemed to take Yankee fans completely out of their euphoria of the night before. Piazza and Clemens squared off in the opening half inning for the first time since the

beaning earlier in the summer, and to the seeming delight of the network television play-by-play crew, fireworks soon exploded. Mayhem struck when Piazza broke his bat while fouling off a first-inning Clemens splitter, and the barrel end of the war club landed a few feet in front of the pitcher's mound. Clemens was clearly mayhem's author this time, as he picked up the splintered bat end and hurled it angrily back in the direction of Piazza, who was running toward first base. Responding to Clemens's aggressive gesture, Piazza advanced menacingly in the pitcher's direction before umpire Charlie Reliford hastily restored order. The Yankee hurler would receive a $50,000 fine from the commissioner's office, but the Mets and Piazza would undoubtedly much rather have had a few more base hits and a game victory as their con-

2000 Subway Series Yankees Composite Box Score

Yankees Batting	G	AB	R	H	2B	3B	HR	RBI	BA
Luis Polonia, PH	2	2	0	1	0	0	0	0	.500
Paul O'Neill, OF	5	19	2	9	2	2	0	2	.474
Derek Jeter, SS	5	22	6	9	2	1	2	2	.409
Tino Martinez, 1B	5	22	3	8	1	0	0	2	.364
Scott Brosius, 3B	5	13	2	4	0	0	1	3	.308
Luis Sojo, 3B-2B	4	7	0	2	0	0	0	2	.286
José Vizcaino, 2B	4	17	0	4	0	0	0	1	.235
Jorge Posada, C	5	18	2	4	1	0	0	1	.222
David Justice, LF	5	19	1	3	2	0	0	3	.158
Bernie Williams, CF	5	18	2	2	0	0	1	1	.111
Chuck Knoblauch, DH	4	10	1	1	0	0	0	1	.100
Orlando Hernández, P	1	2	0	0	0	0	0	0	.000
Glenallen Hill, PH-LF	3	3	0	0	0	0	0	0	.000
Denny Neagle, P	1	2	0	0	0	0	0	0	.000
José Canseco, PH	1	1	0	0	0	0	0	0	.000
Mariano Rivera, P	4	1	0	0	0	0	0	0	.000
Clay Bellinger, PH-LF	4	0	0	0	0	0	0	0	.000
Andy Pettitte, P	2	3	0	0	0	0	0	0	.000
David Cone, P	1	0	0	0	0	0	0	0	——
Roger Clemens, P	1	0	0	0	0	0	0	0	——
Jeff Nelson, P	3	0	0	0	0	0	0	0	——
Mike Stanton, P	4	0	0	0	0	0	0	0	——
YANKEES TOTALS	5	179	19	47	8	3	4	18	.263

Yankees Pitching	G	W-L	SV	IP	H	ER	BB	SO	ERA
Roger Clemens	1	1-0	0	8	2	0	0	9	0.00
Mike Stanton	4	2-0	0	4.1	0	0	0	7	0.00
David Cone	1	0-0	0	0.1	0	0	0	0	0.00
Andy Pettitte	2	0-0	0	13.2	16	3	4	9	1.98
Mariano Rivera	4	0-0	2	6	4	2	1	7	3.00
Denny Neagle	1	0-0	0	4.2	4	2	2	3	3.86
Orlando Hernández	1	0-1	0	7.1	9	4	3	12	4.91
Jeff Nelson	3	1-0	0	2.2	5	3	1	1	10.12
YANKEES TOTALS	5	4-1	2	47	40	14	11	48	2.68

All-Time Mets-Versus-Yankees Series Standings

	Mets Victories	Yankees Victories	Ties
Spring Training Games (1962-2000)	32	45	0
Mayor's Trophy (Exhibition Games)	8	10	1
Mayor's Challenge (Exhibition Games)	2	2	0
Big Apple Series (Exhibition Games)	1	2	0
Official Interleague Play (1997-2000)	7	11	0
2000 World Series	1	4	0
Official Record	8	15	0
Overall Record (with Exhibitions)	51	74	1

solation in the wake of the Rocket's obvious lapse in sportsmanship.

Clemens was given plenty of early breathing room when the Yankees jumped out for two in the home first and another tally in the second off NLCS MVP Mike Hampton. Through eight innings, Clemens was altogether brilliant, as he walked none, struck out nine, and completely silenced the Mets' bats. Three add-on runs by the Yanks in the fifth, seventh, and eighth seemed to be only icing on the cake. But in the game's final half inning, there was a switch in momentum and an altogether quirky turn of events.

Jeff Nelson relieved Clemens for the mop-up duties in the visitor's ninth, and everyone—Mets and Yankees fans alike—expected the visitors to go quietly, as they had all evening. But with Clemens and his fastball now gone from the scene, Mets bats suddenly awoke with a vengeance. Piazza opened the fireworks when he blasted a two-run homer deep off the foul pole. Fans heading for the exits were again stunned a few batters later, when Jay Payton added an exclamation point with a three-run opposite-field shot against the usually untouchable Mariano Rivera. But it all proved too little too late, and when Rivera regained his composure and disposed of light-hitting Kurt Abbott to squelch the rally, the Yanks had earned their home sweep of the opening two games. But a Mets team that could have been demoralized had now also been handed new inspiration and new life by its late uprising against the cream of the Yankees' elite bullpen corps.

The National Leaguers had failed to win on the road and had actually given away the opening encounter by running themselves out

New York Yankee Derek Jeter slides safely across home plate as Mike Piazza fields a high throw. (AP/Wide World Photos)

of at least one certain run that would have nailed down a nine-inning victory. Yet they had also played even and lost each game by only a single run. And Valentine's crew had proven in Game 2 that the vaunted Yankee bullpen was not completely invincible in the late innings. There was thus considerable optimism in the air as the Mets headed back to more friendly territory only one borough and a few miles away, at Shea Stadium.

When the Series moved to Shea, the Mets were finally able to take full advantage of the few opportunities the stingy Yankees were handing them. Orlando Hernández spun another postseason near-masterpiece for the Yankees as he labored to keep his playoff and World Series unbeaten string alive. And on this evening, Hernández was matched pitch for pitch and run for run through six innings by Rick Reed. Robin Ventura's solo homer launched the Mets in the second. But the breakthrough was delayed until Benny Agbayani's double broke the knotted game open in the bottom of the eighth. Another piece of the Yankees' mystique now took a hit when both the club's 14-game Series unbeaten streak (dating to 1997) and El Duque's perfect 8-0 postseason record simultaneously went by the boards.

The Mets' Game 3 victory had rekindled hope for the Shea Stadium faithful and also for the Mets' players and coaches. But the euphoria would prove to be short-lived. The following night, the cool and collected and always businesslike Yankees were back to their old winning ways. The Mets had hoped to even the Series, riding atop both the considerable boost of a boisterous home crowd and the previous night's newfound momentum. But the Yankees seemed ready to ruin the National Leaguers' hopes from the game's first pitch, a loud blast by Derek Jeter that arched high over the Yankees' left-field bullpen.

In what was truly the turning-point of the Series, the Yankees scored solo runs off Bobby Jones in each of the first three innings. It was all they would need. Jones settled into his rhythm after the third, and Rusch, Franco, and Benitez held the Yankees in check once the bullpen got the call. But the again-silent Mets' bats could muster only a pair of runs on a home run by Piazza in the third frame. Lefty starter Denny Neagle was pulled before he completed the required five innings to qualify for a cher-

---

2000 Subway World Series Mets Composite Box Score

Batting	G	AB	R	H	2B	3B	HR	RBI	BA
Rick Reed, P	1	1	0	1	0	0	0	0	1.000
Bubba Trammell, PH	4	5	1	2	0	0	0	3	.400
Todd Zeile, 1B	5	20	1	8	2	0	0	1	.400
Jay Payton, CF	5	21	3	7	0	0	1	3	.333
Benny Agbayani, LF	5	18	2	5	2	0	0	2	.278
Mike Piazza, DH-C	5	22	3	6	2	0	2	4	.273
Kurt Abbott, SS-PH	5	8	0	2	1	0	0	0	.250
Robin Ventura, 3B	5	20	1	3	1	0	1	1	.150
Edgardo Alfonzo, 2B	5	21	1	3	0	0	0	1	.143
Timo Pérez, RF	5	16	1	2	0	0	0	0	.125
Mike Bordick, SS	4	8	0	1	0	0	0	0	.125
Lenny Harris, DH	3	4	1	0	0	0	0	0	.000
Darryl Hamilton, PH	4	3	0	0	0	0	0	0	.000
Bobby Jones, P	1	2	0	0	0	0	0	0	.000
Todd Pratt, C	1	2	1	0	0	0	0	0	.000
Matt Franco, 1B	1	1	0	0	0	0	0	0	.000
Joe McEwing, LF-PR	3	1	1	0	0	0	0	0	.000
Armando Benitez, P	3	0	0	0	0	0	0	0	——
Dennis Cook, P	3	0	0	0	0	0	0	0	——
John Franco, P	4	0	0	0	0	0	0	0	——
Mike Hampton, P	1	0	0	0	0	0	0	0	——
Al Leiter, P	2	2	0	0	0	0	0	0	.000
Glendon Rusch, P	3	0	0	0	0	0	0	0	——
Turk Wendell, P	2	0	0	0	0	0	0	0	——
Rick White, P	1	0	0	0	0	0	0	0	——
METS TOTALS	5	175	16	40	7	0	4	15	.229

Pitching	G	W-L	SV	IP	H	ER	BB	SO	ERA
John Franco	4	1-0	0	3.1	3	0	0		10.00
Dennis Cook	3	0-0	0	0.2	1	0	3		10.00
Glendon Rusch	3	0-0	0	4	6	1	2		22.25
Al Leiter	2	0-1	0	15.2	12	5	6		162.87
Rick Reed	1	0-0	0	6	6	2	1		83.00
Armando Benitez	3	0-0	1	3	3	1	2		23.00
Bobby Jones	1	0-1	0	5	4	3	3		35.40
Turk Wendell	2	0-1	0	1.2	3	1	2		25.40
Mike Hampton	1	0-1	0	6	8	4	5		46.00
Rick White	1	0-0	0	1.1	1	1	1		16.75
METS TOTALS	5	1-4	1	46.2	47	18	25		403.47

---

ished victory. But the Mets saw their championship hopes fade, when they could do absolutely nothing with the subsequent quartet of Yankee relievers.

The final game of the 2000 season—in fitting World Series fashion—once more provided the most unlikely of postseason heroes. Journeyman infielder Luis Sojo—a Yankees' late-season roster addition—would provide a shocking climax to the tense game, which wrapped up the 26th World Series for the visiting Yankees. With Jorge Posada on second and Scott Brosius on first and two down, the Yankee second sacker slapped a ball between short and second that scored Posada and allowed Brosius to scamper home as well when an outfield relay throw struck the sliding Posada and eluded catcher Mike Piazza. Sojo's dramatic ninth-inning single (coming in his only at-bat of the game) brought a bitter end to what had been a gutsy nine-inning attempt by southpaw Al Leiter to extend the Mets' season at least one more night.

In the end, the Mets' bats had gone silent for most of the Series in the face of superior Yankee pitching. Alfonzo (.143) and Piazza (.273) and Timo Pérez (.125) and others who had carried the club with timely hitting against the Giants and Cardinals were fairly impotent against the likes of Clemens, Pettitte, Nelson, and Stanton. Mariano Rivera had finally proven he wasn't invincible, as had El Duque. But in the long haul, the gutsy, yet outmanned Mets simply squandered too many opportunities to win games that were available for the taking.

Three games were one-run affairs, and the other two were both decided by a pair of tallies. The difference was that the timeliest hitting always seemed to fly off the bats of the battle-worn, world-champion Yankees.

Despite the outcome, it had been a glorious and historic 2000 Mets season. The National League pennant was now once more flying atop Shea Stadium. The Mets were league champions for the first time in a decade and a half. There would, of course, be questions that needed answers before the 2001 season. Mike Hampton remained unsigned and was a prime candidate for free agency. Robin Ventura was fading at third, and there were attractive players such as Seattle's Alex Rodriguez and Baltimore's Albert Belle to be courted in the off-season. But there was also much optimism that the Mets might now be well on the road to launching a National League dynasty of their own.

CHAPTER 1
Mets at the Millennium

If Mets history—like that of most big-league clubs—has been an endless roller coaster of exhilarating peaks and depressing valleys, century's end has definitely witnessed one of the more hopeful upturns. For two seasons now, the Mets have appeared to be sitting close to the cusp of a dramatic return to the glories of a not-so-distant Davey Johnson era. But so far, the corner has not quite been turned. The resurrection of the New York Mets is still very much a work in progress.

An exciting pursuit of the team's first-ever NL wild-card berth and potential return to postseason play kept Mets fans perched on the rims of their seats throughout the final stages of the 1998 campaign—at least until the team crashed and burned during the final week of an exhausting, upbeat season. The summer of '98 was noteworthy for an explosion of home runs and a corresponding flood of fan interest spurred by pursuits of one of baseball's most cherished records. All across the nation, fans tuned back into baseball, as Mark McGwire and Sammy Sosa electrified them with their unprecedented joint pursuit of legendary home run milestones reached by Babe Ruth and Roger Maris. But in New York, all eyes were focused more narrowly on the hometown Mets and the dream of their first postseason visit in more than a decade. The collapse in the final week—five straight losses to Montreal and Atlanta—may have been sufficient to cede a wild-card prize to the Chicago Cubs, but it was hardly enough to dull widespread hopes for a true Mets rebirth-in-progress. The 1999 season proved a near carbon copy, with McGwire and Sosa still ringing

up record home run numbers and the Mets still tantalizing their fans with the hope of October playoff success. The second time around, the promised land indeed seemed a step closer, even if the Mets' late-season run would again fall just a few steps short of World Series pay dirt.

The Bobby Valentine years would be characterized from the start by a constantly improving ball club that has repeatedly shown its mettle as a pennant contender. Only the ominous presence in the same NL East Division of the nineties' best outfit, the Atlanta Braves, and runaway free-agent spending by the expansion Florida Marlins dulled more grandiose dreams for potential postseason play. But on-field collapses and off-field chaos have also been franchise staples during most recent seasons. The 1999 campaign wasn't much more than a month old before chaos arose in the clubhouse. The drill-sergeant manager was reportedly unpopular with some of his veteran players, especially Rickey Henderson and Bobby Bonilla; and early-season injuries to starters Bobby Jones and Rick Reed and the team's sluggish May and June performances did little for club morale. When the Mets dropped eight straight between May 28 and June 5, the beleaguered manager remained standing, but three of his handpicked coaches—Bob Apodaca, Randy Niemann, and Tom Robson—were reassigned to minor league duties. Valentine added his own chapter to the reigning calamity when he was suspended for two games and fined $5,000 for returning to the dugout in disguise after being ejected for umpire baiting. The Mets' disappointing overall performance had again raised the specter of Valentine's possible dismissal, but when the dust settled, the manager was still in place, even if his coaching staff had been partially dismantled. What seemed apparent throughout such trials was that the Mets, just like their crosstown rival Yankees, led by noisome owner George Steinbrenner, now seemed to thrive on such off-field upheavals. So far, in Bobby Valentine's managerial tenure, the lasting optimism has always somehow managed to slightly outpace the lurking pessimism.

The sudden arrival of Mike Piazza and the resulting second-half run toward a 1998 wild-card postseason ticket had kept the overachieving Mets in the headlines throughout one of the most memorable seasons in major league baseball history. Piazza's mid-season acquisition was indeed one of the biggest stories to surround the Mets' camp in years. The trade with Florida's Marlins in late May generated the kind of hoopla that had surrounded earlier acquisitions of slugging backstop Gary Carter in the off-season of 1985 and All-Star Keith Hernandez in mid-season 1983. Those trades had led directly to a

Edgardo Alfonzo may well be the best all-around major leaguer in New York. (NY Mets)

world championship, and there was now rampant optimism that the Piazza deal would likely do the same. At the very least, this was exactly the kind of superstar acquisition so desperately needed to compete for fan and media attention against the rival Steinbrenner Yankees, who were now ensconced in another spectacular dynasty. The Yankees were busy racking up the largest win total in modern baseball history, as they ran roughshod over American League opponents; the Mets, with Piazza's potent bat in the lineup, appeared suddenly equipped to hang in a pennant race with the Yankee-like Atlanta Braves. Before the ink was dry on the headlines that greeted the Piazza trade, New York City was abuzz with giddy talk about a possible Subway World Series.

Piazza indeed proved to be everything that the Mets fans and front office had hoped. His contract disputes with the Dodgers and his short, embarrassing sojourn with the dismantled Florida Marlins now behind him, the muscular backstop continued the relentless slugging that had made him the best-hitting catcher in baseball annals. His .348 average over the season's last 100-plus games powered an offense that nearly carried the ball club to the wire. Piazza posted the league's fourth-best batting average, added his fifth season of 30-plus homers, and banged in more than 100 runs for the fourth time. But the stretch run of the 1998 campaign was more than just a solo Mike Piazza show. Baseball's most fearsome catcher also had plenty of help from an offense surrounding him that was one of the most potent the New York Mets had ever fielded. In his second year with the club, lefty-swinging first baseman John Olerud was the league's runner-up in the batting race; Edgardo Alfonzo took another step toward major stardom while manning third with career bests in homers and RBIs. And the pitching—still the team's Achilles' heel—was at least more respectable, thanks to 17 wins and a 2.47 ERA from Al Leiter, 16 victories and 212.1 innings of durable work from Rick Reed, and 38 saves from veteran John Franco.

The stretch run between the Mets and Cubs was the most intense in the short history of the wild card. Both teams entered the final weeks with no realistic hopes of catching division leaders Atlanta and Houston, but both were running neck-and-neck with the West Division Giants for the fourth postseason slot. And the dramatic race to the postseason wire came in the midst of what had become one of baseball's most celebrated summers in almost a decade. In the pennant-race background loomed the ongoing drama of the McGwire-versus-Sosa home run chase, which had captured the nation's fancy and restored millions of fans to the occupation of baseball fanatic. And it was the home run saga and the pursuit of Roger Maris's magic total of 61 that garnered most of the nation's headlines—even in New York, where the Yankees were on pace for a record 114 wins, and the Mets were playoff contenders for the first time in a decade.

After a brilliant August run, in which the club took 20 of 32 and kept pace with the red-hot Cubs, the Mets would falter in the season's final weeks and drop nine of their final 16 games. But the Cubs had an ill-timed slump of their own and didn't run away and hide from the Mets. Chicago actually opened the door one final time when it gave away a crucial game in Milwaukee on a dropped outfield fly in the ninth inning that handed over a sure win and kept the wild-card chase wide open. But the Mets failed to meet the challenge when they bungled two final games at home with weak Montreal (a team 30 games under .500) and then couldn't right the ship during the final weekend series on the road against playoff-bound Atlanta. The final playoff slot was not settled until the final weekend of the summer season, with the Cubs grabbing a pair in Houston while the Mets fell by counts of 6-5, 4-0, and 7-2.

In the end, the Mets' failures could be laid at the doorstep of pitching. It was only a high-powered offense carried by Piazza and Olerud that had kept the team competitive down the stretch. The Mets had no dominant staff ace who could be a stopper every fourth or fifth day; and in the several big September series on which the season turned, this would prove a fatal flaw. The rotation, with Leiter and Reed the only double-figure winners, was solid but not spectacular and also not always dependable in the clutch. The bullpen was also lacking the top closer and reliable setup men that other playoff-ready teams could boast. Franco surpassed his own team record with 38 saves, but the New Yorkers could not stack up against the Braves, Cubs, or Padres when it came to healthy and effective arms. In the end, the schedule didn't do the Mets any favors, either, with home (three

wins in four games) and away (three straight defeats) clashes against powerhouse Atlanta on the docket for the final four weeks. Atlanta had little at stake in late September, with a division title clinched and a postseason home-field advantage already assured, but the proud Braves were certainly not about to roll over and play dead against their bitter New York rivals.

The last-minute collapse in 1998 would be a stiff challenge for the Mets to put aside for the next hope-filled season. One weighty tribute to manager Bobby Valentine was the fact that his next ball club was fully prepared by opening day to focus only on the present and to dismiss all bunglings of the past.

The Mets' front-office team of GM Steve Phillips and assistant GM Omar Minaya played a significant role in resurrecting 1999 hopes from the 1998 ashes. Off-season roster moves would now put in place other obvious elements to enhance the acquisition of Piazza and rebuild the Mets' fortunes in short order. The December free-agent signings of veteran third baseman Robin Ventura (Chicago White Sox) and Hall of Fame–bound outfielder Rickey Henderson (Oakland A's) were bold moves, as was the 1999 off-season trade of Todd Hundley to the LA Dodgers for outfield prospect Roger Cedeño. Hundley had been excess baggage ever since the Piazza deal, and something had to be done while the injury-slowed spare backstop still had some market value. The Hundley-for-Cedeño deal proved brilliant, as the young Venezuelan quickly became the team's most versatile star. Cedeño started at all three outfield posts, filled the leadoff slot while Henderson was injured, served as an excellent late-inning defensive replacement, and came close to leading the circuit with 66 steals. The deal with LA provided an additional bonus: The three-way transaction, which also involved Baltimore, put flame-throwing Dominican Armando Benitez in the Mets' bullpen. With Benitez and Franco, New York would now have the best righty-lefty closer duo in baseball. And the pitching staff was also further strengthened, first by the free-agent addition of veteran Orel Hershiser and later by a July trade for experienced southpaw Kenny Rogers.

The arrival of Robin Ventura marked a watershed in team reconstruction. The immediate result was an infield that proved throughout the 1999 season to be one of baseball's all-time best. Shortstop Rey Ordoñez didn't hit his weight, but he was as good a defender as could be found anywhere. Olerud had supplied a big bat ever since coming over from Toronto, but was also a top defender at first base. Edgardo Alfonzo dutifully accepted a switch from third to second to accommodate Ventura and mastered his new position in surprisingly rapid fashion. More important, Alfonzo was just as quickly becoming one of the best clutch hitters in the league and thus provided an offensive force at second that resurrected images of the legendary Rogers Hornsby. And the addition of Ventura provided another solid hitter. The Mets now offered a truly frightening lineup, with Henderson, Cedeño, Ventura, Alfonzo, and Olerud aligned in the batting order to protect the always-active bat of rock-solid offensive pillar Mike Piazza.

With their own modern-day version of Murderers' Row, the 1999 Mets were poised to launch a season that would boast more record-book milestones than had been reached in years. On the defensive side, the club would establish a major league record for fewest errors in a season, with only 68 miscues. The im-

proved defense was largely due, as expected, to the crack infield, whose season-long error total of 33 was also a big-league record. Rey Ordoñez contributed mightily to the glue-gloved effort by ending the season with 100 straight error-less games, another new entry on the major league record blotter. The pitchers got into the act when John Franco became the second player ever to reach the 400-save plateau and Turk Wendell posted a club mark by appearing in 80 games. But it was the big bats that made the loudest noise. For the first time ever, the Mets had three 100-RBI men (Alfonzo, Piazza, Ventura), with Alfonzo also tying a handful of records for single-game hitting performance (including hits, total bases, and runs scored). The club slugged a record eight grand slams, and Ventura became the first player in big-league history to whack bases-loaded homers in both ends of a doubleheader. Almost unnoticed in all this artillery display were Mike Piazza's efforts in tying the team standard for streak hitting (24 consecutive games) and setting a new record for RBIs (124).

Despite all the obvious improvements, the new season wasn't destined to be any easier than the last when it came to earning a spot in the postseason playoff derby. The Chicago Cubs had fallen from single-season grace, but were quickly replaced by the Cincinnati Reds as a Central Division contender. It had to be assumed that the Mets would not likely overhaul Atlanta for a division title and thus again would have to battle the Central Division and West Division runners-up for a wild-card slot. Either Houston or Cincinnati in the Central would have to be outpaced, and so would the suddenly potent expansion Arizona Diamondbacks, along with the Dodgers and Giants out West.

From the start, it was apparent that the Mets would likely be in the hunt in 1999, but also that the road traveled would be a rough one from April to October. The team proved early on to be streaky, capable of bunching strings of victories on the heels of strings of losses. One bad spell in June caused not only the coaching shakeup that brought Dave Wallace on board as the new pitching coach and original Met Al Jackson as the bullpen mentor, but also set in motion a busy mid-summer of roster adjustments. On the eve of the July trading deadline, there were a few minor but important deals that restructured the outfield and

Rey Ordoñez, baseball's most sure-handed shortstop. (NY Mets)

mound corps. Darryl Hamilton was acquired from Colorado, and although his impact was not like that of Piazza—the previous year's arrival—he was nonetheless a vital addition to the batting order. And Billy Taylor also seemed an important addition in the bullpen when he was plucked from the Oakland A's. But Taylor was not an immediate success; he never duplicated the fast start in which he saved 26 games for the A's through July, and he was rarely used in important games during the final seven weeks of the season.

As the summer progressed, Valentine solidified his reputation as a survivor. He got through the mid-season upheavals that had cost three coaches their jobs. He then survived another late-year slump—seven straight mid-September losses that nearly put Cincinnati squarely in the wild-card driver's seat. Again, the Mets had seemed to fade at the worst possible time—in the summer's closing days. Cincinnati had emerged as the chief rival for postseason honors among non-division-winners, and the Reds had hung with the Mets all summer long. Cincinnati even threatened to overhaul the Houston Astros for the top Central Division spot, but the Reds ran out of gas down the stretch. The Queen City outfit actually helped the Mets' cause, just as the Cubs had done the previous September, dropping two of three on the final weekend to the same Milwaukee team that had almost scuttled Chicago a year earlier. But this time Valentine and company had the experience and fortitude to hang on, if only barely.

In the end, the entire 1999 pennant chase for both the Mets and Reds came down to a single, extra regular-season game played at Cincinnati's Cinergy Field. The vital playoff game was an unscheduled affair needed to decide the wild-card postseason issue between two teams with identical records. Now the Mets' starting pitching, which had on so many recent occasions faltered, came through in spades when it was most desperately needed. The hero was Al Leiter, who hurled the best game of his season and perhaps his career. The crafty southpaw authored a complete-game two-hitter with four walks and seven strikeouts. Leiter received all the support he would need in the 5-0 season-making victory from a pair of long balls off the bats of Edgardo Alfonzo (two-run homer) and Rickey Henderson (solo homer).

Bobby Bonilla returned to his hometown for his swan song with the Mets in the late '90s. (NY Mets)

In earlier postseason visits, the Mets had always seemed to be carried by unlikely heroes. Ron Swoboda and Donn Clendenon had been the prototypes back in the 1969 "miracle" season. And Len Dykstra was a later model during the 1986 uprising against Houston and Boston. Now it would be six-year veteran Todd Pratt, an unheralded reserve who had played for three National League clubs and never played more than 41 games before the current campaign. Pratt would luckily step to the fore when needed and save the opening playoff-round series.

The Mets got off to a fast start against the West Division champions from Arizona. The Diamondbacks had been a season-long surprise, but none doubted their legitimacy after 103 victories in only their second season of existence. With Cy Young hurler Randy Johnson in its arsenal, Arizona was not an unreasonable choice to go all the way. But the Mets were now back on track, and they shocked Johnson and the D-Backs out in Phoenix in the division series opener. A pair of homers by Edgardo Alfonzo

Dave Mlicki never fulfilled his pitching promise in the Big Apple.
(NY Mets)

were the big blows in an 8-4 romp. Surrendering eight hits and seven earned runs to mute his 11 strikeouts, Johnson would lose his sixth straight postseason game.

Arizona quickly rebounded, and the vaunted Mets offense was completely stymied in the second outing at Bank One Ballpark by veteran right-hander and former Cardinal ace Todd Stottlemyre. It was a game that handed the momentum back to Arizona. Another win in New York would now set the stage for handing the ball back to the overpowering Randy Johnson, with only a single win separating Arizona from advancing to the next round. But as fate would have it, Johnson was not destined to again toe the pitching rubber this postseason.

It was not only the prospect of another bout with Johnson that sent the Mets reeling after Game 2. Mike Piazza had injured the thumb on his throwing hand and would be stripped from the heart of the lineup for at least several games. The Mets' prospects immediately sank drastically. The replacement backstop would have to be the inexperienced Todd Pratt, a capable defensive catcher, perhaps, but certainly not a hitter with very imposing numbers. Fortunately, the absence of Piazza was not felt immediately

in Game 3 back at Shea Stadium. The New Yorkers unloaded a big six-run sixth inning on Arizona pitching to build a safe margin. Rick Reed hurled a clutch game, which buoyed the Mets' clubhouse. It was now New York that stood one game away from victory, and the pressure was certainly there to eliminate Arizona once and for all so the Mets wouldn't have to revisit both Bank One Ballpark and the difficult Randy Johnson.

The final game of the divisional playoffs was a barn burner—one of the most unforgettable in club history. This game seemed to have it all, especially a heavy dose of nail-biting drama and late-inning heroics. There were several lead changes and some strange managerial moves along the way. There was a full-scale rhubarb late in the contest that featured the ejection of Mets third-base coach Cookie Rojas. And there was a crucial error by converted Arizona outfielder Tony Womack that allowed the Mets back into the game and also into extra innings. With the D-Backs only six outs from knotting the series, Womack dropped a routine fly off the bat of John Olerud, putting the Mets in position to wriggle off the hook with a game-tying eighth-inning run. Then lightning struck at Shea Stadium as it had hardly ever struck before. As though the script had been drafted in Hollywood, Piazza's replacement, Todd Pratt, stepped to the plate in the 10th with the game on the line. Rarely a long-ball threat, Pratt unloaded in dramatic fashion with a homer to center that instantly ended the series. The round tripper was a historic one—only the fourth to end a playoff game in sudden-death style—but it was also destined to be long remembered by Mets fans as one of the sweetest blasts in the team's annals.

The team that had collapsed at the wire in 1998 had now a year later transformed itself into a ball club adroit at clutch play whenever the chips were down. First, Leiter had come through with a masterful mound effort when the team most needed a stopper to plug opposition bats. Second, unheralded Todd Pratt had enjoyed his rare moment in the sun, joining the long list of unlikely postseason heroes who have so often enriched baseball's playoff lore. And thus Valentine's crew was still very much alive and about to enjoy a crack at the powerhouse Braves and thus at the National League pennant.

Against the Braves there was never much doubt from the early innings of the first NLCS game that the Mets were not yet quite ready to supplant the reigning National League dynasty. The series, in the end, would prove much closer in reality than the six-game scenario might suggest. The opener was decided by two runs and proved to be the most one-sided affair of the entire set. A surprising comeback and the heroics of the final game at Shea were enough to demonstrate that Valentine's team would not simply roll over. But then the magic finally ran out, and superior overall talent—not aimless luck—proved to be the final deciding factor.

Greg Maddux simply baffled Mets hitters from wire to wire in the series opener. The masterful Maddux worked seven innings, giving up a solo run on but five tame hits. Maddux was clearly on top of his game and threw only 83 pitches to the handcuffed Mets batters. Meanwhile, the Braves were busy scratching across single runs in the first, fifth, and sixth, and again in the eighth. The tally in the sixth came on a solo homer by eventual series MVP Eddie Pérez, who was filling in behind the plate for the injured Javier Lopez. Flame-throwing Atlanta closer John Rocker did allow an unearned ninth-inning New York run but retired the final four batters to earn the opening-game save.

Kevin Millwood proved every bit as stingy in the second NLCS matchup. The 18-game winner allowed but a pair of New York scratch runs, which came on a walk and two singles in the second and Melvin Mora's first big-league homer in the fifth. But Millwood's effort proved sufficient in the sixth, when things suddenly collapsed for Mets starter Kenny Rogers, who offered up a pair of two-run homers to Brian Jordan and catcher Eddie Pérez. Rocker then took over out of the bullpen and stranded the potential tying and go-ahead runs in the eighth. Manager Bobby Cox next surprised observers by turning to one of his starters for the closer role, and John Smoltz pitched a perfect 1-2-3 inning to finish out the ninth.

The third game unfolded as a classic matchup between top lefties. Tom Glavine and Al Leiter dueled effectively and equally mystified opposing batters inning after inning. The game's only marker came in the top of the first frame without benefit of an RBI, and Glavine and relievers Mike Remlinger and Rocker then made it stand up for the full nine-inning course.

Leiter surrendered only three hits in his seven frames and nearly matched his clutch outing two weeks earlier in the vital tie-breaker game with Cincinnati. But this time it was all for naught, as the Mets' bats could not provide their ace southpaw with even a single necessary run.

New York finally came to life in the fourth game of the series when the knockout count had reached the mandatory eight. An embarrassing sweep was staring the snakebitten New Yorkers squarely in the face when eighth-inning solo homers by Brian Jordan and Ryan Klesko turned a 1-0 New York lead into an apparent series-ending 2-1 deficit. New York was not yet dead, however, roaring back in its own half of the inning after two batters had already been retired. Olerud, who had provided the only earlier run with a homer, now drove home the deciding tallies (Cedeño and Mora) with a clutch single to center off nemesis southpaw John Rocker. It was only the second hit the Mets had managed off Rocker in his four appearances, and at the moment, it loomed as the biggest hit of the fast-fading season.

Nagging injuries have repeatedly sidetracked Bobby Jones's efforts to become a bona fide Mets mound ace. (NY Mets)

The fifth game—the final game of the year in New York, unless a miraculous turnaround could somehow still salvage a Subway Series—proved to be a truly wild affair. Despite a largely one-sided series up to this point, the air had been charged by the on-field behavior and public pronouncements of Atlanta reliever John Rocker. Rocker had been a thorn in the side of New York fans throughout the series with his show-stopping, late-inning sprints from the outfield bullpen and his rally-stopping mound performances. He had also been quite vociferous in openly condemning New York fans in the press as uncouth and unruly. Against the backdrop of Rocker's blasts at New Yorkers, the Mets' last desperate stand turned into a marathon contest that involved 45 total players, 15 pitchers, and as many managerial moves on both sides as in a high-powered chess game.

Each team scored twice early, but those early runs were only distant memories by the time the battle reached its dramatic conclusion almost five hours later. Atlanta broke the extra-inning ice first, taking a 3-2 lead in the top of the 15th. Braves manager Bobby Cox was down to his final reliever, rookie Kevin McGlinchy, and for some reason was unwilling to turn to starters Greg Maddux and Tom Glavine in the bullpen, even though the pennant was now within easy grasp. McGlinchy remained on the hill despite a shaky performance which saw him load the bases with but one out. The struggling McGlinchy next walked across the tying run when he issued four wide pitches to Todd Pratt. With still no move back to the bullpen by Cox, Robin Ventura sensed a chance for instant redemption as he stepped to the plate in the midst of a 1-for-18 series slump. Ventura promptly unloaded on a McGlinchy fastball, driving the pitch over the right-field fence for an apparent game-ending grand slam. But Ventura's blast would quickly become something other than it appeared to be. As bedlam consumed the entire field, Ventura was mobbed on the basepaths by a torrent of teammates and never touched any bag but first. The dramatic blow was credited as a game-winning single, and only one run was counted. The exhausting game itself had stretched for 5 hours and 46 minutes, easily a postseason record.

The spunky Mets had one last chance back in Atlanta, and they nearly made the most of it. It was a game in which the New Yorkers might well have packed it all in and faded quietly after falling behind 5-0 in the first inning. Yet the Mets gamely rallied for three runs in the sixth inning and then pulled into a 7-7 tie on the strength of a Mike Piazza homer in the seventh. There were even two brief leads for New York in the top of the eighth and the top of the 10th, but the bullpen couldn't make those leads stand up. The tide eventually turned in the bottom of the 11th, when Gerald Williams doubled and then finally scored the game-winner when Kenny Rogers issued a final walk to Andruw Jones with the bases jammed. New York had battled right to the end to make a legitimate contest out of what had started as a one-sided series. In the end, the bullpen had once more let Bobby Valentine down in the clutch.

It seemed once more that the Mets might have a hard time rebounding from season-ending defeat. A most unfortunate incident in the late stages of the final postseason game seemed once more to point in the direction of disintegrating team harmony. Rickey Henderson and Bobby Bonilla had left the dugout and were playing cards in the clubhouse while their teammates went down for the final time in the 11th frame at Atlanta. The rest of the ball club had already pulled together on that final night and had fought bravely with its back to the wall in a fifth consecutive one-run game. Henderson (released early in the 2000 season) and Bonilla (released outright in January) would quickly prove not to be part of the mix that would carry the torch into the next season.

The new century thus opened in Mets country with sufficient reasons for guarded optimism. Houston ace and Cy Young runner-up Mike Hampton, one of the National League's most effective southpaws, had been acquired at year's end in still another off-season front-office move of bold proportions. Stalwarts John Olerud and Roger Cedeño and pitching prospect Octavio Dotel had all departed, the former to free agency and the latter pair to Houston as part of the Mike Hampton deal. Veteran Kenny Rogers was given his release during the winter months. But the rest of the lineup was intact, and some vital reinforcements had been brought on board. Most notable among the newcomers was outfielder Derek Bell, who accompanied Hampton in the landmark Astros exchange and promised to add more lumber to one of the league's heftiest lineups. There was also much

Mike Piazza's arrival in Shea Stadium launched a new era of championship dreams for the hordes of Mets faithful. (NY Mets)

hoopla surrounding the new season when it opened with a historic two-game series versus the Chicago Cubs in Japan's distant Tokyo Dome. The event marked the first time official big-league play had been staged outside the North American continent and also signaled Major League Baseball's commitment to exploiting the sport's newfound international dimensions. Mets fans now had plenty of reason for optimism as a new millennium unfolded. If the powerhouse Atlanta Braves faltered anytime soon at the top of the National League pack, the retooled New York Mets would certainly be waiting hungrily in the wings.

CHAPTER 2
Concise History of the New York Mets

They started out as lovable losers, and they were indeed the most beloved persistent losers in all of baseball history. Never before or since has a team that couldn't win even occasionally and couldn't even look good when it was losing received such charity from the local press or such unwavering devotion from its huge fandom. Nor has any other hapless big-league basement dweller ever boasted such a loyal following. The expansion New York Mets of the riotous early sixties were indeed baseball's most popular success story—by just about any measure.

There were obvious explanations for such seemingly wrong-headed support, to be sure. It was not at all that New Yorkers were untutored baseball rubes willing to accept any excuse for a major league ball club; nor were the cranks of Gotham an especially masochistic lot. Rather, if you couldn't manage to have fun watching the 1962 or 1963 expansion New York Mets, then it was likely you couldn't find joy anywhere in

Choo Choo Coleman typified the colorful, if inept, expansion Mets. (NY Mets)

the nation's pastime. Those first Mets editions managed by septuagenarian trickster Casey Stengel and featuring daily lineups of last-time-around-the-circuit old-timers and still-wet-behind-the-ears underachieving prospects were never very artistic or glamorous on the diamond—as colorful as they may often have been in the clubhouse. They didn't thrill with many victories or many outstanding individual pitching or batting exploits. But they were always joyously and enthusiastically unpredictable.

And their presence also meant that National League baseball was back in town, and for a while at least, that in itself was more than enough.

CAN'T ANYBODY HERE PLAY THIS GAME?

New York ballpark denizens, many of whom are baseball's greatest fans, had only recently been left with an unexpected, devastating void at the end of the 1957 season. Two rival National League clubs that had been a part of the city's fabric since the 1880s and who carried on a rivalry that was, in the words of *New York Times* baseball writer George Vecsey, more like the soccer rivalries of British or Italian

Richie Ashburn capped his Hall of Fame career in the Polo Grounds. (Brace Photo)

neighborhoods than like American sports, had suddenly departed from the scene. Dodgers owner Walter O'Malley and Giants owner Horace Stoneham had pressed the city fathers for several years for some plan that would relocate their ball clubs out of economically floundering neighborhoods and into new stadiums that would draw fans from Gotham's increasingly suburban middle-class population. Eventually, both gave up on the hope to rebuild franchise fortunes in New York and escaped to more promising west coast venues, following a cataclysmic big-league trend started by Lou Perini's 1953 Braves (Boston to Milwaukee), Bill Veeck's 1954 Browns/Orioles (St. Louis to Baltimore), and Connie Mack's 1955 Athletics (Philadelphia to Kansas City).

The sudden flight of the Dodgers and Giants after the 1957 season was all the more painful for New Yorkers when set against the backdrop of all the delirious baseball thrills that had been experienced in the dozen postwar years. In these twelve years, the Yankees had visited the World Series nine times (1947, 1949, 1950, 1951, 1952, 1953, 1955, 1956, 1957). The city's two National League clubs were also regulars in the Fall Classic: the Giants having entered

twice (1951 and 1954), and the Dodgers having qualified half a dozen times (1947, 1949, 1952, 1953, 1955, 1956). That meant that in seven of the past 12 Octobers, the greatest show in baseball had been an all-New York Subway Series affair. And larger-than-life diamond stars such as Willie Mays, Joe DiMaggio, Gil Hodges, Duke Snider, Mickey Mantle, Leo Durocher, Jackie Robinson, Yogi Berra, and Pee Wee Reese had been fixtures on the New York baseball scene.

For half a century, the fans of New York lived and died with the city's two arch-rival NL ball clubs, often carrying out their nonstop baseball debates in the local taverns as well as in ballpark bleachers. Vecsey noted that National League baseball's special charm in New York for decades had been that "Dodger and Giant fans were close enough to get their hands on each other—and frequently did." And then almost overnight there was, shockingly, a hopeless void. Motivated perhaps equally by potential profit and by Mayor Robert Wagner's refusals to offer a sweet stadium deal, Walter O'Malley had decided on a scheme to pull his Dodgers out of town and flee to the gold-paved venues of Southern California. Horace Stoneham was quick to follow the same line of thinking. The Giants actually announced first, on August 19, 1957, that they would take up new residence alongside San Francisco Bay. By early October, O'Malley confirmed his deal with the city fathers of faraway Los Angeles. In one short autumn, the baseball world that had remained constant for half a century was dismantled forever.

On the heels of the Dodgers' and Giants' departures, the hopes for resurrecting National League baseball in the nation's largest city seemed quite bleak. Prominent lawyer William Shea—Mayor Wagner's choice to head a committee charged with finding replacement teams—had approached existing franchises in Cincinnati, Pittsburgh, and Philadelphia without success. What existing franchise would likely pull up roots in the hinterlands to compete openly with the popular and successful Yankees in New York? And today's constant promise of expansion franchises was not part of the tradition-driven baseball universe at midcentury. Yet the times were nevertheless changing, and the winds were now blowing in a different direction everywhere in the baseball universe. What O'Malley had triggered was soon to become New York's baseball salvation, as

Jack Fisher lost an unenviable 24 games with the 1965 edition of the Polo Grounders. (Brace Photo)

New York's Polo Grounds fans may be fanatical followers of the home club, the Mets, but they can't forget the exploits of Willie Mays when the Giants were the local club. Now with the San Francisco Giants, Willie is still the favorite son of the fans, who gathered around the popular outfielder during pregame ceremonies on May 3, 1963. (AP/Wide World Photos)

much as its apparent baseball ruination. Branch Rickey was among those who teamed with William Shea to force the issue. Rickey and Shea launched a scheme for a new Continental League that quickly found financial backers in eight major cities.

The ingenious maneuver—coupled with Rickey's and Shea's announced plan to challenge big-league baseball's favored antitrust status in Washington—seemed a serious enough threat to the existing baseball establishment to spur immediate action from big-league moguls. Before the 1959 summer was out, the commissioner's office announced plans for the first modern-era baseball expansion, with four new clubs to be drawn from the stable of proposed Continental League owners. When these first changes to the size and shape of the base-

ball map were soon unveiled, they contained the expected news that New York City would be a cornerstone of the new construction. Two expansion teams were brought into the American League in 1961, and the immediate impact was a shattering one on the record book. A diluted junior circuit probably helped Roger Maris's headline-grabbing home run onslaught, which overtook Babe Ruth's long-standing record of 60. A year later there would also be a pair of additions to the senior circuit, and once more New Yorkers would receive the direct benefits. The New York Mets would now join the Houston Colt .45s as baseball's newest infant franchises.

Now hope sprang once more to life with the fledgling Metropolitans—heirs to decades of Ebbets Field and Polo Grounds heroics. In real-

THE NY METS ENCYCLOPEDIA

Original Mets Chosen in
October 1961 NL Expansion Draft

Player	Original Team	Position	Draft Price Paid
Jay Hook	Cincinnati Reds	Pitcher	$125,000
Bob Miller	St. Louis Cardinals	Pitcher	$125,000
Lee Walls	Chicago Cubs	Outfielder	$125,000
Don Zimmer	Chicago Cubs	Infielder	$125,000
Craig Anderson	St. Louis Cardinals	Pitcher	$75,000
Gus Bell	Cincinnati Reds	Outfielder	$75,000
Ed Bouchee	Chicago Cubs	First Baseman	$75,000
Chris Cannizzaro	St. Louis Cardinals	Catcher	$75,000
Elio Chacón	Cincinnati Reds	Infielder	$75,000
Joe Christopher	Pittsburgh Pirates	Outfielder	$75,000
Choo Choo Coleman	Philadelphia Phillies	Catcher	$75,000
Roger Craig	Los Angeles Dodgers	Pitcher	$75,000
Ray Daviault	San Francisco Giants	Pitcher	$75,000
John DeMerit	Milwaukee Braves	Outfielder	$75,000
Sammy Drake	Chicago Cubs	Infielder	$75,000
Gil Hodges	Los Angeles Dodgers	First Baseman	$75,000
Al Jackson	Pittsburgh Pirates	Pitcher	$75,000
Hobie Landrith	San Francisco Giants	Catcher	$75,000*
Felix Mantilla	Milwaukee Braves	Infielder	$75,000
Bobby Gene Smith	Philadelphia Phillies	Outfielder	$75,000
Jim Hickman	St. Louis Cardinals	Outfielder	$50,000
Sherman Jones	Cincinnati Reds	Pitcher	$50,000

*Hobie Landrith is the Mets' first pick. Houston's top selection and first overall is San Francisco Giants infielder Ed Bressoud.

ity, of course, the optimism for true replacement of the Dodgers and Giants was transparently ill founded. Fans perhaps had once again been handed raw hope and the bare trappings of big-league baseball, but they hadn't been given much else by the baseball lords. The existing mechanisms for expansion baseball didn't offer much prospect for building a competitive or even respectable team overnight. The fans might not notice or care out in Houston if they were fed a season-opening lineup of career minor leaguers or big-league washouts such as Joey Amalfitano, Bob Aspromonte, Al Spangler, and Roman Mejias, or presented with a pitching staff populated by the weak arms of journeymen Hal Woodeshick, Russ Kemmerer, Jim Umbricht, and George Brunet. But you couldn't so easily fool the baseball-savvy crowds in tradition-rich New York.

An expansion draft held in Cincinnati in the wake of the Yankees-Reds World Series promised the new clubs ragtag rosters to begin their maiden National League journeys. Each existing NL ball club was required to place 15

men in the pool for the October 10 lottery, and each expansion club was allowed 16 picks, two from each established team. The price was $75,000 per player. A second round allowed both New York and Houston one final pick from each sister team for $50,000, and then a selection of no more than four veterans from a premium pool carrying a $125,000 price tag. In New York a bit of front office foresight would manage to sprinkle the new club with some old and respectable heroes to make the package seem a little more palatable, some coming with signings and trades outside of the staged draft, and a few not arriving until partway into the second season. There would thus be names like Hodges, Snider, Spahn, Berra, and Ashburn dressed in Mets colors over the first few summers. Lesser former stars (often with solid New York connections), such as Roger Craig, Clem Labine, Gene Woodling, "Vinegar Bend" Mizell, Tracy Stallard, Felix Mantilla, and Charlie Neal, also provided some household names and some tested big-league talent.

And the wisest move of all came with the hiring of the new field manager. For that role, the Mets ownership was able to resurrect the managerial career of a living New York baseball legend named Casey Stengel, an immense fan favorite, even after having been unceremoniously dumped by the crosstown Yankees on the heels of a 1960 World Series loss to the Pirates. Perhaps only John "Muggsy" McGraw—the architect of "scientific" baseball—might have been a more propitious choice if one had the pick of colorful and charismatic bench leaders from the sport's entire first century. For a dozen years, Charles Dillon Stengel had loomed almost larger in his own right than one of baseball's grandest teams. He had piloted the invincible Yankees to 10 American League pennants and seven world titles, a record five in succession. He spouted endless Stengelese (his unique brand of double-talk) and thus gave a human face to a relentless corporate winner. Early on, he aggravated the great DiMaggio when he boasted after his first World Series triumph in '49 that he couldn't have done it without help from his players. But Casey was, from the start, a huge hit with the New York media, even if sometimes a mixed blessing to his ballplayers. And you couldn't argue with his on-field successes. He managed some of the game's brightest stars in a golden era—Mantle, Ford, Berra, and DiMaggio—and he frequently stole center

Duke Snider was only a shadow of the great "Duke of Flatbush" when he donned Mets togs in 1963. (NY Mets)

stage from the entire lot of them. Now he was being given a barren stage, where he himself would be the entire main attraction. And Casey was still capable of providing quite an entertaining show all by himself.

The choices to fill the rest of the roster were not quite so exciting. In the ceremonial draft that was clearly designed to stuff the pockets of the existing owners rather than the rosters of the new ones, New York came away with a broken-down catcher as its first lineup choice. Hobie Landrith had logged a dozen seasons in the big leagues without ever impressing anyone with his soft Louisville Slugger (he was a .233 lifetime hitter with little power and no foot speed) and his barely adequate receiving skills (only twice had he ever been used in as many as 100 games). Manager Stengel greeted the news with a classic utterance of Stengelese philosophy—"You gotta start with a catcher or you'll have all passed balls." And the rest of the October selections were equally dismal. The four premium players bought for the $125,000 highway-robbery fee were hardly the stuff of a big-league starting lineup. Jay Hook had only once won in double figures during five years of mound work in Cincinnati and that came in a

season when he lost 18 times. Bob Miller, another journeyman right-hander, carried a 9-9 career record in St. Louis. Outfielder Lee Walls (destined to be promptly traded to Los Angeles for dependable infielder Charlie Neal) was the best of the lot and had once batted .304 with the Cubs and also once appeared on an All-Star Game roster. And future coaching legend Don Zimmer had never been more than a dependable utility man with the Dodgers and the Cubs. This was destined to be a team composed of overpriced castoffs and overvalued journeymen.

Club ownership fortuitously seemed to fall into far more capable hands than did the on-field responsibilities for fielding ground balls or hitting pitched ones. The new club was first to be owned in equal one-third shares by three former members of the New York Giants Board of Directors. The imposing troika consisted of Joan Whitney Payson, Dwight F. Davis Jr., and Mrs. Dorothy Killian; but Joan Payson almost immediately bought out the others and set up Donald Grant as her chief of on-field baseball operations. Grant wasted little time in demonstrating his own savvy by turning to recently ousted Yankees front man George Weiss as his general manager. It was Weiss, in turn, thanks to a huge assist from Mrs. Payson herself, who promptly lured his old Yankee colleague Stengel out of temporary retirement. Weiss was clearly committed to a notion that if early victories were unlikely to become regular fare, then a healthy dose of ex-Dodgers and ex-Giants were the order of the day to fill up seats in the Polo Grounds. Using this tactic, which was designed to shape the club's fate for its first six seasons, Weiss supplemented his draft selections of Zimmer, Hodges, and Gus Bell by purchasing the contract of Braves slugger Frank Thomas, swapping Lee Walls for Charlie Neal, and also acquiring future Hall of Famer Richie Ashburn from the Chicago Cubs.

Off the field there unfolded the circus surrounding the choice of a fitting name for the new ball club, which only inherited the label "Mets" a few weeks before the October draft to fill out a playing roster. The new owners made a ceremonious affair of the naming ritual by inviting the press to a September 1961 cocktail party for an "unofficial" vote on the club moniker. Nearly 500 different names had been suggested in fan letters that had poured in over the summer, and the working list was winnowed to

10 by the press corps that gathered at Mrs. Payson's Long Island home—Continentals, Burros (originally spelled "Boros" so as to suggest the city's five boroughs), Skyliners, Skyscrapers, Mets (short for Metropolitans and the top vote getter by a narrow margin), Bees, Rebels, NYBs, Avengers, and Jets. The final choice was Mrs. Payson's, and she liked Mets best, though she reportedly also had a fondness for Meadowlarks, with its not-so-subtle suggestion of the club's planned city-financed ballpark scheduled for construction in Flushing Meadows.

The 1962 season, which opened in St. Louis on April 10, was an ongoing circus and a full-blown sideshow from beginning to end. Manager Stengel entertained the press with his charm and unsurpassed wit, and his charges entertained the faithful ballpark customers with their unmatched incompetence and unrivaled enthusiasm. But there was never much fundamental baseball played that first season in the Polo Grounds. How could there have been much of a team with the stacked expansion deck that

the new kid on the block had been handed by the other National League owners? There was enough hitting (Frank Thomas cracked a total of 34 homers, which would stand for 13 seasons as a club record, and Ashburn hit his usual .300-plus), but the fielding would usually break down and the pitching collapse just in time always somehow to snatch defeat from the jaws of victory.

Fittingly, the season's opening game set the tone for everything that was to follow. The originally scheduled debut at Sportsman's Park in St. Louis was rained out in a grand piece of theatrical foreshadowing. Once the Mets took the field, however, there was no delay on a unanimous jury verdict on the type of ball club Casey and the Mets fans had inherited. Opening night witnessed the club's first homer—off the bat of Gil Hodges—and another by Charlie Neal, but a third ex-Dodger, Roger Craig, failed in his starting pitching assignment and never got past the third inning. The final count was 11-4 in favor of the Cardinals, and Stengel's en-

Recently fired Yankees manager Yogi Berra poses with Mets GM George Weiss in November 1964 after being hired by the expansion club as a player-coach. (AP/Wide World Photos)

tire three-man relief corps that night—Clem Labine, Bob Moorhead, Herb Moford—would be released by the team before the first month was out. The next eight games would follow suit, with the string of season-opening losses including a disappointing 4-3 whipping by the Pittsburgh Pirates in the Mets' first-ever home game. Finally, the team won a game in Pittsburgh on the strength of Jay Hook's complete-game five-hitter, and champagne was uncrated "pennant-celebration-style" in the Mets' clubhouse to mark the historic occasion. The way the rest of the season subsequently played out, that Forbes Field celebration on April 23 may indeed not have been overly excessive.

The entire first Mets season in the Polo Grounds was a string of milestones. The great majority of these could only be characterized as downright embarrassing. And throughout the summer, the on-field foibles and gaffes were always entertaining, even if they didn't represent the solid brand of baseball that New Yorkers had always been accustomed to—at least in recent postwar decades. The 120 losses and mere 40 victories compiled by season's end were both modern records. But it was the manner of losing that was often most noteworthy. The

Lefty Al Jackson suffered through not one, but two 8-20 ledgers. (Brace Photo)

team made a habit of extremes, either impressing early with solid play and a tantalizing lead, only to collapse in the later innings, or falling far behind at the outset, then rallying nobly to resurrect the possibility of victory before finally bungling away all that had been gained in the final inning or two.

The '62 Mets did have some impressive bats in their patchwork lineup. Ashburn could still reach base with regularity, and in his final season, the two-time batting champ stroked enough of his trademark singles in limited duty (135 games and 389 at-bats) to record his ninth .300-plus season, his first in four years. Gus Bell (released to Milwaukee after only 30 games) and Gil Hodges could be frightening to some inexperienced pitchers, although they were now both mere shadows of what they once had been. And Frank Thomas could slug home runs with the best in the league. His impressive total of 34 was not only the sixth best in the senior circuit, but would not be matched by anyone in a Mets uniform until Dave Kingman came along a dozen years later. But the lumber was hardly sufficient to compensate for woefully weak pitching or a ceaseless comedy of errors in the infield and outfield. Several epic losing streaks were endured and stretched to brutal lengths of 17, 11, and 13 games. The cousin novice team over in Houston was also an understaffed expansion outfit. But that group had a few more healthy arms (Turk Farrell, Ken Johnson, and Hal Woodeshick among them) and won 24 more games, even beating out the venerable, if often sad-sack, Chicago Cubs in the league standings. The Mets in turn set a record losing course that left them farther behind the rest of the pack than any big-league club in the previous 50 years.

One player, Marv Throneberry, emerged as a perfect archetype for the entire defeat-laced enterprise. Baseball has always had its bungling antiheroes and overwrought clowns, and Throneberry was destined to be one of the most celebrated. He had not been an original Met, but had been acquired from Baltimore on May 9 in exchange for Landrith, the catcher on whom the first draft pick had earlier been squandered. It was a deal that seemingly only proved the Mets could manage to turn any ill fortune into something even worse. The Throneberry legend began with a single inning on June 17, 1962, not much more than a month after he pulled on the Mets uniform. He opened that fateful frame against the Cubs with a memorable interference play. The bungling first sacker had gotten in the way of a Chicago base runner to sabotage an apparent double play. Given a chance at redemption for such tomfoolery, in the bottom of the same inning, the stumbling first baseman managed to outdo himself. He tripled into the right-field corner but was promptly called out for failing to tag a base on his way to third. When manager Stengel argued the call, he was quietly informed by the men in blue that his base runner had actually missed the other sack as well. In the space of an inning, the Mets' clown prince had cost his team four runs on defense and at least one more on offense. It was Throneberry more than any other individual in his lineup whom Stengel had in mind when he later moaned, "Can't anybody here play this game?"

But it was not just comic ineptitude when it came to fundamentals in the field and in the batter's box that spelled constant disaster. It was also weak pitching that made inevitable a long course of epic losing. Roger Craig and Al Jackson headed the parade of woeful arms, as both reached the 20-loss plateau. Jay Hook came within an eyelash of joining them in the ignoble ranks by ringing up 19 defeats and posting a figure for runs allowed (137) that was destined to withstand the test of time as a club record. Craig Anderson wasn't that far off the mark either (3-17) and perhaps only missed out on 20 losses because his meager talents didn't allow him as many starts. But Anderson took full advantage (or disadvantage) of the starts he had: After becoming the first Met to capture both ends of a doubleheader (May 12 versus Milwaukee), he subsequently dropped the last 19 straight decisions of his brief major league career before fading from the scene in 1964. And the team's $125,000 prize in the expansion draft, Bob Miller (one of a righty-lefty pair of Mets roommates with exactly the same name), had one of the worst records of all. Losing in double figures, Miller won only a single game (1-12) and barely missed the distinction of becoming the first big leaguer ever to drop as many as 13 games without a victory when he somehow hung on for a complete-game, 2-1 triumph, which was the team's final win of the year.

Yet for all the bungling—perhaps largely because of it—this team captured the hearts of New Yorkers and also of baseball fans everywhere across the land. They cracked triple dig-

Journeyman infielder Felix Mantilla became a regular in his one New York season. (Brace Photo)

its in losses before the end of August, tied the 1935 Boston Braves for the most NL losses (115) on September 20, and less than a week later, overhauled the 1916 Philadelphia A's for the worst big-league losing mark. The year's final rally fittingly ended in Wrigley Field, when Joe Pignatano banged into a season-ending triple play. Nonetheless, the Mets were soon outdrawing the staid Yankees, housed up in the Bronx and on their way toward 100 wins (they finished with 96) rather than 100 losses—and also en route to a third straight AL pennant and 12th in 14 seasons. The 922,530 passing through the Polo Grounds turnstiles represented the biggest draw ever for a last-place team. Apparently, baseball in the National League basement was somehow a more pure and thus more appreciated form of sporting entertainment. Yankee fans across the river expected victory and suffered disappointment anytime the Bombers fell short. Mets fans expected defeat and only hoped for a fair share of thrills to lace each new day's debacle. With that mind-set—some called it the Mets Mystique—they were rarely, if ever, disappointed. And veteran New York journalist Leonard Koppett was quick to point out that the first-year Mets had established an indelible iden-

tity, amassed a huge following, grabbed non-stop attention, and made reams of history. What could better rank as unqualified success?

THE MIRACLE METS

Three teams alone stand apart as big-league baseball's true "miracle" ball clubs—clubs whose climb to the pinnacle of a world championship was so unexpected and shocking that their feats became legendary. The first was the heretofore sad-sack Boston Braves outfit of the altogether unlikely 1914 National League season, a perennial tailender which again occupied the basement of the eight-club circuit as late as July and then went on an improbable tear straight to a championship celebration. Another was the 1951 New York Giants, whose charge from 13 1/2 games back in the final month culminated in baseball's most famous and dramatic home run, slugged by Bobby Thomson. And the third team was the Miracle Mets, whose 1969 championship chase was so unlikely and unanticipated that this final club seems to have ultimately appropriated the "miracle" label as something all its own.

The 1969 Gil Hodges Mets, of course, were quite different in the scope of their achievement from the 1914 "worst-to-first" Braves or the 1951 "Shot-Heard-'Round-the-World" Giants. The two earlier ball clubs had recovered from season-long slumps and switched fortunes in the middle of seemingly disastrous campaigns. While the Boston Nationals of the century's first decade had been regular losers on a grand scale, they never stood out as a nonpareil of baseball futility. The Mets, on the other hand, were rebounding from a history of unmatched folly and futility. This was a franchise that had tasted defeat 100 or more times in every one of its previous seasons, save two, and on both of those occasions had missed the mark by fewer than 12 defeats. And therein lies a huge difference.

New York's new National League team spent the better part of its early history building the image of a hopeless loser. The first season in the Polo Grounds was as full of ineptitude as any single campaign ever suffered by a hapless big-league nine. And the second summer didn't show much improvement on any front except soaring attendance figures. The team was as lovable as ever, nonetheless, from opening day until the final shadows of late September, and it was also just as much of a train wreck when it came to viewing results in the National League standings.

The 1963 campaign brought little visible improvement in the ramshackle-style game the New York Mets played daily in their rundown and rickety Polo Grounds. For one thing, the hometown bats were considerably weaker. Ashburn had quickly realized the futility of extending his career in such surroundings and had walked away to the broadcast booth back in Philadelphia, partly at least to keep his lifetime .308 average and his Hall of Fame credentials intact. Frank Thomas was now over the edge and suffered a massive power outage with but 15 homers and 151 fewer plate appearances. He was still the club's top RBI man, but with 34 fewer this time around. The top home run producer was the unimposing Jim Hickman, and his total (17, to go with his 120 strikeouts) was half of what Thomas had posted a year earlier. Madcap Jimmy Piersall and noble Duke Snider arrived to enliven the outfield but with little overall impact. Piersall was quickly in Casey's doghouse—especially after his celebrated backwards baserunning stunt—and had earned a one-way ticket out of town after only 40 games; Duke was now only a shadow of the one-time fence-busting Flatbush prince, his 14 homers providing rare occasions for lusty cheering but never seriously intimidating opposing pitching staffs. Only newcomer Ron Hunt seemed to offer relief to Mets fans. The hustling second sacker was barely edged out for top rookie honors by a slightly more dynamic hustler in Cincinnati named Pete Rose. This, on the whole, could hardly be called progress. There were more record-book milestones, of course, and most of them were still related to bungling. Roger Craig, for example, lost more relentlessly and without interruption than just about any pitcher before him. With more than a little help from his inept teammates, Craig managed to drop 18 straight, a feat that captured more national attention than any other Mets achievement of the summer. And the club's two-year loss total of 231 games had no precedent in more than eight decades of big-league play.

The second-year pitching staff, especially, was once again remarkable for its total lack of performance. Craig, as noted, again lost more than 20 games and this time spiced the herculean effort with his record string of 18 straight. This was not such an exceptional feat

on a ball club that itself dropped 22 straight road games in one unprecedented span. Al Jackson again lost close to 20 (13-17) but began looking more and more like a legitimate big-league ace; Jackson's only apparent fault was a visible lack of support from his teammates on both the offensive and defensive fronts. Carlton Willey was now on board after five disappointing seasons with the Braves, and his ERA of 3.10 (183 innings) was quite impressive, even if his won-lost mark (9-14, as the club's top winner) wasn't.

Nineteen sixty-four turned out to be a crucial transition year for New York City baseball, even if that fact only became apparent in retrospect. The powerhouse Yankees were suddenly approaching the end of their remarkable reign, and a great collapse for the Bronx Bombers lay just around the corner. The Mets, by contrast, were only at the very beginning of their own bold, new National League adventure. For the city's National Leaguers, the only possible direction was upward. But the different paths these two teams were already traveling were hard to decipher from such close range. With Mantle, Maris, and Bobby Richardson on their last legs, the Yankees were still fielding a juggernaut lineup in 1964, while the Mets were still anything but a powerhouse—or even a respectable big-league outfit. But when the vaunted Bronx Bombers nose-dived after their last-hurrah World Series tour of 1964, the door was suddenly thrown wide open for the team newly outfitted with a state-of-the-art ballpark out in Flushing. New York City baseball was more than ready for a fresh set of diamond heroes.

The opening of Shea Stadium in time for the 1964 season provided the first gigantic steps in a positive direction. Located adjacent to the sprawling World's Fair complex that was now drawing throngs to western Long Island, the glittering triple-tiered ballpark was ideally located to attract fans from all five city boroughs. But if the stadium was new and glitzy, the talent in the dugout certainly wasn't. The building of a minor league support system takes time and patience, and the Mets' fledgling farm system clearly wasn't yet ready to produce many needed reinforcements or future frontline stars. Marginal talent was still the order of the day in the Mets' camp, and their opening-day lineup featured such soon-to-be-forgotten has-beens and never-weres as Amado Samuel (2B), Dick Smith (1B), Jim Hickman (CF), Al Moran (SS),

Charlie Neal was another ex-Dodger favorite exiled back to Gotham and the Polo Grounds in 1962. (Brace Photo)

and Sammy Taylor (C). Only Hickman remained with the club for more than three seasons, and his tenure stretched only to five.

Ron Hunt was still the only standout ballplayer in Mets colors during the third franchise season. The solidly built second sacker pumped up his average by 30 points and was the club's only batter to finish above .300. Hunt also made his mark in the trivia books in July when he became the first Met ever to gain a starting lineup spot in the mid-summer All-Star Classic. That traditional game was fittingly housed in the Mets' spanking new ballpark, with the host National Leaguers coming out on top 7-4 and Hunt collecting one single in his three plate appearances. Ron Hunt was already developing a reputation as a gritty batsman who knew how to get on base the hard way. Specializing in maneuvering his body into the path of pitched balls, the spunky infielder would eventually set a career record (since broken by Don Baylor) for being hit by pitched balls. Six seasons down the road, playing for Montreal, he would be whacked an amazing 50 times in the course of a single season.

But with no bigger-name stars and little quality pitching, the result was once more a final record of 100-plus losses. The fans were al-

Ron Hunt became the first legitimate Mets All-Star when he finished second to Pete Rose in balloting for the league's top 1963 rookie. (NY Mets)

ready becoming restless—hapless losing and a daily dose of Stengelese might have been palatable and even fun for a while, but not as a steady season-in and season-out diet. If it was at all possible, the 1965 edition of the Mets was actually something of a step backwards. First came the dismal failure of one last experiment aimed at attempting to retread still another long-since-collapsed Hall of Famer now struggling at career's end. Southpaw Warren Spahn proved even less of an addition in the pitching rotation than either Duke Snider or Richie Ashburn had been in the outfield corps, or a much-reduced Gil Hodges had been at first base. And as a result, Spahn—purchased from Milwaukee for cash in November with the idea that he would also serve as part-time coach—didn't hang around long in New York. Spahn managed only four victories among his 16 decisions and thus reached the vaunted 360-win plateau (the most ever by a lefty), but he was released on waivers early in July. One of Casey's final decisions at the helm was to rely more heavily upon his fresher, if less experienced, pitching prospects.

By 1965, the one thing that had started changing was the personnel. There were now some promising home-grown youngsters with true big-league potential occupying roster spots for the first time. Ron Swoboda seemed to be one of those, though his star would lose some of its luster in rather short order. The hefty outfielder proved almost as much of a rookie sensation as Ron Hunt two seasons earlier and caught everyone's eye around the league with a first-month power-hitting outburst that left him temporarily leading the league in homers. He would hit only 19 for the year, but it was a club rookie mark that would stand for some time and also outdid the first-year feats of Mickey Mantle, Stan Musial, and Roger Maris. The bad news eventually turned out to be that it was also Swoboda's career high for a season. Southpaw Tug McGraw was another youngster who showed considerable promise with a healthy left arm that served both bullpen and starter's duties and posted a solid 3.32 ERA. And when it came to changes in personnel, there was also the demise of beloved manager Casey Stengel. On the eve of his 75th birthday, the tireless Ol' Perfessor suffered a nasty late-night spill at his favorite Toots Shor's watering hole, which left him with a broken hip and thus incapacitated enough to block any hope of a return to his managerial duties. This final parting with the ball club's brief past was indisputably the biggest and saddest (if also not the most timely) departure of all.

New manager Wes Westrum was a sharp contrast to Casey Stengel when it came to both personality displays and managerial savvy. Not that Westrum didn't have his own peculiar talents as a bench boss. During his 11 years as a backstop, he had been a dedicated student of the game, compiling enough insight to sustain a 17-year career as both coach and manager. Westrum had served admirably a decade earlier as a starting catcher with the pennant-winning New York Giants of Bobby Thomson fame. He was especially adroit in his handling of pitchers both from behind the plate and from the manager's seat on the bench. But without many quality arms in his stable, the one-time catcher certainly didn't work any instant miracles during his tenure as Mets manager. He did lift the club out of the league basement for the first time ever in his one full season. And he stopped the 100-loss bleeding with a 1966 edition that featured the team's first two winning pitchers in Bob Shaw and Dennis Ribant. But beyond that, it was still pretty much business as usual around Shea Stadium. Attendance continued to soar in the new park and approached two million. And more future promise was put on display when a pair of talented rookies—shortstop Bud Harrelson and catcher Jerry Grote—received their first trials in the starting lineup.

For the first five years, there had been no true superstars on the New York expansion ball club. Stars from previous generations (Ashburn, Snider, Hodges, Spahn, Ken Boyer) were often paraded before the fans in a display of lingering nostalgia; but these were heroes from the past—not modern wunderkinds. Nonetheless, by 1966, there was some raw talent awaiting proper polishing, such as outfielder Cleon Jones, who set a club record with 16 steals and finished second on the team in hits, BA, and RBIs, and catcher Jerry Grote, who flashed enough potential on defense to win the starting job in spring training. And Bob Shaw (a smart mid-season pickup from the Giants) and Dennis Ribant (the closest thing the Mets had to an ace, with a 3.20 ERA) were a pair of pitchers who actually had winning seasons. It was a start, even if not much of one. Then, suddenly, everything seemed to change overnight with the arrival of a true franchise savior—the truly dominant pitcher needed to anchor any success-

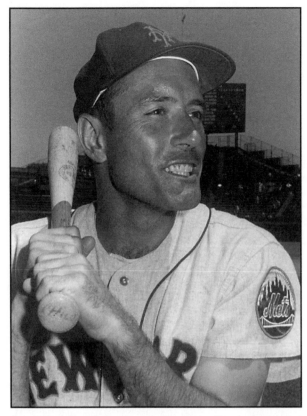

Jimmy Piersall made headlines in New York with a backwards trot around the base paths. (Brace Photo)

The stars truly seemed to align themselves favorably for the first time for the Mets when it came to the circumstances surrounding Seaver's signing and the eventual awarding of his contract to New York via the good fortune of casting lots. Once the Mets had their new prospect on board for the 1967 season, things would soon be noticeably different around Shea Stadium. The team still lost regularly, so regularly that Wes Westrum quit his post before season's end. But Seaver won, and he won with displays of brilliance. He won 16 games, hurled 18 complete games, and struck out 170 batters. Mets fans had never before seen such numbers from one of their own. And Seaver also walked off with the NL Rookie of the Year trophy, the first time a player from a last-place team had earned such a distinction. The handsome right-hander possessed not only a blazing fastball and assortment of unhittable breaking pitches, but he also displayed an innate pitching wisdom far beyond his tender years. And more than the numbers or the raw talent, Tom Seaver brought the Mets' clubhouse a winning attitude. He was a battler who refused to accept defeat. And such an attitude is often contagious.

The Mets' farm system was now also finally about to start paying off big time. The club had done the job right in at least one area, and that was the process of stockpiling tomorrow's prospects throughout its minor league organization. The next promising arrival from the farm was 25-year-old southpaw Jerry Koosman, who launched the 1968 campaign with four straight victories and a string of 21 scoreless innings, which made him the first Mets pitcher ever to throw consecutive shutouts. The latest rookie mound sensation never flagged all summer and even outdid Seaver's early debut with a 19-12 ledger and a major league record for rookie shutouts. Koosman failed to capture the team's second straight top rookie trophy by only a single vote when he was nipped at the ballot box by Cincinnati's future Hall of Famer Johnny Bench. Seaver and Koosman together now suddenly gave the struggling New York club the best righty-lefty one-two punch in either league. And what made it all the better was that the frontline duo was joined by a third fabulous young prospect named Nolan Ryan (also a 1968 rookie with a 6-9 record and 133 strikeouts), who could heave one of the most impressive fastballs ever, even if he struggled early to find ways of

ful mound corps. And the Mets acquired their instant hero almost by accident.

The man they would call "Tom Terrific" enjoyed an extraordinary rookie year—all the more remarkable for the teammates he had clustered around him. What was also remarkable was the way Seaver ended up being a New York Met in the first place. The Atlanta Braves had drafted him in January 1966, but in doing so, violated an MLB rule that prevented signing players who were college juniors or seniors once their collegiate seasons had begun. Seaver had just joined the USC team as a transfer from Fresno State and had not pitched for the Trojans. But his team had begun play by the time he inked an Atlanta contract for $50,000, a fact that did not go unnoticed in the commissioner's office, which promptly voided the deal and also ruled the youngster ineligible for further collegiate action. When Seaver's father threatened a lawsuit, the commissioner, Charles Eckert, hastily designed a plan that would award the promising righty to any big-league club willing to match Atlanta's original bonus. When the Phillies, Indians, and Mets all entered the hunt, a lottery was held, and the National League cellar dwellers were drawn from a hat as the charmed lottery winners.

putting that fastball over the plate and somewhere near the strike zone.

Other vital pieces of a potential champion were also put in place in 1967 and 1968, and most of these pieces also came in the form of home-grown farm talent. None of the building blocks were any more vital than the stellar young outfield the team had almost accidentally patched together behind a sterling mound corps and a still-shaky infield. Swoboda had been the first of that fly-chasing trio to arrive on the scene with his heavy-hitting debut three seasons earlier, and he still offered hope as a true franchise slugger. Cleon Jones debuted back in 1963 but didn't stick until 1966; by 1968, he was hitting near .300 and slugging 14 homers. Jones was something of a rarity among non-pitchers, being a lefty thrower who batted right-handed. The final and only imported member was the swift Tommie Agee, who was acquired from the Chicago White Sox in the aftermath of his 1966 American League Rookie of the Year season. Agee immediately flopped in 1968 with an 0-for-34 early-season slump and anemic .217 overall average, but the dip could at least in part be attributed to a spring training beaning by Cardinals ace Bob Gibson. One of the most stunning features of the Mets' upcoming "miracle" season that lay just around the corner would be the miracle resurrection of fellow Mobile, Alabama, natives Cleon Jones and Tommie Agee.

One additional huge boost to Mets fortunes was the astute decision to hire Gil Hodges in the 1967-68 off-season as the new manager. The Mets would now once again push the right buttons to get the right bench boss for the right moment, just as they had done earlier in the decade with Casey Stengel. The Mets' front office had actually wanted Hodges on board as Casey's replacement in mid-season 1965 but was rejected in its efforts to pry the Brooklyn hero loose from his post with the Washington Senators. The ex-Dodger had learned the managerial craft well with the Senators and had slowly elevated the AL basement ball club to respectability. In the most recent campaign—his fifth—his club had climbed all the way to sixth place and a season's record only nine games under the break-even point. If the Senators were willing to listen to overtures from New York this time around, perhaps it was only because Senators GM George Selkirk and Mets vice president (and soon-to-be GM) Johnny Murphy had been teammates on the great Yankee teams of the '30s: Selkirk was willing to listen, and the Mets were ready to deal.

With Hodges hired away from Washington, dividends now rolled in even faster than could have been anticipated as the Mets approached the decade's end. Hodges's first season was enlivened by the new hurling tandem of Seaver and Koosman, enough of a presence to lead a mound corps that was second in the NL in shut-outs (25) and fourth in ERA (2.72). The young Mets pitching staff—which also included Nolan Ryan and Dick Selma—was the talk of the league, despite another ninth-place finish. Even the temporary scare resulting from Hodges's mild heart attack in September was not enough to derail the growing optimism now surrounding the Mets' fortunes. From the earliest weeks of the 1969 season, the Mets surprisingly found themselves immersed in the uncharted waters of a league pennant race. Despite another opening-day loss (to the expansion team in Montreal), the team hovered around .500 as the weeks stretched from spring to summer. The Mets were only five games off the pace at the

Tim Harkness ably manned first base in the brief span between Throneberry and Kranepool. (Brace Photo)

end of April, eight games out at the end of June, and once again, five games in arrears late in August.

The last campaign of the '60s was a topsy-turvy season of unprecedented proportions. Baseball's reigning lords had followed their earlier tinkerings with tradition by unleashing the biggest revamping of the game's structure to date. With the introduction of the new divisional alignments, each league now featured two pennant races, and while the Braves and Giants battled to the wire in the West, the Mets overhauled the crumbling Cubs in the East and sprinted away from the entire pack with a rousing 38-11 finish down the stretch. Hodges brilliantly platooned at five positions, but nothing bolstered club fortunes more than the comeback seasons enjoyed by outfielders Cleon Jones and Tommie Agee. Agee redeemed his lackluster start in New York by turning into the team's most productive offensive weapon with 26 HRs, 76 RBIs, and a record 97 runs scored. Jones posted a career season by batting .340. And benefiting from the newfound offensive fireworks,

Tom Seaver outdid himself with 25 victories and a much-deserved NL Cy Young Award.

Under the new format, the Mets, as division winners, would square off with the Atlanta Braves in a new baseball event known informally as "the playoffs" and labeled more officially as the National League Championship Series (NLCS). The first-ever edition of the NLCS never developed into much of a crowd pleaser since the pitching-rich and suddenly confident New Yorkers were able to manhandle the hard-hitting but pitching-thin Braves with relative ease. When Seaver was banged around by Braves bats in the opener, the Mets' lineup struck back with even more lumber and coasted by a 9-5 count. New York was even more explosive at the plate in the second outing and romped 11-6 behind blasts by Agee, Jones, and Ken Boswell. Nolan Ryan emerged from the bullpen to close the door on the clincher as the Mets prevailed again, 7-4, despite Hank Aaron's third round tripper of the series.

The biggest "miracles" of the Miracle Mets season were, in the end, saved for baseball's grandest stage—the World Series. And it would indeed take a miracle to get past a team that boasted 109 victories and its own Cy Young ace in lefty Mike Cuellar. The muscular opponent standing in the way of one final miracle chapter was the powerhouse Baltimore Orioles, a team managed by yet another former New York baseball hero, Hank Bauer. It was during the surprise-filled World Series, however, that unlikely new heroes seemed to spring up almost everywhere. Ron Swoboda made a marvelous diving catch that saved Game 4 in the ninth. J.C. Martin produced the winning run in the same game by beating a throw to first, even though he ran illegally inside the base line. Tommie Agee saved Game 3 with two of the most memorable "impossible" catches in World Series history. And Donn Clendenon slugged a record three homers in the five-game Series and walked off with the *Sport* magazine World Series MVP trophy.

The final scene of the Mets' "miracle" was played out during Game 5 like a carefully orchestrated script. It was a game destined to live forever in the baseball consciousness of New York City—right alongside the epic Bobby Thomson homer, the Don Larsen perfect game, and the Sandy Amoros desperation grab, which provided Brooklyn with its only world-championship frenzy. Koosman took the mound at Shea

Wes Westrum led the Mets out of the NL cellar for the first time in club history. (Brace Photo)

Stadium with a chance to slam the door on the slumping Orioles but instead seemed to provide Baltimore with new life when he yielded early-inning homers to Frank Robinson and rival pitcher Dave McNally. The game turned on the famous "shoe polish incident" in which Cleon Jones was awarded a free pass when Hodges emerged from the dugout with a stained ball he claimed to be the one that had clipped the batter's instep. Jones's gift pass was followed by Donn Clendenon's homer, which pulled New York back within a run, at 3-2. An unlikely circuit blast by Al Weis followed—his first in the home park all season—to knot the score in the seventh. The game was decided on a pair of doubles in the eighth by Jones and Swoboda, along with a crucial Orioles infield error. The last hurrah came when future Mets manager Davey Johnson lined harmlessly to Jones in left for the final out, which set off a frenzied on-field celebration in which thousands of fans poured from the grandstands to join the erupting delirium.

A team that had never finished higher than ninth place suddenly rising like the phoenix and winning a World Series was a sports success story almost too good to be true. This was indisputably the sports story of the year, if not the entire decade. The titanic celebration that followed in the nation's largest city was one of unprecedented proportions, complete with the traditional downtown ticker tape parade and endless public ceremonies. Every Mets player was an instant celebrity. And it seemed that every sportswriter in town took typewriter in hand to pound out a New York Mets book guaranteed to capitalize on the instantaneous new market by explaining the New York Mets' meteoric rise. Leonard Koppett's *The New York Mets: The Whole Story* was easily the most thorough and entertaining contribution to the new literature, yet it had to fight for shelf space in 1970 with a dozen similar knockoff volumes. What had started a few years earlier as a comedy of errors had, by the end of baseball's most tumultuous decade, become a Horatio Alger tale of the unlikeliest proportions.

THE AMAZIN' METS

If the sixties closed with the lusty thrill of improbable victory, the seventies were, at the very outset, marked by disillusionment and the ugly specter of true tragedy. The first blow to the still-giddy Mets family was the sudden death

Nolan Ryan wilted in the shadow of Seaver and Koosman at Shea Stadium. (SPI Archives)

of GM John Murphy, who had been the main architect of the ball club's miracle rise. When Murphy was felled by a first heart attack on December 30, the front office was thrown into chaos, since no heir for the general manager's slot was apparent. When a second attack proved fatal on January 14, the post was handed over to a reluctant Bob Scheffing, who had been heading up the team's scouting operations. Just before his death, Murphy had completed a trade, sending youngster Amos Otis to Kansas City for Joe Foy, who was earmarked to shore up the constantly troublesome third-base slot. The swap looked sound at the time, but would soon prove to be the first of a series of bad 1970s deals when Otis sprang to stardom in the junior circuit and Foy became one of the Mets' all-time busts.

Things began brightly enough in the 1970 season to satisfy most ball clubs, with a record performance by Tom Seaver (19 Ks versus the Padres) highlighting the opening month, and a first-ever victory in the inaugural game ending 11 years of frustration on opening day. But overall, it was a year of streaks (good and bad) and

inconsistency. The three-way pennant race between the Mets, Cubs, and Pirates lasted all the way to the final week. Yet the final results were disappointing for a team coming off a world championship. Even another year of record attendance (2,697,479) was insufficient consolation for the quick drop from winners to has-beens.

With the exception of the trio of top pitchers—Seaver, Koosman, and Ryan—it was becoming apparent that the young talent in camp consisted in the main of overachievers who were never destined to be lasting big-league stars. That proved to be the case again in 1971 with another almost carbon-copy season for Gil Hodges and crew. The Mets won at exactly the same pace (83-79) and again finished third, yet dropped eight full games in the standings. The only highlight was Seaver's 20-10 record, which featured a sterling 1.76 ERA and 289 strikeouts and may have been the best year of his career. Jones hit above .300 for the second time, and Bud Harrelson earned a second All-Star selection and second Gold Glove at short. But Agee was plagued by injuries, age overtook Donn Clendenon, and Swoboda had already been peddled to Montreal.

An ongoing bane of the club was the year-to-year problem at third base, which had reached new urgency by the time the team turned to the business of rebuilding a world champion. One mistake had already been made when, on the heels of the 1969 World Series success, Ed Charles was quickly dumped and Joe Foy was handed the responsibility for guarding the hot corner. In his one-season trial (1970), Foy hit an anemic .236 with little power and proved a less sure-handed fielder than Charles. Bob Aspromonte was the next experiment—when light-hitting prospect Wayne Garrett was called to army reserve duty—and performed poorly enough to prompt retirement at season's end. A bigger blunder now emerged, with a major trade orchestrated at the December 1971 winter meetings to fetch Jim Fregosi from the Angels as the 46th third-base prospect in the team's 10-year history. Still-developing pitching phenom Nolan Ryan and three minor leaguers were sent to the California club as ransom for Fregosi, who was reportedly overweight and had slumped horribly in the previous season, notching only five homers and 33 ribbies. The ill-fated deal, engineered by new GM Bob Scheffing, was easily the worst in franchise history and would

for the next several decades send Mets fans into periodic outbursts of rage and remorse.

The Ryan trade shocked New York fans, even if it was true at the time that the future Hall of Famer's ongoing struggles with control of his fastball and a New York lifestyle seemingly made him the most expendable among the Mets' young pitchers. But the shock was not nearly as great as the tragic circumstances that followed closely on the heels of the unpopular deal. On the eve of the late-starting 1972 season, beloved manager Gil Hodges would be felled by a second heart attack. The episode occurred near the end of a spring training session interrupted by the first general players' strike in big-league history. The massive coronary came on the golf course in West Palm Beach two days short of Hodges's 48th birthday, and this one was fatal.

Yogi Berra, another celebrated New York baseball fixture, was now handed the daunting task of rebuilding. The announcement of Berra's two-year contract to manage came only hours after the somber burial of Gil Hodges in his beloved Brooklyn. There were some big trades in Berra's earliest weeks on the job—trades that helped to put the ball club back on the winning track. Rusty Staub came on board, adding a hefty bat to the lineup. A rotund slugger, Staub had emerged as an overnight franchise hero in Montreal with the expansion Expos, thus the price to gain his services was steep: The Mets gave up versatile utility infielder Tim Foli and heavy-hitting prospects Mike Jorgensen and Ken Singleton. And best of all, Willie Mays was lured back to New York. The last of the old Dodgers and Giants stars to be brought back home to Gotham would quickly prove the most popular and the most productive of the lot. Mays was a sure bet to rekindle fan interest as baseball's best all-around player. But unlike the earlier deals for has-been heroes of yore, this one would also have some positive on-field results.

The measurable progress of 1972 rapidly transformed into tangible triumphs a mere summer later. The irony here was that the club didn't necessarily perform any better than it had the previous year, at least not when measured by the raw data of wins and losses. The victory total in 1973 was actually a one-game dip from the previous two summers and thus only a hair over .500. The rest of the division simply seemed to slip back and join the Mets. Mays brought down the curtain on his remarkable ca-

Gil Hodges had a brief playing stint with the fledgling New York Mets. (NY Mets)

Dave Mlicki is only the latest in a long line of Mets pitchers who failed to fulfill their promise. (Brace Photo)

reer by boosting his lifetime home run count to 660. Seaver paced the circuit in ERA and Ks for the third time and garnered his second Cy Young Award as the first non-20-game winner ever to pocket the trophy. The Mets, Cardinals, Pirates, and Cubs all seemed incapable of pulling away from each other or playing much above the break-even point. The result was an exciting pennant race that thrilled fans all summer long, but which left the Mets, in the end, as baseball's least impressive postseason entrants.

Postseason play against Cincinnati's emerging Big Red Machine provided one of the most acrimonious championship series in baseball annals. Especially eye-catching was the incident involving Reds star Pete Rose and the scrappy Bud Harrelson. Fisticuffs broke out between the two in the fifth inning of Game 3 after Charlie Hustle upended Harrelson in an effort to break up a potential double play. Enraged Shea Stadium partisans pelted Rose with garbage the following inning before order could be restored and a 9-2 Mets rout played to conclusion. But the entire series was bitterly fought, and Rose gained a measure of revenge on New York rooters in Game 4 with a series-evening

12th-inning homer. The sloppily played tie-breaker at Shea was finally won by the Mets, 7-2, on the strength of a six-run inning that bailed out an ineffective Tom Seaver pitching performance. The pennant-clinching game was hardly as notable as its aftermath, when a most memorable, if truly regrettable, on-field scene ignited the postgame championship celebration. Hordes of crazed fans stormed from the grandstands, gleefully ripping up chunks of infield turf and tearing down sections of outfield fence. It was a sinister and shocking display of mob violence that quickly evoked universal condemnation from newspaper editorials throughout the city and even across the nation.

The World Series that followed was in every way an anticlimax to the Mets' second NL pennant victory. Mets pitching, in the guise of Seaver and Koosman, effectively shut down the heavy lumber of Reggie Jackson and his Oakland teammates and held the power-packed American League lineup without a homer in the first six games. Game action was largely overshadowed by the reprehensible behavior of Oakland owner Charles Finley, who attempted to ban his second baseman Mike Andrews from play after two costly errors in Game 2. But in the deciding seventh game, the booming Oakland bats closed the championship door when homers by Bert Campaneris and Reggie Jackson—both stroked off Jon Matlack—put punctuation marks on Oakland's second consecutive World Series victory. This time there was no miracle to be celebrated at Shea Stadium.

The overnight fall from grace by Yogi Berra's 1974 New York Mets was almost as rapid and stunning as the club's improbable ascent to a world championship had been only five seasons earlier. Willie Mays had retired, his final hit coming in Game 2 of the World Series. But the real loss in the Mets' outfield was the player they didn't get in a proposed off-season trade with Houston. Scheffing was wary of being burned again in a repeat of the Nolan Ryan fiasco and had therefore nixed an offered exchange of slugger Jim Wynn for New York pitching veteran George Stone and prospect Craig Swan. Wynn promptly went to the Dodgers, where he sparked a pennant drive with 32 homers and regular clutch hitting. On the pitching front, Seaver overtook Koufax's NL record by striking out 200-plus for the seventh straight season, yet stumbled to his lowest career win total (11) and highest ERA (3.20). Koosman was the top winner with 15, but missed out on seven more that were blown in late innings by the bullpen. It was all a formula for disaster, and the tumble to 20 games below .500 and a fifth-place finish was a distinct franchise embarrassment.

Berra was finally gone in 1975, and his two replacements didn't survive the turmoil for very long either. Interim skipper Roy McMillan rode out the final third of the uninspiring 1975 third-place finish, and full-time replacement Joe Frazier made it only a third of the way into his own second season before becoming another victim of the constant losing. And the entire franchise seemed to be sent reeling even farther when the longtime individual "Franchise"—Tom Seaver—was suddenly traded in the midst of the 1977 season. On the eve of the June 15 trading deadline, the baseball world was set on its heels by the news that baseball's best pitcher was departing New York for Cincinnati, in exchange for a pitcher (Pat Zachry) and infielder (Doug Flynn) with big-league credentials and two minor league outfielders (Steve Henderson and Dan Norman). The deal ended a bitter standoff between the Mets' front office and its top star over the structuring of a new contract and had followed in the wake of increasingly personal attacks on Seaver and his family by a caustic New York press. Tom Terrific had, in the end, been driven out of town by a front office lacking in tact and by an overly vicious New York press corps.

Seaver's departure came only two weeks after another front-office maneuver, which saw veteran infielder Joe Torre elevated to the role of player-manager as Joe Frazier's bench replacement. With Joe Torre at the controls, there was at least a marked change in clubhouse atmosphere, if not much of an upswing in team performance. But Torre's five seasons were a throwback to the frustrations of the mid-sixties. Torre would, if nothing else, be one of the longest-surviving Mets skippers. But his milestones over the next five campaigns were largely those earned by losing. His teams never suffered as many as 100 defeats, yet in each of his four full seasons (including the one he inherited from Frazier in late May) they came within five losses or fewer of accomplishing that unadmirable feat. (Torre's last year on the job was a strike-shortened campaign that also found the club on a pace to challenge the embarrassing 100-loss plateau.) The Cooperstown-caliber managerial successes that would eventually arrive for Joe Torre were still years away.

What can only be characterized as transition seasons under two-year manager George Bamberger were more of a holding pattern than anything else. There were some faint signals of future promise, thanks to events outside New York. A young right-handed pitcher from Tampa's Hillsborough High School named Dwight Gooden was the Mets' fifth overall choice in the June 1982 amateur draft. And a 1980 pick with the improbable name of Darryl Strawberry had been turning heads down in the farm system. Strawberry broke into the big time in May 1983, after an impressive spring training, and the Mets seemed to have another superstar on the way. But most of the other changes were largely cosmetic. A state-of-the-art Diamond Vision scoreboard was installed in Shea Stadium. Big Red Machine home run threat George Foster was acquired from Cincinnati, but disappointed in his first go-around with only 13 homers and 70 ribbies. Dave Kingman had been reacquired and tied his own club home run mark, but had little impact on the team's dismal performance. Only the exchange of problem-child pitcher Neil Allen for All-Star St. Louis first sacker Keith Hernandez resembled real progress on the rebuilding front, but that move came 12 days after Bamberger had already resigned with the club still faltering in June of 1983.

Darryl Strawberry's arrival on the big-league scene, however, was so spectacular, it even evoked memories of the arrival in New York of Mickey Mantle. And for a while at least, Strawberry indeed looked every bit like another multi-tooled Mantle. Cracking the starting lineup with 26 homers and 74 RBIs, Strawberry opened enough eyes to walk away with the Mets' third Rookie of the Year honor (Seaver, 1967; Matlack, 1972). A year later, there was an even more spectacular breaking-out party—the most notable in team history. This one revolved around Gooden, who had blazed his way to the majors in less than two years and still hadn't reached his 20th birthday. Gooden's debut managed to overshadow those of both Seaver and Koosman before him, as well as just about every other first-year pitching performance on record by a long country mile. Averaging 11.4 Ks per nine innings, the phenomenal teenager struck out more batters (276) than any rookie before him, and in the process, became the first

John Franco was the mainstay of the New York bullpen throughout most of the 1990s. (NY Mets)

teenager ever to reign as a big-league strikeout king. Needless to say, Gooden mirrored Strawberry in claiming top NL rookie honors.

The beginning of the Doc Gooden era at Shea was also the beginning of the Davey Johnson era. Johnson wouldn't waste much time joining Gil Hodges as the two most successful managers in club history. Johnson's first two years at the helm were laced with countless successes, not the least of which were two solid second-place division finishes and the first two 90-win seasons since the Hodges miracle. His third campaign was even more remarkable. With their powerful revamped lineup and their matchless young pitching star, the Mets were now, overnight, the toast of the entire National League. The first two Mets National League champions had managed to sneak up rather unexpectedly on their unwary league rivals. No one had expected either the Hodges squad of 1969 or the Berra-led crew of '73 to have much impact on the seasons they eventually dominated. But Johnson's well-stocked team spent two years serving notice that it was the best outfit around and thus a solid bet to win everything when it opened the franchise's Silver Anniversary season.

The 1986 Mets ran away and hid from the rest of the NL East before mid-season and, in the process, established just about every conceivable club record for winning and productivity—108 victories, 55 home wins, 53 road wins, 148 homers, .263 club BA, and 2.76 million in attendance. The 21.5-game lead over runner-up Philadelphia was the biggest in divisional history; the September 7 clinching date was also the earliest ever (since the 1969 change in pennant format). And that was just the beginning of a truly charmed season. The subsequent NLCS against Houston largely rivaled the 1973 Mets-Reds series for nonstop thrills and heroics. It may have been even better when judged from a pure baseball standpoint. The seesaw matchup featured three one-run games in the first five, and the Mets were severely pressured to end the affair in Game 6 rather than risk facing Mike Scott a third time in the Game 7 tiebreaker. The vital sixth game at the Astrodome is still considered by many as the greatest postseason game ever played and stretched out to 16 frames before the Mets rallied for three and Jesse Orosco finally closed out the third NL pennant in Mets history.

The World Series that followed will always reduce in the fans' collective memory to the single improbable event of Game 6 in which Bill Buckner disappointed a generation of Boston rooters by fulfilling their worst nightmares and once more "snatching defeat from the jaws of certain victory" in true and tragic Bosox fashion. This time around, the Mets were yet again fortunate winners, thanks to a "miracle" of rather remarkable proportions. But there were plenty of thrills even before Game 6 and Buckner's Series-turning 10th-inning miscue. On the heels of the dramatic New York-Houston NL series and the even more improbable Boston comeback in ALCS action against the California Angels, opening World Series play was rather slow and even anticlimactic. Bruce Hurst twirled a shutout for Boston in the opener, with the only score resulting from a Tim Teufel infield bobble. But the drama increased when both teams took two on the road and Hurst staked his claim for Series MVP with another complete-game mastery of New York in Game 5. Boston's snakebitten Red Sox were now a game away from their first world championship in seven decades.

The final two Series games were exercises in ceaseless momentum shifting. The Mets would come back from the dead more than once. And it all did seem somehow fated—perhaps another preordained chapter in Boston's "Curse of the Bambino" run of endless postseason bad luck. The Red Sox were one pitch away from the world title that had so long eluded them and their fans, when Mookie Wilson dodged a wild toss from Bob Stanley that allowed Kevin Mitchell to scamper home from third with the tying run. Wilson next drilled the fateful ground ball that eluded the usually glue-fingered Buckner and thus handed New York one final chance at redemption in an unanticipated rubber game. The Bosox had their opportunities once more, as they posted an early three-run lead behind Hurst in the deciding match, but the Mets again stormed back and finally salted away the victory with three in the sixth, three in the seventh, and two more in the eighth. For the second time in their 25-year history, the New York Mets had won all the marbles in the most improbable fashion imaginable.

BACK TO THE FUTURE

Davey Johnson's Mets powerhouse didn't simply go away overnight after the pinnacle of

a 1986 world championship, the way Yogi Berra's team of aging winners had done a dozen seasons earlier. Throughout the final summers of the eighties, the Mets remained, year-in and year-out, one of the National League's most feared teams. The New Yorkers might well have performed an encore, if injuries to the pitching staff had not ultimately derailed a 1987 club that posted 92 victories and limped home with the fourth-best winning percentage in the majors. A year later Johnson and company fell a single game short of a second pennant, and the 1989 campaign was also ruined by a muscle tear in Doc Gooden's right shoulder that forced the staff stopper to miss the entire second half of the season. Even when Johnson's fragile house of cards finally collapsed around him in 1990, the team that was managed for much of the year by replacement skipper Bud Harrelson still finished 20 games above water and only four games off the division-winning pace.

The differences between Davey Johnson's successful club and the winners produced by Hodges and Berra in previous decades were all too obvious to even the casual fan. Earlier Mets championship editions had both been carried to victory by the same two star pitchers—Tom Seaver and Jerry Koosman—with the remainder of the adequate but hardly eye-popping roster coming sufficiently to life and simply being carried along for the ride. The 1973 NL champions, for example, didn't boast anyone with more than 23 homers or 76RBIs, and Felix Millan was the top hitter at a barely respectable .290. The 1969 world champions didn't have much more when it came to power in the middle of the lineup, and the incredible 38-11 stretch run was made with manager Hodges platooning at three infield positions, one outfield post, and behind the plate. The mid-eighties winners were, by sharp contrast, a deep ball club with both more-than-adequate pitching (especially after lefty Bob Ojeda joined Gooden, Darling, Fernandez, and Aguilera in the starting rotation) and all the other requisite elements. There were five league all-stars on that

Hall of Famer Willie Mays demonstrates a proper batting grip to John F. Kennedy Jr. during the youngster's June 1972 visit to Shea Stadium. (AP Wide World Photos)

roster (Carter, Hernandez, Strawberry, Gooden, Fernandez), and Tim Teufel, rookie Kevin Mitchell, and Danny Heep provided exceptional bench strength. The acquisitions of Keith Hernandez (1983) and Gary Carter (1985) had filled in the only real lineup holes by the time new manager Johnson had settled into his steamroller stretch of winning 90 or more in each of his first five full seasons. With such a balanced and potent roster across the board, the winning seemingly should have continued unabated for some time to come.

By and large, the expected successes did continue for a while at least. For the next four years, the club never fell below second place in the division scramble. Only in 1987, however, were the Mets within three games of the top spot when the season shut down. Another division title lay just around the corner in 1988, and once more the team would also claim 100 victories and win by a gaping margin of 15 full games over runner-up Pittsburgh. If Johnson and company didn't repeat their 1986 title immediately, they did have a follow-up season full of milestones and achievements. The 92-70 won-lost mark of 1987 had only been bested on three occasions in club history; by boosting his personal victory total to 388, Johnson became the winningest skipper in team history; Strawberry enjoyed his best season and broke club records in five offensive categories (runs, home runs, extra-base hits, total bases, slugging); and for all the injuries that racked the pitching staff, the mound corps still featured five double-figure winners (Aguilera, Darling, Fernandez, Gooden, Leach). The combined 457 days that Mets pitchers spent on the disabled list and a hot St. Louis Cardinals ball club were all that prevented a string of three straight division flags.

The team also did not stand pat in the front office or on the playing field. Kevin McReynolds was obtained from San Diego (at the cost of hard-hitting youngster Kevin Mitchell), and he proved to be highly productive, even if he was never very popular with the fans or the media. The 27-year-old righty swinger had already proven he could sock 25-plus homers and produce 95-plus RBIs and was counted on as an everyday star in left field. McReynolds was never disliked by the New York partisans, but merely overshadowed by the likes of Strawberry, Carter, and Hernandez. He nonetheless filled up the remaining outfield hole in grand style. Touted prospect David Cone was also brought over from Kansas City to further bolster an already impressive battery of pitching artillery. The only roster casualty was World Series MVP Ray Knight, who fled after an off-season contract squabble and who might easily have been retained with more delicate maneuvering in the front office. Switch-hitting Howard Johnson nevertheless filled in with a great offensive season to compensate for Knight's absence in the batting order, if not in the locker room. Intangible but vital leadership in the clubhouse had definitely been sacrificed with Knight's angry departure, and the Knight-for-HoJo flip-flop was a lineup swap that soon came back to haunt the residents of Shea Stadium.

There were also some rather obvious and disturbing storm clouds gathering on the horizon. The most ominous surrounded the chaotic personal life and on-field slippage of Dwight Gooden. Gooden perhaps could not be expected to maintain his pace of early seasons when he bolted out of the starting gate faster than any teenage phenom in baseball history. But the fall-off now was more than merely casual. Although Doc was still winning at a phenomenal clip (he had the league's best winning percentage in 1987), there had already been a first visit to a drug rehab session and a delayed season's start, which had cut his strikeout total and innings pitched by nearly 40 percent. The youngest everything else (Rookie of the Year, All-Star Game performer, league strikeout leader) was now threatening also to become one of baseball's youngest washouts. The impact of Doc Gooden's dip in effectiveness was quickly magnified in the post-championship year by an epidemic of other health-related problems among a large segment of the Mets' pitching staff. The biggest collapse came when Bob Ojeda, an earlier 18-game winner, needed elbow surgery in April for an inflamed nerve and spent the rest of the year disabled. Ron Darling's season was ended in the heat of the September pennant chase by torn thumb ligaments. Youngster David Cone, counted on as a fifth starter, was also out from mid-April to mid-August with a broken finger on his pitching hand. The total impact was enough to hand the division flag to the talented but beatable St. Louis Cardinals.

Even the failure to defend their NL pennant didn't dim very much the claim that the Mets still owned one of the best lineups anywhere in baseball. Strawberry was now reach-

ing his career peak and Gary Carter was protecting him in the center of the batting order. Keith Hernandez was also a tough out at the plate and even more impressive on defense. And HoJo had now also peaked as a first-rank league slugging star whose value was only increased by the fact that he was a switch-hitter. Johnson joined Strawberry as baseball's first pair of 30-homer and 30-steal teammates. McReynolds (posting career highs in homers and doubles, as well as three double-figure hitting streaks) had a monster season but was once more lost in the shuffle. The fans duly appreciated all the offensive fireworks and were tantalized all summer long by a nip-and-tuck pennant race that dragged out until the final week. If there was disappointment, it certainly wasn't felt at the turnstiles, where partisans flocked into Shea Stadium at a record three million clip.

With so potent a lineup and with the pitchers finally staying healthy for the duration, Davey Johnson's 1988 edition was almost the equal of his 1986 world champions. After riding a five- or six-game first-place cushion for nearly four months, New York finally ran away from the field in September (winning 20 of 26 games) and claimed the division title over Pittsburgh by a margin of 15 games. An important late-season boost was contributed by rookie Gregg Jefferies, who was called up from Tidewater on August 28 with the simple idea that he might add bench strength for the postseason. Jefferies shocked the Mets almost as much as he shocked opponents by wearing out league pitching for the entire final month. When the dust settled, the Mets had won 100 games for the third time and no one failed to notice that the other two such seasons had both been capped with World Series rings. So there was, understandably, much optimism everywhere in the Mets' camp on the eve of the upcoming postseason playoffs.

But this time around, the optimism was quickly derailed by a charmed LA Dodgers ball club boasting the oft-injured but dangerous Kirk Gibson (25 homers, 76 RBIs) and the seemingly invincible Cy Young pitching ace, Orel Hershiser. Hershiser especially was on a late-year roll and had finished the campaign with a record-setting 59 consecutive scoreless innings in one of the most impressive mound performances witnessed in years. The Mets did seem to be in the driver's seat, nonetheless, when they took two of the first three NLCS meetings. Es-pecially impressive was the opener in Dodger Stadium, when the New Yorkers rallied from a 2-0 hole in the eighth against the LA bullpen and thus negated a masterful seven-inning outing by Hershiser. Then everything seemingly unraveled in the fourth game when Gooden couldn't hold onto a 4-2 lead in the ninth in the game that might have stretched New York's lead to an invincible 3-1 series margin. Mike Scioscia's two-run blast in the ninth off Gooden knotted the count, and Hershiser (with a surprise bullpen appearance) and Gibson (with the game-winning blast in the 12th) turned out to be the extra-inning heroes who turned the postseason around for the freewheeling Dodgers.

The Mets did rebound and make a series of it before the death knell sounded. After dropping a crucial final game in New York, Johnson's team struck back to deadlock the series out in LA. Cone was the stopper with a masterful five-hitter, and unheralded Kevin McReynolds did the heavy work on offense. But Game 7 turned out to be perhaps the worst display of clutch effort in team postseason history. The Mets simply handed away the NLCS and thus the entire season with one atrocious inning in the field. Five second-inning runs put the deciding game

Todd Hundley reached new milestones for slugging by a catcher before being derailed by injuries and the arrival of Mike Piazza. (NY Mets)

completely out of reach early when errors by Gregg Jefferies and Wally Backman (the latter on a routine double-play ball) opened the flood-gates against Ron Darling and surprise reliever Doc Gooden.

No one could have predicted it at the time, but this was to be the final postseason fling in Shea Stadium for more than a decade. It was also a final personal mountaintop for Davey Johnson's all-too-brief, if highly successful, New York Mets tenure. And as it would turn out, there were also some other unfortunate endings now in sight: Gooden, Strawberry, Hernandez, and Carter were also nearing the end of the road. Only once more in his career (two seasons down the road) would Dwight Gooden flirt with the charmed 20-victory circle; Strawberry had only two seasons of true power-hitting left, and only one would be in New York; and Carter and Hernandez had already slipped as everyday contributors well before the 1987 pennant chase had run its course. An era was winding down, and it didn't require any particular genius to predict that the impact of all these farewells would soon play out with nothing but disastrous results.

The season that ended the '80s was one of the most disappointing in club history. This was especially the case on the heels of some of the loftiest performances in Mets annals. The Mets' division winners of 1988 had made Davey Johnson the first manager ever to claim 90 victories annually for five seasons running. Now, in what was destined to be his last full go-around with the club, all the relentless success would suddenly begin to unravel. There simply was no team cohesiveness left in the clubhouse or on the field for a team of oversized personalities that had for some time been a powder keg waiting to ignite. Darryl Strawberry now griped publicly about his "inadequate" contract for most of the year. Keith Hernandez and Gary Carter, and to a lesser extent Doc Gooden, were no longer what they once were as dominant weapons or clubhouse leaders. Len Dykstra and Mookie Wilson also were agitated about platooning in center field, and each was quite vocal in the media about wanting either a regular starting assignment or a trade to some team more desirous of their services.

One experiment with the youngster Gregg Jefferies at second base failed miserably and led to widespread second-guessing about the off-season deal that had cleared the lineup spot for

him. Jefferies had taken the city by storm the previous fall with a sensational month of September after his emergency call-up; he also had remained torrid at the plate during postseason frays (.333), and his predicted stardom had over-crowded the Mets' talented infield. If Jefferies was to crack the starting lineup—which seemed inevitable—someone had to go, and that someone turned out to be the popular fireplug Wally Backman. Backman was dealt to Minnesota for a trio of minor league pitching prospects, but the exchange left a bad taste when Jefferies opened the season in a 1-for-28 slump and remained a yearlong disappointment. Another experiment with Juan Samuel in center was also a failure when the converted second baseman batted only .228 for his half year in town before being booted over to Los Angeles. The trade with Philadelphia for Samuel was an ill-fated venture with a high price tag—the popular Lenny Dykstra, who would blossom with the Phillies and pace the NL in hits the very next year. But the season's biggest blow by far was a devastating shoulder injury to Gooden that put the staff ace on the shelf shortly after his 100th career win in June. The team finally limped home amidst all of these setbacks a disappointing half-dozen games off the pace. In the aftermath of so much acrimony, Johnson would last only another partial season at the helm. And the four great franchise stars of the eighties—Strawberry, Gooden, Hernandez, and Carter—were also soon making hasty exits out the door.

By the early 1990s, the Mets were once again in the midst of a major rebuilding program. The managerial position was itself a constantly revolving door that admitted Bud Harrelson (274 games), Jeff Torborg (200 games), and Dallas Green (312) for extended, if not lengthy, tenures in the skipper's office. Ex-catcher Torborg could never get his edition untracked the way he had with the White Sox as 1990 AL Manager of the Year, and ex-pitcher Green could not reverse the sliding team fortunes either. The decade launched with this managerial merry-go-round would, in the end, house the longest dry spell (13 seasons) without a league pennant to reward the hometown faithful. Major front-office deals like the one that brought Cy Young winner Frank Viola from Minnesota in 1989 were stopgap measures at best and often mortgaged the club's future. Viola's 38 victories over three seasons were purchased at the cost of a fleet of young arms that included Rick Aguilera, David West, and Kevin Tapani. Another deal for John Franco that worked to fill the closer's role a year later had a far more lasting value. Exciting players did pass through Shea during half a dozen seasons of sub-.500 baseball: Hall of Famer Eddie Murray, future Giants standout Jeff Kent, and switch-hitting infielder-outfielder Bobby Bonilla were foremost among them. But between flamboyant sluggers Darryl Strawberry and Mike Piazza, there were no genuine superstars to assuage the constant losing.

Dallas Green's tenure, especially, never did live up to expectations. This was true, even though the club made a remarkable turnaround during his first full season, which was also the strike-shortened campaign that witnessed the first World Series cancellation in nine decades and that most baseball fans in New York and elsewhere thus preferred to forget. The 20.5-game improvement in the standings between 1993 and 1994 was the third-best reversal in team history. It was not hard to improve, after all, on a year that resulted in 100 losses for the first time in a quarter century. But a lineup featuring David Segui, Jeff Kent, Joe Orsulak, and Bobby Bonilla could not match the heavy hitting of a few years earlier; and aside from Bret Saberhagen (14-4 for the league's best winning percentage) in the starting rotation and John Franco (an NL-best 30 saves) in the bullpen, the pitching staff was again largely in shambles.

Green's replacement, Bobby Valentine, did not always have a smooth relationship with either his ballplayers or his front-office bosses and at times seemed even to thrive on the controversies that swirled around his office door. But during the second half of the decade, Valentine quickly began reestablishing a winning attitude in the clubhouse and a respectable lineup on the field. He produced the first winning season in half a dozen years for starters and then twice duplicated the effort without the slightest backsliding. The acquisition of 1993 AL batting champ John Olerud from Toronto and slugging third sacker Robin Ventura from Chicago via free agency provided an instant lineup boost. Latin imports Edgardo Alfonzo (Venezuela) and Rey Ordoñez (Cuba) developed rapidly to give the club new infield pizzazz. The four combined in the inner garden to provide a defensive alignment for the 1999 campaign that one *Sports Illustrated* cover story touted as the best around-the-horn quartet ever assembled. And if the starting pitching wasn't overwhelming, it eventually became stable enough behind southpaws Al Leiter and Kenny Rogers and righties Orel Hershiser, Bobby Jones, and Rick Reed to complement a very potent and productive offense.

The biggest event in Shea Stadium at the end of the 1990s was the acquisition of Mike Piazza, one of the game's most glamorous stars and baseball's heaviest-hitting catcher ever. With Piazza entrenched behind the plate, and with the best infield in the game to add both offense and defense, the Mets were back in the thick of the pennant chase for both the 1998 and 1999 seasons. (Details of these recent seasons were the subject of Chapter 1.) In the first of the Piazza-led seasons, the club posted a second straight 88-74 mark, but stumbled in the final two weeks after a gutsy August-September run at a wild-card berth and fell one game short of a postseason slot. A year later, the final collapse didn't come until NLCS action versus the powerhouse Atlanta Braves, although a wild-card slot was earned only on the strength of a dramatic one-game tie-breaker in Cincinnati. But if late-season slumps have blocked recent championship drives, the future nonetheless seemed once again exceedingly bright in Shea Stadium by the time the new millennium had rolled around.

METS CHRONOLOGY
125 Most Memorable Moments in New York Mets History

September 2, 1961—Press release from headquarters of expansion National League ball club introduces team name as "Mets . . . just plain Mets." Names on list approved by owners and voted on by thousands of newspaper readers included colorful monikers like Burros (or Boros, for New York's five boroughs), NYBs, Meadowlarks, Jets, Continentals, Rebels, Skyscrapers, Skyliners, and Avengers.

October 10, 1961—National League expansion draft held in Cincinnati with Houston winning coin flip and garnering first pick of Giants infielder Ed Bressoud. Mets elect catcher Hobie Landrith with second overall pick and Casey Stengel quips, "You've got to start with a catcher or you'll have all passed balls."

April 10-11, 1962—In portentous fashion, first-ever regular-season game of the New York Mets is rained out in St. Louis. Worst loss-filled season in baseball history is thus delayed by

one night, with the Mets instead opening April 11 against the Cardinals and falling 11-4. Ex-Dodger Roger Craig suffers first franchise loss, and Gil Hodges and Charlie Neal, also former Dodgers, slug first two homers. Opening-night lineup for inaugural game also includes popular NL veteran outfielders Richie Ashburn, Gus Bell, and Frank Thomas.

April 13, 1962—Mets' first home game and return of senior-circuit baseball to New York City is witnessed by only 12,000 in the Polo Grounds amongst snow flurries. Roberto Clemente makes sliding mud-spattered snag of a Richie Ashburn foul fly to thrill fans, and the Mets lose to Pittsburgh Pirates 4-3.

April 23, 1962—Mets finally win their first game with 9-1 triumph in Pittsburgh's Forbes Field. Jay Hook tosses complete-game five-hitter and club pops champagne to celebrate first-ever franchise victory.

May 9, 1962—Mets trade catcher Hobie Landrith and cash to Baltimore Orioles to acquire promising first baseman Marv Throneberry. Throneberry quickly takes on funfilled mantle of "Marvelous Marv" and comes to symbolize ball club's enthusiastic but frustrating season-long offensive and defensive ineptitude.

May 30, 1962—Largest baseball crowd of year and largest Polo Grounds throng since 1942 jams park to witness return of exiled Dodgers to New York City. Overflow crowd of 56,000 (some reportedly sitting on top of telephone booths) has identity crisis as former "Bums" come out on top in both ends of twin bill, 13-6 and 6-5. First Mets triple play executed.

June 17, 1962—Marvelous Marv etches his legend forever in the minds of New York ball fans with what later became known as Throneberry's "unforgettable maneuvers" (the words were Jimmy Breslin's). During 8-7 loss to Cubs, Throneberry chooses to illegally block Chicago runner Don Landrum on base paths, even though he doesn't have the ball. Cubs' Lou Brock smacks memorable homer into Polo Grounds centerfield bleachers.

September 30, 1962—One of strangest plays in club history brings end to three major league careers and caps off Mets' woeful inaugural season. The most bizarre triple play in team annals occurs when Joe Pignatano's blooper behind second is snagged by Ken Hubbs, whose relay to infield nabs both base runners. Richie Ashburn and Sammy Drake (the runners), along with Pignatano, never play in another big-league contest.

June 23, 1963—Jimmy Piersall wins clubhouse bet with Duke Snider by celebrating his 100th career homer with backwards trot around Polo Grounds base paths. Most famous of Piersall's many zany on-field stunts is not at all amusing to Casey Stengel, who releases Piersall shortly after incident. Stengel apparently felt that one clown (himself, obviously) in Mets' dugout was more than enough.

August 7, 1963—Jim Hickman becomes first New York Met batter to hit for cycle, collecting single, double, triple, and homer in same game versus St. Louis Cardinals in Sportsman's Park.

April 17, 1964—First game (also season's home opener) played in Shea Stadium before near-capacity crowd of 50,312, with Pittsburgh's Willie Stargell belting first Shea homer in second inning and Pirates coming out on top 4-3.

May 31, 1964—Only six weeks after Shea Stadium opening, Mets and San Francisco Giants play longest doubleheader in history with total of 32 innings. In typical fashion, Mets manage to lose both games of historic Memorial Day twin bill, played before 57,000-plus throng, with 23-frame nightcap also featuring a Mets triple play.

June 21, 1964—Philadelphia's ace, Jim Bunning, pitches perfect game against Mets in Shea Stadium on Father's Day. It is ninth perfect game in MLB history and final score is 6-0.

July 7, 1964—Ron Hunt is first Met to start an All-Star Game as National League defeats American League in Shea Stadium. Philadelphia outfielder Johnny Callison smacks three-run homer to spark four-run ninth-inning rally for winners.

October 2, 1964—In perhaps the most brilliant mound display of Mets' early years, southpaw Al Jackson allows only five hits to break Cardinals' eight-game winning streak. Ed Kranepool knocks in only tally in 1-0 victory over St. Louis ace Bob Gibson.

April 27, 1965—Mets drop first visit to Houston's spectacular new Astrodome 3-2 when outfielder Joe Christopher loses routine fly in milky glow of indoor park's Plexiglas skylights.

June 14, 1965—Jim Maloney of Cincinnati no-hits Mets for 10 innings but suffers 1-0 defeat anyway when Johnny Lewis smacks solo homer over center-field wall at Crosley Field in 11th frame.

Yogi Berra quickly rebuilt championship dreams at Shea Stadium in the aftermath of the death of Gil Hodges. (Brace Photo)

July 24-25, 1965—On weekend of 75th birthday celebration, Casey Stengel suffers fall in men's room at Toots Shor's restaurant and fractures hip, thus ending long and colorful baseball career. Casey picks pitching coach Wes Westrum as his replacement.

September 3, 1965—Outfielder Jim Hickman again makes history, this time as first Mets slugger to power three homers in single game, again versus Cardinals, and with all three blasts coming off same pitcher, future Met southpaw Ray Sadecki.

April 17, 1966—Veteran third sacker Ken Boyer accounts for three RBIs and paces team to 5-4 victory over Atlanta in Shea, their second defeat of Braves in three days. With 2-1 record in opening series, Mets stand above .500 for first time in team history. But New Yorkers quickly drop next five straight to launch another season below sea level.

July 31, 1966—With manager Wes Westrum constantly tweaking starting lineup, Mets achieve first winning month with 18-14 July ledger. Month finishes with one seven-game winning streak, followed by another three straight in Houston and two of three in Chicago versus Cubs.

October 2, 1966—Mets complete fourth campaign at 66-95 and only 28.5 games out of first. This is 13-game improvement on previous best ledger and represents first time ball club avoids losing 100 or finishing dead last. Chicago Cubs trail Mets by 7.5 games in NL basement.

April 25, 1967—Young Tom Seaver first flashes brilliant potential with 2-1 complete-game victory in Wrigley Field. Five days earlier, Mets sterling rookie right-hander had won his first major league game.

July 11, 1967—At All-Star Game in Anaheim, Tony Pérez smacks dramatic 15th-inning homer to lift NL to 2-1 win. NL skipper Walter Alston's choice to save victory is Mets' rookie Tom Seaver, who walks Carl Yastrzemski but strikes out Bill Freehan to preserve game.

September 20, 1967—Wes Westrum, second Mets manager, resigns with 11 games left after frustrating season marked by growing player discord. Coach Salty Parker finishes out dismal final two weeks 4-7 as interim pilot.

October 1, 1967—Mets finish season using record 54 players and record 27 pitchers, prompting broadcaster Ralph Kiner to later re-

mark that "never had any big-league team accomplished so little with so many."

April 15, 1968—At Houston, Mets endure 24 innings of scoreless tie in longest night game in history, eventually losing 1-0 on bad-hop infield grounder. No previous NL game had gone longer than 20 frames without a score, and this was also longest NL game ever played to completion.

April 17, 1968—Mets win first home opener ever before 52,079 in Shea Stadium. Rookie southpaw Jerry Koosman blanks Giants 3-0, becoming first Met to toss two consecutive shutouts.

April 19, 1968—Another rookie sensation, Nolan Ryan, becomes ninth pitcher in major league history to strike out side on nine pitches but nonetheless loses to Dodgers 3-2.

May 14, 1968—Nolan Ryan strikes out 14 Cincinnati Reds at Shea Stadium for new club record. Previous mark of 12 was shared by Dick Selma and Tom Seaver.

July 9, 1968—In All-Star Game at Houston's Astrodome, Jerry Grote is second Met named as starter in Midsummer Classic. Seaver shines as All-Star for second straight summer with two scoreless innings.

September 13, 1968—With three-hit, 2-0 blanking of Pirates at Shea Stadium, Koosman matches NL record for whitewashes by rookie. Last rookie with seven shutouts was legendary Grover Cleveland Alexander with Philadelphia Phils in 1911. Victory is No. 67 of season for team and surpasses franchise record of 66 in 1966.

September 24, 1968—During game in Atlanta, manager Gil Hodges suffers minor heart attack. Hodges sits out final few days of season but is cleared by doctors to return for springtime action.

April 8, 1969—Opening-day jinx continues with 11-10 embarrassment at hands of league's newest team, expansion Montreal Expos. Seaver is blasted for five runs in six innings as Montreal captures its first-ever franchise game.

May 28, 1969—At Shea Stadium, Jerry Koosman matches Nolan Ryan's team record with 14 Ks in nine innings versus San Diego Padres. Koosman registers 15th K in 10th, then gives way to bullpen as Mets win 1-0 in 11th on Bud Harrelson's bases-loaded single.

June 4, 1969—Mets beat Dodgers 1-0 in 15 innings in game featuring impossible game-

Bobby Valentine had little impact on the Mets' outfield in the late '70s. (Brace Photo)

saving fielding play by Al Weis at second that broadcaster Ralph Kiner would later remember as greatest he ever saw.

July 9, 1969—Capacity throng of 59,083 on hand at Shea for game Seaver would later claim was the best he ever pitched. Mets win 3-0 over rival contenders, the Chicago Cubs, but Tom Terrific loses perfect game when unheralded Jimmy Qualls singles in ninth.

July 30, 1969—During late stages of second game in rain-soaked doubleheader loss to Astros, manager Hodges sends message by pulling Cleon Jones from lineup for not hustling while running down a double in the left-field gap. Incident grabs entire team's attention and dramatically turns around club fortunes for remainder of season.

September 8, 1969—Another turning point in pennant chase against Cubs comes when Jerry Koosman's "retaliation" pitch nails Ron Santo. Showing they could not be intimidated after Billy Hands' "message" knockdown of Tommie Agee, Mets bounce back to beat Chicago 3-2 on Agee's own two-run homer.

September 15, 1969—In St. Louis, Steve Carlton sets new major league mark with 19 Ks (Sandy Koufax and Bob Feller had 18), but pen-

nant-bound Mets win anyway by 4-3 count on pair of two-run shots by Ron Swoboda.

October 4, 1969—In first-ever postseason game, Mets squeak by Braves in Atlanta 9-5, scratching back for victory in late innings after Seaver is blasted for five runs in seven frames.

October 6, 1969—Miracle Mets claim National League flag with 7-4 win over Atlanta to punch their first-ever World Series ticket. Ryan is the pitching hero in relief, and Tommie Agee and Ken Boswell homer in biggest game to date in franchise history.

October 11, 1969—Orioles capture Mets' first-ever World Series game 4-1, as Brooks Robinson makes several memorable fielding plays at third base, including a rally-killing scoop of a Rod Gaspar dribbler in the seventh.

October 12, 1969—Mets earn first-ever World Series victory, 2-1, on brilliant mound performance by Koosman, who gets vital bullpen aid from Ron Taylor in the ninth.

October 14, 1969—Tommie Agee dominates first World Series game played in Shea Stadium. Agee's heroics include leadoff homer against Jim Palmer and two outfield circus catches (against Elrod Hendricks in the fourth and Paul Blair in the seventh) that still rank among best Fall Classic fielding gems of all time.

October 16, 1969—Miracle completed with 5-3 victory behind Koosman best remembered for shoe-polish incident in sixth inning that put Cleon Jones aboard ahead of Donn Clendenon's rally-starting home run. Davey Johnson lines to Cleon Jones for final out of Series, and greatest frenzy in New York baseball history engulfs Shea Stadium.

January 14, 1970—Popular GM and team architect John Murphy struck down by second heart attack within a month. Super-scout Bob Scheffing immediately named as Murphy's replacement.

April 7, 1970—Mets open new decade in Pittsburgh by winning first season opener ever with 5-3 11-inning victory against Pirates. Opening-day losing streak thus stopped at eight, with Ron Taylor emerging as winning pitcher and Tug McGraw earning save, both in relief of starter Tom Seaver.

April 18, 1970—Nolan Ryan reclaims club strikeout record by ringing up 15 versus Philadelphia Phillies in Shea Stadium. Denny Doyle's slap single to open game is Phillies' only base hit.

April 22, 1970—Seaver obliterates Ryan's short-lived strikeout mark with 19 Ks in Shea Stadium versus Padres. String includes final 10 batters and ties major league mark. Seaver's performance considered one of great pitching outings of entire 1960s-1970s.

October 1, 1970—Despite struggling in season's second half, Seaver tops NL with 283 Ks, a new record for righties. Ken Boswell also finishes strong with record 85 consecutive errorless games at second base.

May 29, 1971—Mets sweep early-season doubleheader in San Diego on strength of combined 26 Ks from Seaver (10) and Nolan Ryan (16). Ryan walks only four and throws only 130 pitches in most controlled outing ever for Mets.

September 30, 1971—Seaver completes strong season with new record for NL strikeouts by right-hander (289) and outstanding 20 wins plus fabulous 1.76 league-best ERA.

December 10, 1971—In worst trade of franchise history, Mets ship young fireballer Nolan Ryan (baseball's future all-time strikeout king), along with Leroy Stanton, Don Rose, and Francisco Estrada, to California Angels for Jim Fregosi, veteran infielder who would hopefully solve club's long-standing third-base problems.

April 2, 1972—Darkest moment of team history occurs when Gil Hodges dies suddenly of massive heart attack on West Palm Beach golf course after day's outing with coaches Ed Yost, Rube Walker, and Joe Pignatano. New York legend Yogi Berra named new Mets manager four days later.

May 11, 1972—Board chairman M. Donald Grant arranges deal with San Francisco Giants to bring Willie Mays back to New York City in Mets uniform.

May 14, 1972—After two nights riding bench, Mays makes first appearance in Mets uniform on Sunday afternoon, Mother's Day, starting in center field against his old Giants team, walking in his first at-bat and socking a game-winning solo homer in the fifth.

October 2, 1972—At end of frustrating third-place season, Mets are embarrassed one last time, being no-hit 7-0 by Expos righty Bill Stoneman in Montreal's frigid Parc Jarry.

July 3, 1973—Club endures one of most humiliating defeats ever in 19-8 pounding at Montreal. Ex-Mets Ken Singleton, Mike Jorgensen, and Ron Hunt all contribute heavily to Expos onslaught.

September 21, 1973—After Seaver's 10-2 victory over Pirates in New York, Mets reach .500 level and take over division lead on same night. Team would hold on to win lackluster NL East race that seemed at times headed for five-way tie of sub-.500 clubs.

October 8, 1973—Mets grab 2-1 NLCS lead in Shea Stadium with 9-2 pounding of Cincinnati Reds. But game most renowned for ugly incident at second base when Bud Harrelson and Pete Rose square off after vicious slide by Cincinnati's Charlie Hustle and thus incite full-scale bench-clearing brawl.

October 10, 1973—Pandemonium reigns in Flushing after pennant-clincher against Reds during NLCS Game 5. Contest evolves into one of most memorable for postseason mayhem, with crush of rowdy fans already collapsing temporary foul-line box seats before game's end. When Tug McGraw gets final out of 7-2 victory, hordes of destructive celebrating fans invade the Shea Stadium infield and outfield and up-root much of ballpark playing surface.

October 13-14, 1973—Series opener lost to Oakland A's 2-1 in west coast ballpark containing more than 4,000 empty seats. Fall Classic from start seems anticlimactic after acrimo-

Felix Millan contributed to a championship in his first Mets season. (Brace Photo)

nious NLCS between New York and Cincinnati. Mets' 10-7 Game 2 win next day in four-hour-plus marathon still remembered as one of sloppiest and most unfocused World Series performances ever.

October 16, 1973—Series Game 3 overshadowed by off-field controversy when Oakland team owner Charles Finley suspends and threatens to fire second sacker Mike Andrews for two errors previous day. Commissioner acts swiftly to reinstate Andrews, and A's outlast Mets in 11-inning showdown between Catfish Hunter and Tom Seaver.

October 18, 1973—Mets take 3-2 Series lead on three-hit shutout by Jerry Koosman, with Tug McGraw saving 2-0 Shea Stadium victory.

October 21, 1973—A's complete two-game comeback and finish off Mets' Series hopes 5-2. A's also escape fate of becoming first homerless team in seven-game Series, with crucial game-deciding homers by light-hitting Bert Campaneris and strongman Reggie Jackson.

February 21, 1974—On heels of second Cy Young Award in 1973, Tom Seaver re-signs

John Stearns handled Mets pitchers for nearly a decade. (Brace Photo)

for $175,000, making him highest-paid player in baseball.

September 11, 1974—Mets play their longest game, which stretches to 25 innings and lasts 7 hours and 4 minutes. Also set team record for players used (24) and runners stranded (25) in 4-3 marathon loss to St. Louis Cardinals.

October 1, 1974—Seaver breaks Koufax's NL record and matches AL immortals Walter Johnson and Rube Waddell by reaching 200 Ks for seventh straight season.

April 6, 1975—Small opening-day crowd (18,527) at Shea Stadium turns out mostly to witness newly arrived home run threat Dave Kingman's debut in Mets uniform. "Sky King" deliver a 400-foot bleacher blast in his second at-bat against Steve Carlton.

August 5, 1975—Board chairman Donald Grant fires manager Yogi Berra after doubleheader shutout losses to Montreal Expos. Tom Seaver had met with Grant hours before to reveal that players had lost faith in Berra's leadership abilities.

August 24, 1975—Team suffers no-hit embarrassment in San Francisco at hands of undistinguished Giants right-hander Ed Halicki. At the time, Halicki owned an 8-18 career record in 29 starts.

September 28, 1975—Shortstop Felix Millan completes season by playing in all 162 games, becoming first Mets player to accomplish this iron-man feat.

June 4, 1976—Kingman enjoys most productive night in Mets flannels by slugging three homers and driving home club-record eight runs in 11-10 victory in Dodger Stadium. King Kong's outburst ended 1-for-18 slump and matched Jim Hickman's 1965 three-HR feat in St. Louis.

August 16, 1976—Jerry Koosman reaches 20 wins for first time in midst of career season. Milestone comes against St. Louis Cardinals and also features southpaw's season-high 13 strikeouts.

May 31, 1977—Grant fires manager Joe Frazier in midst of losing steak that reaches six games. Joe Torre takes over as first player-manager in NL since Solly Hemus in 1959 with Cardinals. Torre will remove his name from active roster on June 18, after less than three weeks of double duty.

June 15, 1977—In perhaps Mets' second-worst trade ever (and certainly most immediately unpopular), Seaver is dealt to Cincinnati

for outfielders Steve Henderson and Dan Norman, utility infielder Doug Flynn, and bullpen hand Pat Zachry.

July 24, 1978—Cincinnati's Pete Rose visits Shea Stadium in midst of NL-record 44-game hitting streak and thrills fans by tying modern NL mark of 37 set by Tommy Holmes of Boston Braves in 1945. Blow comes off former Red Pat Zachry, acquired in Seaver trade and now Mets' top starter.

December 8, 1978—Mets part with second top mound star of '70s when Koosman is traded to Minnesota for another southpaw, Jesse Orosco. With more potent Twins, Koosman rejuvenates for another 20-win season and 82 more career victories in final seven campaigns.

April 5, 1979—Orosco ("player to be named later" in Koosman exchange) makes big-league debut, getting final out of season's opener in Wrigley Field. Twenty-one years (and 1,090 games) later, Orosco sets ML record for pitching appearances.

July 12, 1979—High point of disappointing Mets season comes in All-Star Game when center fielder Lee Mazzilli thrills Seattle fans as late-inning defensive replacement, bashing game-tying homer in eighth and walking with bases jammed to force in game-winner in ninth.

September 30, 1979—Ed Kranepool calls it quits, ending longest Mets playing tenure. Kranepool leaves after 18 seasons as club's career leader in numerous categories: games (1,853), at-bats (5,436), hits (1,418), doubles (225), HRs (118), RBIs (614), total bases (2,047), and extra-base hits (368).

February 21, 1980—Frank Cashen hired to replace Joe McDonald as GM. New boss makes best move of year with use of nation's first overall amateur draft pick in June to pluck Darryl Strawberry from LA's Crenshaw High School.

September 30, 1980—Smallest crowd in Shea Stadium history, as 1,754 casual bystanders witness 10-5 loss to Pittsburgh Pirates.

February 28, 1981—Cashen brings Kingman back to New York for second Mets tour in deal with Cubs involving popular but disappointing and unproductive outfielder Steve Henderson. King Kong had led NL with 48 round trippers two seasons earlier.

October 4, 1981—Skipper Joe Torre and entire coaching staff fired on final day of disappointing strike-interrupted, two-part season. Torre leaves with highest (today still unsur-

Wally Backman emerged as a fan favorite in the mid '80s. (Brace Photo)

passed) Mets total for managerial defeats (420), as well as third-highest win total (286, behind Hodges and Berra).

June 9, 1982—Kingman establishes all-time club home run leadership en route to NL crown with 37 dingers. On April 30 he smashed 300th of career off Rich Gale of San Francisco Giants and also set new Mets record with 19 round trippers in home park.

June 1982—Front office selects Dwight Gooden from Tampa's Hillsborough High School as fifth overall pick in Amateur Player Draft. Shawon Dunston was nabbed out of Brooklyn by the Chicago Cubs with the top overall choice.

April 5, 1983—Tom Seaver makes emotional Mets return in front of biggest opening-day crowd (48,682) since 1968. In face-off with old rival Steve Carlton, Seaver blanks Phillies for six frames on way to 2-0 win. Mets' ninth straight opening-day victory, tying 1937-45 skein by St. Louis Browns.

May 16, 1983—Hot 21-year-old prospect Darryl Strawberry launches Mets career in Pittsburgh with first big-league homer, a two-run shot off Lee Tunnell.

June 15, 1983—Mets pull off perhaps their best-ever trade to acquire all-star first baseman Keith Hernandez from the Cardinals in exchange for Neil Allen and Rick Ownbey.

Lee Mazzilli was both a matinee idol and an offensive spark plug in two tours of duty with the Mets. (Brace Photo)

October 1, 1983—Second-year submarine right-hander Terry Leach tosses 1-0 10-inning one-hitter at Philadelphia Phillies, which remains the only extra-inning one-hitter in club history.

April 7, 1984—Dwight Gooden makes first big-league start in Houston. Teenage prospect impresses with five Ks in five innings and picks up win thanks to Strawberry's mammoth center-field home run.

September 7, 1984—Gooden loses no-hitter in ninth against Cubs on Keith Moreland dribbler, yet nonetheless passes Grover Cleveland Alexander's rookie strikeout record with 235 and counting. Ten nights later, Gooden breaks Koufax's NL record for most Ks in two games and also ties major league mark.

December 10, 1984—Cashen again transforms team into instant contender with trade bringing All-Star catcher Gary Carter from Montreal in exchange for Hubie Brooks and three others. Carter brings team both big bat and valuable experience necessary to handle top young mound phenom Doc Gooden.

April 11, 1985—Second season under manager Davey Johnson begins with storybook moment when new hero Gary Carter homers for exciting opening-day win in bottom of 10th against St. Louis Cardinals.

June 11, 1985—Most one-sided Mets contest staged in Philadelphia's Veterans Stadium as home team creams New Yorkers by 26-7 count. Pitching staff so injury riddled that reliever Tom Gorman starts this game, with disastrous results.

July 4, 1985—Keith Hernandez hits for cycle (single, double, triple, homer) in 16-13 extra-inning marathon win over Braves in Atlanta. Holiday fireworks show postponed until 4:30 a.m., when several rain delays and poor defense extend farcical contest to 19 innings.

July 22, 1986—Mets climb into thick of pennant race with chaotic three-game sweep of Cincinnati Reds. Headline-grabbing middle game of series features wild and woolly 10th-inning brawl kicked off by third-base fisticuffs between Ray Knight and Eric Davis that earns national headlines.

October 5, 1986—Mets finish as East Division champions with franchise-record 108 wins and mammoth 21.5-game margin over runner-up Phillies. Clincher comes on Doc Gooden complete-game victory in Shea Stadium.

October 11, 1986—Lenny Dykstra's dramatic and unexpected ninth-inning line-drive homer turns around NLCS with Houston. Before his blast, Dykstra had poked only eight homers all season.

October 15, 1986—NL pennant clinched in Houston with one of most memorable battles of NLCS history. Jesse Orosco, after giving up game-tying homer to Billy Hatcher in 14th, strikes out Kevin Bass with two aboard in bottom of 16th to finally end seesaw, heart-stopping affair, which some have insisted on hyping as "the greatest game ever played."

October 25, 1986—One of the most famous (or infamous) moments in both Mets and Bosox history unfolds when Mookie Wilson's easy grounder slips through Bill Buckner's legs at first base and stuns Boston team that was one out from first World Series triumph since 1918. Buckner's misplay breaks Boston hearts and is trumpeted everywhere as firm proof of Boston's hopeless "Curse of the Bambino" World Series jinx.

October 27, 1986—Mets wrap up second World Series title with exciting 8-5 Shea Stadium finale over demoralized Red Sox. Jesse Orosco again is bullpen savior and ices deciding game with final strikeout of Marty Barrett.

March 26, 1987—Doc Gooden's career begins to unravel when troubled ace tests positive for cocaine use. Mets' top mound star enters alcohol and drug rehabilitation program and is lost until June 5.

August 19, 1987—Strawberry and Howard Johnson bang 30th homers on same night against San Francisco Giants in Shea Stadium to become baseball's first 30-homer and 30-steal teammates.

September 30, 1987—Mets finally slip from contention for another division title with 4-3 loss to Philadelphia Phillies. Stopper Jesse Orosco is this time a goat, surrendering game-deciding pinch homer to Luis Aguayo in 10th.

April 4, 1988—Division title-winning season is launched with big game and big blast from Darryl Strawberry in Montreal. Straw homers in season's first at-bat for second straight year and adds second round tripper (one of longest ever seen in Olympic Stadium) plus two singles and a walk in 10-6 drubbing of Expos.

September 21, 1988—Division title clinched at home with 4-3 victory over Phillies. Stadium celebrations are muted, however, by heavy show of mounted police aimed at squelching duplication of 1973 and 1986 fan outbursts.

October 12, 1988—Tense seven-game series for NL flag finally falls to Los Angeles after 6-0 Dodgers victory in rubber match. Orel Hershiser is LA pitching hero with complete-game effort. Mets contribute to own downfall with shoddy fielding displays, especially in second inning, when several misplays open floodgates for five unearned Dodger runs.

June 19, 1989—Doc Gooden becomes third-youngest pitcher to win 100 games when he bests Montreal Expos to reach milestone at 24 years and seven months. Bob Feller, who reached 100 victories at only 22, remains baseball's youngest triple-digit winner.

June 25, 1989—Fans witness rarest of baseball feats in Shea Stadium when Mets record all 27 putouts against Philadelphia Phillies without a single recorded assist.

August 20, 1989—Howard Johnson makes history by reaching 30-homer and 30-steal plateau for second time in career. Two seasons later, HoJo will reach this milestone for a third and final time.

October 1, 1989—Keith Hernandez finishes seventh Mets season in top 10 in 10 different career offensive categories, including a .297 team-best lifetime batting average. He would nonetheless be released during off-season.

April 30, 1990—Davey Johnson fired as manager early in trouble-marred season. Much of turmoil involves Darryl Strawberry, who battles drug addiction and several run-ins with the law. At season's end, Strawberry flees ball club as free agent bound for Los Angeles Dodgers.

September 13, 1996—Derek Wallace becomes first Met to strike out four in one inning (ninth) as he picks up save in 6-4 victory against Atlanta Braves. Victims are Terry Pendleton (who reaches base on passed ball), Chipper Jones, Ryan Klesko, and Mike Mordecai.

September 14, 1996—Switch-hitting catcher Todd Hundley, in midst of career year, smashes 41 homers to pass Roy Campanella's 43-year-old record for backstops. This total also passes NL mark for switch-hitters, previously posted by Mets' Howard Johnson in 1991. Mickey Mantle (1956, 1958, 1960, 1961) and Ken Caminiti (1996) remain only other switch-hitters to reach 40.

September 29, 1996—Outfielder Lance Johnson finishes season with 227 hits for new Mets' single-season record. Johnson paces NL hitters after leading AL with 186 for 1995 White Sox and thus becomes first and only player in baseball history to lead both leagues in this department.

June 16, 1997—First regular-season meeting with crosstown rival Yankees staged at Yankee Stadium in inaugural season of interleague play. Mets win, 6-0, behind Dave Mlicki. Right-hander throws first complete game and first career shutout before mixed crowd of 56,188.

May 22, 1998—Mets pull off shocking trade to acquire slugging catcher Mike Piazza from the Florida Marlins in exchange for talented minor leaguers Preston Wilson and Ed Yarnall, an outfielder and pitcher. Time may yet prove that this deal outranks the acquisition of Keith Hernandez in 1977 as the best trade in Mets franchise history.

September 27, 1998—Mets fall one game short of earning first postseason wild-card slot by squandering season-ending series in Atlanta and losing final five games after strong closing month (12-7 before final losing string). Two of final five defeats are shutouts, and disastrous closing week allows Chicago Cubs to sneak into wild-card berth.

August 15, 1999—Kenny Rogers pitches Mets' first complete game of the season with a 12-5 victory over Giants in San Francisco. The solo effort by southpaw Rogers stops the New York string at 139 outings without a complete game, one game short of the major league record set by Anaheim Angels earlier the same season.

October 9, 1999—Reserve catcher Todd Pratt becomes unlikely postseason hero by smashing game-winning 10th-inning homer in Shea Stadium to close out National League Division Series against West Division–champion Arizona Diamondbacks.

October 17, 1999—Robin Ventura keeps Mets' pennant hopes alive with one of the most unusual game-winning blasts in postseason history. Ventura's bases-loaded blow against Atlanta in Shea Stadium settles a 16-inning affair that extends the NLCS to Game 6, but his dramatic poke into right-field seats is ruled only a single when Ventura is mobbed at first base by the entire Mets dugout.

METS' OPENING-DAY LINEUPS AND RESULTS

1962

St. Louis—Cardinals 11, Mets 4—LP: Roger Craig
(first New York Mets franchise game)

Richie Ashburn, CF
Felix Mantilla, SS
Charlie Neal, 2B
Frank Thomas, LF
Gus Bell, RF
Gil Hodges, 1B
Don Zimmer, 3B
Hobie Landrith, C
Roger Craig, P
Casey Stengel, Manager

1963

Polo Grounds—Cardinals 7, Mets 0—LP: Roger
Craig

Larry Burright, 2B
Choo Choo Coleman, C
Ed Kranepool, RF
Duke Snider, CF
Frank Thomas, LF
Tim Harkness, 1B
Charlie Neal, 3B
Al Moran, SS
Roger Craig, P
Casey Stengel, Manager

1964

Philadelphia—Phillies 5, Mets 3—LP: Al Jackson

Dick Smith, 1B
Amado Samuel, 2B
Ron Hunt, 3B
Frank Thomas, LF
Jim Hickman, CF
Bob Taylor, C
Joe Christopher, RF
Al Moran, SS
Al Jackson, P
Casey Stengel, Manager

1965

Shea Stadium—Dodgers 6, Mets 1—LP: Al Jackson

Billy Cowan, CF
Roy McMillan, SS
Johnny Lewis, RF
Ed Kranepool, 1B
Joe Christopher, LF
Charley Smith, 3B

Bobby Klaus, 2B
Chris Cannizzaro, C
Al Jackson, P
Casey Stengel, Manager

1966

Shea Stadium—Braves 3, Mets 2—LP: Jack
Fisher

Cleon Jones, RF
Ron Hunt, 2B
Ken Boyer, 3B
Dick Stuart, 1B
Jim Hickman, CF
Ron Swoboda, LF
Jerry Grote, C
Roy McMillan, SS
Jack Fisher, P
Wes Westrum, Manager

1967

Shea Stadium—Pirates 6, Mets 3—LP: Don
Cardwell

Don Bosch, CF
Cleon Jones, RF
Ken Boyer, 3B
Tommy Davis, LF
Ron Swoboda, 1B
Jerry Buchek, 2B
Jerry Grote, C
Bud Harrelson, SS
Don Cardwell, P
Wes Westrum, Manager

1968

San Francisco—Giants 5, Mets 4—LP: Danny
Frisella

Bud Harrelson, SS
Ken Boswell, 2B
Tommie Agee, CF
Ron Swoboda, RF
Ed Kranepool, 1B
Art Shamsky, LF
J.C. Martin, C
Ed Charles, 3B
Tom Seaver, P
Gil Hodges, Manager

1969

Shea Stadium—Expos 11, Mets 10—LP: Cal
Koonce

Tommie Agee, CF
Rod Gaspar, RF
Ken Boswell, 2B

Cleon Jones, LF
Ed Charles, 3B
Ed Kranepool, 1B
Jerry Grote, C
Bud Harrelson, SS
Tom Seaver, P
Gil Hodges, Manager

1970
Pittsburgh—Mets 5, Pirates 3 (11)—WP: Ron Taylor

Tommie Agee, CF
Bud Harrelson, SS
Joe Foy, 3B
Cleon Jones, LF
Art Shamsky, 1B
Ron Swoboda, RF
Wayne Garrett, 2B
Jerry Grote, C
Tom Seaver, P
Gil Hodges, Manager

1971
Shea Stadium—Mets 4, Expos 2 (5)—WP: Tom Seaver

Tommie Agee, CF
Bud Harrelson, SS
Cleon Jones, LF
Art Shamsky, RF
Donn Clendenon, 1B
Ken Boswell, 2B
Bob Aspromonte, 3B
Jerry Grote, C
Tom Seaver, P
Gil Hodges, Manager

1972
Shea Stadium—Mets 4, Pirates 0—WP: Tom Seaver

Bud Harrelson, SS
Ken Boswell, 2B
Tommie Agee, CF
Rusty Staub, RF
Cleon Jones, LF
Jim Fregosi, 3B
Ed Kranepool, 1B
Jerry Grote, C
Tom Seaver, P
Yogi Berra, Manager

1973
Shea Stadium—Mets 3, Phillies 0—WP: Tom Seaver

Bud Harrelson, SS
Felix Millan, 2B
Willie Mays, CF
Rusty Staub, RF
Cleon Jones, LF
John Milner, 1B
Jim Fregosi, 3B
Duffy Dyer, C
Tom Seaver, P
Yogi Berra, Manager

1974
Philadelphia—Phillies 5, Mets 4—LP: Tug McGraw

Wayne Garrett, 3B
Felix Millan, 2B
Rusty Staub, RF
Cleon Jones, LF
John Milner, 1B
Jerry Grote, C
Don Hahn, CF
Bud Harrelson, SS
Tom Seaver, P
Yogi Berra, Manager

1975
Shea Stadium—Mets 2, Phillies 1—WP: Tom Seaver

Gene Clines, LF
Felix Millan, 2B
John Milner, 1B
Joe Torre, 3B
Dave Kingman, RF
Jerry Grote, C
Del Unser, CF
Bud Harrelson, SS
Tom Seaver, P
Yogi Berra, Manager

1976
Shea Stadium—Mets 3, Expos 2—WP: Tom Seaver

Wayne Garrett, 3B
Felix Millan, 2B
Ed Kranepool, 1B
Dave Kingman, RF
John Milner, LF
Del Unser, CF
Jerry Grote, C
Bud Harrelson, SS
Tom Seaver, P
Joe Frazier, Manager

1977

Chicago—Mets 5, Cubs 3—WP: Tom Seaver
   Lee Mazzilli, CF
   Felix Millan, 2B
   John Milner, LF
   Dave Kingman, RF
   Ed Kranepool, 1B
   John Stearns, C
   Roy Staiger, 3B
   Bud Harrelson, SS
   Tom Seaver, P
   Joe Frazier, Manager

1978

Shea Stadium—Mets 3, Expos 1—WP: Jerry
Koosman
   Lenny Randle, 3B
   Tim Foli, SS
   Steve Henderson, LF
   Willie Montañez, 1B
   Ken Henderson, RF
   Lee Mazzilli, CF
   John Stearns, C
   Doug Flynn, 2B
   Jerry Koosman, P
   Joe Torre, Manager

1979

Chicago—Mets 10, Cubs 6—WP: Craig Swan
   Lee Mazzilli, CF
   Kelvin Chapman, 2B
   Richie Hebner, 3B
   John Stearns, C
   Willie Montañez, 1B
   Steve Henderson, LF
   Elliott Maddox, RF
   Doug Flynn, 2B
   Craig Swan, P
   Joe Torre, Manager

1980

Shea Stadium—Mets 5, Cubs 2—WP: Craig Swan
   Alex Taveras, SS
   Elliott Maddox, 3B
   Lee Mazzilli, 1B
   Steve Henderson, LF
   Mike Jorgensen, RF
   John Stearns, C
   Jerry Morales, CF
   Doug Flynn, 2B
   Craig Swan, P
   Joe Torre, Manager

1981

Chicago—Mets 2, Cubs 0—WP: Pat Zachry
   Mookie Wilson, CF
   Alex Taveras, SS
   Lee Mazzilli, CF
   Dave Kingman, LF
   Rusty Staub, 1B
   Alex Treviño, C
   Hubie Brooks, 3B
   Doug Flynn, 2B
   Pat Zachry, P
   Joe Torre, Manager

1982

Philadelphia—Mets 7, Phillies 2—WP: Randy
Jones
   Mookie Wilson, CF
   Bob Bailor, SS
   George Foster, LF
   Dave Kingman, 1B
   Joel Youngblood, RF
   John Stearns, C
   Hubie Brooks, 3B
   Ron Gardenhire, SS
   Randy Jones, P
   George Bamberger, Manager

1983

Shea Stadium—Mets 2, Phillies 0—WP: Doug
Sisk
   Mookie Wilson, CF
   Bob Bailor, SS
   Dave Kingman, 1B
   George Foster, LF
   Hubie Brooks, 3B
   Mike Howard, RF
   Brian Giles, 2B
   Ron Hodges, C
   Tom Seaver, P
   George Bamberger, Manager

1984

Cincinnati—Reds 8, Mets 1—LP: Mike Torrez
   Wally Backman, 2B
   José Oquendo, SS
   Keith Hernandez, 1B
   George Foster, LF
   Darryl Strawberry, RF
   Mookie Wilson, CF
   Hubie Brooks, 3B
   Ron Hodges, C
   Mike Torrez, P
   Davey Johnson, Manager

1985

Shea Stadium—Mets 6, Cardinals 5 (10)—WP: Tom Gorman

    Wally Backman, 2B
    Mookie Wilson, CF
    Keith Hernandez, 1B
    Gary Carter, C
    Darryl Strawberry, RF
    George Foster, LF
    Howard Johnson, 3B
    Rafael Santana, SS
    Dwight Gooden, P
    Davey Johnson, Manager

1986

Pittsburgh—Mets 4, Pirates 2—WP: Dwight Gooden

    Len Dykstra, CF
    Wally Backman, 2B
    Keith Hernandez, 1B
    Gary Carter, C
    Darryl Strawberry, RF
    George Foster, LF
    Howard Johnson, 3B
    Rafael Santana, SS
    Dwight Gooden, P
    Davey Johnson, Manager

1987

Shea Stadium—Mets 3, Pirates 2—WP: Bob Ojeda

    Mookie Wilson, CF
    Tim Teufel, 2B
    Keith Hernandez, 1B
    Gary Carter, C
    Darryl Strawberry, RF
    Kevin McReynolds, LF
    Howard Johnson, 3B
    Rafael Santana, SS
    Dwight Gooden, P
    Davey Johnson, Manager

1988

Montreal—Mets 10, Expos 6—WP: Dwight Gooden

    Len Dykstra, CF
    Tim Teufel, 2B
    Keith Hernandez, 1B
    Darryl Strawberry, RF
    Kevin McReynolds, LF
    Gary Carter, C
    Howard Johnson, 3B
    Kevin Elster, SS
    Dwight Gooden, P
    Davey Johnson, Manager

1989

Shea Stadium—Mets 8, Cardinals 4—WP: Dwight Gooden

    Mookie Wilson, CF
    Gregg Jefferies, 2B
    Keith Hernandez, 1B
    Darryl Strawberry, RF
    Kevin McReynolds, LF
    Gary Carter, C
    Howard Johnson, 3B
    Kevin Elster, SS
    Dwight Gooden, P
    Davey Johnson, Manager

1990

Shea Stadium—Pirates 12, Mets 3—LP: Dwight Gooden

    Gregg Jefferies, 2B
    Keith Miller, CF
    Howard Johnson, 3B
    Darryl Strawberry, RF
    Kevin McReynolds, LF
    Mike Marshall, 1B
    Barry Lyons, C
    Kevin Elster, SS
    Dwight Gooden, P
    Davey Johnson, Manager

1991

Shea Stadium—Mets 2, Phillies 1—WP: Dwight Gooden

    Vince Coleman, CF
    Gregg Jefferies, 3B
    Dave Magadan, 1B
    Hubie Brooks, RF
    Howard Johnson, SS
    Kevin McReynolds, LF
    Tom Herr, 2B
    Charlie O'Brien, C
    Dwight Gooden, P
    Bud Harrelson, Manager

1992

St. Louis—Mets 4, Cardinals 2—WP: Jeff Innis

    Vince Coleman, LF
    Willie Randolph, 2B
    Bobby Bonilla, RF
    Howard Johnson, CF
    Eddie Murray, 1B
    Bill Pecota, 3B

Kevin Elster, SS
Todd Hundley, C
David Cone, P
Jeff Torborg, Manager

1993

Shea Stadium—Mets 3, Rockies 0—WP: Dwight
Gooden (first Colorado Rockies franchise game)
 Vince Coleman, LF
 Tony Fernández, SS
 Eddie Murray, 1B
 Bobby Bonilla, 3B
 Howard Johnson, 3B
 Joe Orsulak, CF
 Jeff Kent, 2B
 Todd Hundley, C
 Dwight Gooden, P
 Jeff Torborg, Manager

1994

Chicago—Mets 12, Cubs 8—WP: Dwight Gooden
 José Vizcaino, SS
 Todd Hundley, C
 Kevin McReynolds, LF
 Bobby Bonilla, 3B
 Jeff Kent, 2B
 David Segui, 1B
 Jeromy Burnitz, RF
 Ryan Thompson, CF
 Dwight Gooden, P
 Dallas Green, Manager

1995

Denver—Rockies 11, Mets 9 (14)—LP: Mike
Remlinger
 Brett Butler, CF
 José Vizcaino, SS
 Rico Brogna, 1B
 Bobby Bonilla, 3B
 Jeff Kent, 2B
 David Segui, 1B
 Carl Everett, RF
 Todd Hundley, C
 Bobby Jones, P
 Dallas Green, Manager

1996

Shea Stadium—Mets 7, Cardinals 6—WP: Jerry
DiPoto
 Lance Johnson, CF
 Bernard Gilkey, LF

Rico Brogna, 1B
Butch Huskey, RF
Jeff Kent, 3B
Todd Hundley, C
José Vizcaino, 2B
Rey Ordoñez, SS
Bobby Jones, P
Dallas Green, Manager

1997

San Diego—Padres 12, Mets 5—LP: Yorkis Pérez
 Lance Johnson, CF
 John Olerud, 1B
 Bernard Gilkey, LF
 Todd Hundley, C
 Butch Huskey, 3B
 Carlos Baerga, 2B
 Carl Everett, RF
 Rey Ordoñez, SS
 Pete Harnisch, P
 Bobby Valentine, Manager

1998

Shea Stadium—Mets 1, Phillies 0 (14)—WP: Turk
Wendell
 Hal McRae, CF
 Edgardo Alfonzo, 3B
 Bernard Gilkey, LF
 John Olerud, 1B
 Carlos Baerga, 2B
 Butch Huskey, RF
 Tim Spehr, C
 Rey Ordoñez, SS
 Bobby Jones, P
 Bobby Valentine, Manager

1999

Florida—Marlins 6, Mets 2—LP: Al Leiter
 Rickey Henderson, LF
 Edgardo Alfonzo, 2B
 John Olerud, 1B
 Mike Piazza, C
 Bobby Bonilla, RF
 Robin Ventura, 3B
 Brian McRae, CF
 Rey Ordonez, SS
 Al Leiter, P
 Bobby Valentine, Manager

CHAPTER 3
The Great, the Memorable, and the Colorful:
Profiles of 100 Unforgettable Mets Players

Even one- and two-act plays have their leading men and boast supporting casts. Although the four-decade-long history of the New York Mets is admittedly short in its scope when laid side-by-side with that of more venerable and long-toothed teams like the Yankees, Red Sox, Cubs, Tigers, Cardinals, or any other of the dozen or so "original" ball clubs that have hung around for the full century of National League and American League play, the current senior circuit ball club in New York nonetheless boasts its own rather considerable pantheon of true immortals, oversized superstars, colorful lesser lights, and some just plain cherished unforgettables. A few of them—like Snider and Spahn and Mays and Hodges—were only passing through for one weak curtain call at career's end. Others—like Nolan Ryan and Mike Scott—launched their fame-bound careers in Shea Stadium, yet never hung around long enough to attach their personal glories to the Mets' franchise star. Others—like Seaver and Gooden and Strawberry—will always be most intimately connected with the considerable fortunes of the beloved hometown ball club. Together their stories are sometimes the very heart and sometimes only the entertaining footnotes that comprise the always-expanding volume that is New York Mets baseball history.

TOM "TERRIFIC" SEAVER
(1967-77, 1983, Pitcher)

If any hard evidence is needed to clinch the argument that Tom Seaver was the first true superstar in Mets history—or bolster the case that he is the closest thing the club has ever

had to a franchise ballplayer—it is found in the fact that over the span of his 10 seasons in New York, the flame-throwing right-hander won 25 percent of the Mets' total games. Tom Terrific left behind, after 10 New York seasons and another 10 in Cincinnati, Chicago, and Boston, an unimpeachable Hall of Fame résumé that included 311 career wins, a big-league-record 10 total seasons with better than 200 strikeouts (nine of those in a row), and a rarely duplicated three Cy Young Awards, all with the Mets. Only Roger Clemens and Greg Maddux have garnered

Tom Seaver, the Mets' franchise pitcher. (NY Mets)

more Cy Young hardware, and only Jim Palmer and Steve Carlton have equaled Seaver's proficiency at capturing baseball's top pitching award. More notable still, only 16 immortals had ever reached the 300-victory plateau before Tom Terrific did so on August 4, 1985. In October of that same season he moved past Walter Johnson and into third place on the career strikeout list, and today only Ryan, Carlton, and Bert Blyleven lead him in that category. Finally, when it comes to the New York Mets' record book, Seaver still remains the franchise pacesetter in career wins (198 with New York), starts, complete games, innings pitched, ERA (2.57), strikeouts (2,541), walks, and shutouts (44).

The Mets' greatest-ever pitcher came on board with the franchise early in its expansion history under some of the strangest circumstances in modern contract history. Atlanta's Braves had originally offered the USC mound phenom a $40,000 signing package in 1966, but the NCAA and baseball commissioner William Eckert were both quick to void the tainted deal which violated rules governing athletes with college eligibility (juniors and seniors couldn't be signed once their team's season was in progress). Eckert declared that Seaver could re-sign with any team inclined to match the Braves' underhanded offer and three clubs—Cleveland, Philadelphia, and the still-struggling expansion Mets—jumped to seize the opportunity. A lottery "ceremony" ensued in the commissioner's office, and it was the Mets who rejoiced to see their name card fortuitously pulled first from the ceremonial hat. Thus it was a rather convoluted and fortuitous set of developments that had to unfold for one of the country's hottest young pitching prospects of the mid-sixties ever to wind up as a New York Met in the first place.

Once in a Mets uniform, the California right-hander wasted little time in demonstrating his unmatched value as a franchise pitcher. His first year's performance in the big time was nothing short of spectacular and garnered the hearts of both New York fans and beat writers as well as league-wide accolades in the form of the "official" 1967 Rookie of the Year honor and also a berth in the NL All-Star Game lineup in July. The rookie picked up 16 victories for a basement ball club that posted only 61 wins. The victory total was bested by only four other league pitchers, and only Fergie Jenkins of the Cubs, with 20, rang up more than Seaver's 18 complete games. But it was at the end of the

decade that everything came together for both Seaver and the Mets simultaneously. After duplicating his 16-win total with a team that improved a dozen games in the win column but only a single slot in the NL standings, Tom Terrific was a runaway success story in 1969—collecting 25 victories, leading everyone in winning percentage, trailing only three others (Marichal, Carlton, and Gibson) in ERA, and outdistancing the field in the Cy Young balloting. En route to the club's "miracle" year World Series upset of Baltimore, Seaver was also a postseason mainstay. He earned a crucial win in the NLCS against Atlanta when New York rallied to victory in Game 1 and also claimed World Series Game 4 on Swoboda's circus catch in the ninth.

Seaver's second remarkable season and second corresponding Cy Young honor came not surprisingly in the year the Mets made their return to the World Series. It was during the 1973 charge that Tom Seaver became the first-ever non-20-game winner to capture the coveted Cy Young honor. He did so by leading the circuit in ERA (2.08), strikeouts (251), and complete games (18). It was Tom's third crown in strikeouts and upped his string of 200-plus strikeout seasons to half a dozen. During postseason play, the Mets' ace lost a heartbreaker in the NLCS opener but bested Cincinnati in the clincher by allowing only a single earned run. But in that year's World Series, he suffered the kind of hard luck that often plagued him on account of the Mets' sometimes impotent offense and earned only a no-decision (in Game 3, with an 11-inning, 3-2 defeat) and an unjust Game 6 loss (3-1, after surrendering only two runs in seven frames).

Seaver suffered a fall-off due to injury on the heels of the 1973 season. The ball club won 11 fewer games and slid to fifth; Seaver tumbled to .500 at 11-11 and was nowhere to be found among league leaders in any important category. The culprit was a painful hip injury, and the unfortunate result was Seaver's first 3.00-plus ERA (3.20) in eight big-league seasons. But there was still plenty of glory to come, and much of it would be played out in Shea Stadium with the New York Mets before the unpopular trade of 1977 that sent the franchise hurler packing to Cincinnati. The comeback 1975 season saw another Cy Young built on the circuit's highest win total and winning percentage and still another NL strikeout crown. But eventually

trouble would set in with the front office. Never one to hide his feelings, despite his consummate professionalism, Seaver was vocal about his stalled contract negotiations and also about the way GM Donald Grant was managing team affairs. There were private confrontations and even public taunts traded in the newspapers. And these ugly conflicts would, of course, lead eventually to one of the worst and most publicized player trades in New York City baseball history. The bombshell June 1977 deal with Cincinnati that ended Tom Seaver's Mets career (discounting the brief one-season swan song return of 1983) was enough to sour many die-hard Mets boosters for the remainder of a three-year string of basement-dwelling seasons which closed out the roller-coaster decade.

DWIGHT "DOC" GOODEN
(1984-94, Pitcher)

If anyone ever seemed destined to unseat Tom Seaver from the top of the heap among Mets pitching stars, it was surely Dwight "Doc" Gooden, who burst onto the baseball scene in 1984 with one of the most spectacular rookie campaigns found anywhere in big-league annals. For a handful of seasons, five, in fact, it appeared that Gooden might even be a legitimate rival to immortals like Cy Young or Christy Mathewson or Nolan Ryan and not just the equal of modern-era star Tom Seaver. The Tampa native's rookie season was as full of dizzying overachievement as any other debut on record during baseball's first full century.

Record-breaking is hardly sufficient to describe the kind of opening outing Gooden enjoyed the year he jumped straight to The Show from the Mets' Lynchburg team in the lowly Class-A Carolina League. As the fifth overall player selected in the June 1982 amateur draft, Dwight Gooden held seemingly unlimited promise from the outset, but few could have expected quite so much quite so soon. Having struck out 300 in only 191 innings in the bottom-rung minors in 1983, Gooden found big-league swingers to be hardly more challenging, as he constructed a major league rookie record with 276 Ks in only 218 National League innings. It was a summer-long performance that earned him the nickname "Doctor K" and soon had delirious Shea Stadium denizens hanging red-printed letter Ks on the facing of a special fan club section of the right-field upper deck. Other strikeout feats of the season were a tied major league mark for whiffs in consecutive games (32 on September 12 and 17) and a new record of 43 in three straight contests. The new Mets ace was also the youngest National League All-Star ever.

The sensational youngster was anything but a one-year or two-year flash in the pan. His second Mets season was even more head-spinning than his first. For starters, he walked off with the pitching "Triple Crown" by pacing the National League in victories (24), ERA (1.53, the lowest since Gibson's 1.12 in 1968's "Year of the Pitcher"), and strikeouts (268). He was also a league leader in complete games (with 16), and his exploding fastball continued to dominate hitters so thoroughly that there was little doubt he was the most feared pitcher in either circuit. Though he was still a few months short of reaching the age of majority by season's end, Dwight Gooden was already on the fast track to Cooperstown.

Those first two seasons were a hard act to follow, and there was little surprise when Gooden had trouble maintaining so dizzying a pace much further into his career. He was never quite the same dominating pitcher after his sophomore campaign. On only a single occasion would he again pace the league in any individual pitching category, and this came when he posted the best 1987 NL winning percentage (15-7, .682). But there was certainly no immediate collapse. That was still a few years down the road even if bouts with substance abuse and scrapes with law enforcement were already forming ominous storm clouds on the horizon. If Gooden was not unhittable in 1986, he was still the matchless ace of one of baseball's best teams. The personal victory total dropped to 17 on a ball club that was only the ninth in modern history to win as many as 108 games. His 200 strikeouts made Gooden the first hurler ever to reach that plateau in each of his first three seasons. And the powerful right-hander also rang up an NLCS record for a seven-game series with 20 strikeouts, despite not personally picking up a single postseason victory. Despite the signs of diminishing dominance, Gooden continued his mastery in his third storybook season and played a major role in carrying the ball club to its first World Series victory without Tom Seaver.

Dwight Gooden started faster than perhaps any other pitcher in baseball history. (Brace Photo)

Perhaps Dwight Gooden and his early success was just too good to be true. Perhaps his teenage triumphs all came too easy and far too early. Or perhaps there is no single explanation for the nearly as rapid demise that started as early as his fourth big-league season. But by 1987, Gooden's career was already beginning to unravel and his life was beginning to spin out of control. At the center of the collapse were problems with drugs and alcohol—the latest tragic chapter of a timeworn baseball saga. The league's best winning ratio of 1987 was rung up only after the Mets' slipping star had returned to action from his first drug rehabilitation program. A narrow loss in the division race that season might justifiably be blamed on Gooden's early-season absence. What followed in the subsequent summers (and off-seasons as well) was often not very pretty. Despite 18 victories in 1988 and 19 in 1990, the diminished Gooden was no longer the league's best, and his loss in the 1988 All-Star Game tied the career record for defeats in the Midsummer Classic. The 1988 postseason was another case of solid pitching for Gooden without achieving any all-important NLCS victories. He barely won in double figures on three other occasions before his Mets career finally ended in wreckage after the strike year of 1994—at age 30 and 41 victories short of Seaver's franchise benchmark.

There would be a few brief hurrahs down the road (including a 1996 no-hitter with the Yankees and a surprising hometown comeback with expansion Tampa Bay early in the 2000 season), but these were only encouraging rebounds rather than epic milestones. A shoulder injury in mid-1989—the first of his career—also contributed to the slide. In the end, it was the tragic demise of an altogether rare talent that for a short span had seemed bound on a fast track for a gilded spot in Cooperstown. First, Gooden found himself struggling to save his Hall of Fame credentials, and all too soon he would grapple simply to keep his big-league career afloat. Once it became apparent that personal demons and the evils of alcohol lay at the heart of his problems, it became equally apparent that the greatest struggle of all for Doc Gooden might simply be that of keeping his very life intact.

KEITH HERNANDEZ
(1983-89, First Baseman)

Keith Hernandez will likely never end up in Cooperstown or even draw more than passing support for future ranking as one of the game's all-time best all-around first sackers. For one thing, his 17-season offensive totals were never nearly impressive enough for a position that usually assumes consistent power numbers. While he hit over .300 on six occasions and racked up 90 or more RBIs half a dozen times, these were hardly numbers to put at the heart of the batting order. He was never George Sisler with his 15th-best all-time batting mark, to take one example. And he never approached Lou Gehrig, who was an awesome enough hitter to protect Babe Ruth in an unparalleled Murderers' Row lineup. Perhaps two-time AL batting champion Ferris Fain of the '50s Philadelphia Athletics would be a better parallel. Hernandez did hit well enough, however, to earn widespread respect as the best all-around first baseman of the late seventies and most of the eighties. And when his glove is taken into account, there is little argument that he was one of the best of his own era.

The handsome and personable San Francisco native had established stardom in St. Louis with several super seasons well before coming over to the Mets under somewhat less than stain-free circumstances. All-Star campaigns in both 1979 and 1980 produced one NL batting crown (he outdistanced Pete Rose by 13 percentage points in 1979) and a number of other league-best performances at the plate. The same season he had the league's top numbers for doubles (48) and on-base percentage. Hernandez also twice (1979 and 1980) scored the most runs in the senior circuit. The lefty swinger and thrower achieved better than 200 hits one year (1979, when he trailed only his teammate Garry Templeton by one) and twice running had the league's top figure for on-base percentage. It was all enough to suggest the best defensive first sacker around was also one of the game's most clever batsmen. But after 1980 Hernandez did not seem to keep up the pace on the offensive side of his game.

After leaving St. Louis in a trade for pitcher Neil Allen, Hernandez showed renewed enthusiasm in New York. In the end, the trade may well have served as an ironic emotional boost that assured further stardom for Hernandez and certainly paid large dividends for his new employers. Hernandez was an immediate hit in Shea Stadium, regaining his lost All-Star slot and again posting worthy offensive numbers, which

Keith Hernandez, possibly the slickest-fielding first baseman in the history of the game. (Brace Photo)

included three consecutive summers of .300 hitting. The trifecta of outstanding personal seasons also overlapped a long-awaited Mets world championship, as well as a second run to postseason play two years later. But the storybook run was relatively short-lived and had already wound down by the start of a fifth season in New York. In 1989 Hernandez hit only .233, and in 1990 he was taking a final bow as a bench player in Cleveland.

In the end, there is little argument that Hernandez was the best first-base defender of his own era and perhaps one of the three or four best of all time. His top hitting seasons in New York were supplemented by the league's best fielding percentage at his key infield position. And Hernandez's talents with the glove could not entirely be measured adequately with mere numbers or even with his accumulation of 11 consecutive Gold Gloves. He developed an aggressive style of defensive play that was highlighted by his bold efforts at charging the first-base line on sacrifice bunts in order to cut off potential advances to second base. It was a pioneering style previously mastered by Ferris Fain—his earlier prototype—but now made into Hernandez's own special personalized trademark. In the face of such combinations of consistent offensive production and eye-catching

defensive consistency, the argument is hard to deny that in all phases of the game, Keith Hernandez was, during his own era at least, one of the best first basemen baseball had to offer.

DARRYL STRAWBERRY
(1983-90, Outfielder)

Doc Gooden has a clear-cut rival when it comes to the sad saga of a New York Mets superstar who has somehow managed to let a sure date with Cooperstown gradually disintegrate into a lamentable struggle for baseball and personal survival. Darryl Strawberry's schizophrenic big-league career splits right down the middle into two disjointed halves. The first is the tale of a budding superstar maintaining a rapid and steady course in the direction of baseball immortality. The nation's No. 1 pick in the 1980 amateur draft burst onto the scene in 1983 as the NL's top rookie and maintained an eye-popping slugging pace over the next nine seasons, which put his career squarely on par with that of Reggie Jackson. Over that span, the slim but power-packed lefty never socked fewer than 26 homers, only once slugged less than .500, reached triple figures in both runs and RBIs twice, and in 1988 was the NL home run champ with 39 dingers in a season noted for a league-wide drop in power numbers.

The second half of the saga reads more like the tragedy-soaked tale of a big-league has-been trying desperately to resurrect a once-glorious career and seemingly sabotaging his own best comeback efforts at every turn. The last nine seasons—split between the Dodgers, Giants, and Yankees—have witnessed only one power-packed season of 24 round trippers in only 101 games with the runaway-champion 1998 Yankees team that set new standards for relentless winning. Between 1992 and 1998, Strawberry never logged more than 63 big-league games in a season and only once produced as many as 11 homers. The stretch was blighted by substance-abuse problems, drug rehabilitation assignments, numerous second chances from the commissioner's office and from Yankees owner George Steinbrenner, a much-publicized stint in the independent Northern League, and finally a bout with colon cancer. Darryl's 1999 season with the repeat-champion Yankees seemed only a microcosm of his entire career. The sometimes star swung a heavy and timely bat in only 24 September and October games

THE NEW YORK METS ENCYCLOPEDIA

Darryl Strawberry nearly matched Dwight Gooden's heady rookie achievements. (Brace Photo)

after sitting out much of the year on suspension for off-field mistakes; Strawberry had seemingly recovered miraculously from the previous year's cancer treatments, when he curtailed his own season by pleading no contest to charges of solicitation and cocaine possession. After still another fall from grace during the 2000 preseason, resulting in still another year-long suspension for testing positive for drug use, Strawberry's rocky and once-so-promising big-league career now finally seems to have reached its tragic conclusion.

In the early seasons in New York, Strawberry was an always-solid and sometimes-spectacular performer and thus owned a nationwide fan following that earned him a starting All-Star Game spot every season but one in his first decade. His power numbers were truly awesome, even if he remained a streaky hitter whose looping roundhouse swing not only produced numerous opposite-field homers but also Reggie Jackson-like strikeout totals. But if he was an impatient hitter who slumped badly at least one month of every season, he was also a graceful athlete who ran like a gazelle and owned a strong, if erratic, throwing arm. In his fifth big-league season (1987), Strawberry joined with Howard Johnson to become the first 30-30 teammates (homers and steals) in baseball history. Yet the numbers were only part of the story. Immature behavior by the Mets' superstar led to frequent early-career feuds with manager Davey Johnson and numerous highly publicized clubhouse and dugout sulking incidents. Mental lapses in the outfield also led to several costly injuries (such as torn ligaments in his right thumb, which slowed his 1985 campaign) and a league-wide reputation for lack of hustle on defense.

There were thus many negatives for Strawberry in his early seasons with the Mets, and some of these came well before the personal off-the-field problems set in. He suffered mental lapses all too frequently on defense and was also an inconsistent performer in crucial postseason games. Despite a three-run homer in the Mets' Game 3 NLCS triumph in 1986 and a vital Game 6 double that ignited the team's pennant-winning rally, Strawberry also struck out 12 times in 22 at-bats for an NLCS record. His only World Series RBI that year came on a titanic blast in the Mets' Game 7 clincher. His ability to aggravate and incite opposing fans and pitchers led to a daily chorus of bleacher boos

that followed him around the league. And rival pitchers threw at him even in spring training games, inspiring several on-field brawls.

The most tragic chapters in the career of Strawberry were destined to unfold after his free-agent flight out of Shea Stadium to the Dodgers in November 1990. A back injury spelled doom for his second season in LA and seemingly started the downward spiral that has made Strawberry only a part-time player ever since. If he has remained an oversized celebrity with the Dodgers and Yankees (and briefly the Giants in 1994) throughout much of the 1990s, he has long since slid from the ranks of legitimate baseball superstars. For a brief stretch in the '80s, however, Strawberry seemed on the fast track toward 500-plus career homers (he entered 2000 still stuck at 335) and a guaranteed wall plaque displayed in the main foyer at Cooperstown. That once plausible dream has now faded forever.

MIKE PIAZZA
(1998–, Catcher)

Assuming that Mike Piazza even comes close to maintaining the breakneck slugging pace of his first half-dozen seasons, it remains an almost surefire bet that Tom Lasorda's godson will wind up not only residing in Cooperstown but also sporting the reputation as baseball's greatest hitting catcher. While considered a poor defender by some baseball insiders and only adequate by others, the Mets' cleanup hitter possesses batting skills that more than compensate for any throwing or receiving liabilities. An All-Star in each of his eight major league seasons, Piazza has never hit lower than .303, and his .328 career mark is a runaway best among catchers from all eras. He slugs with unparalleled power to all fields and dipped below 30 homers only during the strike-shortened 1994 season. In his first half season with the Mets he reached the 200 plateau in career homers and paced the majors with four grand slams. Enjoying a full season in New York a summer later, he matched career highs with 40 homers and 124 RBIs and did so in only 141 games.

The big-league career of Mike Piazza has been something of an improbable Cinderella story from day one. Here was a youngster who had few, if any, big-league prospects when he left high school in Norristown, Pennsylvania, back in 1986. His only asset seemed to be a

chance family connection, but it turned out to be quite a connection and one that provided the break needed to showcase his hidden talents. Mike's father, Vince, was a personal friend of Dodgers manager Tom Lasorda, and it was as a personal favor to a longtime associate that Lasorda first arranged for the big-league club to draft the youngster (who was playing at Miami-Dade North Community College in Florida) in the 62nd round (1,390th overall pick) of the 1988 amateur talent lottery. When no contract was at first forthcoming, Lasorda again intervened and arranged a private tryout before team brass in Dodger Stadium, then pronounced that his godson would become a catcher, although he had previously been a schoolboy pitcher and college outfielder.

Once signed, Piazza took full advantage of his opportunities in Los Angeles and turned almost overnight into a legitimate superstar of unexpected proportions. It wasn't really quite overnight, of course, since Piazza paid his dues in the hardest way imaginable before becoming a household name for big-league ball fans. In order to learn the catching trade, which was his apparent ticket to the big time, Piazza put in time at the club's famed Campo Las Palmas training center in the Dominican Republic. He was the first U.S. apprentice who had ever been taught there. The unglamorous internship was followed by a whirlwind minor league tour of four seasons, which took the rapidly improving prospect to bush-league stops in the Northwest League (Salem), Florida State League (Vero Beach), California League (Bakersfield), and Texas League (San Antonio). It was evident that Piazza had learned his trade well by the time he reached AAA Albuquerque and had earned a finalist slot for *USA Today* and *The Sporting News* Minor League Player of the Year awards. Once reaching the big time, his 1993 Rookie of the Year season was altogether staggering and featured 35 homers and 112 RBIs (fourth in the league). Strike-shortened seasons the next two years were all that could curtail his numbers, but the drop-off, if there was any, was in home run totals and run production only. The hard-hitting catcher's .346 average in 1995 was second to Tony Gwynn's (.368), and a year later he ranked third. In 1996 Piazza was an All-Star Game MVP during his fourth straight appearance in the Midsummer Classic. But despite all the heroics, LA's top performer surprisingly fell out of favor by 1998 when he balked at re-sign-

Mike Piazza, the best-hitting catcher of all time. (NY Mets)

ing with the Dodgers for a hefty salary increase. Turning a cold shoulder to a reported long-term deal for $80 million, Piazza not only rankled LA officials but seemed to become a symbol nationwide of the ballplayer greed that was turning off fans from coast to coast. In one of the blockbuster trades of the entire decade, Piazza was finally shipped to the Florida Marlins in mid-May in exchange for Gary Sheffield, Bobby Bonilla, and promising catcher Charles Johnson (all three heading out to LA).

If there was negative baggage surrounding Piazza's contract demands in Los Angeles, it was certainly not baggage destined to be enhanced for skeptical fans by any on-field loafing or dip in performance from an unmotivated big-league prima donna. After only five games with the Marlins, Piazza was dealt once more—this time to New York—and immediately set about proving beyond doubt that his game would not suffer from any contract stalemates. Inking the long-term deal he had wanted with the Mets, baseball's leading offensive catcher continued posting numbers identical to those he had rung up with regularity on the other coast. He finished fourth in the league in hitting, rang up

30-plus homers for the fifth time, and walked off with an NL Silver Slugger Award.

Piazza's debut in New York and its immediate aftermath is one of the most dramatic stories in the four decades of Mets history. He broke in with a bang, clubbing a double in his May 23 debut and collecting his first Mets homer on June 1 versus the Pirates. As the summer wore on, his bat kept the team in a pennant hunt that fell one game short of a wild-card berth on the season's final day. For his own part, Piazza hit .318 in June, .326 in July, and .347 with eight homers and 30 RBIs during the dog days of August. He has continued to carry a potent New York lineup in similar fashion for two full seasons and spearheaded the 1999 wild-card winners. Since the wear and tear of a full season behind the plate seemed a culprit in slowing Mike Piazza during the losing NLCS struggle with Atlanta, it now seems likely that a position change to first base is in the offing. Yet, since Piazza was still only 31 on the eve of the 2000 season, the future indeed remains bright for baseball's best-hitting catcher.

1960s—THE DEBUT OF THE BELOVED AMAZINS

The first decade of club history was filled with more pratfalls and misadventures than anything else, and the ballpark heroes of that decade were thus drawn accordingly. Some were once-proud National League stars hanging on for one last embarrassing trip around the senior circuit. Duke Snider, Richie Ashburn, Warren Spahn, and Bob Friend were among the long-toothed heroes of the previous decade who took their last brief bows in a crumbling Polo Grounds or a newly minted Shea Stadium. Other early Mets were beloved only because they were the best that local fanatics had to cheer for. Marvelous Marv Throneberry was an unlikely bungling hero whose numerous errors only further endeared him to the die-hard faithful. And Ed Kranepool soon inherited a similar role without quite as much of the tomfoolery—although Casey Stengel once defended Kranepool's benching by noting that "he's only 17 but already runs like he's 30." They may not have

1960s National League Composite Standings and Pennants (Ranked by Total Games Won)					
Team	Won	Lost	Pct.	NL Pennants	World Championships
San Francisco Giants	738	560	.569	1962	None
St. Louis Cardinals	718	573	.556	1964, 1967 1968	1964, 1967
Los Angeles Dodgers	707	592	.544	1963, 1965 1966	1963, 1965
Cincinnati Reds	700	594	.541	1961	None
Milwaukee (Atlanta) Braves	680	616	.525	None	None
Pittsburgh Pirates	678	617	.524	1960	1960
Philadelphia Phillies	653	641	.505	None	None
Chicago Cubs	611	684	.472	None	None
Houston Astros (Colt .45s)	555	739	.429	None	None
New York Mets	**494**	**799**	**.382**	**1969**	**1969**
Montreal Expos (1969)	52	110	.321	None	None
San Diego Padres (1969)	52	110	.321	None	None

been much at the time, but at least they were all our very own.

RICHIE ASHBURN
(1962, Outfielder)

Throughout much of the late eighties and early nineties, Richie Ashburn was the cause célèbre for touters of overlooked Cooperstown Hall of Fame candidates. The enticing argument always went as follows: One of the game's most dependable outfielders and productive singles hitters—he was often celebrated as "the ultimate singles hitter"—was being given repeated short shrift because he had been unfortunate enough to play in the same epoch as three of the greatest center fielders of all time—Mays, Mantle, and Snider—who all enjoyed a considerable advantage playing in media-happy New York. Ashburn was, thankfully, eventually enshrined with the immortals, yet the true value and stature of his silently productive career will probably never be fully appreciated in an era that ranks the home run as baseball's prime achievement and touts overall offensive production (measured by long balls and runs plated by heavy sticking) as the top role for quality outfielders. Later a longtime popular broadcaster with the Phillies, outfielder Ashburn was a mainstay in the leadoff spot in Philly for a dozen seasons, hitting above .300 in eight of them and salting away two NL batting titles. He gunned down Brooklyn's Cal Abrams at the plate to preserve the pennant for the Whiz Kid Phils in 1950

and once singled eight times in a Sunday afternoon doubleheader. In one swan song season with the expansion Mets at age 35, he was able to remain respectable with a final .300 season and even hit a career-best seven homers that year in the short-porched Polo Grounds.

But even a proud future Hall of Famer like Richie Ashburn was not able to escape altogether from the follies that marked expansion baseball in New York under Casey Stengel. On the final day of the 1962 season, in Chicago's Wrigley Field, the talented veteran outfielder closed out his career with one of the most bizarre moments of an altogether bizarre season. As the woeful Mets marched toward their record 120th loss of the summer, Sammy Drake led off the eighth inning with a pinch single, and Ashburn followed with a base knock in his final career at-bat. But to top the season in fitting fashion, catcher Joe Pignatano next popped to Cubs second sacker Ken Hubbs, whose diving grab produced an inning-killing triple play. Since Ashburn never returned to the field for the ninth frame, this was the last play in which he was ever involved. And a final touch of irony was that neither Drake, Ashburn, nor Pignatano ever appeared in another major league game. The season's final Mets blunder was a triple play that killed off three major league careers.

KEN BOYER
(1966-67, Third Baseman)

One of a trio of big-league siblings, Boyer in his prime in the fifties with the St. Louis Cardinals was one of the best third basemen of his era. Signed originally as a pitcher, but failing quickly in that role, the hard-hitting right-hander was splendid in the field, a regular on the National League All-Star roster for most of a decade, and one of the senior circuit's biggest threats at the plate in almost any clutch situation. Further luster was added by five Gold Gloves and a shared record for leading NL hot corner defenders in double plays five times. All that kept Boyer from top-bill stardom was his rather muted personality—he always led by quiet example rather than clubhouse eloquence—coupled with the fact that the St. Louis teams he played for his first 11 seasons usually stood among the league's tailenders. But there were nonetheless moments when Boyer claimed headlines: His 29-game hitting streak in 1959 was the longest in the majors since

Ken Boyer, All-Star third baseman. (NY Mets)

Musial's in 1950, twice (1961 and 1964) he hit for the cycle, and his 1964 MVP season (when he was the NL's top RBI man with 119) was capped by a clutch World Series performance against the vaunted yet defeated Yankees. Boyer's single peak performance with the Mets was a club-leading 61 RBIs during the first of his two Shea Stadium seasons.

JOE CHRISTOPHER
(1962-65, Outfielder)

A trio of oddities highlights the brief big-league tenure of outfielder Joe Christopher. The first, of course, was his claim of being an "original" New York Met and also his slot as starting left fielder in the ball club's first-ever Shea Stadium season opener. Another was his pioneering role as the first native of the Virgin Islands to make it onto a big-league roster. And a third distinction was Christopher's feat of scoring two runs without an official at-bat as a pinch runner for the Pittsburgh Pirates in the 1960 World Series. But there were also some more substantial contributions in his eight-season sojourn, not the least of which was a solid season (154 games, .300 BA, 16 HRs, 76 RBIs) in 1964 as the regular New York Mets left fielder. It was his only .300-plus campaign and the only time he

Joe Christopher batted .300 in 1964. (Brace Photo)

luster team surrounding him, and if nothing else, Coleman's punchless hitting only seemed to enhance his short-lived charisma as a mainstay on baseball's lovable "worst-ever" team.

Clarence "Choo Choo" Coleman, an original Met. (Brace Photo)

cracked double figures in homers, but he did play more than 100 games on two other occasions, ironically in his first (1962) and last (1965) seasons wearing a Mets uniform.

CLARENCE "CHOO CHOO" COLEMAN
(1962-63, 1966, Catcher)

Colorful Clarence Coleman could always boast one of baseball's most interesting nicknames, even if there was little else about his short stay up in "The Show" that was especially memorable. He did log 106 games as the Mets' regular catcher in 1963 when he also recorded 247 official at-bats—almost half his career total—but he managed largely to discredit the quality of that accomplishment by posting a powder-puff .178 season's batting mark that stands among the lowest ever produced by a starting big-league backstop. And the minuscule offensive production—which also included 44 hits, 22 runs, and an unthinkably low nine RBIs—was hardly enhanced by the distinction of handling a pitching staff that carried the NL's worst ERA, fewest shutouts and saves, and biggest individual loser (Roger Craig, with 22 defeats). Of course, some of this record-setting ineptitude may be laid at the doorstep of the lack-

ROGER CRAIG
(1962-63, Pitcher)

There is an old adage in baseball that you have to be a heck of a pitcher to lose 20 games during a season in the big leagues. The logic follows that any losing hurler who is kept around in the big time long enough to accomplish the feat without demotion is clearly a recognized talent. The hidden subtext is that the losing has more to do with inept teammates than the fortuneless hurler himself. And by these lines of reasoning, this future big-league manager must have been a quality talent indeed when he toiled in the Polo Grounds for the lackluster expansion New York Mets. The rugged right-hander with obviously thick skin not only lost 20 in a single summer, but he did it twice running (24 losses in 1962, 22 in 1963), adding further negative evidence to his stature in the process by becoming the first pitcher in National League annals to pace the circuit in

losses in back-to-back campaigns. To clinch the case of unmatched ill fortune, Craig also tied a league standard in 1963 by dropping eighteen straight.

The evidence of Roger Craig's mound abilities of course did not only consist of the questionable merits of being able to survive a surfeit of defeats. With the pennant-winning LA Dodgers of 1959, he had starred as a dependable arm in both a starter's and bullpen role and tied for the NL lead with four shutouts. He won a World Series game with the Brooklyn Dodgers (1956) and another with the St. Louis Cardinals (1964). And he boasted 74 big-league wins and a career 3.83 ERA during a tenure that stretched a dozen seasons. But Craig's greatest fame would come two decades later as a pitching coach in Detroit and manager in San Diego and San Francisco when he honed his reputation as acknowledged "maestro of the split-fingered fastball" (*Sports Illustrated*) and tutor of eighties aces like Jack Morris and Mike Scott.

JACK FISHER
(1964-67, Pitcher)

Jack Fisher often seemed to find himself in just the right place—the wrong place from a more balanced perspective—to draw headlines and footnotes that would preserve the memory of a thoroughly mediocre, decade-long big-league pitching career. His best season came with the Orioles in 1960 when he turned in his one winning ledger, at 12-11, as well as his highest victory total. But it was a single pitch that year—Ted Williams' dramatic round tripper in the Hall of Famer's final career at-bat on September 28 in Fenway Park—that emerged as Fisher's most likely ticket to trivial immortality. Perhaps figuring that one landmark homer surrendered was not enough to assure a place in baseball lore, slightly less than a year later, Fisher also yielded Roger Maris's clout No. 60 in Yankee Stadium. (Maris socked his 61st off another future Met, Tracy Stallard, who would follow Roger Craig and precede Fisher as the Mets' top loser in 1964.) After he joined the expansion Mets, there were opportunities aplenty to enter into the record books by authoring diamond curiosities. It was Fisher who started the Mets' first-ever game in Shea Stadium, though he escaped defeat in that one with an early exit. And before he was done with the Mets, Fisher also matched the earlier milestones of Roger

Craig when his 24 defeats in 1965 and 18 losses two summers later made him the second New York Mets hurler to pace the senior circuit twice in games lost.

TIM HARKNESS
(1963-64, First Baseman)

A Quebec native who signed a pro hockey contract with the hometown Montreal Canadiens before settling on baseball as a professional occupation, Harkness hung around the big time for only two partial seasons in Los Angeles and two more with the expansion Mets. After being acquired from LA on the eve of the 1963 season along with infielder Larry Burright, the rangy left-handed swinger and thrower distinguished himself in the Polo Grounds with the not-too-difficult feat of unseating popular Marvelous Marv Throneberry from the first-base slot in the lineup, then underscored the accomplishment by giving way himself to the most durable Met of all time, several-season bench fixture and one-time bonus baby, Ed Kranepool. Harkness did enjoy one other brief moment in the spotlight in New York but it was earned only as an innocent bystander. When clownish outfielder Jim Piersall trumped his career-long spate of zany antics by trotting backwards around the basepaths after socking career home run No. 100, it was Tim Harkness whose photographic image was splashed across the nation's sports pages, waiting at home plate (he was the on-deck batter) to greet the backpedaling Piersall. Harkness also later became a prime source for those seeking out the hidden story (involving a clubhouse wager with Duke Snider) behind Piersall's colorful baserunning stunt.

JIM HICKMAN
(1962-66, Outfielder)

As a rookie outfielder with a rookie ball club in 1962, Jim Hickman poked 13 homers while batting .245, and thus provided just enough offensive clout on an impotent club to compensate for his clumsy play in the outfield pastures and his all-too-frequent strikeouts at the plate. Over the next several seasons, he also provided enough heavy lumber to account for several noteworthy franchise slugging milestones. Hickman was the first Met to hit for the cycle (August 7, 1963) and also the first in team history to power three homers in a single game

In 1963 Jim Hickman became the first Met to hit for the cycle. (Brace Photo)

through season, he was acquired by the new-comer Mets in the October 1961 expansion draft and won his lasting niche in franchise annals by earning the team's first victory in the ball club's 10th outing of the maiden 1962 season. Before that campaign was out, Hook had lost 19 times, a mind-boggling tally on most teams in most years. But with the expansion Mets, Hook's 8-19 ledger was only the third worst on a staff which headlined 20-game losers Roger Craig (10-24) and Al Jackson (8-20). Another campaign of double-figure losing the next summer was enough to change the career aspirations of the talented Hook, who had earned an off-season degree in thermodynamics. After a brief 1964 season with only two starts (0-1) and a mere three appearances, the Big Ten alumnus retired at age 28 to pursue an engineering career with Chrysler.

(September 3, 1965). On the heels of the 1966 season, he was packaged with second-base starter Ron Hunt in an unpopular deal which brought former star outfielder Tommy Davis and infielder Derrell Griffith over to New York from Los Angeles. The single long-range benefit of that deal would turn out to be a subsequent trade sending Tommy Davis on to the White Sox one winter later in a more widely applauded exchange that put Al Weis and Tommie Agee in New York Mets uniforms. Hickman, for his own part, almost came back to haunt his old mates in Shea Stadium when he flashed surprising brilliance at the plate for the rival Chicago Cubs down the stretch run of the nip-and-tuck 1969 pennant chase.

JAY HOOK
(1962-64, Pitcher)

Signed as a bonus baby off the campus of Northwestern University by the Cincinnati Reds, right-hander Hook made only four appearances with the big-league club in 1957 and 1958 and lost his only two decisions. But he seemed to come of age in 1960 with an 11-18 record, 10 complete games, and 222 innings hurled. Knocked out by the mumps after that break-

Jay Hook was the first Met pitcher to record a victory. (Brace Photo)

RON HUNT
(1963-66, Second Baseman)

Two-time National League All-Star, career .273 hitter, and the Mets' regular second baseman for three of the first five franchise seasons, "Zeke" Hunt made a career out of getting hit by baseballs rather than hitting baseballs.

THE NEW YORK METS ENCYCLOPEDIA

Quipping that while some give their bodies to science, he donated his to baseball, Hunt retired from a 12-season baseball tenure in New York, Los Angeles, San Francisco, Montreal, and St. Louis with three major league records for being hit with pitched balls: those for most times plunked in a career (243), a season (50 in 1971), and a game (3, tied with several others). He paced the senior circuit in this painful offensive category for seven seasons running. But it was all only part—notably the most intriguing part—of Hunt's overall talent for getting on base. This was a talent he supplemented by twice hitting over .300—once with the Mets in his sophomore All-Star season, and once with the Montreal Expos—and with consistently high totals for bases on balls. He was also a tough out, setting records in Montreal for fewest strikeouts in a season (19 in 1973) and fewest times hitting into double plays (once in 1971). Ron Hunt's crowning achievement, however, came early in his career, in his first full Mets season of 1964, when he became the first player ever to represent the franchise as an All-Star Game starter. An off-season trade to the LA Dodgers in November 1966 would later be remembered by Hunt as unquestionably the most disappointing moment of his big-league career.

AL JACKSON
(1962-65, 1968-69, Pitcher)

One has to wonder what a pitcher with Al Jackson's talent, tenacity, and technical knowledge of the hurler's art might have been able to accomplish had he pitched with a heavy-hitting or defensively skilled ball club like the Yankees or Dodgers during his heyday. Acquired in the expansion draft from the Pirates, the crafty southpaw, in his late 20s, was one of the under-staffed ball club's shining lights when he recorded all four of the team's first-season shut-outs in 1962. His 43 wins in New York were a team high-water mark before "Tom Terrific" Seaver came on the scene. But such was also the fate of one of the most solid arms on one of baseball's worst-ever teams that Jackson also entered the record books with identical 8-20 ledgers in both 1962 and 1965. He did have the partial consolation in both of those seasons of not pacing the ball club in futility. In the first, he trailed Roger Craig (with 24) in the "top loser" department; in the latter, he was runner-up to

Jack Fisher (also with 24). And a telling measure of Al Jackson's underappreciated talents lost within a surrounding sea of ineptitude was also the fact that his seemingly woeful records for three straight seasons (13-17, 11-16, and 8-20) were all ball club bests. Al Jackson was hardly the main culprit during that handful of depressing seasons which had Casey Stengel nightly scratching his head and pondering: "Can't anyone here play this game?"

CLEON JONES
(1963, 1965-75, Outfielder)

Until John Olerud came along, the highest any Mets player had ever finished in a National League batting race was the third-place showing by outfielder Cleon Jones during the Mets' first championship season. It was that very season that also represented a career peak for Jones. And it was a peak that significantly aided the New Yorkers in their season-long championship cause. A starting point certainly was the 10 game-winning hits that Jones rang up that season. Such game-deciding blows were not yet an "official" statistic but they certainly served to tip the season's balance in a tight race which saw the Mets stretch their final margin over the Cubs to eight games. Jones also reached top career marks that season with 92 runs scored and 75 batted home. Those were big numbers indeed for a Mets ball club that did most of its winning with superb pitching and often had to scratch and claw for any significant offensive production.

But for all his productive hitting in 1969, it was a pair of defensive plays—one embarrassing and the other stellar—that cemented Cleon Jones in the history books as a pivotal figure in two Mets championship campaigns (1969 World Series championship and 1973 NL championship). The entire Mets season had seemed to turn around in July 1969 when manager Gil Hodges suddenly woke up his lethargic forces by removing Jones from left field for failing to hustle after a batted ball. Four summers later, it was again Jones who launched a pennant race in an entirely new direction, this time by making a remarkable throw to gun down Pittsburgh's Richie Zisk at the plate, preserving a game which hoisted the pennant-bound New Yorkers into a late-season first-place berth.

JERRY KOOSMAN
(1967-78, Pitcher)

If it hadn't been for Tom Seaver, Jerry Koosman would likely still be celebrated as the original New York Mets franchise pitcher; and if it hadn't been for Koosman, Seaver would likely never have had a chance to show off his talents in baseball's showcase event known as the World Series. Together the two formed the best one-two punch in ball club annals and also one of the most effective righty/lefty duos of their era when it came to the National League pennant wars. Throughout his career, Koosman's lofty success came largely as a result of his remarkable control, which was consistently so precise that his strikeouts for most years of a two-decade career regularly doubled or tripled his bases on balls. And that control led over the years to some rarely paralleled achievements. As the best rookie hurler in the senior circuit in 1968, the Mets' top left-hander trailed only Johnny Bench in balloting for the NL Rookie of the Year trophy. He did so on the strength of new team records with 19 wins, seven shutouts, and a skimpy 2.08 ERA, all good enough to wipe out the team bests posted by Tom Seaver only one year earlier. It was only a beginning for the durable southpaw who eventually won 222 big-league games, struck out 2,556 batters, and posted 20-win seasons in both New York (where he labored for his first 11 seasons) and Minnesota. Koosman contributed heavily to the Mets' pennants in 1969 and 1973 (despite a hard-luck 14-15 mark in 1973) but only peaked in 1976 when his 21-10 effort was the class of the league. The trade of Tom Seaver a year later, however, triggered a total team collapse, and Koosman's low-water mark came that summer when he lost 20 and tied Phil Niekro for the league's most losses. The consecutive 20-game seasons—one winning and one losing (8-20 in 1977)—were a prime piece of evidence for the argument that a pitcher's won-lost statistics often have far more to do with a supporting cast than they do with his own valiant efforts.

ED KRANEPOOL
(1962-79, First Baseman)

Marv Throneberry was indisputably the most beloved and celebrated of the early Mets. But it was another first baseman who followed Marvelous Marv who turned out to be the most durable performer of the Metropolitans' first two decades. Ed Kranepool was a "bonus baby" signed out of the Bronx who reached the expansion club at the tender age of 17 during their first season and was taunted by press accounts as "over the hill" before he was out of his teenage years. Given the regular first-base slot after Throneberry's early departure, Kranepool was a reliable defender and consistent .250 hitter whose home run numbers occasionally stretched into the teens (his high was 16 in 1966) and whose glove was proficient enough to once (1971) lead the entire league in fielding percentage. Dropped to the minors in the wake of the 1969 "miracle," he bounced back in 1971 with his best single offensive showing, posting career highs in RBIs and runs scored. The one-time $85,000 prospect eventually played in each of the ball club's first 18 seasons, and although his career was rather slow in starting, he hung around long enough to leave a very large mark throughout the franchise record book. Kranepool's club records totaled eight at the time of his retirement, and he still holds the franchise lifetime marks for base hits, pinch hits, doubles, total bases, at-bats, and games played. Two decades after hanging up his spikes, Kranepool also still ranks in the Mets' career

Jerry Koosman, the runner-up franchise pitcher. (Brace Photo)

Ed Kranepool logged a record 18 seasons in a New York Mets uniform. (Brace Photo)

top 10 lists for homers (sixth), RBIs (third), extra-base hits (third), runs (fifth), and triples (eighth).

HOBIE LANDRITH
(1962, Catcher)

Fame—even immortality—sometimes comes in the smallest of doses. In the case of Hobie Landrith, 23 games and a mere 45 at-bats wearing a Mets uniform were enough to overshadow everything else in 14 seasons of big-league labor, and even to grant the journeyman backstop a considerable place in New York City baseball lore. Such irony transpired as a result of the Illinois native's rare fortune in being tabbed as the Mets' top pick in the talent-thin 1962 expansion draft, a silly exercise promoted as a means to stock the rosters of the fledgling Mets and Houston Colt .45s, but in reality being a profitable windfall for other league owners, who collected $75,000 a head for castoff "talent" that had no place on their own rosters. Houston won a coin flip and garnered Giants infielder Ed Bressoud, while the Mets wasted their top choice on Landrith, also a Giants has-been sporting a .239 batting mark in 1961. Reputed as mediocre at best defensively and owner of a less-than-adequate throwing arm, Landrith was nonetheless the opening-day catcher when the Mets unveiled their first pathetic NL entry. Nothing that Landrith produced on the field in his short tenure with the club drew nearly the press attention spurred by manager Casey Stengel's draft-day defense of expending a top draft pick on a catcher who couldn't hit or field with regularity. With one of his most memorable tirades of pure "Stengelese," Casey quipped that "you gotta start with a catcher or you'll have all passed balls." Never has faint praise been more damning.

Hobie Landrith's 20-plus games in Mets colors were but a fraction of a big-league career that survived a decade and a half and included backup backstop roles in Cincinnati, Chicago, St. Louis, Baltimore, and Washington for a final partial season in 1963. He played in 772 games, banged 34 homers, and managed to stay far enough above the Mendoza Line to retire with a .233 batting average and .327 slugging mark. But the New York sojourn was brief indeed on the heels of Casey's cogent remark about his new backstop's potential value. Little more than a month after opening day (May 9 to be exact),

Hobie Landrith was shipped off to Baltimore with a supplemental cash payment to acquire promising first sacker Marv Throneberry. The final irony was that the brief role player who was the subject of one of the most notorious quotes in team annals was also involved in the trade that brought to the Polo Grounds the most beloved ballplayer ever to wear a New York Mets uniform.

FELIX MANTILLA
(1962, Infielder)

A journeyman utility player who manned three infield slots and three outfield slots and occasionally hit with power, Mantilla enjoyed a brief touch of fame with the Milwaukee Braves in May 1959 when his ground ball to Pirates third sacker Don Hoak was booted to ruin Harvey Haddix's 12-inning perfect game. Four seasons later, he achieved a somewhat longer run in the spotlight when a trade from the Mets to the Red Sox deposited him in Fenway Park and the new surroundings triggered an uncharacteristic offensive explosion which resulted in a .315 BA in 1963 and 30 homers the next summer, 19 above his previous career best. It was an incredible resurrection which was not long-lived, and despite 92 RBIs in 1965, his average soon plummeted again and the versatile Puerto Rican was soon dispatched to Houston and then into retirement. Mantilla had arrived with the Mets via the 1962 expansion draft and he regularly manned third during the maiden franchise season while hitting a respectable .275 (almost 10 points above his eventual career average) and blasting 11 homers. At the end of a single season in the Polo Grounds he was dealt to Boston for infielders Al Moran and Pumpsie Green and pitcher Tracy Stallard, the sometimes starter most famed for delivering Roger Maris's record-breaking homer on the final day of the 1961 season.

CHARLIE NEAL
(1962-63, Infielder)

Another veteran infielder acquired by the fledgling Mets during the winter which preceded their debut season was Charlie Neal, plucked from the Dodgers in mid-December for outfielder Lee Walls (an expansion draft selection) and $100,000 cash. The acquisition came little more than two seasons after the veteran

second and third baseman had grabbed headlines as one of the heroes of the 1959 World Series with two homers in Game 2, including the game-winner. The versatile Neal was a rookie second baseman with Brooklyn in 1956, played both short and third during the Dodgers' final New York season, then won the regular second-base job in the team's first summer on the west coast. A flashy fielder who led the NL in double plays, putouts, and fielding average several times in the late fifties, Neal also became a potent offensive threat once plunked down in the Los Angeles Coliseum with its tantalizing short left-field screen. He slugged 19 round trippers and, along with teammate Wally Moon, paced the circuit in triples (11) during the LA Dodgers' first pennant-winning season. During his one full season with the Mets, he proved the club's best and most versatile infielder, logging 85 games at second, 39 at short, and 12 at third. But when his .260 average in 1962 tumbled to .225 by the midway point of the 1963 season, he was deemed to be at career's end by Mets management and hastily peddled off to Cincinnati for journeyman catcher Jesse Gonder.

JIM PIERSALL
(1963, Outfielder)

Mention Jimmy Piersall to any long-toothed ballpark crank, and images of lunacy are certain to be conjured up with glee. Everyone with an eye on baseball history knows that Piersall suffered a nervous breakdown shortly after arriving in the big leagues (during his 1952 sophomore season) and that the colorful near-two-decade career which followed his "recovery" and return (featuring a 6-for-6 batting performance on June 10, 1953) was also an endless string of zany stunts, such as hiding behind the Yankee Stadium center-field monuments while performing for the Indians and running out a home run by trotting the basepaths backwards while playing for the Mets. His own personal account of his illness in the best-selling book *Fear Strikes Out* was made into a well-attended Hollywood movie (starring Tony Perkins) while his baseball career was still in full swing and certainly fanned the flames of the growing Piersall legend. And so did his newfound attitude for dealing with fans who taunted him about his instabilities after his June 1953 return to action with the Boston Red Sox;

Piersall relished the oddball attentions of seemingly equally crazed rooters and seemed always determined to "give them their money's worth" with an ongoing parade of staged on-field pranks. Even Piersall's career after his playing days was marked by zaniness and controversy, and he eventually lost his final baseball-connected employment in the early 1980s as an outspoken broadcaster for the Chicago White Sox as a result of his continually criticizing management and lambasting the performances of modern-era players over the airwaves.

Lost in all the high jinks was the solid career that included a .272 lifetime average, 104 homers, and two Gold Gloves earned with some of the best center-field defensive play of his era. He became Boston's regular starter at that position in 1954 when he took over for Dom DiMaggio and dazzled by playing the shallowest center field in the majors. He also pounded the ball regularly in the mid-1950s, posting a league-leading 40 doubles for Boston in 1956, scoring over 100 runs for the same club a year later, and posting the fourth-best AL batting mark (.322) with Cleveland in the offense-happy 1961 campaign. His brief stay with the Mets (after he was waived by Washington in 1963) produced only a .194 hitting mark and provided constant aggravation for equally charismatic skipper Casey Stengel, who released him after only 40 games. The New York stopover earned its greatest notoriety with the backpedaling home run trot (which came off Dallas Green of the Phillies on June 23), but as with most things involving Piersall and his bizarre on-field antics, there was more to the story than the popular "ballplayer as nut case" scenario usually portrayed. It seems that the colorful prankster had made a clubhouse bet with veteran Duke Snider (also a recent Mets acquisition) that his own upcoming 100th homer would garner far bigger New York press headlines than Duke's also-imminent round tripper No. 400. It was one of the easiest bets Piersall ever won.

BOB SHAW
(1966-67, Pitcher)

A 1962 NL All-Star with Milwaukee and the league leader in winning percentage with the AL-champion White Sox of 1959, durable right-hander Bob Shaw was another of the household-name players who passed through the revolving doors of the Polo Grounds and Shea Stadium clubhouses during the Mets' early expansion years. Shaw's late-career stop in New York was for most of the 1966 and 1967 seasons, and he pitched effectively enough on arrival to log 11 victories in 1966, which tied him with veteran Jack Fisher and youngster Dennis Ribant for the club leadership. All told, Shaw claimed 108 wins in the big leagues (against 98 defeats), along with a most respectable 3.52 lifetime ERA and a favorable 880-511 strikeouts-to-walks ratio. He was a student of the pitching art and after retirement penned an instructional manual entitled *Pitching,* which was widely respected in coaching circles. Shaw was also just enough of a reported flake, however, to likely have been most comfortable in his late-career Shea Stadium surroundings of losers and castoffs. Not immune to bizarre behaviors himself, the ace of Bill Veeck's Chicago staff in the late fifties was once so incensed at management for not granting him a raise that he reportedly one day fled the Sox locker room and stood atop a catwalk at Comiskey Park berating arriving fans for showing up to watch a team that was nothing but a loser.

DUKE SNIDER
(1963, Outfielder)

The Duke of Flatbush was an oversized legend in the city of baseball legends during the fabulous fifties. "Willie, Mickey, and the Duke" was baseball's hottest debate, and Snider had his own fervent segment of devoted supporters in the arguments about baseball's greatest living center fielder. No one—not Mantle or Mays or Kiner or anyone else—hit more home runs in the entire decade (Snider hit 326 despite two final slumping years in LA), and no one owned a sweeter home run swing. But when Duke Snider returned to New York early in the following decade for a swan song appearance with the beloved hometown Mets, he was merely a shadow of his former self. And his role in the headlines was often more that of jester than of the dignified epic warrior, and even that of the sometimes tragic hero he had for so long once been. During his single Mets season, the one-time Duke of Flatbush did manage to reach a then-lofty 400 plateau in career homers, finishing his Hall of Fame career with 407.

WARREN SPAHN
(1965, Pitcher)

No southpaw in baseball annals won more games than crafty Warren Spahn and some would argue that there was no better money pitcher in all of baseball history. Perhaps Lefty Grove or Christy Mathewson deserves the honor of top spot in that elevated category, but Spahnie would not rank far behind. Not much of Spahn's winning came with the sadsack Mets, of course. He posted only four New York victories en route to a 7-16 year with the Mets and Giants, which also marked his last trip around the circuit and only his third losing record in 21 seasons of National League wars. But it was something of a colorful footnote to early Mets history that Cooperstown legends like Spahn, Snider, Berra, and Ashburn briefly pulled on the flannels of a team whose very lifeblood was at first based largely on nostalgia.

It is significant perhaps that Spahn was actually the final chapter of the ball club's desperate promotional scheme of handing out often pathetic "comeback laps" to some of yesterday's worn-out greats just to put some extra fans in the stands. After winning better than 350 games in his Hall of Fame, 16-year tenure, baseball's most venerable southpaw had been released over the winter by Milwaukee and was quickly signed on in New York as a short-term player-coach. Yogi Berra had been similarly contracted as a coach during the same off-season and Berra also appeared in two games as a fill-in backstop before pulling the plug on his own career. Surprisingly, Spahn's 20 games with the Mets were slightly more than a mere glossed-over footnote. He pitched well in his debut, even though the club lost in extra innings. He then hurled seven innings of shutout baseball in a second effective outing just three days shy of his 44th birthday and this time held on to best Claude Osteen and the Dodgers. But after four early-season wins, the veteran ran out of gas and lost eight straight. Spahn's final pursuit of Kid Nichols for fifth spot on baseball's all-time winning list was thus destined to play out its final few months with the pennant-contending San Francisco Giants, who eagerly picked him up for a $1 waiver price at the tail end of June.

TRACY STALLARD
(1963-64, Pitcher)

Some pitchers are remembered by history for a single disaster, while others are remembered for several disasters. Ralph Branca, with his gopher ball to Bobby Thomson, is the master of this fraternity, and Ralph Terry with the 1960 Yankees and Donnie Moore of the 1986 California Angels are certainly members in elevated standing. Tracy Stallard was not satisfied with a single moment of epic failure but chose rather to make an entire career of such events, though it was fateful circumstance and not Stallard himself that always seemed to load the deck. At the close of the 1961 season, it was Stallard, toiling for Boston, who grabbed the headlines and spotlight as the pitcher who surrendered Roger Maris's record-setting 61st home run in Yankee Stadium. Three years later, Stallard, now employed by the Mets, again earned notoriety by leading the National League with an embarrassing 20 losses. But Stallard that season in New York didn't just lose an even 20 games; he managed to spice the embarrassing total with some remarkable timing. One of the defeats came during the longest game in major league history, a seven-and-a-half-hour marathon in May with the San Francisco Giants. And a second unluckily unfolded on the afternoon when Philadelphia's Jim Bunning tossed a perfect game against the limp-hitting New Yorkers. Stallard was thus an example of a truly vital lesson for all those seeking public recognition. If you can't do something heroic, at least you can hopefully manage to publicly display your weakness at moments when the entire world is almost certain to be watching.

RON SWOBODA
(1965-70, Outfielder)

The stellar 1969 Mets outfield that boasted slugging Cleon Jones in left and agile Tommie Agee in center also featured hefty-hitting Ron Swoboda in the right-field slot. Of the three, Swoboda was cursed with the largest portion of "potential" and thus automatically doomed to be the biggest disappointment of the three during his later seasons. The disappointing post-championship 1970 campaign was Swoboda's last with the Mets and also the final season in which he appeared in at least 100 games; he never came close to matching the 19 homers he belted as a 20-year-old rookie in 1965; and his career batting average of .242 was hardly a bragging point. Yet during the unforgettable "Miracle Mets" season, the 25-year-old veteran outfielder was as big a contributor as anyone found in the patchwork New York lineup. He collected half of his season's 52 RBIs during the crucial final five weeks of the pennant season's stretch drive. A late-season highlight moment came when he socked two homers off Steve Carlton to produce a Mets victory on the very night when St. Louis's ace southpaw rang up 19 strikeouts. But it was a single defensive play that forever intimately linked Ron Swoboda with the Mets' championship drive. During World Series Game 4, it was Swoboda's improbable diving right-field grab of a vicious liner off the bat of Brooks Robinson that turned back Baltimore's charge and saved both the day and the Series for the charmed upstart Mets.

FRANK THOMAS
(1962-64, Outfielder)

Frank Thomas bragged far and wide that he could catch the hardest-thrown baseball with only his bare hands, and he spent many a spring

Tracy Stallard had a rare penchant for epic failures. (Brace Photo)

training or batting practice session amazing teammates by making good on the claim. It was perhaps a small boasting point for a verified major leaguer, but in the end, it was about all that Frank Thomas had to strut about in his decade and more of big-league ball playing.

The original Frank Thomas suffered the same fate as the original Ken Griffey, that of having his name forever rubbed out of the collective memory of baseball fans by a successor who happened to come along a generation later with exactly the same moniker. And Thomas (unlike Griffey) was not fated to be soothed by any consoling knowledge that his usurper in the history books was at least a next-generation offspring who was only working to keep the family reputation alive. Accustomed early to living in the shadows, the original Frank Thomas was one of the least-appreciated power hitters of the late fifties and early sixties. He was also, during three New York seasons, almost the entire offense for the first couple of editions of big-league pretenders that the Mets organization ran onto the field under manager Casey Stengel.

Thomas began in Pittsburgh as the heir apparent to slugger Ralph Kiner (when the latter was traded off to Chicago), and he largely lived up to his part of the bargain with 12 consecutive seasons of producing double-figure home run totals. He was once the league's HR runner-up behind Ernie Banks when he banged a career-high 35 in 1958. He was even a league All-Star on several occasions, but never boasted a good enough all-around game as an outfielder or third baseman to prevent constant relocation, which took him to seven different clubs in the same number of seasons. With the woeful Mets near his career's end, he became the expansion team's only legitimate power threat, slugging 34 homers and plating 94 runs during the 1962 debut season. When New York peddled him off to the pennant-contending Phillies in August 1964, Thomas suffered yet one more full-scale career disaster at the hands of lady luck. He promptly broke his right thumb during the September pennant chase and thus contributed indirectly, if nonetheless mightily, to Philadelphia's infamous total collapse during the final weeks of his last full big-league season.

MARV THRONEBERRY
(1962-63, First Baseman)

Some ballplayers have an inexplicable knack for simply being in the right place at exactly the right instant, selecting a potentially historic moment to seize the spotlight precisely when kind fate is ready to reward even epic bungling with a special place in the history books or in the hearts of long-memoried fans. There is no better prototype than Marv Throneberry, a journeyman who parlayed his average major league skills into moments of memorable ineptitude once he signed with the most beloved team in baseball history. Throneberry was not technically an expansion Met, even though he, more than any other player, is nearly synonymous with the team's infamous opening seasons at the Polo Grounds. He had already kicked around for three years in New York as a Yankees prospect (viewed by some as a Mickey Mantle look-alike without the results) and had also languished with the A's and O's by the time the Mets first charged unequipped into the National League fray.

Yet once acquired by the "Lovables" from Baltimore a mere month into the first expan-

Marvelous Marv Throneberry was a truly lovable loser. (NY Mets)

sion season, the free-swinging and sloppy-fielding first baseman overnight became a universally adopted symbol for the slapstick drama of New York Mets futility. It is hard not to believe that some perverse higher agent did indeed have a subtle hand in the entire enterprise once it was pointed out that Marvelous Marv's initials actually spelled out M-E-T. Over the course of less than two full seasons, the strikeout-prone southpaw elevated untimely hitting, incompetent fielding, and careless baserunning into an unmatched art form. A single incident that seemed to capsulize Throneberry's image as an extraordinary bungler came when he tripled against the Cubs but was called out for missing first base en route to his rare three-bagger. When manager Stengel attempted a feeble protest, he was quickly assured by umpires that his runner had failed to connect with second base as well. Marv was jovial enough to parlay his on-field disasters into a brief role as a fan favorite and media darling. But he pleased Mets management far less with his antics, and a contract dispute at the end of his second Mets season led directly to his outright release and a fitting end to his comical seven-year big-league sojourn.

CARL WILLEY
(1963-65, Pitcher)

An outstanding rookie performer with the pennant-bound Milwaukee Braves in 1958, Carlton Willey earned a small spot in the lore of the national pastime during the World Series aftermath of his debut season. Future Cuban strongman and reputed fanatical baseball fan Fidel Castro—while on a break from his guerrilla battles in the mountains against reigning dictator Fulgencio Batista—queried a U.S. newsman as to why Warren Spahn instead of Willey had been picked by manager Fred Haney to start a crucial World Series game. Despite such notoriety on the larger world stage, Willey never lived up to the widespread expectations in Milwaukee that he would form a potent starting rotation with veteran aces Warren Spahn and Lew Burdette. He never won in double figures (nine victories in 1958 and again in 1963 with the Mets), and his final two seasons with New York were little more than a footnote to a grandly disappointing career. But he did go out with the distinction of having served on one of the worst pitching staffs in modern major league

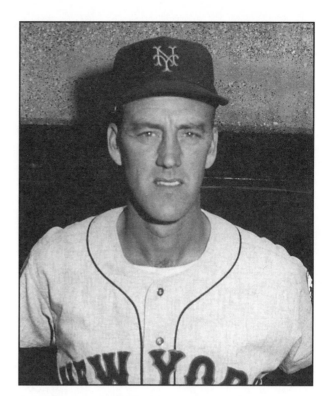

Carl Willey once attracted Fidel Castro's attention. (Brace Photo)

history. Willey was, in fact, the ace (with a 9-14 ledger) of a woeful 1963 Mets contingent that featured half a dozen double-figure losers (Roger Craig 22, Al Jackson 17, Tracy Stallard 17, Galen Cisco 15, Jay Hook 14, Willey 14). And such is the stuff of baseball legends.

1970s—AN EPOCH OF RENEWED MIRACLES

The New York Mets entered their second decade decorated with newfound celebrity status as a defending world champion and also now boasting a roster of headliners that matched any in either league when it came to substantial hometown heroes. It was a turnaround of fairy tale proportions, and the new trappings almost appeared an uncomfortable fit. For the most part, the biggest stars of the latter half of the sixties would continue their reign for much of the coming decade. There was no more dominant or more popular pitcher in the big leagues than Tom Seaver. And before Seaver would depart the Mets' ranks, Jerry Koosman would emerge as one of the league's top southpaws and a first-rank star in his own right. Dave Kingman was also launching mammoth homers by mid-decade, and Rusty Staub was earning a devoted following by "leading the league in idiosyncrasies" and also demonstrating rare artistry with his pure hitting skills. But one-by-one, the decade's heroes were destined to depart: Seaver was traded to Cincinnati, Koosman fled to Minnesota, Nolan Ryan was squandered in an ill-fated exchange with the Angels, Kingman took up residence with San Diego, Staub was inexplicably peddled to Detroit, and Jon Matlack wound up in Texas. The departures not only deflated the Mets' pennant chances by decade's end, but also represented some of the most regrettable and traumatic moments of ball club history.

TOMMIE AGEE
(1968-72, Outfielder)

Tommie Agee's big-league career was slow in picking up momentum, and by the time he captured Rookie of the Year honors in 1966 for the White Sox by smacking 22 homers and leading AL outfielders in putouts, he had already tasted four extended cups of coffee with both Cleveland and Chicago. The latter club acquired his services (along with those of Tommy John and catcher Johnny Romano) in a celebrated three-player deal which also involved Kansas City and engineered the return of matinee idol Rocky Colavito to the Indians. But it was a second trade two years later, with Agee going to the New York Mets (with Al Weis, for Tommy Davis and a trio of throw-ins), that fixed New York's pennant fortunes and also assured the hard-hitting outfielder of a date with baseball destiny.

After another slow start in New York, Agee inexplicably emerged overnight as the center-field speedster who anchored the showcase defensive outfield that was a top boasting point of baseball's greatest-ever "miracle" team. Flanked by Ron Swoboda and Cleon Jones, Tommie Agee proved his mettle in 1969 not only as a skilled defensive fly chaser, but also as a potent offensive force. Having disappointed with an anemic .217 batting performance and only five homers during his first summer at Shea Stadium, the 27-year-old Alabamian authored a huge turnaround by producing the team lead in RBIs (76) as well as homers (26, his career best). The career rever-

sal by their center fielder was perhaps as responsible as anything else for the Mets' ability to sneak up on the rest of the league during one of baseball's most surprising pennant upset seasons. And Agee's value that year was never more pronounced than in World Series Game 3, when he popped a lead-off home run and then further rescued the day with two circus catches that saved his team five runs in the deficit column. Agee's grabs off Elrod Hendricks in the fourth and Paul Blair in the seventh are still remembered as two of the unmatched gems of Series history, and rarely, if ever, has a single player more thoroughly owned a single World Series game.

DONN CLENDENON
(1969-71, First Baseman)

A versatile athlete with uneven baseball skills, Donn Clendenon received contract offers from the NFL Cleveland Browns and basketball's Harlem Globetrotters before finally settling on a baseball deal with the big-league Pittsburgh Pirates. The powerfully built 6'4" righty swinger was most valued throughout his 12 seasons as a long-ball hitter and didn't disappoint the Pirates as a rookie in 1962: He stroked the ball at a .302 clip in an 80-game debut and also banged out a dozen or more homers from 1963 to 1970, peaking with 28 in 1966. As a free swinger, he also twice topped NL swingers in strikeouts, and on three occasions, he paced league first basemen in errors. Clendenon was not a shoddy fielder, however, and it is noteworthy that he also three

1970s National League Composite Standings and Pennants (Ranked by Total Games Won)

Team	Won	Lost	Pct.	NL Pennants	World Championships
Cincinnati Reds	953	657	.592	1970, 1972, 1975, 1976	1975, 1976
Pittsburgh Pirates	916	695	.569	1971, 1979	1971, 1979
Los Angeles Dodgers	910	701	.565	1974, 1977, 1978	None
Philadelphia Phillies	812	801	.503	None	None
St. Louis Cardinals	800	813	.496	None	None
San Francisco Giants	794	818	.493	None	None
Houston Astros	793	817	.493	None	None
Chicago Cubs	785	827	.487	None	None
New York Mets	**763**	**850**	**.473**	**1973**	**None**
Montreal Expos	748	862	.465	None	None
Atlanta Braves	725	883	.451	None	None
San Diego Padres	667	942	.415	None	None

Tommie Agee anchored the memorable Miracle Mets outfield. (Brace Photo)

times led the league's first sackers in putouts and assists and five times in double plays. After leaving Pittsburgh for Montreal with the 1968 expansion draft and then being quickly dealt to the Mets, Clendenon produced his most memorable season as a platoon player during New York's Cinderella pennant pursuit in the last summer of the decade. Alternating with lefty Ed Kranepool, Clendenon provided timely power when his ball club most needed it. Banging only 12 regular-season round trippers (in 72 games), he suddenly came to life with crucial circuit blows in Games 2, 4, and 5 of the World Series. In each contest, Clendenon's homers provided the game-winning margin. For such timely base knocks, Clendenon walked off with that year's prestigious World Series MVP trophy and assured himself a lasting place in New York baseball lore.

NINO ESPINOSA
(1974-78, Pitcher)

This Dominican right-hander achieved more success over in Philadelphia on the eve of the Phillies' 1980 championship than he ever did from 1974 to 1978 with the Mets. This seemingly had more to do with the quality of the team he played for in Philly than it did with Espinosa's own mound efforts. He won a career-best 14 games with the Phillies in 1979 on a club that had Pete Rose and Mike Schmidt in the everyday lineup, Bob Boone behind the plate, finished half a dozen games above the break-even point, and was about to take over the following summer as the league's best outfit. Two previous campaigns in New York had also produced moderate results with 10 and then 11 wins on teams that sat deep in the basement and finished 30 games under. By winning in double figures for the worst two Mets editions in a decade, this workmanlike starter was clearly the best the anemic Mets had to offer in a lackluster mound rotation made up of Craig Swan, Pat Zachry, Espinosa, and washed-up Jerry Koosman. Espinosa nonetheless did briefly flash some considerable promise with 13 complete games and two shutouts (one against Steve Carlton), despite such negatives as the league's fifth-most homers allowed and as many walks as strikeouts. But it didn't last long over in Philadelphia once arm troubles set in and provided an early exit to the DL during the very season when his new team was marching to a surprising and dramatic world championship.

Nino Espinosa twice led the club in wins despite owning losing records. (Brace Photo)

JIM FREGOSI
(1972-73, Third Baseman)

Right-hander Ernie Broglio—for all his mound accomplishments—remains a sour memory among Chicago Cubs boosters simply because he was traded to the North Side team for future Hall of Famer Lou Brock. Cubs fans have long memories when it comes to recounting Broglio's subsequent failures in Wrigley Field and Brock's Cooperstown career with the hated Cardinals. In similar fashion, Jim Fregosi has always been a bitter pill in the throats of all New York Mets fans. It was Fregosi, it turns out, who was acquired back in 1972 as a reported surefire solution at third base, but came at the cost of a young pitching prospect named Nolan Ryan. It looked like a good deal at the time—the eve of the 1972 season when Ryan was still only a strong-armed prospect, and the third-base problem had persistently haunted the Mets throughout the tenures of Ed Charles, Joe Foy, and Bob Aspromonte. Fregosi, after all, had been the best power-hitting shortstop in either league

Jim Fregosi was acquired in the worst trade in New York Mets history. (Brace Photo)

could bestow. Over the second half of his career, Grote indeed was one of baseball's most talented all-around receivers. But it took him quite a while to get there, and his early career was a series of disasters and embarrassments brought on largely by a profound weakness with the bat and a personal penchant for blaming his shortcomings on just about everyone else in sight. As a rookie, Grote hit only .181 with the expansion Houston Colt .45s, which earned him a quick trip back to the bush leagues. He got a second shot with the rival expansion Mets two seasons later, but continued his soft hitting (.237 in 1966 and .195 in 1967) and was less than average at handling pitchers and defending the plate. Shoddy defense and numerous outbursts of anger at umpires and teammates inspired another memorable line about Grote— this one uttered by his own manager, Wes Westrum. "If Grote ever learns to control himself, he might become the best catcher in the game," said Westrum, who himself had been a talented receiver with the Leo Durocher Giants. Fortunately, Grote took the criticism to heart and eventually developed into a key player in Mets fortunes of the late 1960s and early '70s, including the 1969 world championship and the 1973 NL pennant chase. During those two title years, Grote caught every inning of postseason play and even chipped in with a pair of fielding records (most chances handled and most putouts) in the 1973 World Series.

for most of the sixties and was also a recognized clubhouse leader. The addition of such a heavy-hitting infielder seemed just the ticket to wrapping up another NL pennant. But it didn't quite work out that way. Fregosi made the defensive shift from short to third without apparent problem but never hit a lick in a Mets uniform and provided only a .232 average and five homers in his season and a half with New York. The deal, in the end, was bad enough even to obliterate the memory of an earlier trade also aimed at solidifying the Mets' hot corner. That was the deal in which the Mets had picked up Foy (a .236 hitter in his one season on the club) from Kansas City in exchange for Amos Otis, who went on to star big-time for the Royals.

JERRY GROTE
(1966-77, Catcher)

The single quote that best capsulizes Jerry Grote's hard-earned big-league success is attributed to one-time base-stealing king Lou Brock. Hall of Famer Brock labeled the veteran Mets backstop the toughest catcher to steal against anywhere in the league, and considering the source, it was about the highest praise anyone

BUD HARRELSON
(1965-77, Shortstop)

Before the appearance of acrobatic Cuban defector Rey Ordoñez in the mid-nineties, Bud Harrelson was hands-down winner of any poll to pick the all-time New York Mets shortstop. And once Harrelson's all-around game, offensive production, and career longevity are raised as the relevant factors in such debates, it is the diminutive Californian and not the diminutive Cuban who still likely comes out ahead of the field as the ball club's best-ever middle infielder. Like Ordoñez, Harrelson earned his spot in a big-league lineup with his special fielding skills, but he was also a major contributor to the Mets' cause with his speed and agility on the base paths, combined with his ability to reach first via the free pass. Harrelson helped his own cause after hitting only .108 during a 19-game

Bud Harrelson was the franchise Gold Glove shortstop until Rey Ordoñez arrived. (Brace Photo)

trial in 1965 by converting to switch-hitting, but the stolen base was always his top offensive weapon. His two pilferings of home during a brief September call-up in 1966 dealt severe blows to both the Giants and Pirates in that year's late-season pennant chase. He led the Mets in steals in 1971 with 28, the same year he picked up a Gold Glove for sensational short-stop play. He enjoyed his best offensive campaign (.252 with 32 RBIs) while also tying an NL mark with 54 consecutive errorless games. But if there is a single moment that capsulizes the career of the future Mets manager, it would have to be the 1973 NLCS play that earned lasting infamy for Pete Rose among the Shea Stadium denizens. Rose would be booed mercilessly in New York for the remainder of his career as a result of the ugly second-base incident in which bullying Charlie Hustle nearly incited a riot by bowling Harrelson over while trying to break up a double play.

STEVE HENDERSON
(1977-80, Outfielder)

Despite missing out on Rookie of the Year honors by only a single vote in 1977 (edged out by Montreal's Andre Dawson), twice leading the Mets in batting (1979 and 1980), and setting a since-broken club record for single-season triples (nine in 1978), outfielder Steve Henderson was far more notable for how he came to and departed from the Mets roster than he was for anything he accomplished in orange and blue pinstripes. Henderson's arrival came as part of a package of young prospects (including Pat Zachry, Dan Norman, and Doug Flynn) received from Cincinnati in exchange for franchise star Tom Seaver in one of New York's most startling player trades. In 1981 he was shipped off to the Chicago Cubs in exchange for heavy-hitting Dave Kingman, who would soon capture a National League home run title in his second tour of busting down outfield fences at Shea Stadium. Henderson's own numbers in New York were nothing to scoff at and included three batting averages over .290 and one above the .300 mark (.306 in 1979), 35 of his 68 career round trippers, and the ball club's best RBI production in his rookie campaign (65), despite appearances in fewer than 100 games. But it was nowhere near enough to measure up to the gigantic performances of the stars he was exchanged for at both ends of his Shea Stadium sojourn.

DAVE KINGMAN
(1975-77, 1981-83, Outfielder)

No one owning more career home runs than Dave Kingman (442) and featuring a career that ended more than a decade ago is not already sanctioned as an immortal in Cooperstown. At the same time, no one who approaches Kingman's 442 career round trippers is by any stretch of the imagination a less likely candidate for permanent Hall of Fame enshrinement. Not only was Kingman's entire career reduced to a one-dimensional power show, but at every turn, he seemed to demonstrate shortcomings in both on-field talent and off-field behavior inconsistent with one of the game's genuine stars. Kingman could always hit the ball a country mile (and often did), but he had little tolerance for fans or the media and little love either for the discipline of playing defense. With enough power displays to bolster any lineup, "King Kong" was nonetheless never welcome for very long in any of the big league cities he visited and was traded so often that one year (1977) he set a big-league record by playing with four different ball clubs. Like Mark McGwire after him, Kingman started out as a college pitcher but was converted to the outfield by longtime USC coach Rod Dedeaux. But while McGwire later blossomed into a fine all-around performer, Kingman was always content to do little more than swing wildly for the fences. The big blasts and equally big strikeouts that resulted would remain the single calling card of Kingman's entire career, and he rang up numerous milestones for both kinds of attention-grabbing performances. With the Cubs in 1979 (the first of his two seasons as home run champ), he tied major league records for most times homering in consecutive games and most times homering three times in a game. But with the Mets in 1982 (his only other time as home run leader), he also equaled a record by striking out five times in a nine-inning game.

SKIP LOCKWOOD
(1975-79, Pitcher)

Hall of Famer Bob Lemon is perhaps the most famous convert from position play to pitching duties during or immediately preceding a big-league career. A surprisingly small number of others—including former Met John Olerud—have followed the same route. One member of

the exclusive fraternity was Kansas City A's bonus prospect Skip Lockwood, who originally inked a $100,000 pact to man third base and then quickly set to work demonstrating in the Seattle Pilots' organization that he couldn't hit even minor league pitching. Making the drastic career switch to the role of a starting pitcher in the minors, Lockwood soon failed again and had to switch in midstream once more, this time to the role of a reliever while toiling with his transplanted big-league club in Milwaukee. Lockwood's rocky start with the Pilots/Brewers sufficiently demonstrated a talented arm but also left his future on the big-league mound very much in doubt. By the late seventies, Lockwood—now with the Mets—was finally achieving some long-absent success as the ace workhorse of the Mets' bullpen, where back-to-back years of 19 (1976) and 20 saves (1977) put him in the league's top five in that department. It was in this role as reliable reliever that he also established a short-lived club milestone with the since-broken standard for one-season mound appearances (63 in 1977).

Jon Matlack, perhaps the most unsung southpaw in team history. (Brace Photo)

JON MATLACK
(1971-77, Pitcher)

Tom Seaver and Jerry Koosman cast a large shadow over the rest of the Mets' pitching staff throughout the late sixties and most of the seventies. And if that shadow unjustly obscured the mound careers of some other pitchers of considerable talent, perhaps the biggest loser of all was Jon Matlack. Of course, Matlack was also a winner, since what he lost in personal glory was more than offset by the team successes attached to one of the best NL ball clubs of the era. The first pick of the June 1967 draft, the oversized lefty from West Chester, Pennsylvania, enjoyed long-awaited big-league success five summers later with a brilliant Rookie of the Year campaign. In his first full season in 1972, he produced 15 victories and the league's fourth-best ERA (2.32) in his first full tour around the league. For an encore the following summer, he rang up 205 strikeouts—third-best total in the NL—despite a hairline skull fracture which kept him inactive for 11 days. The staff's No. 2 lefty (behind Koosman) lost more that he won in 1973 (14-16) for a Mets team that reached the World Series more on its pitching than its hitting, but he did shine in the postseason with a two-hitter in NLCS Game 2

and a Game 4 World Series win. His best outing may well have been the Series lid lifter, in which he surrendered only two earned runs and fell 2-1. But such early successes were never sustained in future years. Matlack suffered from two debilitating factors that plagued his entire career. One was ongoing shoulder problems that frequently put him on the shelf. And the other was a distinct lack of run support from his team's mediocre offensive lineup during stretches when he pitched some of his best baseball. The 1974 season, for example, saw Matlack top the NL in shutouts (7) and post the third-best ERA (2.41) and still come up on the losing side of the ledger at 13-15. Despite one of the best arms of the 1970s, Jon Matlack's final big-league record (125-126, but 30 shutouts) nonetheless wound up below .500.

WILLIE MAYS
(1972-73, Outfielder)

Many have made the convincing argument that Willie Mays was, by any measure, the greatest all-around baseball player of all time. Perhaps the only better argument might be made for Babe Ruth, who was a Hall of Fame–caliber pitcher as well as the game's greatest slugger, or perhaps Ty Cobb, owner of the best statisti-

Willie Mays capped a Hall of Fame career with a dramatic return to New York in 1972. (Brace Photo)

cal hitting credentials and baseball's highest lifetime batting average. Mays is a close second, if he is second at all, and no one ever boasted a better combination of batting power (660 homers—trailing only Aaron and Ruth), baserunning skills (he was as intelligent on the basepaths as he was swift and daring), and spectacular fielding prowess. The endless highlights of Willie Mays's career feature the following distinctions: His first big-league hit was a mammoth homer off Cooperstown-bound Warren Spahn; he was the rookie slugger waiting on deck when Bobby Thomson smacked baseball's most famous home run; he was the leadoff name of baseball's most hotly debated mid-century issue (Was it "Willie, Mickey, or the Duke" who was New York's, and thus baseball's, greatest center fielder of the Golden Age fifties?); his over-the-shoulder deep center-field grab of Vic Wertz's blast in the opening game of the 1954 World Series at the Polo Grounds is still the most spectacular highlight-film moment in baseball annals; and his 1957 tally of 20-plus doubles, triples, homers, and stolen bases clinched his credentials as perhaps the sport's unparalleled offensive threat.

Mays joined the decade-old New York Mets at the twilight of his career in May 1972 and hung around long enough for a bench role with the surprising 1973 Mets squad that made a World Series appearance against Oakland, despite a season of only slightly better than break-even performance. Willie's contribution to the "You Gotta Believe" New York pennant charge consisted of 66 fill-in appearances, a .211 batting average, his final half a dozen career homers (he hit 14 round trippers in all for the Mets), and two unnoticed World Series singles. "Tom Terrific" Seaver may own the best year-in and year-out Mets career performances, and Darryl Strawberry may have been the team's heaviest slugger, but Willie Mays was unarguably the greatest ballplayer of all time ever to pull on a New York Mets uniform for an inning of big-league action.

TUG MCGRAW
(1965-67, 1969-74, Pitcher)

While Tom Seaver may have been the backbone of the 1973 NL champions in New York, it was flaky southpaw bullpen stopper Tug McGraw who was the team's emotional heart and soul. McGraw coined the team's memorable "You Gotta Believe" rallying cry, which came to symbolize the second and perhaps most improbable "miracle" season for the upstart expansion franchise. And his own magic hurling over the final months of that season was as responsible as anything for the successes of one of the senior circuit's most unlikely pennant winners. McGraw made a career out of late-game and late-season heroics and for nine seasons was a bullpen fixture for the Mets, and then for 10 more, a fireman for the Philadelphia Phillies. His best single season was probably 1972 when the fanatic lefty won eight games, saved 27, and stymied hitters with a 1.70 ERA. And his career peak perhaps came with the World Series heroics he performed for the Phillies in 1980 as that team captured its first world championship in 65 long years. But for Mets fans, the lasting image of McGraw is the one associated with his first trip to a World Series, the one in which he wore a Mets uniform.

FELIX MILLAN
(1973-77, Second Baseman)

A native of Puerto Rico, this sure-handed infielder split his 12 big-league seasons between Atlanta and New York as an original prototype of the light-hitting and glue-fingered middle infielder raised in the sugar cane fields of the sun-drenched Caribbean. One surprise season of .300 hitting (.310 in 1970 for the Braves) and a couple others that approximated that lofty level of offensive proficiency, of course, work to belie the "good field, no hit" stereotype. Yet despite three All-Star Game selections and enough batting talent to once go 6-for-6 in a nine-inning game, it was nonetheless weak hitting in 1972 (.257) that wrote Millan's eventual ticket out of the Atlanta Braves' organization. The trade immediately before the 1973 season that sent Millan to the Mets, along with George Stone, in exchange for hurlers Gary Gentry and Danny Frisella, turned out to be one of the best player exchanges in Shea Stadium history. It was a minor deal of major proportions and one that launched the New Yorkers on the path to a 1973 World Series appearance, while at the same time sending the disintegrating Atlanta ball club sinking in the opposite direction.

JOHN MILNER
(1971-77, Outfielder)

Hank Aaron and John Milner both bore the self-appointed nickname of "The Hammer" during their major league careers, but there the similarity ends rather abruptly. Not that Milner was a total flop as a big leaguer, but he was hardly a Hall of Famer, either, and he never even approached the mammoth career of his childhood idol Aaron, whose moniker and batting stance he had imitated. Milner did hang around for a dozen seasons with the Mets and Pirates and finally Montreal, and he did slug 20 round trippers on two different occasions in early outings with New York (23 in 1973 and 20 in 1974), but he never reached the 1,000-hit plateau (855 total), and his batting average only once edged above the mediocre .275 level. Milner's single more-or-less productive season came during the NL pennant pursuit of 1973, when he banged 23 homers and produced 72 RBIs as the team's regular first sacker. He also contributed 16 homers and a career-high .276 average in a bench

role with the 1979 Pittsburgh Pirates, who walked off with a world championship. But the once-promising outfield prospect never fully materialized, and recurring hamstring injuries were at least one factor that sabotaged his career.

LENNY RANDLE
(1977-78, Infielder)

A talented infielder with considerable and inconsistent batting skills, Lenny Randle etched his name in the collective memories of fans with two incidents which illustrated a rather amazing inconsistency when it came to quick-witted thinking. The second of these came at career's end in Seattle, when his response to a slow roller along the third-base line was to drop to all fours and attempt to blow the potential base hit into foul territory. Such presence of mind escaped Randle altogether several years earlier and with far-reaching consequences. After establishing his value with the Texas Rangers in the mid-seventies with solid switch-hitting performances and fill-in play at seven different defensive positions, the acrobatic infielder was angered by an apparent spring training loss of the starting second base position to

John Milner shared a memorable nickname with Henry Aaron—"The Hammer." (Brace Photo)

Lenny Randle achieved the good, the bad, and the ugly. (Brace Photo)

rookie Bump Wills. Showing uncontrolled rage, the journeyman ballplayer slugged manager Frank Lucchesi in a rare moment of unparalleled modern-era diamond violence. The Texas skipper required plastic surgery as a result of the assault, and the offending ballplayer—normally noted for his good nature—was heavily fined, suspended, and then shipped out to the New York Mets. To Randle's credit, he did rebound from the incident to lead the Mets in five different major offensive categories—batting average (.304), hits (156), runs (78), triples (7), and steals (33)—during the first of two Shea Stadium campaigns (1977 and 1978), before free agency took him elsewhere.

RUSTY STAUB
(1972-75, 1981-85, Outfielder)

Perhaps only Marvelous Marv Throneberry and Ed Kranepool have been more beloved than the lefty-swinging outfielder, designated hitter, and third sacker known affectionately as "Le Grand Orange" and described by one clever wordsmith as looking not so much like a ballplayer but more like "a 205-pound Sherlock Holmes who'd taken an intense interest in the game of baseball" (Ken Turetzky, writing in *The Ballplayers*). Two separate four-year stints in Shea Stadium a decade apart comprise a considerable portion of a near Cooperstown-level career that also played out for 23 seasons in Houston, Texas, Detroit, and Montreal and featured 2,716 base hits, 292 home runs, 1,466 RBIs, half a dozen All-Star Game appearances, and an undisputed career-long league leadership in outrageous eccentricities and amusing idiosyncrasies.

Staub's God-given baseball skills were, at best, only average, and hard work and discipline remained bywords of his overachieving career. The same dedicated studiousness that improved his baseball performance also led to considerable accomplishment as a master chef, restaurateur, and amateur history buff. On the field, it was clear that what Staub did do altogether naturally was hit, and his talents seemed so effortless that opponents, scouts, former players, and coaches could come up with no more fitting label than that of "pure hitter." But in the end, it was remarkable longevity that accounted for most of Rusty Staub's milestones and career highlights. He and Ty Cobb share the distinction as the only players to homer both before

age 20 and after age 40. No other big leaguer has appeared in 500 games and also collected 500 hits for four different teams. While exceedingly popular in two stays with the Mets and one with the Tigers, the rotund lefty became something of a national hero in Canada with the expansion Expos, earning his famed handle ("Le Grand Orange") as a result of his flaming red hair. But his biggest career moment may have come in the 1973 World Series, when he bounced back from a painful shoulder injury suffered in the NLCS versus Cincinnati to sock a game-winning opposite-field homer in Game 4 of the Fall Classic.

JOHN STEARNS
(1975-84, Catcher)

A considerable record of athletic accomplishment already attached to the John Stearns résumé before the catcher ever launched his solid New York Mets playing career or performed as an All-Star-caliber backstop for a handful of seasons at the end of the '70s and outset of the 1980s. A collegiate football star of substantial reputation, Stearns was drafted out of the University of Colorado by the NFL Buffalo Bills; his baseball promise was also substantial enough to earn a Philadelphia Phillies contract as that big-league team's first overall pick in the 1973 amateur baseball draft. Appearing in only a single big-league contest with the Phillies, the solidly built Denver native was shipped to the Mets within a year and had earned a starter slot behind the plate by late 1976. A multi-tooled athlete, Stearns quickly proved an adept bunter and line-drive hitter as well as an adequate handler of a Mets pitching staff featuring Jerry Koosman, Skip Lockwood, Nino Espinosa, Jon Matlack, and the veteran Mickey Lolich. He was also swift enough afoot to once (in 1978) set a league record for lead-footed catchers with 25 stolen bases. But injuries began to take their toll rapidly on a backstop who played with an at-times savage "football mentality," and elbow tendinitis had largely sabotaged Stearns's career by the outset of the eighties. Although he hung around with the Mets for 10 seasons and appeared on four NL All-Star squads, he logged 100-plus games only three times (1977-79), and his tenure as the club's starting backstop barely stretched beyond half a dozen quality seasons.

CRAIG SWAN
(1973-84, Pitcher)

The single career mountaintop for Swan came within the 1978 season, the exact midpoint of his dozen big league campaigns, all spent with the Mets (discounting two final games with the California Angels). Limited that summer by gastroenteritis which cut a month from his season, the stocky right-hander barely logged enough innings with a sixth-place club managed by Joe Torre to capture nine victories and pace the National League in ERA effectiveness (2.43). The accomplishment left him as one of the most undistinguished ERA champions in major league baseball annals. In 1979 he would continue the upswing with a club-best and also career-best 14 victories as the staff's leading starter. These back-to-back solid seasons were achievement enough—at least in the eyes of the front office—to land the staff ace a new five-year contract, which was, at the time, the most lucrative in New York Mets history. But before the ink was even dry on the windfall contract, Craig Swan's pitching career had already begun its downward spiral, and he would see only one additional season of double-figure wins (11 in 1982) before a rotator cuff tear in 1980 killed off his fastball and more or less spelled the end to his big-league pitching effectiveness.

Craig Swan, surprise National League ERA champion. (Brace Photo)

JOE TORRE
(1975-77, Infielder)

When the Mets fired manager Joe Frazier on May 31, 1977, and named infielder Joe Torre to fill the slot, the veteran third baseman became the NL's first player-manager in almost two full decades. No one had played the dual roles in the senior circuit since Solly Hemus turned the trick with the 1959 St. Louis Cardinals. Torre didn't wear both hats for very long and took himself off the active roster on June 18 to concentrate on a managerial career with the Mets that would stretch over five years with mostly tailender ball clubs. Hall of Fame managerial credentials would not be something associated with Joe Torre until much later in his career, and his overall Mets performance as a team leader was never eye-catching. It did, however, mark a seemingly predestined transition to the bench after a playing career of All-Star proportions. That career spanned three teams (Braves, Cardinals, Mets) and three positions (catcher, third base, first base) and featured one memorable league MVP season (1971) when he led the league in batting (.363), hits (230), total bases (352), and RBIs (137). In his playing days with the Mets, Torre was destined to be remembered more than anyone else as yet another failed experiment in solving the team's ongoing third-base problem. After squandering Nolan Ryan in the effort to fill the hot-corner gap with Jim Fregosi, the Mets were at it again when they dealt Ray Sadecki for Torre following the 1974 season. Managerial futures aside, Torre proved almost as big a disappointment as Fregosi, hitting into 22 double plays in 1974, revealing a considerably reduced range at third, and providing (with a .247 BA) no more offensive punch than any of his inadequate predecessors. His best Mets batting average came in 1976 when he hit .306 in 114 games.

DEL UNSER
(1975-76, Outfielder)

Son of a former big-league catcher, Del Unser gained some career notoriety straight out of the box with *The Sporting News* American League Rookie of the Year prize in 1968 while breaking in with the Washington Senators. He garnered the top distinction strictly on the basis of his defensive performance, since he posted a batting average of .230 and an anemic

Del Unser broke in with the Washington Senators as AL Rookie of the Year. (Brace Photo)

total of 30 RBIs for the junior circuit's last place club. As a fly chaser, however, only Baltimore's acrobatic Paul Blair was considered any better that year, and Unser piled up numbers that clinched the chase with the league's best tallies in assists, double plays, and total chances per game. In his sophomore season, his improved hitting was highlighted by the league lead in triples; his total of eight was the fewest ever for a league pacesetter. Unser finally came to the Mets after the 1974 season and after brief career stops in Cleveland and Philadelphia, arriving with Mac Scarce and John Stearns in the deal that sent Tug McGraw to the Phillies.

Unser's stay in Shea Stadium lasted but a year and a half, but he did produce his best all-around offensive campaign in 1975, when he batted .294 while manning the starting center-field slot, and recorded 53 RBIs on 156 base hits. A prolonged batting slump the following spring, however, spelled the end to his career as an everyday outfield starter and signaled the beginning of a final few seasons in Montreal and back in Philadelphia that were most notable for some exceptional pinch-hitting accomplishments.

Mike Vail enjoyed one of the fastest starts ever in Gotham. (Brace Photo)

MIKE VAIL
(1975-77, Outfielder)

Few players have enjoyed any faster start in a Mets uniform, or in any other big-league togs, for that matter. Mike Vail flashed considerable promise in the outfield and at the plate as 1975 International Player of the Year, and in the process, earned a call-up to the majors in August of that same year. The right-handed outfielder immediately seized the opportunity by exploding on the big-league scene with a 23-game hitting string that, at the time, was both a ball club highwater mark and a new modern-era National League rookie standard. But an off-season foot injury the following winter marked the beginning of a just-as-sudden downward spiral that spelled frustration and failure for most of the remainder of Vail's largely unfulfilled baseball career. There would be a short tenure as a much-valued pinch hitter and occasional reserve outfielder with the Cubs during the last handful of seasons in the 1970s. But Vail only logged 100 games in a season twice in his career (once with the Mets) and also only twice (in his super-sub years with the Cubs) hit above .300 for an entire summer.

BOBBY VALENTINE
(1977-78, Second Baseman)

Few fans, especially Mets fans, will ever remember Bobby Valentine for his role as an active player. But the popular, controversial, and sometimes quite successful manager in Texas and New York during the 1990s was also an outstanding playing prospect when he first arrived on the big-league scene with Los Angeles during the very same summer that the Mets shocked baseball with their miracle championship charge across baseball's first expansion season. Unfortunately for Valentine and the Dodgers, the young infielder's penchant for reckless all-out play was reminiscent of another sterling Dodger prospect of three decades earlier, and the results were also the same. Like Pete Reiser, Valentine was robbed of a lustrous career by serious injury caused by his own daring play. In Valentine's case, the injury was a single disastrous collision with an outfield fence while playing with the California Angels in May 1973. It left his leg fractured and misshapen and his career largely in shambles. There were a series of comeback attempts, including 100-plus games with the Angels a year later, a brief sojourn in San Diego, and a two-season stint with the Mets as an infielder in the late seventies.

But Valentine's role had been reduced to a journeyman's lot, as he rarely cracked the regular lineup. In 1978, his final season with the Mets, he hit .269 with one home run and 18 RBIs.

JOEL YOUNGBLOOD
(1977-82, Outfielder)

Infielder Joel Youngblood made more news and a bigger splash in the record books on the day he pulled off his Mets uniform for the final time than he did in any of the seasons while he had worn it. This irony transpired on August 4, 1982, when Youngblood earned the trivial distinction of becoming the first major league player ever to perform for two different teams in two different cities on the very same day. He also managed to spice the events by collecting a base hit in each of the two geographically distant ball games. Enjoying his final performance with the Mets during an afternoon affair at Wrigley Field, Youngblood managed to pick up a scratch single off future Hall of Famer Ferguson Jenkins, who was toiling for the Cubs. Traded to the Montreal Expos only

Joel Youngblood played for two different teams in two different cities on the same day. (Brace Photo)

moments after the final out in Chicago, Youngblood immediately hopped on a commercial flight and arrived promptly enough in Philadelphia to collect yet another single that same evening off another Cooperstown-bound mound opponent, the Phillies' Steve Carlton. While he was with the Mets, Youngblood was best known perhaps for being the team's only All-Star Game participant in 1981, a year when the game was delayed until August by a mid-season players' strike. Youngblood made a token appearance in that showcase game, largely due only to the fact that managers elected that year to use a record 56 different players.

1980s—ONE PEAK AND NUMEROUS VALLEYS

Seaver, Kingman, McGraw, and company would soon be giving way to a brand new collection of heroes wearing Mets pinstripes. And before the decade of the 1980s would run its course, the New York National League fans would have a whole new generation of idols about whom they could wax nostalgic. Strawberry and Gooden were the top headliners, of course, but there were others to boast about with equal fervor. Gary Carter briefly set new standards for offensive and defensive play at the catcher position. Lenny Dykstra also briefly entertained with his tattered-uniform playing style before slumping badly and then taking his act to rival Philadelphia. Lee Mazzilli flashed across the scene as New York's most popular ballpark matinee idol since Mickey Mantle, and a colorful contingent of fresh arms kept Shea Stadium well stocked with some of baseball's most reliable and also most colorful late-inning firemen. Regrettably, there was only one championship to cheer because, as in the previous two decades, mid-decade and late-decade heroics came only after a vast wasteland of early-eighties seasons buried deep in the NL East basement. But when it came to individual diamond stars, Shea Stadium remained, for another decade, home to some of baseball's biggest and brashest on-field entertainers.

RICK AGUILERA
(1985-89, Pitcher)

In a hidden corner of Rick Aguilera's baseball career is the trivial fact that he was a third baseman for Brigham Young University on the same team with Wally Joyner, Cory Snyder, and

Scott Nielsen. That fact may serve to explain an apparent talent for hitting once sufficient enough to produce a hefty .278 batting average as a big-league rookie pitcher, and it also explains Aguilera's occasional use as a major league pinch hitter. The better-known side of Rick Aguilera's story, however, is a solid 15-year career with the Mets, Twins (twice), Red Sox, and Cubs that has now produced 318 career saves—12th on the all-time list—and has also featured some memorable early-career post-season heroics while wearing the uniform of his first team, the New York Mets. Breaking in as New York's fifth starter, the 6' 4" right-hander recorded exactly 10 wins in each of his first two seasons and also delivered three crucial innings of scoreless relief during a memorable 16-inning NLCS-clinching game versus the Houston Astros which capped the 1986 title drive. And when Mookie Wilson's grounder dribbled through Bill Buckner's legs at the climactic moment of unforgettable Game 6 in that year's World Series, it was Aguilera who would reap the benefits as the winning pitcher in perhaps the most famous game in Mets postseason history. After 1986, Aguilera would only once more post double figures in victories—in 1987 with 11 (against three losses)—and the bulk of his career since then has been devoted to the valuable closer's role he occupied with the 2000 Chicago Cubs.

NEIL ALLEN
(1979-83, Pitcher)

For fans appreciating exotica, it should be noted that Neil Allen once pitched a big-league shutout on a day when he was not credited with a complete game. The strange circumstance resulted from a scorer's decision that was made when Allen entered a game for the Yankees late in his 11-year career with none out but a man aboard in the first frame. The right-hander immediately picked the runner off base, then continued unscored upon for the duration. Official scoring procedure allowed the shutout, since the same hurler had worked through a full nine innings and all 27 recorded putouts; but the

1980s National League Composite Standings and Pennants
(Ranked by Overall Winning Percentage)

Team	Won	Lost	Pct.	NL Pennants	World Championships
St. Louis Cardinals	825	734	.529	1982, 1985, 1987	1982
Los Angeles Dodgers	825	741	.527	1981, 1988	1981, 1988
New York Mets	**816**	**743**	**.523**	**1986**	**1986**
Houston Astros	819	750	.522	None	None
Montreal Expos	811	752	.519	None	None
Philadelphia Phillies	783	780	.501	1980, 1983	1980
Cincinnati Reds	781	783	.499	None	None
San Francisco Giants	773	795	.493	1989	None
San Diego Padres	762	805	.486	1984	None
Chicago Cubs	735	821	.472	None	None
Pittsburgh Pirates	732	825	.470	None	None
Atlanta Braves	712	845	.457	None	None

complete game could not be credited to a pitcher who was not the announced starter and had not tossed the opening pitch on that rare afternoon.

It was all only a minor footnote, however, to a decade of quality hurling divided almost evenly between the two leagues and featuring stops with two NL ball clubs (Mets and Cardinals) and three junior circuit outfits (Yankees twice, White Sox, and Indians). Debuting in 1979 as a part-time starter with eight saves, Allen de-

Neil Allen once earned a piece of trivial distinction. (Brace Photo)

veloped quickly into a first-flight closer with the Mets, and his string of 22 (1980), 18 (1981), and 19 (1982) saves early in his career was not only a personal high-water mark but also one of the few bragging points of the early-1980s Mets franchise. Allen's career with the Mets tenure came to an end in June 1983 when he was dispatched to St. Louis with fellow pitcher Rick Ownbey in a blockbuster deal for first sacker Keith Hernandez.

WALLY BACKMAN
(1980-88, Infielder)

Teaming with rough-and-tumble Lenny Dykstra as half of the Mets' "Partners in Grime" duo during the 1986 world-championship season would constitute Wally Backman's greatest moment of big-league notoriety. It was a distinction well earned by the pair of spunky hitters at the top of the Shea Stadium lineup (Backman batted second), whose all-out style of play and ability to get on base ahead of sluggers Keith Hernandez, Gary Carter, and Darryl Strawberry provided the backbone of one of the best and most entertaining National League teams ever fielded in New York. Backman, at the time, was in his seventh big-league season but only his third as a regular. It was also the exact midpoint of a career that would record only one additional season after 1986 (1990 with the division-winning Pittsburgh Pirates) in which the spunky switch-hitter would manage to log as many as 100 games. Backman batted a lifetime-best .320 during the Mets' title season and was also a league leader for the only time in his career, hanging up the best fielding percentage (.989) among NL second basemen. A platoon player used mainly against right-handers, Backman topped the club by scoring five runs during the 1986 NLCS showdown with Houston. He also logged key hits in each of the final three contests of that wild series and scored the final run of his team's heart-stopping 16th-inning winning rally. With his exceptional baserunning speed and high on-base percentage, Backman was always far more of an offensive contributor than a defensive standout (despite the high fielding average of 1986), and it may have been his defensive shortcomings, in the end, that year-in and year-out prevented him from ever winning a regular second-base job during his nine National League seasons in New York.

HUBIE BROOKS
(1980-84, 1991, Infielder and Outfielder)

The third player plucked in the June 1978 amateur draft, Hubie Brooks would play several different roles in the ongoing efforts to re-build ball club fortunes during the lean seasons of the early eighties. At the top of his career he supplied some much-needed and heretofore long-absent stability at the hot corner, batting a solid .283 in 1984 before a late-season shift to shortstop aimed at opening a lineup spot for the newly acquired Ray Knight. At season's end—when Knight seemed to have wrested away the third base job—Brooks featured in the Mets' rebuilding plans in a much different manner when he was traded to Montreal with Floyd Youmans (a minor leaguer), Mike Fitzgerald, and Herm Winningham in order to acquire All-Star catcher and potential franchise-maker Gary Carter. It turned out to be a costly move for the Mets—despite Carter's obvious value—since Brooks immediately blossomed with his new team and soon turned heads in Montreal with some outstanding clutch hitting that awoke the second guessers back at Shea. In 1985 with the Expos, Hubie Brooks became the first NL short-stop since Ernie Banks to drive home better than

Hubie Brooks is best remembered for a blockbuster trade. (Brace Photo)

100 runs. And there might have been even more head scratching back in New York over the next several seasons if not for a series of unfortunate injuries which soon muted Brooks' subsequent successes. Hitting a career best .340 in 1986, Brooks suffered torn thumb ligaments and also bone chips in his left thumb which shortened his season to but 80 games. Earning a repeat NL All-Star slot the following season, he continued to struggle with the injury bugaboo that affected his playing time but never totally neutralized his consistently effective hitting. Despite a specter of constant injury, Brooks earned Silver Slugger Awards in both 1985 and 1986 as one of the league's best run producers. But his fragility, coupled with a reputation for sloppy fielding, eventually justified the earlier Mets trade and also eventually forced the shift of Brooks from infield to outfield duty in the Montreal lineup.

GARY CARTER
(1985-89, Catcher)

Between Johnny Bench and Mike Piazza stood Gary Carter, perhaps baseball's best catcher of the late '70s and early '80s and certainly one of the most popular and celebrated backstops during that brief period. Carter's reputation was always a mixed bag, however, and both the negative and positive sides of his reputation were guaranteed to generate reams of press coverage and endless minutes of radio and television air time. To his detractors (some of whom were also his teammates), he was a publicity-hungry "camera hound" whose every on-field action and off-field reaction appeared somehow self-serving rather than team oriented. To his legions of champions, by contrast, he was an exuberant ambassador of the game, plus a dependable clutch hitter (with 10 career grand slams) and durable defender unequaled elsewhere around baseball. On the defensive side, it was noteworthy that Carter always supplemented his throwing and receiving credentials with substantial skill at handling the pitching staffs with which he worked, first in Montreal (featuring Steve Rogers, Bill Gullickson, and Scott Sanderson) and later in New York (featuring Dwight Gooden, Sid Fernandez, and Ron Darling).

With the Expos, Carter had once paced the senior circuit in RBI production (106 in 1984) and was twice the top backstop in terms of field-

ing percentage. His home run totals climbed above 20 on half a dozen occasions and once even topped 30. He was a regular in the NL All-Star lineup, seven times elected to the Classic, including his last six seasons in a row with the Expos. Further measures of greatness were a pair of All-Star Game MVP trophies garnered in 1981 (when he clubbed two homers) and 1984 (when he banged yet another). Across the first three of his five seasons with the Mets there was little if any reduction in production, and his 24 dingers and 105 RBIs were major contributions to the team's 1986 pennant climb. The previous season—his first in New York—was filled with the most eye-catching, Carter-generated events, including a game-winning grand slam on opening day, three consecutive blasts in a September game, and 18 game-winning hits throughout the campaign. And for all the offense in his debut Mets season, Carter also played an often underappreciated, yet nonetheless invaluable, role as the savvy veteran receiver who handled flamethrower Doc Gooden during the young superstar's own amazing "Triple Crown" performance, which was the height of Gooden's short-lived and meteoric New York career. If Gary Carter is a bona fide Hall of Famer (a point open to debate), most of his credentials were admittedly earned up in Montreal. But his one treasured moment on the unmatched stage of postseason play nonetheless came in New York with the bright-lights Mets.

RON DARLING
(1983-91, Pitcher)

Ron Darling's considerable major league career never produced a spotlight moment that quite equaled the highlight event of his amateur days. This came when the Hawaiian-born right-hander was a collegiate star at Yale and hooked up with future big-league teammate Frank Viola (then toiling for St. John's University) in one of the most memorable pitching duels in NCAA history. Darling no-hit St. John's for 11 frames before losing both his masterpiece and the game itself to future teammate Viola in the 12th. At the time, it was the longest no-hitter in collegiate history. It was also a springboard to a first-round pick by the Texas Rangers in the June 1981 draft, followed by a 13-year big-league sojourn in which he earned 136 victories, posted an overall winning ledger, and

Ron Darling stood in the shadows of Dwight Gooden's rookie season. (Brace Photo)

logged eight campaigns of 10-plus victories with first the Mets of the mid- and late eighties and later the Oakland A's of the early nineties. Darling was an excellent fielder and also earned notoriety for one of the game's best pickoff moves among right-handed pitchers. His eight-plus seasons in New York were also marked by a tendency toward wildness and a reputation for picking up many bad-luck "no decisions" (especially in his rookie year, when he was forced into the shadows by fellow newcomer Dwight Gooden). Twice he rang up more than 100 walks in a season, and on the second occasion (1985) was a league leader in this dubious category. A footnote to Ron Darling's Mets career came when he recorded the final strikeout of a 19-inning 16-13 victory over Atlanta that remains the latest-ending baseball game (3:55 a.m.) in major league history.

LENNY DYKSTRA
(1985-89, Outfielder)

Len Dykstra appeared to play major league baseball in a time warp, always seeming like some historical relic that had been unaccountably lifted straight out of the Gas House Gang 1930s and then dropped down in the midst of the relatively cosmetic eighties and nineties. A gritty tobacco-stained, devil-may-care hustler reminiscent of the old-school era of reckless and daring outfield play, Dykstra entertained modern-era fans in both New York and Philadelphia (where he was traded in the middle of the 1989 season for Juan Samuel) with diving and sliding outfield catches and intelligent baserunning (stealing 30 or more bases in five different seasons) plus surprising power from the leadoff spot in the batting order. Viewed from a distance, Dykstra almost passed for a modern-era version of Richie Ashburn—a speedy singles hitter with underrated outfield defensive skills—but, of course, on closer inspection, he had none of Ashburn's quiet class and certainly didn't match up when it came to long-term offensive productivity. Yet for a brief spell in the mid-eighties, Dykstra's spunky and enthusiastic outfield play made him almost as big a fan favorite in New York as Ashburn had once been in Philly. It was a fitting irony, in that light, that Len Dykstra's final baseball stop was with a pennant-contending club in Philadelphia, a team for which he twice led the National League in base hits.

SID FERNANDEZ
(1984-93, Pitcher)

The list of native Hawaiian big-league pitchers is a short one that seems to start and end with Ron Darling and Sid Fernandez, and it is one of baseball's lesser ironies that both natives of the Hula State enjoyed the bulk of their major league triumphs while wearing uniforms of the New York Mets. Fernandez was conscious enough of his special geographic origins to wear Mets uniform number "50" in recognition of his homeland's claim to statehood history. He was also a large enough blip on the big-league radar screen to emerge as one of the Mets' biggest mound stars during the mid-eighties revival under manager Davey Johnson. The Dodgers had earlier given up entirely on Fernandez because of his perceived weight problems and despite his two eye-catching minor league no-hitters. Once in a Mets uniform, he quickly displayed his talents in 1985 with 180 strikeouts in only 170 innings. He was the league leader in Ks per innings pitched and hung up a team record for lefties with 16 in a losing effort against Atlanta. A season later, his 16-6 record was a significant contributor to the

Sid Fernandez, a rare Hawaiian big-league headliner. (Brace Photo)

Mike Fitzgerald was the second Met to homer in his first at-bat. (Brace Photo)

team's NL pennant drive. Because of Davey Johnson's aversion to using a southpaw in Fenway Park, Fernandez lost his chance at a World Series start that year, but did contribute a 1.35 Series ERA and 2.1 scoreless innings in crucial Game 7 while working out of the bullpen. While he may never have pitched up to his full potential for an entire season and would never again match his 16 wins of 1986, Fernandez did log 110 career victories and often helped his own cause on the mound with his better-than-average skills as a left-handed hitter.

MIKE FITZGERALD
(1983-84, Catcher)

Some diamond careers begin in glowing promise and then slide rapidly toward near oblivion. Catcher Mike Fitzgerald enjoyed a heady debut with the Mets in the early eighties, entering with a bang by whacking a homer off the Phillies' Tony Ghelfi in his very first big-league plate appearance on September 13, 1983. Taking over the starting catcher's assignment the following spring, the solidly built right-handed swinger and thrower seemed to signal future stardom by tying a team record for fielding percentage set earlier by Jerry Grote

(Fitzgerald's .995 led the league) and earning further plaudits as Topps Bubble Gum's leading rookie receiver in the senior circuit. But it was seemingly only enough to shore up Fitzgerald's value as trade bait, and that spring he was shipped with Hubie Brooks and two journeymen to Montreal to acquire Gary Carter. Fitzgerald would subsequently fail miserably in Montreal as Carter's replacement, a pressure-packed role that was submarined by a string of unfortunate injuries and a distinct lack of star talent on his own part. The California native did hang on for seven seasons of inconsistent performance with the Expos, but he never again flashed the promise of that first fall and subsequent summer of overachievement in Shea Stadium.

DOUG FLYNN
(1977-81, Infielder)

Utility infielder Doug Flynn belonged to that considerable fraternity of big-league journeymen who are able to exploit a glue-filled glove effectively enough to compensate for a powderpuff bat and thus extend a 10-year big-league career far beyond its appropriate boundaries. The former University of Kentucky basketball star and excellent all-around athlete was

Doug Flynn owned a Gold Glove and a powder-puff bat. (Brace Photo)

never adroit enough with the lumber when facing major league flamethrowers to hit much above .230 and thus qualified as a genuine "Mendoza Line" big-league hanger-on. He batted only a paltry .197 in 126 games split between the Reds and Mets in 1977, and his .255 mark in 1980 was his best effort in a New York uniform. Only once did he stroke more than a single homer in a full season (four in 1979). But what will always be remembered most about Doug Flynn among the hometown faithful—and this is equally true in both New York and Cincinnati—is that he was one of four young Reds prospects shipped over to Shea Stadium in June 1977 as part of the most unpopular trade in New York Mets history. That was the regrettable and ill-received deal that prematurely ended Tom Seaver's tenure as the original New York Mets franchise player.

GEORGE FOSTER
(1982-86, Outfielder)

By century's end, the roster of players boasting better than 50 homers in a single season had exploded to 17, eight in the National League and nine in the junior circuit. Eight (McGwire, Ruth, Foxx, Kiner, Mantle, Mays,

Griffey, and Sosa) can now claim the distinction more than once, and even lesser lights among big-league lumber toters—Brady Anderson, Greg Vaughn, and Cecil Fielder—are now part of this history-making wrecking crew. George Foster was a valued member of Cincinnati's Big Red Machine teams of the 1970s, despite his acknowledged weaknesses as a mediocre outfielder and only average base runner. He was not a household name like Rose, Bench, Pérez, Morgan, Concepción, or even the senior Griffey. But he was a powerful and productive hitter in the middle of the lineup for three NL champions and may have enjoyed five of the most productive run-producing seasons of any player in his era. His 52 dingers in 1977 were followed by another league best (40) the following year; his three consecutive NL RBI titles tied a major league record; the 31 road homers during the year he cracked 52 was a big-league record for right-handers; and he also led the senior circuit during the stretch (1975-79) once in runs scored and once in slugging average. Perhaps it was only the charisma of teammates like Rose, Bench, Morgan, and company that robbed Foster of some of the luster he might have held in other towns. Dealt to the Mets in 1982, he was still productive enough to bang 20-plus homers on three occasions and ring up 90 RBIs once (missing by only four a second time). But a $10 million deal in New York doomed such otherwise hefty performances to the status of major "disappointments," and Foster was released by the Mets in August of their own 1986 championship season.

DANNY HEEP
(1983-86, Outfielder)

The Mets have certainly made solid—even great—trades down through the years, and many of them were deals that brought quality pitching to the New York roster. The best deals, however, always seemed to be for potential slugging stars like Keith Hernandez, Donn Clendenon, Tommie Agee, George Foster, and recently Mike Piazza. But then there are also the deals that relinquished Tom Seaver, Nolan Ryan, and future Cy Young winner Mike Scott, who was sent to Houston for a reserve outfielder named Danny Heep. Scott admittedly had not overwhelmed in New York with two early seasons of double-figure losses, but in Houston, of course, he blossomed into the staff ace. What

George Foster never equaled his Cincinnati slugging exploits with the Mets. (Brace Photo)

Danny Heep arrived at Shea Stadium in another ill-fated Mets trade. (Brace Photo)

arrived at Shea Stadium in return for Mike Scott was a hefty left-handed bat ideal for pinch-hitting service, as well as a utility fly chaser who might offer spot outfield duty. Danny Heep was an immediate success in these roles. Four pinch-hit homers in 1983 led the league and set a new franchise record; the pinch-hitting contribution was also notable during the 1986 world championship season with a 9-for-30 performance, which led the ball club. But in the end, it wasn't much in exchange for a dominant right-handed fastballer who would walk off with the NL Cy Young trophy that same year.

HOWARD JOHNSON
(1985-93, Infielder and Outfielder)

For a five-year stretch between 1987 and 1992, Howard Johnson established himself as one of the heaviest-hitting switch-hitters in baseball annals. He twice earned NL All-Star honors, pacing the senior circuit in both round trippers (38) and RBIs (117) during a career-year 1991 campaign. Johnson also posted the NL's top figure for runs scored (104) in 1989, when he also slugged 36 homers and again topped the lofty 100 RBI standard (101). Though the onslaught did not last long (he only once reached

double figures in homers after the high-water-mark 1991 season), it was responsible for enough offensive output to entrench HoJo as the New York Mets' club record holder for single-season extra-base hits (80 in 1989) and leave him second in career homers (192), RBIs (629), stolen bases (202), extra-base hits (424), runs scored (627), and doubles (214), as well as third in career total bases (1,823). Much of HoJo's slugging success seemed to come from a singular skill: His ability to hit almost any fastball on the nose, no matter what speed or how much hop the ball might carry. It was a talent that served him well in late innings against opposing closers who, more often than not, were little more than overpowering flamethrowers. Johnson's penchant for late-game homers especially victimized one of the league's top relief specialists, Todd Worrell of the St. Louis Cardinals, who alone surrendered five late-game blasts to the Mets' top clutch-situation slugger.

RAY KNIGHT
(1984-86, Third Baseman)

Some players, despite a small mountain of noteworthy achievement, nonetheless seem to pile up trivial distinctions that are the delightful if useless dross of barroom debate far more easily than they compile any of the true stuff of baseball legend and lore. Ray Knight, 1986 World Series MVP and solid third sacker of the late-'70s and mid-'80s, is a perfect example of the type. Knight's memorable Series performance for the Mets capped a season in which he was also tabbed as the older circuit's Comeback Player of the Year for his 80-point elevation in batting average (.218 in 1985 to .298 in 1986) and valued hot corner play as a platooning regular alongside Howard Johnson. But a bitter contract dispute at the close of the year soon sent him packing to Baltimore, a twist that left the part-time third sacker as the first-ever World Series MVP to join a new team for the subsequent summer. Five solid seasons with the Cincinnati Reds at the outset of Knight's big-league journey were also overshadowed, in the end, by a single, charming footnote: He was also the man who had replaced local hero Pete Rose at the hot corner in Cincinnati at the end of the seventies.

THE NEW YORK METS ENCYCLOPEDIA

TERRY LEACH
(1981-82, 1985-89, Pitcher)

A unique sidearm delivery and an over-achieving summer when his ball club was most in need of a lift are the two features that provided Leach with a ticket to Mets immortality. Listing far to the right with each delivery, the right-handed control specialist would submarine the ball toward home plate while scraping a padded right knee across the pitcher's rubber; it was an effective enough style in the short haul to befuddle most opposing hitters. For a brief spell during the spring and summer of 1987, it also allowed Leach to reach his moment of glory with an injury-wracked ball club struggling to defend its world championship. It was precisely those debilitating injuries to a large contingent of the Mets' staff that year which gave Leach an unanticipated opportunity to shine during his second stint with the ball club. Posting 12 starts (more than half of his 11-year career total of 21), Leach garnered an eye-popping 11-1 record and also struck out twice as many opposing hitters (61) as he walked (29). It was the only time he would win in double figures and truly the only season of note on his big-league résumé. A year later, he was again

successful with a 7-2 mark and three saves, but only after converting back to spot bullpen duty. A Mets record of 10 straight wins at the beginning of a season in 1987 thus remained his single boasting point, outside perhaps of a second rare footnote to Mets history. That came five years earlier, on October 1, 1982, when Leach tossed the only extra-inning one-hitter in club annals, a 1-0 10-inning masterpiece against the Philadelphia Phillies.

LEE MAZZILLI
(1976-81, 1986-89, Outfielder)

Lee Mazzilli rivals Ed Kranepool as the biggest Met fan favorite of all time, at least among those long-term hometown ballplayers who never reached true star status on the national level. The Brooklyn native, whose father, Libero Mazzilli, had been a professional prizefighter, was enough of a talented all-around athlete to win eight national speed skating championships. It also didn't hurt that he was a handsome enough matinee idol—even an obvious sex symbol—to be heavily promoted by the Mets' front office in the late 1970s as a franchise megastar despite only a single NL All-Star Game selection (1979) during his first six-year stint with the club. Finally, he was fortunately enough of an on-field contributor to justify the front-office promotions and still appear on the Mets' career top 10 lists in stolen bases (fourth), total bases (11th, 1,192), extra-base hits (10th, 238), games played (eighth, 979), at-bats (ninth, 3,013), runs scored (10th, 404), base hits (10th, 796), doubles (10th, 148), triples (ninth, 22), and pinch hits (tied for fifth, 38).

Mazzilli also enjoyed some rather outstanding and eye-catching individual moments early in his pro baseball career. Two years after his selection as the Mets' first-round amateur draft pick of June 1973, the fleet switch-hitting outfielder set a professional record (believed to remain unique to date) when he pilfered seven bases in a seven-inning minor league game (June 8, 1975) for Visalia (California League) versus San Jose. A little more than a year later, he broke into the majors with a considerable splash, first clubbing a pinch-hit three- run homer off Cubs reliever Darold Knowles in his second plate appearance, and 12 days later clubbing a ninth-inning game-winning circuit blast that eliminated the rival Pittsburgh Pirates from pennant contention.

Terry Leach had a unique sidearm delivery and one sensational summer. (Brace Photo)

ROGER MCDOWELL
(1985-89, Pitcher)

Cincinnati native Roger McDowell hurled in the big leagues mostly as a relief specialist who started only two of his 723 games across a full dozen seasons. He split his 140 career decisions right down the middle (70-70), saved 159 career games, and saw service with first three National League teams (Mets, Phillies, and Dodgers) and later two AL ball clubs (Rangers and Orioles). He laced all that journeyman duty with a center-stage reputation as one of baseball's chief merry pranksters—a role that often falls to hurlers who spend the bulk of their careers in the right-field or left-field corner, waiting for irregular late-inning fireman duty. Moe Drabowsky, Dan Plesac, and Dick Radatz were shining examples of the breed, but none was any better at the art than McDowell. McDowell was often called a latter-day Drabowsky by those apprised of the special art of bullpen mayhem, and he was reported to carry his own "mischief kit" loaded with stink bombs, exploding cigarettes, hand buzzers, and cherry bombs. Outside of the occasional and not-so-occasional high jinks, however, there were some noteworthy pitching accomplishments, especially during McDowell's stay in New York, and especially during the 1986 and 1987 National League campaigns. In the 1986 world-championship year, he set a short-lived club record with seven straight wins to open the season; in the famous 16-inning Game 6 of the NLCS with Houston he contributed five innings of one-hit relief; and despite a mediocre performance, he also picked up the victory during the Game 7 World Series clincher against the Red Sox. He even left New York for Philadelphia (in the same trade with Len Dykstra) as the No. 2 man on the franchise career saves list. None of it was enough, however, to override the image of McDowell once wearing his uniform upside down in the Mets dugout (his pants over his head and his shoes on his hands) during a nationally televised game.

KEVIN MCREYNOLDS
(1987-91, 1994, Outfielder)

As the sixth player chosen (by San Diego) in the June 1981 amateur draft and also minor league player of the year the next two summers (1982 and 1983), Kevin McReynolds seemed a can't-miss bet as a big-league superstar with his combination of raw batting power, blazing foot speed, and more-than-adequate outfield defensive skills. Yet despite eventually logging 211 homers and remaining a solid slugger in the middle of Padres and Mets lineups for more than half a dozen seasons, McReynolds was destined to be a middle-level big leaguer whose career distinctions would always be found buried in the fine print and never trumpeted in the headlines or the record books. As a regular center fielder on the Padres team which captured the pennant in 1984, he paced all NL fly chasers in putouts both that season and the next. He tied for the team leadership in home runs with 20. He also contributed one of the season's clutch hits in 1984 when his three-run homer in NLCS Game 3 ignited San Diego's valiant comeback against the hard-luck Chicago Cubs. Part of a seven-player deal, he arrived with the Mets the season after New York's own trip to the World Series in 1986 and immediately contributed with 29 homers and 95 RBIs. In the process, he anchored the middle of a powerful Mets lineup also featuring Keith Hernandez, Howard Johnson, Darryl Strawberry, and Gary Carter. During the Mets' 1988 run to a division title, he contributed still further by leading NL outfielders in assists (18 from the left-field slot, a rarity) and setting a major league record by stealing 21 times without being gunned down. The record string would extend to 33 a season later. McReynolds earned one final distinction during the 1988 season when he became the first player ever to produce three straight 95-plus RBI totals (96 in 1986, 95 in 1987, and 99 in 1988) while, at the same time, never reaching triple digits in the run-production department. It was an impressive boatload of distinctions, but most were of the kind most relished by baseball's many trivia hounds.

RANDY MYERS
(1985-89, Pitcher)

The aging southpaw bullpen ace who shares the NL single-season record for saves was still hanging around with the San Diego Padres at the outset of the 2000 season, and his steadily growing career saves total of 347 (through 1999) has now vaulted him into the all-time top five (trailing only Lee Smith, John Franco, Dennis Eckersley, and Jeff Reardon) in baseball's newest and most respected specialist role. Most of the bullpen success has come after leaving the Mets, where "Randall Kirk" (a favorite handle for play-by-play broadcasters) logged his first five seasons (1985-89) and became a major contributor with lofty save totals of 26 and 24 during the final two seasons of the eighties. With the Cubs in 1993 (53) and again in 1995 (38) he paced the senior circuit in games saved, then duplicated the accomplishment in the junior circuit (45 in 1997) after free agency took him off to Baltimore. The highlight of Myers' Mets tenure was undoubtedly his two victories in the 1988 NLCS, which New York lost to the LA Dodgers. That same summer he placed second in the senior circuit with a sterling .897 saves percentage. Of all the talented closers who have become a modern-era baseball trademark, perhaps none threw harder than Myers in his prime. The rubber-armed southpaw was several times timed by radar with velocities close to 100 miles per hour.

BOB OJEDA
(1986-90, Pitcher)

Bob Ojeda sprinkled his 15-year big-league career with a string of bizarre circumstances and off-beat distinctions. Most memorable and tragic was a spring training Florida boating accident which resulted in the untimely deaths of Cleveland Indian relievers Tim Crews and Steve Olin, while leaving Ojeda severely injured and casting a dark pall over the entire 1993 summer, which was also the Indians' last campaign within cavernous Municipal Stadium. On a lighter note, there was also the southpaw starter's reputed "dead fish" change-up that acted like a screwball and, although colorfully named, was not much protection during his early seasons in Boston. Pitchers relying on such finesse deliveries often struggle in claustrophobic Fenway Park, and Ojeda's early-career ups and downs in one of baseball's best hitters' ballparks eventually spelled a free ticket out of Boston; the Red Sox unloaded Ojeda to the New York Mets in 1985 as part of a memorable eight-player exchange that also sent Calvin Schiraldi and Wes Gardner to Boston. In his new and less hitter-happy surroundings with the New York club, Ojeda appeared to turn his career around overnight by posting 18 victories and the senior circuit's best won-lost percentage (.783, 18-5) his first season out of the American League. It was a heady campaign with a championship

ball club that Ojeda would never quite be able to duplicate, though he did win 10 in 1988 and 13 in 1989 before being shipped to the Dodgers at the end of 1990. Most of his steady downslide in New York seemingly resulted from the same penchant for bizarre accidents which plagued most of his career. A pinched ulnar nerve in his elbow sabotaged the 1987 summer, and in 1988, he also severed the middle finger of his left hand while trimming a hedge at home. The latter accident was much celebrated when Ojeda deliberately had the detached digit sewn back on crooked in an effort to aid his curveball throwing.

JESSE OROSCO
(1979, 1981-87, Pitcher)

The ageless and rubber-armed Jesse Orosco is seemingly the Pete Rose of the pitching trade, a tireless and personally driven performer who eventually reeled in one of baseball's most prized records for noteworthy longevity simply by refusing to hang up his glove or listen to his body's clear signals that a young man's game was finally beyond his rather average skills. Late in the century's final season, the 42-year-old Baltimore reliever finally overhauled Dennis Eckersley to take possession of the career standard for games pitched, closing out his 1999 campaign with a phenomenal record 1,090 total appearances. (Hoyt Wilhelm, Kent Tekulve, Lee Smith, and Rich Gossage complete the exclusive six-man list of 1,000-game pitchers.) Armed with a deadly slider and a backdoor curve, both of which he manipulates with pinpoint control, Jesse Orosco has survived not only on willpower alone, but equally on a finely tuned talent that continues even after 21 full seasons to make him one of baseball's best situational left-handed moundsmen. Such southpaw savvy is a skill guaranteed to stretch out any big-league career well beyond the expected limits. Orosco has never made his splash with big numbers; he has won only 84 games total (about four per year) and boasts but 141 career saves. He has only twice (13 in 1983 and 10 in 1984) enjoyed 10-plus victories in a single season, and those occasions both fell during his eight initial seasons with the Mets. And surprisingly, only once has baseball's most often used pitcher ever paced the league in games logged (65 in 1995 with Baltimore). But like Rose, Orosco just never seems to go away. A December 1999 off-season trade that sent Chuck

Jesse Orosco was the Pete Rose of the big-league pitching trade. (Brace Photo)

sons—was productive enough to earn him slots as all-time club leader in two speed departments, with 281 career stolen bases and 62 career triples. But all the details of Wilson's solid major league career are obliterated for most Mets fanatics by one indelible image of what was one of the most memorable single at-bats in team annals. It came in the 10th inning of 1986 World Series Game 6 and was actually an opportunity gifted rather than earned—a shot at immortality unexpectedly handed to Wilson by a pair of unaccountable Boston Red Sox blunders. The switch-hitting New York outfielder first dodged a two-ball, two-strike wild heave from Bosox reliever Bob Stanley, which brought Kevin Mitchell scampering home from third with the tying run. On the very next pitch, the fate-kissed Wilson sent a harmless dribbler toward first base, which crept through Bill Buckner's legs and plated Ray Knight with the improbable winning tally, forcing a crucial and fateful Series Game 7. A handful of hitters in the game's postseason history have been decidedly more heroic in the clutch—Bobby Thomson and Bill Mazeroski spring first to mind—but none has ever been any luckier at the plate in situations with the entire season squarely on the line.

1990s—A DECADE OF UNDERACHIEVEMENT

Despite its many highlights and a decade-closing return to postseason play, the fourth epoch of team history was destined in the end to be the only 10-season span that seemingly offered more outright disappointments than clear-cut triumphs. For the first time in franchise history, the new decade would fail to produce a pennant flag to fly proudly above Shea Stadium. And the Mets' yearly rosters throughout the nineties would also fall a good bit short of those from three earlier eras, especially when it came to totaling up genuine franchise heroes or even potential Hall of Famers. Yet even the championship-barren 1990s would nonetheless witness their appointed share of colorful and even memorable stars—enough always to prick the interest of Gotham's die-hard faithful and thus also to continue entertaining and occasionally even thrilling New York Mets fans everywhere around the globe. Mike Piazza arrived on the scene at the end of the '90s to head the biggest power show in ball club annals. For one brief season, the best defensive infield baseball

McElroy to Baltimore once again put Orosco back in a Mets uniform for the 2000 campaign, but Orosco's stay was short-lived as, on March 18, 2000, he was traded to St. Louis for Joe McEwing.

MOOKIE WILSON
(1980-89, Outfielder)

A 12-year big-league veteran whose entire career (minus two-plus final seasons in Toronto) was spent with the Mets, Mookie Wilson still remains a valued figure in the Mets' camp a full decade after closing down his stint as an active player. In 2000, Wilson served his fourth season as the ball club's popular and effective first-base coach and doubles as a knowledgeable instructor of base runners and hitters during spring training. Mookie's stepson, Preston, was a first-round Mets pick in the June 1992 free-agent draft and now stars as a center fielder with the rival Florida Marlins. And Mookie himself was a second overall pick by the Mets back in the 1977 version of the same big-league talent lottery. His own sojourn in the big time with the Mets—a spell of slightly less than 10 sea-

THE NEW YORK METS ENCYCLOPEDIA

has ever seen was trod onto the field wearing Mets uniforms. And a handful of skilled Spanish-speaking stars also brought the New York Mets squarely into the mainstream of baseball's ongoing Latin American invasion. The pennants may have fallen by the wayside in a decade so thoroughly dominated by Atlanta's pitching-rich Braves. But the baseball thrills that have long been a Shea Stadium staple were never for very long in short supply.

EDGARDO ALFONZO
(1995–, Infielder)

One of the sterling representatives of a recent bumper crop of Venezuelan big-league talent, Edgardo Alfonzo entered the new decade and the new century as one of baseball's biggest stars. During the Mets' 2000 season, he hit a robust .324 in 150 games, including 25 home runs, 40 doubles, and 94 RBIs. Alfonzo's 1999 performance at second base with the Mets included impressive power numbers, topped by 27 homers and 108 RBIs, and also a new ball club single-season record for runs scored with 123. It also established Alfonzo as a key member (along with third baseman Robin Ventura, shortstop Rey Ordoñez, and first baseman John Olerud) of what many chose to call the best defensive infield in all of baseball at century's end. While such a notable offensive explosion was not entirely unexpected, given Alfonzo's .315 batting mark of 1997 and his 17 homers and 78 RBIs of 1998, the sudden blossoming was all the more impressive, coming, as it did, in a season of defensive transition. The acquisition of Robin Ventura in the off-season had mandated a shift of Alfonzo back to second from third, where he had starred for two years after playing all three infield slots during his first two seasons. The added defensive adjustment was also handled brilliantly, as Alfonzo gave Cincinnati's Pokey Reese a strong yearlong challenge for the National League Gold Glove at the difficult keystone position.

Through the 2000 regular season, Alfonzo ranked high in several of the Mets' career categories, including doubles (sixth with 164), RBIs (seventh with 433), runs scored (seventh with 472), base hits (ninth with 874), and batting average (third at .296).

Edgardo Alfonzo has emerged as one of the most potent and reliable hitters in club annals. (NY Mets)

CARLOS BAERGA
(1996-98, Second Baseman)

There were moments when Carlos Baerga performed solidly in a New York Mets uniform, like the stretch in May 1997 when he batted .368 during the 25 games played that month, or the late-season upswing that year which boosted his season's average from an anemic .161 in April all the way to a final, respectable .281 mark. He was even more solid in Cleveland during his first seven seasons, sometimes brilliant enough, in fact, to leave his mark on the baseball record book. During 1995, he was the second-hardest batter in the entire junior circuit for pitchers to strike out, fanning an average of only once every 19.4 plate appearances. And on April 8, 1993, he earned a piece of true immortality as the first (and still only) batsman ever to sock homers from both sides of the plate during the same inning. The historic homers occurred in New York and came at the expense of southpaw Steve Howe and righty Steve Farr. But most of the switch-hitting second baseman's promise was displayed only in Cleveland, several seasons before his largely unproductive sojourn in New York, and almost all of it was crammed into four seasons (1992-95) of .300 hitting, three of those campaigns crowned with American League All-Star Game selections.

Once dealt to New York in July 1996 (along with Alvaro Espinoza, in exchange for Jeff Kent and José Vizcaino) Baerga's career took a sudden and dramatic detour southward. Already suffering from a lower abdominal strain before the trade from Cleveland, he appeared in only 26 games with New York during his first partial season there. A year later, Baerga stoically climbed out of his early-season slump with sufficient success to hold onto the second-base job for the bulk of the season. But by 1998, he was barely a .260 hitter, and in two New York seasons, he never managed as many as 10 homers or 60 runs batted in. In the end, Carlos Baerga rivals Butch Huskey as perhaps New York's biggest disappointment of the past baseball decade.

BOBBY BONILLA
(1992-95, 1999, Infielder and Outfielder)

No matter how good the numbers he posted sometimes were, switch-hitting Bobby Bonilla has always been an exemplar of under-achievement—fairly or unfairly—among numerous fans, as well as among many members of the sporting press and even among baseball insiders. The numbers posted for offense have often been exceptional and include a league-best 44 doubles for the Pittsburgh Pirates in 1991, 30-plus home run seasons in both Pittsburgh and New York, four years (one in Baltimore and three with the Pirates) of knocking home better than 100 runs, a fifth (with the Florida Marlins) that just missed that standard, and five plus-.500 slugging performances. And there were also five All-Star Game berths to pad the career résumé of one of the more productive third-base and outfield performers of the second half of the eighties and first half of the nineties.

				NL	World
Team	**Won**	**Lost**	**Pct.**	**Pennants**	**Championships**
Atlanta Braves	925	629	.595	1991-1992, 1995-1996, 1999	1995
Houston Astros	813	742	.523	None	None
Cincinnati Reds	809	746	.520	1990	1990
Los Angeles Dodgers	797	757	.513	None	None
San Francisco Giants	790	766	.508	None	None
Montreal Expos	776	777	.499	None	None
Pittsburgh Pirates	774	779	.498	None	None
New York Mets	**767**	**786**	**.494**	**None**	**None**
St. Louis Cardinals	758	794	.488	None	None
San Diego Padres	758	799	.487	1998	None
Chicago Cubs	739	813	.476	None	None
Philadelphia Phillies	732	823	.471	1993	None
Colorado Rockies (1993-99)	512	559	.478	None	None
Florida Marlins (1993-99)	472	596	.442	1997	1997
Arizona Diamondbacks (1998-99)	165	159	.509	None	None
Milwaukee Brewers (1998-99)	148	175	.458	None	None

1990s National League Composite Standings and Pennants (Ranked by Overall Winning Percentage)

But for all the heavy hitting—which now includes a legitimate shot at 300 career homers, with 282 and counting—Bonilla never quite lived up to his highly publicized hefty contracts or his adopted label as a franchise player. This rap as a disappointing clutch performer was

Bobby Bonilla was doomed to a career of unfulfilled promise. (NY Mets)

likely born of a single disappointing postseason performance with Pittsburgh, when he hit only .190 (in the 1990 NLCS, when teammate Barry Bonds also collapsed at .167), but seems highly unfair in light of his role in carrying his team during postseason play (hitting .304 while Bonds struggled at .148) a season later. Further debits against the Bonilla ledger have been numerous injuries (both his 1992 and 1993 seasons with the Mets ended in arthroscopic shoulder surgery) and a reputation for inconsistent fielding in both the outfield and at third base. While the powerful switch-hitter elevated his BA to .325 just before being traded from the Mets to Baltimore in mid-season 1995 and also socked 34 homers with the Mets in 1993, it also didn't help his Big Apple reputation when he slid to .249 and .265 at the plate in his first two Mets seasons after ranking as one of the league's most potent batsmen the previous three years in Pittsburgh and also finishing as runner-up to Barry Bonds in the 1990 NL MVP polls.

RICO BROGNA
(1994-96, First Baseman)

Flashes of brilliance have often marked Rico Brogna's career as a heavy-hitting and glue-gloved first sacker with the Detroit Tigers (nine games in 1992), Mets (three seasons in the mid-nineties, featuring a league-leading .998 fielding percentage in 1995), and Philadelphia Phillies (three straight years of 20-homer production and two with better than 100 RBIs). His 24 long balls and team-best 102 runs knocked home in the 1999 campaign were not quite enough for recognized stardom since they were compromised by both on-base-percentage and slugging-average numbers that were substantially below the average of NL starters at his position, and also by arthritic knees and a noticeable lack of success against left-handed pitching. Traded away by the Mets in the off-season of 1996-97 for pitchers Toby Borland and Ricardo Jordan, Brogna was never missed for a single moment in New York since talented batsman John Olerud was immediately obtained from Toronto as a replacement that very same winter. His only notable Gotham season had been the post-strike year of 1995, when he had slugged 22 homers and knocked home 76 runs, as well as playing the league's best defense among first basemen. Yet while Brogna's incon-sistent offense has never been headline-grabbing around the senior circuit—nor pleasing to bleacherites comprising baseball's toughest fans in both New York and Philadelphia—nonetheless, his agile glove and surprising range have quietly made his stellar defensive talent at first base one of baseball's best-kept secrets.

DAVID CONE
(1987-92, Pitcher)

There haven't been many better or more consistent right-handed pitchers in the major leagues throughout the decade of the 1990s than Royals, Mets, Blue Jays, and Yankees ace David Cone. And even in an age of rampant free agency, there haven't been many staff aces who have traveled quite as much, jumping every few seasons from one contending ball club to another. Or at least it seems that way. Cone, in reality, has toiled for only four clubs—the Mets, Royals, Blue Jays, and Yankees—and has seen postseason action with three of the four. The fact that he has hooked on twice each with both the Jays and Royals seems to accent the gypsy character of his career. Wherever he has been, however—either for a long stint or a short stop-

David Cone, one of baseball's best money pitchers.
(Brace Photo)

Rico Brogna is a solid first baseman and potential big-time slugger who has, nevertheless, remained a baseball vagabond. (Brace Photo)

over—Cone has consistently toiled with rare effectiveness and thus has piled up numerous milestones along the way, as evidence of his dominance. These include a 1994 Cy Young Award, two 20-win seasons (20-3 with the Mets in 1988), and also two league leaderships in strikeouts (233 in 1990 and 241 in 1991, both with the Mets). And it has now all been capped off by World Series rings earned with the most recent edition of Dynasty Yankees, and also by a single storybook afternoon in 1999 when Cone pitched the third perfect game in New York Yankees history. A key to such endless successes has been the variety of Cone's arsenal: two different fastballs, two distinct types of curves, a slider and a splitter, and also a wicked cutter. Equally effective is his uncanny ability to change both speeds and arm angles as well as anyone now in the pitching business. Those same abilities were already at the forefront during the six seasons Cone spent with the Mets, working to produce a 20-3 season in 1988, which represented the sixth-best winning percentage of all time for a pitcher winning at least 20 games (.870).

Kevin Elster logged 88 straight errorless games at shortstop. (Brace Photo)

KEVIN ELSTER
(1986-92, Shortstop)

It hasn't taken long for the brilliant defensive shortstop play of Rey Ordoñez to obliterate memories of his New York Mets predecessors at that position, a crew that includes Howard Johnson, Tony Fernández, José Vizcaino, and Kevin Elster in the 1990s. Of that crew, Elster hung around the longest at the position (four seasons of regular duty with the Mets), flashed the most temporary brilliance and eye-catching potential, and in the end perhaps also disappointed the most with his inability to become an everyday star or even a heavily contributing starter. The career highlight for Elster came in the 1988 and 1989 seasons, when he set a major league record with 88 straight errorless games (294 chances) at baseball's most challenging defensive slot. The string stretched across the final 60 games of the first campaign (commencing after a final error in Cincinnati in July) and finally came to a halt in early May the next year (also in Cincinnati). The old record had been held by Detroit's Ed Brinkman; Elster's record stood for two seasons, until it was extended to 95 games by Baltimore's Cal Ripken.

Beyond that one flawless string, Kevin Elster's only other temporary blip on the baseball map came with the Texas Rangers in 1996, when he suddenly became one of the best exhibits for a juiced baseball by socking 24 homers, a full third of his 12-year career total.

JOHN FRANCO
(1990–, Pitcher)

It took John Franco 16 quality big-league seasons to finally reach playoff action, where he secured a berth in the 1999 Division Series (versus Arizona) and NLCS (versus Atlanta) with the Mets, helping by making his usual heavy contributions out of the bullpen. Although he finally lost his spot as the team closer (to Armando Benitez) during the highly successful Mets wild-card campaign of 1999, he nonetheless continued to pad his personal record book, which has now left him as runner-up for the title of baseball's all-time saves leader (his 420 total trails only Lee Smith, who had 478) and also as the most frequently used pitcher (with 547 appearances) in New York Mets history. Franco is also obviously the Mets' all-time saves pacesetter with an 11-season tally of 272 and

John Franco, the most frequently used pitcher in Mets history.
(NY Mets)

above .300 his first two full seasons and then recovered from a strike-season malaise to pace the Cardinals in batting in 1995 while also displaying solid everyday defense. Apparent difficulty in seeing the ball (a defect eventually corrected by laser eye surgery in late 1998) caused a shocking fall-off in both 1997 and 1998, however, when Gilkey's average plunged first to .249 and then to .227. Consequently, his status fell to that of a part-time outfielder, and he was eventually dumped on the expansion Arizona Diamondbacks (for pitcher Willie Blair and part-time catcher Jorge Fabregas) late in his third Mets season. Gilkey rebounded in Arizona, where he filled in as a 1999 part-timer and posted a .333 BA as a frequent pinch hitter. He played for the Boston Red Sox in 2000. Highlights of a brief stint with the Mets include two straight seasons of leading the National League in outfield assists and a cumulative New York batting average of .285.

RICKEY HENDERSON
(1999-2000, Outfielder)

Few position players of the modern era have made more headlines than all-time base-stealing king Rickey Henderson, and fewer still have made them without slugging home runs. Henderson, of course, did earn a bit of lasting notoriety for his long-ball feats when he first set, and then continued to extend, a record for career homers hit leading off ball games (75 through the 2000 season). But the man who remains perhaps baseball's greatest-ever leadoff specialist is more noted for his spectacular baserunning feats (1,370 stolen bases), and his overall offensive productivity, which has also left him as one of baseball's all-time leading run scorers.

During two twilight seasons with the Mets, Henderson became something more of a distraction than a major lineup contributor, though his presence at the top of the batting order at times enhanced an already potent array of run-producing sluggers that was one of the most fearsome in the National League. His continued ability to get aboard ahead of such productive bats as those belonging to Edgardo Alfonzo, John Olerud, Robin Ventura, and Mike Piazza produced a bevy of runs and kept the Mets in solid pennant contention. Yet, in the long run, Henderson's final chase for personal milestones

still counting. The Brooklyn-raised southpaw has always pitched more like a wily veteran starter than a flamethrowing closer: His fastball has movement but not overwhelming velocity; he tantalizes hitters with deceptive sliders, change-ups, and sinkers rather than overpowering them with invisible heat; he succeeds most often with his ability to induce ground outs and his talent for putting the ball in play but keeping it in the ballpark. A startling fact about Franco's late-inning successes is that it has been six full seasons since he last gave up a home run to a left-handed batter.

BERNARD GILKEY
(1996-98, Outfielder)

Obtained from the St. Louis Cardinals for a bunch of minor leaguers (none of whom has yet logged any big-league playing time of consequence) on the eve of the 1996 season, the hefty right-handed-hitting outfielder immediately flashed surprising promise with a solid .317 average (among the league's top 10) and a club-record 44 doubles. The surprise was not too startling, perhaps, as Gilkey had already proven his offensive value in St. Louis, where he batted did not seem to compensate for the clubhouse distractions that were also part of his baggage. At the conclusion of the 1999 season, when the Mets fell short in postseason wars with the pitching-rich Atlanta Braves, Henderson grabbed headlines not by starring on the field but instead by aggravating teammates and the front office with such unwelcomed stunts as playing cards in the clubhouse during the final innings of the season-ending NLCS loss. That single event stirred numerous rumors throughout the winter that Henderson was on the way out in New York. The Mets opened the 2000 season on a historic road trip to Japan with trade rumors still swirling and a disgruntled Henderson eventually spent the bulk of the season as a Seattle Mariner. Henderson (2,178 runs) eventually passed Hank Aaron (2,174), Babe Ruth (2,174), and Pete Rose (2,165) for all-time career runs scored. Even leader Ty Cobb's (2,246) record may not be entirely out of reach.

TODD HUNDLEY
(1990-98, Catcher)

The Mets' backstop who preceded current club hero Mike Piazza was not exactly a one-season wonder, yet he comes awfully close. The heady single season that put Hundley square on the National League map was his fifth full campaign in 1996, when he blasted 41 homers, drove in 112 runs, and set a new major league record for homers by a catcher, beating Roy Campanella's standard, which had stood for 43 summers. Hundley did follow up his 41 round trippers with 30 a year later, but several seasons down the road, the overnight outburst by the switch-hitting backstop now appears more like a single, inexplicable career peak than any onset of true big-league stardom. Two subsequent seasons brought a major fall-off in production: Hundley appeared in only 53 games in 1998, hitting a mere three homers and knocking in a paltry dozen runs. He rebounded with 24 homers for the Dodgers in 1999, but rang up only 55 RBIs and batted an anemic .207. The culprit was injury, with surgeries (one for a wrist bone spur and the other for elbow bone chips) following both the 1996 and 1997 seasons. And Mike Piazza had come along in New York, closing Hundley out of the backstop picture and finally initiating a trade with Los Angeles. Hundley has been anything but an instant success with the Dodgers, and the three-team trade

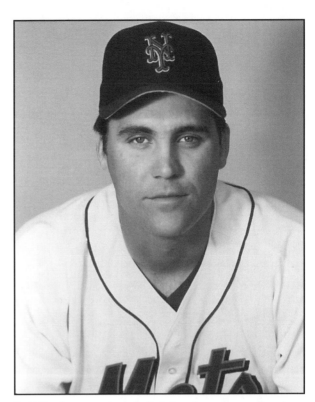

Todd Hundley was not exactly (but almost) a one-season wonder. (NY Mets)

that brought him to the west coast at the cost of outfielder Roger Cedeño and catcher Charles Johnson was one of the main reasons for a team collapse in LA. Hundley is now struggling to rebuild his career as a frontline big-league backstop with the Chicago Cubs.

BUTCH HUSKEY
(1993, 1995-98, Outfielder and Infielder)

Termed a "classic mistake hitter" by baseball insiders, Butch Huskey finally enjoyed the kind of offensive season in Boston during the second half of 1999 (22 homers, 72 RBIs, .282 BA, .492 SA) that might yet produce a solid big-league career as a valued platoon player, if never as a dependable starter. A solid second season with the Mets in 1997 featured 24 homers and 81 RBIs and provided one small boasting point at the outset of Huskey's still-promising career. The only Met ever to hit more homers in his second full campaign was Darryl Strawberry with 26 in 1984. But the comparisons with past greats seemed to stop there. A season later, Huskey's average tumbled to .252, and his homers dipped to 13 in 131 games. He played for four different teams from 1999 to 2000, stopping in Seattle, Boston, Minnesota, and Colorado.

GREGG JEFFERIES
(1987-91, Infielder)

Gregg Jefferies launched his pro baseball career with seemingly endless potential, headlining as the New York Mets' first-round pick in the 1985 amateur draft and then turning in MVP performances in each of his first three minor league outings. He also debuted in the Big Show with an outstanding stretch after being called up late in 1988, hitting .321 and socking six homers in only 109 September and October at-bats. It was during that stretch that Mets manager Davey Johnson stirred controversy in New York and especially elsewhere by deliberately holding his prized newcomer out of potential at-bats so that Jefferies might still qualify for rookie honors during the upcoming 1989 National League season.

But the potential never fully materialized for a versatile ballplayer who has always flashed enough batting skill over the years to maintain roster spots down to the present with six different teams, but has also never broken through with consistent year-in and year-out All-Star performances. This despite considerable hitting talent, which has left Jefferies a lifetime .289

Gregg Jefferies remains one of the franchise's biggest disappointments. (Brace Photo)

hitter through his 14 major league seasons. In New York, Jefferies did once pace the NL in doubles with 40 (1990) and was also one of the league's toughest strikeouts in 1991, but he lasted only five seasons in Shea Stadium before being peddled to Kansas City. There eventually were two near-brilliant All-Star seasons with the St. Louis Cardinals in 1993 and 1994, and Jefferies ranked as the NL's third-leading hitter during the first of these two peak campaigns. But two subsequent free-agent stints in Philadelphia and Detroit have witnessed a dramatic slide from the ranks of the game's clutch batsmen, and career's end now seems to be close at hand for an underachieving player who has surprisingly never returned to postseason play since the one-time late-season heroics of his short, "unofficial" rookie campaign with the Mets.

LANCE JOHNSON
(1996-97, Outfielder)

Repeated injuries and advancing age have robbed Lance Johnson in recent seasons of his short-term prowess as a solid slap hitter, high-percentage base stealer, and solid center fielder with superb speed and range. The 2000 season may, in fact, have signaled the end of the left-handed speedster's 14-year big league sojourn. Acquired via free agency by the Mets in December 1995 after six seasons as a regular with the White Sox, Johnson enjoyed a single "career-year" campaign in New York when he exploded at the plate for league "bests" in both hits (227) and triples (21), stole 50 bases, and posted a sterling .333 batting mark, which ranked fourth in the entire league. He also scored 117 runs, and his 75 multiple-hit games and 682 at-bats where both unmatched in the majors that year. Further landmarks of Johnson's best campaign were the club record for single-season triples and a rare distinction as the first player ever to pace both circuits in total hits, having been the AL leader with 186 a summer earlier in Chicago. But the sudden stardom in Gotham was unfortunately brief. A rash of injuries set in a season later, which pared nearly 25 points from Johnson's batting average and soon sent him packing in August to the Chicago Cubs, in exchange for valuable relief pitcher Turk Wendell and still-promising (but soon failure-bound) outfielder Brian McRae.

Lance Johnson, the first player in history to pace both leagues in total hits. (Brace Photo)

BOBBY JONES
(1993–, Pitcher)

Any balanced assessment would have to label Bobby Jones as a mostly limited, if useful, starter, as far as big-league hurlers go. His fastball of 85 mph is barely adequate by major league standards, yet he compensates when healthy with an effective range of deliveries and also with excellent command of his varied arsenal of off-speed pitches. Having missing the bulk of the '99 campaign with an injured shoulder, Jones compiled an 11-6 record in 27 starts, including victories in seven of his last eight appearances. The highlight came in the 2000 NL Division clincher versus San Francisco on October 8, when Jones spun a one-hit, 1-0 masterpiece. An injury-ruined 9-9 season in 1998 was his first full campaign that didn't boast a winning ledger. His 15 wins in 1997 were the most by a Met since Frank Viola was the team's last 20-game winner seven summers earlier. He also joined the select company of Greg Maddux, Tom Glavine, and Ramon and Pedro Martínez as the only NL hurlers between 1994 and 1997 to reach double digits in victories annually without also showing a losing record somewhere in the stretch. Two final achievements are also boasting points for an otherwise run-of-the-mill pitching career. When Jones reached double-digit victory totals in four straight seasons, he was the first Met to accomplish the feat since Doc Gooden (1990-93). And his eight straight wins in a starting role also tied a team record shared by David Cone and Tom Seaver.

JEFF KENT
(1992-96, Infielder)

For at least half of the past decade, Jeff Kent has been one of the most underrated and underappreciated second sackers in all of baseball. During the 2000 campaign for the San Francisco Giants, Kent enjoyed his career's best single season, hitting .334 with 33 homers and 125 RBIs. Kent's nine-season big-league career kicked off in Toronto in 1992, deposited him with the Mets that same season as part of a blockbuster trade featuring David Cone, passed through Cleveland for only 39 games in 1996, and has subsequently anchored in San Francisco since 1997. The tenure has, through 2000, featured 194 homers, a solid .284 batting mark, six seasons above 20 round trippers, and slugging marks that have now soared above .500 three years running. In New York, he twice slugged 20 or more homers, knocked in as many as 80 runs, and once hit .292 for a full season. Yet he

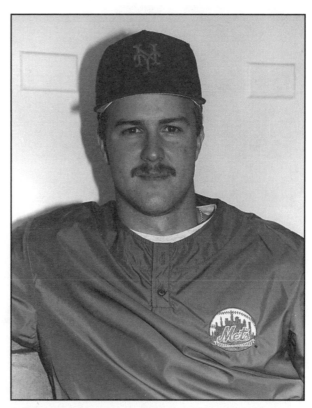

Jeff Kent flashed promise in New York before achieving true stardom in San Francisco. (Brace Photo)

Bobby Jones, a big-league pitching star despite his admittedly limited mound arsenal. (NY Mets)

never managed the kind of noteworthy numbers or achieved the kind of substantial, if underappreciated, stardom that has highlighted his career since relocating to the west coast.

AL LEITER
1998–, Pitcher)

Eight partial seasons in the major leagues before posting a campaign with a double-figure winning ledger does not bode well for true big-league stardom. Throwing his first big-league pitches with the Yankees in 1987, Al Leiter battled numerous debilitating injuries during his early seasons (including a sore shoulder and arthroscopic surgery in 1989, irritation of the ulnar nerve in his left elbow in 1991, blisters on his pitching hand in 1993, and a groin strain in 1994) and struggled just to stay in the majors with the Yankees (1987-89) and Blue Jays (1989-95) before turning his career around with an 11-11 mark at Toronto in '95, a season in which he also cracked the league's top 10 in ERA (3.64). But there were early flashes of promise, such as the fact that he was the only Yankee hurler to record more strikeouts than innings pitched during his sophomore major league summer (1988). But things really turned around for Leiter when he joined the Florida Marlins in 1996, won 16 games, finished third in the NL with a 2.93 ERA, and tossed that fledgling ball club's first-ever franchise no-hitter. The whitewash came at home against the heavy-hitting Colorado Rockies in May of 1996 and remains a career highlight. But Leiter's 17-6 (2.47 ERA) debut season with the Mets in 1998 was solid enough to earn a sixth-place finish in the NL Cy Young balloting. And while knee problems ruined early-season performances in 1999, the Mets' top southpaw was still able to rebound sufficiently to gain 13 victories and also toss a vital two-hit shutout in a single-game playoff with Cincinnati to gain his team a postseason wild-card playoff spot.

Leiter's 16-8 mark with a 3.20 ERA and 200 strikeouts in 208 innings again helped lead the Mets to the 2000 playoffs.

DAVE MAGADAN
(1986-92, Infielder)

The younger cousin of longtime big-league manager Lou Piniella has always been a solid-enough defender (he led NL first sackers with a

Dave Magadan, a journeyman infielder who once made a run at a league batting title. (Brace Photo)

.998 fielding percentage in 1998) and skillful enough at reaching base (his .425 OBP was tops in 1990 in the senior circuit) to assure a long-lived journeyman's career as a part-time platoon player. Magadan also logged enough quality time with the Mets in his first seven big-league seasons to wind up third on the club's career top 10 list in batting average (.292) and also on the best single-season list for BA (.328 in 1990). A versatile glove man, he also logged time at both corners of the infield and appeared in more than 100 games four different times. But it was precisely his orientation as a third baseman and first baseman that cost Magadan any chance at a regular lineup spot with the Mets, since the infield corners during his tenure were already capably covered by a pair of NL All-Stars, Howard Johnson and Keith Hernandez. There were two brief bursts of glory for Magadan nonetheless, the first coming with a huge offensive performance during the team's division-clinching game in 1986, and the second coming when he filled in for the injured Hernandez in 1989 and went on a hitting tear to close at .286. The latter performance was enough for manager Davey Johnson to experiment for a spell with Howard Johnson at shortstop in order to cram the potent bats of HoJo,

Hernandez, and Magadan into the same Mets lineup.

Since leaving the Mets, Magadan has played for six different teams, including finally the San Diego Padres in 2000.

BRIAN MCRAE
(1997-99, Outfielder)

The Mets had lofty expectations for the son of former big-league All-Star Hal McRae when they picked him up from the rival Cubs as part of the August 1997 trade including outfielder Lance Johnson and relievers Turk Wendell and Mel Rojas. After a less-than-head-turning four-year tryout in the Kansas City Royals' lineup, Brian McRae had displayed some early offensive clout in Chicago with a career-best .288 BA in 1995, along with the senior circuit's second-leading total for doubles and fourth-highest number of base hits (172) that same season. There did seem to be some signals of a career turnaround on the heels of McRae's arrival in Shea Stadium when he settled in with the regular center fielder's job in 1998 and put up some impressive power numbers by blasting 21 homers and both driving home and scoring 79 runs. The home run number would make McRae only the second Mets center fielder to register 20 round trippers and 20 steals in the same season, equaling the 1970 feat of Tommie Agee. But it was more of a last hurrah than a sign of promise. By July of the next season, McRae had played himself onto the bench and then out of the Mets' clubhouse altogether. His career was in such a downspin by August of 1999, in fact, that the one-time top prospect was traded away by both the Mets and the Rockies in a single nine-day span and then also released outright by a third club (Toronto) at season's end.

EDDIE MURRAY
(1992-93, First Baseman)

Eddie Murray may well have been the most underrated big-league superstar of the final quarter of the 20th century; he certainly was one of the game's most soft-spoken offensive threats, a quiet clubhouse presence whose on-field consistency was often unfairly overlooked in the absence of any blockbuster single-season numbers for long balls or run production. Murray's final 21-year ledger of 504 home runs, 3,255 hits, 1,917 RBIs, and 1,627 runs scored

make him a guaranteed first-ballot Hall of Famer and link him with Mickey Mantle as baseball's two best switch-hitters in history. At the same time, Murray is the only member of the 500-home run club never to reach 35 round trippers in any single season. He captured only one home run crown (with a mere 22 homers in the strike-shortened 1981 season), and he boasts only three other occasions in two decades when he finished a season as the league's offensive leader (with 78 RBIs, again in 1981, 107 walks in 1984, and also a .415 on-base percentage that same season). Murray joined the Mets—his third of six teams—for two brief seasons (1992 and 1993) that were perhaps subpar by his own career standards, but productive enough by almost any measure. He produced 93 RBIs in 1992 and followed up with 100, supported by 27 round trippers, in 1993. His first year in Shea saw him pace an injury-riddled sub-.500 club in most offensive categories and also in games played. His 100-RBI campaign that followed drew few headlines on a team that lost an embarrassing 103 games and also featured a record 27-game losing streak by pitcher Anthony Young, the firing of manager Jeff Torborg, and the resignation of GM Al Harazin.

JOHN OLERUD
(1997-99, First Baseman)

The New York seasons of John Olerud were unfortunately extremely limited, but nonetheless crammed with as many highlight-reel moments and record-book achievements as almost any Mets résumé in recent or ancient team history. Arriving from Toronto in late 1996 in exchange for touted pitching prospect Robert Person, the former AL batting champion (.363 in 1993) and quality first sacker let loose with a late-season batting explosion that left him as the team leader in both runs scored (90) and RBIs (102). In 1998, his further adjustments to NL pitching produced the highest batting mark in ball club history (.354) and barely missed out on a second career league batting title. Colorado's Larry Walker would outdistance the Mets' first sacker by nine points in the batting race, but Olerud's mark was 14 digits better than the club standard of .340 posted by Cleon Jones back in the year of the 1969 miracle. Olerud thus became the first Met ever to rank second in the NL in hitting (Dave Magadan and Cleon Jones each once finished third), and his 197 hits

Eddie Murray toiled briefly in Shea Stadium on his circuitous route to Cooperstown. (Brace Photo)

were also the second-best club mark, behind Lance Johnson's record 221. Olerud's flawless textbook swing produced another solid season in 1999, and while his batting average dipped to .298, his effectiveness at getting on base and driving in runs in the middle of a lineup touting Piazza, Alfonzo, and Ventura helped make the Mets one of baseball's most fearsome lineups. In the age of free agency, however, stable rosters are a thing of the past in big-league baseball. By 2000, Washington native John Olerud had left New York and signed on with the Seattle Mariners, hoping to finish out a brilliant career with his hometown ball club.

REY ORDOÑEZ
(1996–, Shortstop)

One of the most notable members of a small but nonetheless headline-grabbing contingent of recent Cuban defectors now toiling in the major leagues, flashy Rey Ordoñez is also one of the most outstanding middle-infield de-

fensive performers of baseball's recent past. He is also something of a mystery figure on a number of unrelated counts. First, there is the issue of his true age, a constant black hole with the current crop of Cuban immigrants now playing big-league baseball. The Mets list his birthdate as November 11, 1972, when the actual date (published in Cuba) of January 11, 1969, reveals that the prized four-year veteran has already crossed the 30-year age barrier. There is also the garbled background of the shortstop's playing career and status in his native Cuba, where he once held down a spot on the Cuban junior national team before defecting to the United States during the 1993 World University Games in Buffalo. Since Ordoñez was already stuck behind two even more brilliant shortstops named Germán Mesa and Eduardo Paret in the Cuban national team pecking order, his prospects for stardom back home were indeed limited. This fact, as much as any other, may have prompted his flight to the major leagues. Furthermore, there is the ongoing mystery of his inconsistencies as a big-league batter, a single element that seems now to threaten to short-circuit any true big-league stardom. While he upped his season's average to .258 in 1999 from a three-year career .242 mark, he still justifiably wears the label of the worst-hitting regular infielder in the majors. And his mediocre batting average sometimes actually masks his true impotence with the lumber, since he also swings freely and even wildly, rarely walks, produced fewer RBIs in '99 (60) than all but two other NL starters at shortstop, and has virtually no consistent power to compensate for a low on-base percentage.

Midway through the 2000 campaign, Ordoñez fractured his left arm, sidelining him for the remainder of the season. He was hitting just .188 at the time.

RICK REED
(1997–, Pitcher)

Before settling in as the Mets' third or fourth starter in the final years of the decade, Reed was an eight-year journeyman right-hander with the Pirates, Royals, Rangers, and Reds, and he even pitched some replacement-roster spring training innings during the 1995 strike-interrupted season in a desperate attempt to keep his professional career alive. He had posted only eight big-league wins before busting into the New York rotation early in 1997 and surprising that year with the NL's sixth-best ERA (2.89) and second-best walks-per-innings ratio (behind Atlanta's Greg Maddux). A 1998 All-Star Game roster choice, Reed has had an inconsistent career that was slowed in 1999 when a pair of injuries shelved him for better than a third of the Mets' season. When he was more or less healthy in 1997, 1998, and 1999, however, this gritty West Virginia native was considered one of the most precise control pitchers in the game and a master at painting the corners of the strike zone with his moderate fastball, after the fashion of Atlanta ace, Maddux. Other pluses for Reed and factors that kept him a Mets starter for several campaigns were his considerable defensive prowess, his skill at holding base runners near the bag, and his talents as a hitter—especially as a situational bunter.

In 2000, Reed recorded his fourth straight winning campaign for the Mets (11-5), boosting his career mark in New York to 51-30.

BRET SABERHAGEN
(1992-95, Pitcher)

Throughout much of the eighties, it seemed as though Bret Saberhagen was a charmed pitcher unaccountably destined to perform brilliantly in odd-numbered years and then tail off to mediocrity in even-numbered seasons—a pattern that was finally reversed when he came over from the American League Kansas City Royals to the National League New York Mets. In the junior circuit, Saberhagen had racked up win totals of 20, 18, 23, and 13 (all winning years) in the odd-numbered years and boasted only 10, 7, 14, and 5 (all losing totals) in the even-numbered summers. He had established his brilliance with a 20-6 sophomore campaign in 1985, making him the youngest Cy Young winner ever, and a second Cy Young accolade in 1989, when he bested the circuit in both winning percentage (.793) and total victories (23), as well as complete games (12), innings pitched (262.1), and ERA (2.16). It was not until he donned a Mets uniform that the alternate-year jinx was snapped, but only after a fashion. Only once in three-plus seasons with the Mets did the control artist maintain his brilliance for a season-long spell, and that occasion was the even-numbered season of 1994 (a strike-shortened campaign), in which his 14-4 ledger was, once more, the best winning ratio in the circuit. Shoulder problems (he had his third major surgery in 1999) have largely accounted for Saberhagen's career-long inconsistencies. But when he was on, he was dazzling with his command of pitch location; and his uncanny control of his fastball allowed him to pitch 119 innings in 1999 with the Boston Red Sox while issuing a mere 11 free passes. Over 15 full and partial seasons, the occasionally brilliant right-hander has posted a remarkable 1,705-471 strikeouts-to-walks ratio, and this stinginess with bases on balls has remained his prime calling card.

ROBIN VENTURA
(1999–, Infielder)

After a decade of solid achievement at third base with the Chicago White Sox, Robin Ventura joined the New York Mets for the 1999 season in one of the year's most valuable free-agent signings. A career .274 left-handed hitter in Chi-

cago with five Gold Gloves to his credit, Ventura easily handled the pressure of a transition to the media limelight in New York and even seemed to improve upon his solid offensive and defensive prowess in the process. He copped yet another Gold Glove in his first Mets season as the anchor of what may have been for a single season the best defensive infield in all of baseball. He hit .301, pounded 32 homers, his second-highest number ever, and reached a career high with 120 runs batted in. Hobbled by a torn cartilage in his left knee throughout the latter part of the 1999 season, Ventura nonetheless nobly gutted out a heroic Mets postseason run and continued to contribute with both his offensive and defensive clutch performances. He even provided one of the year's highlight moments when he stroked the apparent extra-inning, game-winning grand slam that lifted a seemingly moribund New York ball club into Game 6, after faltering New York had earlier trailed in the NLCS, three games to none.

Ventura's dramatic blast against Atlanta was indeed the game-winner, but ironically was ruled a single when the heroic batsman was swamped by celebrating teammates at first base and never allowed to complete his home run trot. But if Ventura lost his most memorable grand slam on a technicality, he remains noteworthy nonetheless for more than a dozen other four-run shots he has stroked over his first dozen seasons. A 14th career grand slam he hit against Milwaukee in Shea Stadium early in the 2000 season made Ventura the all-time grand slam leader among active big leaguers. Ventura was previously locked in a four-way tie with Harold Baines, Ken Griffey Jr., and Mark McGwire for the top spot in this most impressive of clutch-hitting categories. His final stats in an injury-plagued 2000 showed him with 24 home runs and 84 RBIs.

FRANK VIOLA
(1989-91, Pitcher)

During the late '80s, there was no more effective southpaw in the American League than Frank Viola, ace of the 1987 world-champion Minnesota Twins and Cy Young winner during the Twins' title-defense season of 1988. And in a short two-year-plus stopover with the Mets, Viola would continue his magic, if only

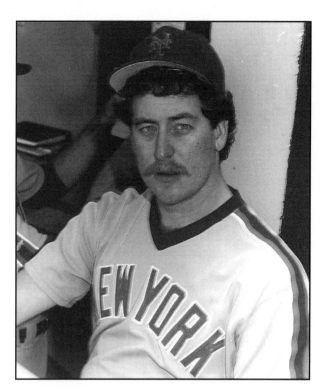

Frank Viola, former Cy Young winner who shone only too briefly in New York. (Brace Photo)

briefly, in the senior circuit with his only other 20-win campaign (20-12 in 1990) and the NL lead in innings pitched (249.2). During his 1988 career season, the 6'4" southpaw was not only the league's biggest winner (tops in victories with 24 and percentage at .774), but he also finished third in ERA (2.64) and strikeouts (193). A season earlier, he had mastered hitters effectively enough with his tantalizing change-up to post a 17-10 mark as staff ace for the world champions and then garner World Series MVP honors by winning twice in the Fall Classic, the second time on three days' rest in Game 7. His trade to the Mets in the middle of the 1989 season for Rick Aguilera, David West, and a handful of no-name prospects generated plenty of media attention, if only because the deal provided New York with a pitching staff owning a higher aggregate salary than the entire roster of the downsizing Chicago White Sox. A footnote to Viola's arrival in New York was his union on the same staff with Ron Darling, a pitcher he had bested in one of the legendary games of collegiate baseball history. In that contest, Darling had tossed an 11-inning no-hitter for St. John's, but Viola had triumphed for Yale 1-0 in the 12th frame.

ANTHONY YOUNG
(1991-93, Pitcher)

If Roger Craig, Al Jackson, Jack Fisher, and Tracy Stallard all had to have talent in order to be continually handed the ball enough times to suffer more than 20 humiliating single-season defeats with the woeful expansion Mets clubs of the early sixties, the same would have to be said in defense of Anthony Young, who posted an even more eye-catching ledger of pitching futility with a pair of almost-as-embarrassing New York ball clubs three decades later. Manager Jeff Torborg, an ex-catcher, must have had considerable faith in the physical skills of his 26-year-old prospect to offer him the baseball repeatedly enough for the ill-starred 6-2 right-hander to establish an unenviable major league mark for mound futility—27 defeats without a single intervening victory. A 3.77 ERA posted over 100 innings of Young's 1-16 1993 season (the one in which his consecutive losses finally reached record proportions) suggests that his basement-bound team's inability to produce timely runs during his mound stints—or to provide much solid defense behind him—were the largest culprits during his personal run of mound misfortune. Fifteen saves during a 2-14 1992 performance offer another yardstick leading to a similar conclusion. Things did, in fact, improve ever so slightly once Young finally departed Shea Stadium and donned the uniforms of the Chicago Cubs and Houston Astros during subsequent seasons, and he was even a near-.500 pitcher (10-13 overall) when employed for occasional middle-relief chores across his three final big league seasons.

Anthony Young holds one of baseball's most dubious career pitching records—24 consecutive losses. (Brace Photo)

CHAPTER 4
Unforgettable Moments
in Mets History

Baseball is simply a matter of rooting faithfully (and in most cases and for most seasons, quite hopelessly) for the cherished hometown nine. Long-favored stars retire, and quaint ballparks are replaced by shopping mall stadia; high-priced free agents come and go, and popular performers are traded away; but it all matters very little in the long haul. Loyalty in baseball is to a logo and a uniform alone. We may grouse, groan, and whine, but we seldom ever trade in our favorite team for a new one.

Such loyalties are formed early in life and often have most to do with simple geography. They supersede and survive the ebb and flow of individual seasons, as well as the comings and goings of individual star players (one reason why free agency and its constant player shuffling has little negative impact on the game's continuing popularity). Part of the baggage is attachment to a particular ballpark and thus a deep connection with the events played out in that park over the course of many child-

Ron Swoboda was a key contributor to the Mets' 1969 miracle finish. (Brace Photo)

hood summers. Ernie Banks will always move gracefully in the Wrigley Field sunshine; a revamped Yankee Stadium still houses palpable ghosts of Mantle, Maris, Ruth, and the stoic Yankee Clipper. It was the loss of Ebbets Field itself, and not just the Brooklyn nameplate alone, which disenfranchised all those former Flatbush Faithful, whose own adult lives eventually took them to such distant corners of the nation. The Tigers would no longer quite be the Tigers without Tiger Stadium; nor would the Bosox seem legitimate anywhere but on the hallowed turf of ancient Fenway Park.

Baseball memories are thus highly personalized matters. As a nation of ballpark addicts, we often mark the mundane events of our lives—especially our early lives—against a nostalgic baseball backdrop. Each fan is intimately attached to the ballplaying styles and diamond events of his youth. This explains the prevalent belief in a baseball "golden age"— that period when we were young and carefree, when our heroes were above any taint, when the hitters were more muscular, the pitchers more relent-

Mets manager Casey Stengel mugs with two of his great Yankees stars, Roger Maris and Mickey Mantle, during the expansion club's first spring training camp. (AP/Wide World Photos)

lessly unhittable, the infield and outfield play far more pleasingly aesthetic, and the ballplayers themselves much more spirited and dedicated. Our health, well-being, and very state of mind all seemed somehow inexorably bound up with the fortunes of a favored hometown team. We all see the sports world of our youth this way, through the rose-colored filter of our own fandom. And all big-league teams provide their fans with a gallery of irrepressible ballpark memories. Even relatively young franchises like the New York Mets are no exception to this universal baseball rule.

Football lures its legions of bloodthirsty fans with unrelenting violence. The pigskin game is spiced by the "corporate metaphor" of team play and individual sacrifice in the name of cohesive progress for the militaristic unit. Basketball has reached its current popularity through the appeal of the larger-than-life (quite literally) celebrity and fantasy superhero. Baseball's appeal, by contrast, has always rested firmly on the drama of the hometown team. We live and die with the summertime adventures of the Dodgers, the Cubbies, the Redlegs, or the Tigers. The quixotic fortunes of a local ball club, serving as our alter ego, provide us with lasting early lessons about the ebb and flow of a life in which sobering defeat always comes

hard on the heels of almost any euphoric victory.

Thus while we have carbon copy "football fans" (of both NFL and collegiate variety) and MTV-generation basketball "hero worshippers" loyal to Air Jordan, Magic, Bird, Shaq, or Kobe, baseball's myriad followers come in two dozen or more species. There are Cub fans and Met fans and Yankee rooters and Tiger and Cardinal fanatics. Each inherits a colorful legacy passed down lovingly from generation to generation; each swoons summer after long summer over the ins and outs, ups and downs, pennant pursuits, and endless droughts of the favored hometown team.

1962—FIRST FRANCHISE GAMES (DEBUT GAME, HOME OPENER, FIRST VICTORY)

True ball fans are always gripped by the lure of arcane trivia. And franchise "first" games are one of the richest sources of such cherished, if useless, data. Especially the very first franchise games of an inaugural season, or first games held in a new ballpark. Who collected the first base hit? Who stroked the first-ever homer? Who scored the first-ever run for the home team? Who recorded the first strikeout, balk, or triple? These are the fodder of years of

THE NEW YORK METS ENCYCLOPEDIA

Yankee manager Yogi Berra and Mets skipper Casey Stengel chat amiably before an inaugural spring training exhibition meeting between the new and old New York ball clubs. (AP/Wide World Photos)

future barroom debates. The first scheduled Mets game, of course, never actually happened. The new franchise was rained out of its inaugural match in St. Louis on opening day 1962 in what had to be taken as a foreshadowing of the depressing events to follow throughout the remainder of the team's first lengthy season stuffed with countless disasters. When the debut game of the 1962 NL season was finally played a day late, the actual franchise opener was about what might have been expected. Roger Craig, former Dodgers journeyman and projected Mets staff ace, opened the proceedings for the visitors in the home half of the first when he allowed the first-ever run scored against the newest NL club by balking home a Cardinal runner from third. The final count was 11-4 in the Cardinals' favor, and three Mets hurlers called upon to relieve Craig—Bob Moorhead, Herb Moford, and Clem Labine—all found other employment before the first month of the season had run its course. The first pair of franchise round trippers by another pair of ex-Dodgers—Gil Hodges and Charlie Neal—were the night's only bright spot.

The Mets' home opener two days later also ran true to expectation. It was another loss, but much closer in its final count. Yet it was a loss of the kind that would haunt the team all season long—one booted away by a whisker with the help of a series of infield and outfield defensive blunders. Two late-inning wild pitches by Ray Daviault provided a 4-3 victory for the visiting Pittsburgh Pirates. The loudest crowd response of the afternoon came in the form of raucous booing that greeted lineup introductions, when it was announced that Jim Marshall would man first base in place of an injured Gil Hodges. Only 12,000 turned out to watch the homecoming for National League baseball in New York City, and those who did attend had to endure the most uncooperative type of April baseball weather. There were snow flurries and bitter winds throughout the contest. But if the nasty springtime conditions were inappropriate for baseball, the calendar date for the affair was nonetheless absolutely perfect. League schedule makers had displayed an inspired flair for the ironic by penciling in the Mets' first-ever Polo Grounds game for Friday the 13th.

A first franchise victory, on the other hand, had plenty of tantalizing buildup. It had indeed begun to appear to the hordes of new Mets fans during the first couple of weeks of franchise life

that this hastily assembled collection of big-league pretenders might actually be so bad that they would never actually win a game. By the end of week two, the club had reeled off nine straight failures and were now matched up on the season's second weekend with a hot Pittsburgh Pirates outfit that had themselves burst out of the gate with 10 straight wins. Then on April 23 in Pittsburgh's ancient Forbes Field, the New York bats finally came to life with a 14-hit outburst that was good enough for nine runs. And this time out, there was some pitching and defense to actually support the run production. Promising right-hander Jay Hook (an 18-game loser two years earlier in Cincinnati and now launched on a season that would eventually bring 19 setbacks) lasted the full nine frames of the historic and surprising 9-1 Mets rout.

1963—ROGER CRAIG'S LOSING STREAK

Roger Craig was not a horrible pitcher or even a moderately bad pitcher. In fact, he was a rather good moundsman, even by the most arduous big-league standards. In truth, he was so good that he was able to earn a rare opportunity to hang around in the big time long enough to seize a chance at some memorable feats of record-setting futility. With the Brooklyn Dodgers, Craig had been a most effective role player as part-time starter and rugged bullpen fixture. He twice won in double figures—once in Brooklyn and again in Los Angeles—and also posted an important Game 5 World Series win that launched the Brooklyn team toward its only championship.

But pitching for the "Boys of Summer" in Ebbets Field or the LA Coliseum was a far cry from toiling for an expansion train wreck of a team in the Polo Grounds. The Mets' biggest loser reached his full momentum in the team's second season, not an easy feat, since he had already lost 24 times and paced the league in humiliation during the team's inaugural outing. Craig had lost big in 1962, but he would lose bigger still, once some of the first-year hitting (in the form of Richie Ashburn, Gil Hodges, and a still-productive Frank Thomas) was taken out of the New York lineup. Before the '63 summer progressed far, the Mets' "ace" found himself in the midst of a losing streak that began to draw national attention as it reached record proportions. The string began with a horrible outing

Roger Craig proved the old adage that you have to be a most talented pitcher to lose 20 games in one major league season. (Brace Photo)

Stengel clowns a farewell gesture before the Mets' final game in their temporary Polo Grounds home on September 18, 1963. (AP/Wide World Photos)

frame. Then in the bottom of the final inning, Lady Luck at last turned another cheek. The Mets loaded the bases, the final runner reaching on a walk to Tim Harkness, who had pinch hit for an exhausted and arm-weary Roger Craig. Jim Hickman would now have to deliver if Craig was to gain a decision in one of his ripest chances at victory all summer. Hickman promptly lifted a fly ball that barely nicked the left-field upper-deck overhang for an improbable grand slam. The suddenly lucky hurler raced from the dugout to personally direct each runner around the basepaths, making sure that no sacks were somehow missed. (No precaution was too great when the Mets were on the field!) Craig later commented to surrounding media in the joyous Mets clubhouse that the rare win indeed felt just like any earlier World Series victory with the proud Brooklyn Dodgers.

on May 4, during which the Giants drubbed the Polo Grounders 17-4. From that point on, Craig didn't pitch nearly as ineffectively, but the string of defeats eventually stretched through 17 more games. Craig couldn't win, simply because he couldn't shut down the opposition completely every time out of the box. His own team only averaged a piddling 1.6 runs per outing for the luckless Craig. Eight times he lost to an opposing pitcher's shutout. When the string reached 18, he had finally tied the National League record set by Boston's Cliff Curtis way back in 1910. Craig was also now only one loss shy of the major league mark set by Jack Nabors of the 1916 Philadelphia Athletics.

But this was one standard for epic futility that the Mets would not be destined to collect. Craig changed his uniform to "unlucky" No. 13 for the August 9 encounter with the Chicago Cubs, and the well-chosen symbol of reverse luck may have been his first stroke of good fortune all summer long. The ninth of August was apparently destined to finally be Craig's night, but no Mets victory that year would ever come easily. The weary New York staff ace was handed an early lead and once more struggled gamely to hold onto a 3-3 tie going into the ninth

1964—OPENING OF SHEA STADIUM AND TWO MOST MEMORABLE METS GAMES

Shea Stadium was seemingly enough to make a sadsack New York National League club buried deep in the league basement suddenly appear legitimate. They may have still been hopeless losers on the field, but at least the fledgling Mets now had a state-of-the-art facility in which to entertain fans in the nation's baseball capital. Patrons could now watch their beloved stumblebum Mets in considerable luxury and could boast one of the finest stages for watching big-league games anywhere in the nation. And if there was no other advantage to the new digs, at least now it was the ballpark and not the tenants that might draw the bulk of the media and fan attention. It also didn't hurt Mets fortunes any that the crosstown, powerhouse Yankees were now suddenly finding themselves in a disastrous tailspin of their own. The days of nostalgia in the decrepit Polo Grounds were

148 METS

THE NEW YORK METS ENCYCLOPEDIA

finally over, and the spanking new venue signaled a new direction aimed at hopefully building a pennant contender. The first positive sign of a changing aura around the club was the surge in attendance, with 1.7 million paying customers drawn into the new park, a dramatic increase of nearly 700,000 over the final Polo Grounds season. Over in the Bronx, the pennant-winning Yankees were packing only 1.3 million into the House That Ruth Built. It was the first but not the last time that the turnstiles now officially showed the Mets and not the Yanks to be the city's favored ball club.

It also didn't take long for the new venue and the club that occupied it to witness some unique games. Shea Stadium itself celebrated a noteworthy, if not entirely successful, debut on April 17, 1964, when Willie Stargell's second-inning homer (the first ever at Shea) was the difference in a 4-3 Pittsburgh victory. A near-capacity throng of slightly over 50,000 witnessed the Mets' Tim Harkness register the first base hit and Jack Fisher hurl a called strike on the historic game's first pitch. The first in a series of truly momentous games, however, came on the road at Chicago's Wrigley Field. On May 26, the sadsack Mets inexplicably rose up and routed the more potent Cubs by a shocking 19-1 count. Little-used outfielder Dick Smith fell only a homer short of hitting for the cycle, the Mets chalked up a club-record 23 safeties, and Jack Fisher decided to make the issue indisputable by tossing a four-hitter. The story would circulate throughout New York the next day that when some disbelieving Mets fans heard their team had somehow posted 19 runs, they immediately phoned newspaper sports departments to find out whether the team had actually won. Back at home on May 31, the Mets made sure that the new park also had its first taste of the truly historic. In the nightcap of a Sunday doubleheader, it would take 23 innings for the home club to finally lose 7-6 to the San Francisco Giants. This may have been the most unforgettable single game of early club history; it featured a Mets triple play (initiated in the 14th when Roy McMillan snagged a liner off the bat of Orlando Cepeda) and a marathon relief stint by the Giants' Gaylord Perry, who entered in the 13th and stayed on for 10 innings. Three weeks later, there was another taste of the rarest of moments when Jim Bunning threw a perfect game at the Mets on Father's Day, only the ninth such masterpiece in big-league his-

tory. No matter how bad their team still was, Mets fans didn't lack for considerable entertainment during that inaugural summer of precedent-setting baseball in Shea Stadium.

1965—END OF CASEY'S HALL OF FAME CAREER

Many probably thought that Casey Stengel would eventually die—or maybe simply fade graciously into the history books—while still wearing his always baggy-legged flannel baseball uniform. The thought of a "retired" Casey Stengel almost seemed a classic oxymoron. The Yankees were surely wrong in thinking that their colorful top clown had grown too old for dugout strategy or for keeping a team in the spotlight as front-page fodder. Three Mets seasons of constant diamond entertainment, despite epic-proportion losing, had already established that the game had not yet passed the old master by. As he approached his 75th birthday the Ol' Perfessor seemed to be rolling along strong as ever and still seemed to be sharp as a proverbial brass tack. The ceaseless comedy surrounding the Mets appeared more than anything else to be keeping him forever young. He had been one of the game's most rock-solid fixtures—in Brooklyn, New York, Boston for a spell, and then back in Gotham—for nearly half a century. Only Connie Mack had ever seemed a more timeless or indelible baseball figure.

But then the cruel fates shamelessly intervened in the most unexpected manner conceivable. On the eve of his landmark 75th birthday Casey was felled by a bizarre accident which occurred far away from the ballpark. For an old-timers' celebration at Shea on July 25, the beloved manager had donned his yellowed Brooklyn Dodgers playing uniform, and more birthday festivities were planned for Casey between games of the next day's doubleheader. Stengel retired on Saturday evening to his favorite after-hours haunt at Toots Shor's restaurant for more sessions of private partying with intimates that lasted late into the night. Before the evening was over, Casey somehow slipped and fell in the men's room, an accident to which he at first paid little heed. But after heading home with a companion (Mets comptroller Joseph DeGregorio) who lived only a few miles from Shea (perhaps assuring his chances of making it on time to the Sunday festivities), Casey discovered that his injuries were far more serious: a sharp pain in his hip indicated that he would be hospital-bound and not ballpark-bound in the wee hours of the next morning. It was quickly concluded that Casey was now left in no condition to carry on with his managerial duties. It was Casey himself, not surprisingly, who quietly picked his own immediate successor—trusted coach Wes Westrum, who was hastily named as interim manager. Casey Stengel would live for 10 more years and make numerous public appearances at Shea Stadium and elsewhere around the city. But the New York Mets were never again quite the same lovable clowns or the same tolerated losers after Casey's perhaps overdue but certainly unanticipated 1965 departure.

1967—ARRIVAL OF TOM TERRIFIC

The complex story of Tom Seaver's signing as a top collegiate prospect has been told and retold on numerous occasions. It is recounted several times in the pages (e.g., see Chapters 2 and 3) of this very book. Had young Mr. Seaver's improper signing in February 1966 with the Atlanta Braves been allowed to stand unchallenged, then obviously, the face of National League baseball would have looked quite different throughout the late 1960s and all of the 1970s. Tom Terrific would certainly have ended up as a permanent resident in Cooperstown, no matter which team he pitched for. But if he had not worn the Mets' blue and orange jersey from the start of his career, it is likely that the charming saga of the Miracle Mets would never have occurred, at least not quite so early on.

Seaver's first season in the big time was not as eye-catching as that of some other rookie phenoms. He didn't lead the league in anything outside of top rookie ballots, despite breaking every club record in sight for the six-year-old franchise. Dwight Gooden's debut was certainly better from a numerical standpoint and from every other angle. Gooden's 17-9 mark edges Seaver's 16-13 ledger, and the ERA and strikeout totals of the former easily best those of the latter. Gooden's strikeout total was better than Seaver's by nearly a hundred whiffs (276 to 170). The following year's rookie phenom, Jerry Koosman, also posted victory and ERA numbers better than those of Seaver's debut campaign. But then it has to be noted that the 1967 Mets, who had slipped back into the league cellar, didn't exactly offer much support for the

wet-behind-the-ears star pitcher. Gooden and Koosman both pitched for much better teams. Yet from the first day Seaver arrived in New York with the Mets, one thing was clear. Here was the ball club's entire future hopes wrapped up in one sensational arm and in an athlete who was wise far beyond his years in the craft of pitching. Indeed, never has it been any more crystal clear that a single player held the key to an entire franchise future. And never have such outrageous expectations heaped on the shoulders of an untried rookie been better met in the few short years to follow.

1969—FIRST CHAMPIONSHIP CELEBRATION

Photos of Shea Stadium taken moments after the Game 5 World Series clincher against Baltimore looked strangely like scenes from the aftermath of another landmark event that had transpired in New York State only a few months earlier—the weekend-long August rock 'n' roll lovefest at Woodstock. But for all the chaos that broke out on the field that afternoon, the joyous celebration was still remarkably innocent. There was the obligatory hysterical clubhouse celebration with wild backslapping and champagne baths all around. Fans climbed over the railings and dugouts and did their best to tear up the infield dirt and the outfield turf. It was a city's shared delirium in response to an impossible dream coming true in a single afternoon. Most on the scene could hardly believe what had just transpired before their eyes. It was an eruption of joy not surpassed in New York City since the Times Square celebrations that rang out World War II. But all this would change drastically the next time a championship was celebrated on the same field at the conclusion of an NLCS showdown with Cincinnati four years later.

Before the final out of the 1973 NLCS was recorded at Shea Stadium by Tug McGraw, an ugly grandstand scene had already been brewing for several innings. The Pete Rose and Bud Harrelson affair of two days earlier was still simmering for vengeful New York rooters, and with the Mets comfortably in front 7-2 with three frames remaining, the boisterous crowds were already pushing toward the field. The temporary wall of on-field box seats was knocked down, causing a game delay and evacuation of the official Cincinnati entourage in the seventh; firecrackers were echoing throughout the

Mets Jerry Grote (left) and Rod Gaspar (#17) douse Mayor John Lindsay after the once-dreadful New Yorkers clinch their first pennant on October 7, 1969 with an NLCS victory over Atlanta. (AP/Wide World Photos)

Frank Thomas, the original slugger with that name. (Brace Photo)

Ron Hunt was proud of his propensity for getting beamed.
(Brace Photo)

Roger Craig, sporting "unlucky" uniform #13, warms up for a game with the Chicago Cubs that broke his lengthy losing streak.
(AP/Wide World Photos)

stands. With McGraw's final pitch, the players fled the field and the wild hordes descended, bent on destruction. While Rose raced for safety, his teammates stood on the dugout steps armed with bats. This time around, it was anything but a pure celebration marked by innocent joy; this was an embarrassing excuse for a full-fledged riot. Damage was so severe by the time the mobs were cleared that the field was barely repaired in time for the World Series home opener six days later. Baseball has always been one of our society's most perfect mirrors. The Mets and the nation as a whole had entered a very different epoch by fall 1973, and the NLCS Shea Stadium uprising was ample evidence, if any more were needed, that a great deal of America's innocence had been lost forever.

1972—TRAGIC LOSS OF GIL HODGES

One can debate endlessly about the brightest Mets moment. Many would opt for the final out of the 1969 World Series, when the impossible dream suddenly came true. Others would contend it was the club's birth itself which filled the intolerable National League void in New York City back in 1962, and still others might pick the improbable 1986 championship comeback against the Boston Red Sox spiced by Bill Buckner's lamentable gaffe. But when it comes to the darkest moment of ball club history, there is no debate and certainly no hesitation in choosing. That tragic episode is the one that arrived on the eve of the 1972 season, when beloved fifth-year manager Gil Hodges was suddenly and sadly felled by a fatal heart attack. Even if Hodges had not created a true Mets miracle in the autumn of 1969, he would still have been sorely missed. Few figures in the game have exuded such leadership on the field, inspired such confidence and respect in the clubhouse and on the bench, or generated such love from the grandstand partisans. But given what Hodges had, in fact, done for team fortunes in recent seasons, the sudden loss was all the more devastating to everyone in the New York Mets' family.

The ball club didn't handle the aftermath of the tragic death very well at all. The front office alienated many of Hodges' devoted fans almost overnight when they too hastily announced that Yogi Berra had been signed up as a replacement and that the club was already preparing for business as usual. Perhaps it was a necessary front-office stance to ward off a potential paralysis that might well have gripped the stunned franchise. But what appeared as callousness on the surface didn't sit very well with ball fans all around the city and the country. It all seemed so cold and impersonal when the day after 36,000 mourning fans had attended the wake in Hodges' neighborhood in Brooklyn, the ball club excitedly announced it had just closed a deal to obtain Rusty Staub, Canada's first baseball hero, from the rival Montreal Expos. And once the season unfolded, things went from bad to worse on the field of play. While the club enjoyed one of its fastest-ever starts under Berra, injuries soon wiped out any hopes of a serious pennant revival. Newcomers Staub and Willie Mays made contributions, but Jim Fregosi (obtained in the unpopular trade for Nolan Ryan the previous winter) immediately flopped at third. Berra's first club won the same number of games as the last two editions under Gil Hodges. But that fact was accompanied at year's end by very little celebrating anywhere around the environs of Shea Stadium. The Mets' ball club may have been due for some unraveling under even the best of circumstances in the third season of the seventies. But with the inspiring Gil Hodges still on the job, it likely would not have been quite so painful or somber a scene.

Gil Hodges, the most beloved Met of all. (Brace Photo)

1973—THE INCREDIBLE STRETCH RUN

Even if the competition wasn't quite the Boys of Summer Dodgers, the Mets edition of 1973 was sufficiently reminiscent of Bobby Thomson's rags-to-riches '51 New York Giants. Of course, it has to be admitted that they looked more like a poor man's version of the courageous club managed by Leo Durocher. When the Durocher Giants stared at a 13 1/2-game gap looming between themselves and the front-running Dodgers on August 11, 1951, they certainly didn't have to hang their heads because of the way they had played most of the summer. They were seven games over .500 themselves at the time, and the width of the Brooklyn lead had mostly to do with the Dodgers' torrid 70-35 clip, which had obliterated all competition up to that point of the pennant race. Then, down the stretch, the surprising Giants suddenly grew so hot themselves that everything simply withered in their sight, the front-running Dodgers included. This was not quite the case with the last-to-first Mets team two decades later. It would not be too far off the mark to suggest that the Yogi Berra ball club actually backed into the division top spot on its last-minute dash—which at times was more like a crawl—out of the league basement.

The Mets escaped the East Division cellar for the final time on the final day of August. But when they did, they were suddenly staring at only a very small slope between themselves and the mountain's summit. Writer Roger Angell referred at the time to the dwindling divisional race as being most like "a crowded and dangerous tenement." Heading into September, only the front-running Cardinals even had their heads above water. The other five struggling clubs were all sub-.500 losers. Only 6 1/2 games separated first from worst, and each new day brought another shuffling of positions among the combatants. The Phillies were the first to drop dead along the wayside, but the rest of the contenders and pretenders remained locked in a hopeless death grip. After the Mets won three of four from the moribund Phillies and moved into the fourth slot, there were only 21 games left on the schedule. Berra attempted the final three-week stretch run with a four-man rotation of Seaver, Koosman, Matlack, and George Stone. But Tug McGraw, out in the bullpen, was Berra's real ace in the hole. The effusive lefty appeared in 19 games down the stretch, win-

Veteran Willie Mays receives a champagne shower in the aftermath of the 1969 division-clinching victory in Chicago's Wrigley Field. (AP/Wide World Photos)

ning 12 and saving five. Only twice did he falter under the pressures of relief duty. Delaying his first victory of the season until August 22, McGraw now posted an ERA of 0.88 and rang up 38 strikeouts in 41 tense late-game innings. It was one of the most remarkable season-ending bullpen steaks anywhere on record.

The Mets found a second hero in catcher Jerry Grote, who had returned from the injury list on August 21. Once the steady veteran backstop had regained control of the Mets' staff, New York pitchers seemed to find a newly inspired confidence. They threw eight shutouts once Grote was again calling signals behind the plate. And Grote's bat was also a factor, as he hit .300 and drove in 18 big runs over the final 18-game stretch. Two other saviors down the stretch were Cleon Jones, who reserved 17 of his year's total of 48 RBIs for the final dramatic month, and Wayne Garrett, who also drove in 17 and hit .333 across the final four weeks. Yet, even for all the heroics by McGraw and Grote and a large supporting crew, it looked for all the world like the race to the wire might nonetheless end in an improbable five-way tie. When the Mets, behind Tom Seaver, tromped the Pirates at Shea on September 21 to finally gain first place, the same game also miraculously marked the team's first climb above .500. It was that kind of an unprecedented finish—a delight for casual fans perhaps, but nothing short of a nightmare to baseball purists. The Mets had come to life when it most counted, but neither they nor anyone else exactly burned up the league during the final wild month of sometimes botched baseball. Only one team in the bunch won even half of its games in September, and that was Berra's crew, which managed to take 19 of the final 27 contests. The Mets had not shown much of an ability to win consistently all season long. But they were, fortuitously, the one team that did so when the victory line was finally looming within easy sight.

1975—SEAVER'S THIRD CY YOUNG TROPHY

It is difficult to say which was the best individual season of Tom Seaver's brilliant career. Tom Terrific won three Cy Young honors and led two successful pennant drives in a brief six-year span. For a record nine straight seasons, he struck out more than 200 batters. Twice with the Mets he was the league's top winner, three times the ERA leader, and five times the Na-

tional League strikeout king. His 1.76 ERA of 1970 was one of the stingiest in modern baseball history. And his first Cy Young trophy was the first ever awarded to a pitcher toiling for a miserable last-place ball club.

But his final Cy Young season may well have been Tom Seaver's best outing ever. This seems especially the case when one considers the team around him that season—a third-place also-ran club that barely played at a .500 pace from wire to wire. Without Seaver in the rotation that summer, the Mets were assuredly destined to be a last-place ball club. The big righthander's accomplishments were, in fact, about all the Mets faithful of 1975 had to boast about. His 22-9 record represented the most wins in the senior circuit. His 243 strikeouts were also tops, and his 2.38 ERA trailed only San Diego's Randy Jones and LA's Andy Messersmith. Stretching his string of 200-strikeout years to eight that summer he overtook the longstanding major league record. He also led the New York staff in starts (36), complete games (15), shutouts, and innings pitched. And for toppers, he reached another personal milestone when he passed 2,000 career strikeouts. The only per-

Tom Seaver posted a string of "best-ever" seasons.
(SPI Archives)

Donn Clendenon seemingly turned the 1969 World Series into his own personal stage. (Brace Photo)

sonal failure for Seaver seemed to come in the All-Star Game in Milwaukee's County Stadium, where he surrendered a three-run homer to Carl Yastrzemski and, in the process, became the first Mets pitcher to allow an earned run in the traditional Midsummer Classic. And all this came on top of the fact that Tom Terrific had experienced a dreadful slide to 11-11 only one season earlier. It was one of the best comebacks ever, and also one of the best end-to-end pitching performances ever witnessed from a mound ace wearing a New York Mets uniform.

1976—THE SLUGGING OF DAVE KINGMAN

Dave Kingman would have fit much better on the New York Mets ball clubs of 1963 or 1964 than he did on the ones he toiled for in the mid-seventies and early eighties. Here, after all, was a ballplayer cut from a truly lopsided mold. He was a genuine baseball "character," if not exactly a shining role model, and was always good for more than his fair share of negative press. He often created more headlines in the clubhouse with his abrasive personality than he did on the field of play with his booming fly balls, and once he took the field, his slugging prowess was always considerably muted by the fact that he was a huge defensive liability and owned both a minuscule batting average and mountainous strikeout total. But all that aside, Kingman arrived in Shea Stadium in the bicentennial year custom designed to be one of the biggest gate attractions the franchise would ever boast. The Mets had been showcasing great pitching for the better part of the decade. Tom Seaver was a superlative mound ace and as big a hometown hero as could be found anywhere in baseball. But even a quarter century ago, it was home runs—especially mammoth home runs—rather than shutouts or other displays of mound artistry that guaranteed to put hordes of fans into the grandstands.

When it came to a ticket-selling slugger, Kingman certainly filled the bill. His blasts were usually mammoth and awe inspiring—the kind only Mark McGwire is now providing. And he supplied fans with large numbers of such entertaining missiles—36 in his first New York season and 37 in his second (with 30 by the All-Star break before a torn thumb ligament wiped out much of the second half of his season). It was a huge boost the weak-hitting club needed at the time, coming off its worst season in seven

years. Thus it didn't take King Kong long to start winning over the Gotham fans. In spring training, he stroked one memorable blast off Catfish Hunter that immediately took on the aura of legend. The titanic smash hugged the left-field line and, in Roger Angell's words, "left the park five feet inside the foul pole and three palm trees high." Even Mickey Mantle, who was working the game as an instructional coach for the Yankees, said he never saw a ball hit quite so far. The prodigious blasts continued to come in clusters all summer long, as King Kong banged out a homer every 13.94 visits to the plate. It was a frequency rate good enough to wipe out Frank Thomas's 12-year-old Mets record for single-season homers.

And the onslaught also continued for a second year, even though Kingman played an injury-reduced season in 1977. He again set a club record for slugging percentage, as well as another new homer milestone. One of his mid-season blasts in Wrigley Field reportedly traveled an astonishing 630 feet. It was enough fireworks, in the end, to earn a starting spot on the National League All-Star squad, and in such a lean franchise period, that in itself was quite a significant prize. Yet, if the strapping slugger turned on the fans at Shea Stadium, he just as quickly turned off the media assigned to cover the club. Hot in pursuit of Ruth and Maris, and also threatening Hack Wilson's NL home run record by mid-season, Kingman turned a cold shoulder on press attention to his feats and became increasingly sullen and reclusive in the clubhouse. A third season in New York was only half over before King Kong was requesting another trade. That was not all bad news to disillusioned Mets management. Once Kingman was injured and missed much of the second half of the 1976 campaign, it was clear that the Mets' "home run or nothing" offense was dead in the water with or without him. Kingman's trade to San Diego in mid-June garnered relatively little press attention and spurred few fan protests, coming as it did in the immediate aftermath of the more earthshaking deal only hours earlier which banished Tom Seaver to Cincinnati.

1977—TWO UNFORGETTABLE TRADES

June 15, 1977, brought with it the biggest shakeup in club history. After a handful of seasons of floundering in the middle of the pack, it seemed time for some rather drastic changes.

Dave Kingman inspired slugger-turned-broadcaster Ralph Kiner to marvel, "He can hit them out of any park—including Yellowstone Park!" (Brace Photo)

But when they came, the changes were more drastic than almost any New York fan could possibly have been ready for. Franchise star Tom Seaver had not been getting on well with the Mets' front office for some time. The club also still seemed to be reeling from disappointments surrounding the end of Yogi Berra's tenure and the nosedive following the 1973 pennant. But what seemed to contribute more to the malaise than anything else was the way the front office, under GM Joe McDonald, seemed to flounder in the face of a new era of free agency. There were many areas of the club crying for repair or upgrade—Harrelson was slowing down at shortstop, and young Lee Mazzilli had not shown that he was the answer in center field. The biggest problem was that the great Mets pitching (the team ERA was the league's best in 1976) was constantly being undercut by powderpuff hitting and stone gloves in the infield and outfield. McDonald and his staff seemed to be sitting on their hands and ignoring opportunities to retool the sagging ball club. Fans were also now worried that if a deal were eventually made, the team would again squander some of its top pitching, as it had done in the Nolan Ryan deal—especially with Seaver now apparently unhappy in New York and talking about testing the free-agent waters himself.

However, when the news came that Seaver had been traded, a true pall was cast over the entire franchise. And Tom Terrific's sudden departure was itself only the tip of the iceberg. Seaver had not only been let go—inconceivable in itself—but on the surface, the deal that finally was made had not seemed to bring very much in fair exchange. There was no big-name star headed to New York—a Pete Rose or Reggie Jackson or Mike Schmidt or Dave Parker—to replace baseball's top pitcher. Instead, the Mets had picked up what appeared to be no more than a handful of unheralded prospects, the best of whom was an unrecognized minor league outfielder named Steve Henderson, who supposedly glistened with star potential. But the Mets were not yet done dealing in the aftermath of the blockbuster Seaver trade. The same evening, New York brass traded infielder Mike Phillips to St. Louis for Joel Youngblood and sent another utility player (Roy Staiger) to the minors. And then in a third deal, one that would itself have been a major headline had it not come on the same day as the Seaver trade, another problem child was purged from the roster. Dave Kingman was shipped to San Diego for a pair of unpromising replacements named Bobby Valentine and Paul Siebert. The Mets had axed another player who had been grousing about his contract all spring. But they also eliminated the club's only other legitimate gate attraction in the process.

Never had a team so drastically overhauled its roster in a single day of scatter-shot dealing. And rarely had one created such a public relations nightmare with its faithful fans. Outbursts of protest from ticket holders and the local press were so vitriolic that for a short time, front-office boss Donald Grant had to travel the streets with a personal bodyguard. The remainder of the season, not surprisingly, proved to be a disaster in the wake of such a roster upheaval, with the Mets slumping in the box scores and in the standings. A 17-game deficit at the end of June had increased to 37 under new manager Joe Torre by the time the team settled into the division basement at the end of September. Seaver, meanwhile, enjoyed a banner summer and fall with his new club in Cincinnati, ringing up the league's second-best victory and innings-pitched totals and the top mark for shutouts. Things, of course, only got worse in the standings and at the turnstiles the following year, when Seaver's expected replacement, Pat Zachry, proved largely a bust on the hill, and other young players acquired from Cincinnati, such as Henderson and Doug Flynn, never developed much beyond the journeyman level.

1979—RETIREMENT OF ED KRANEPOOL

Ed Kranepool replaced a gigantic, if short-lived, legend. He did so when in May of 1963 he took over for the ever popular but always inept Marv Throneberry as the New York Mets' new hope at first base. Only a season earlier, Marvelous Marv Throneberry had built a quaint reputation for bungling that capsulized an entire opening Mets season. But what was tolerated as charming by giddy first-year fans wore out its welcome in short order when legitimate expectations of on-field progress soon set in. Early in the second Mets season, Marvelous Marv was demoted to Triple A Buffalo for good, and Kranepool got his initial chance. Ed had been signed up straight out of high school as an 18-year-old bonus baby and saw little first-year action while a permanent bench rider: He got into only three games and rang up a single base hit. Even when he got a shot as a result of Throneberry's permanent banishment, his own status with the ball club was at first largely an up-and-down affair. Kranepool was himself demoted before the end of 1963 in a well-measured attempt to save his career. The youngster had started fast, then slumped with a .190 batting average in mid-July; he also showed distressing signs of becoming a problem child when he sulked in the clubhouse and refused to take batting tips from veteran teammates like Duke Snider. But the temporary demotion back to Buffalo worked its magic, and the big lefty was soon back in the New York lineup, with his major league act showing considerable renovation. Once back upon the scene, he would remain at Shea Stadium for what eventually proved to be the longest and most productive tenure in club history.

By the time he was ready to hang up his spikes, Ed Kranepool had constructed an oversized New York baseball legend all his own. But unlike Throneberry, Kranepool built his own Mets legend at a measured walking pace. His best single season would come down the road in 1971 when he put up career hitting numbers (.280 BA and 14 homers) and was the league's best defensive first sacker. There were other

Ed Kranepool replaced a short-lived legend and then built a long-lived legend of his own. (Brace Photo)

years when he paced the club in various categories, though the numbers were never very grand. The most remarkable feature of his career was his longevity. By the time he was done at the end of a second decade, he had walked away with a bigger piece of the Mets' record book than anyone before or since. Many small contributions had added up to a place atop numerous team career categories. Kranepool had earned his reputation step-by-step as "Steady Eddie" in the New York lineup. In fact, no Met, Yankee, Dodger, or Giant was ever any steadier for quite so long a haul.

1981—THE RETURN OF KINGMAN

Dave Kingman made two noteworthy arrivals in New York. The first provided the Mets with their first legitimate power hitter since the demise of Frank Thomas at the end of the ball club's first outing a dozen seasons earlier. Dave Kingman was purchased from the San Francisco Giants during spring training on the eve of the 1975 season for $150,000 cash with the hope that he would resolve the team's long-standing home run production problems. And the lanky right-handed swinger didn't disappoint in immediately filling at least some of those expectations. He improved on his earlier performances, banged over 30 homers (36) for the first time, and wiped out Thomas's earlier team record. A season later, he broke the record again and lost the league home run crown to Mike Schmidt by the margin of a single dinger, despite missing 39 games. But after two years of pounding the baseball with Ruthian effort, the one-dimensional slugger had quickly worn out his welcome on a ball club bent on an image overhaul. In the middle of year three, Kingman was on his way back out of town, dumped from the Mets' roster the same fateful day as Tom Seaver.

The second tour of duty with the Mets was nearly as productive for the oversized free-swinging banger with the notoriously bad attitude. But that second tour also exposed the nature of Kingman's limited value in any lineup bent on winning many ball games. Kingman had been picked up from the Cubs in February 1981 (for Steve Henderson and cash) at a time when Mets fortunes had dipped to an all-time post-sixties low. And there was some irony attached to his reacquisition. Kingman had, four years earlier, been dealt away on the same day Seaver

Winning Traditions . . .

the *New York Mets* and
the United States
Postal Service

 **UNITED STATES POSTAL SERVICE.**

Continuing the winning tradition with United States Postal Service's Priority Mail

WHAT IF NEW YORK HAD A BRIDGE
THAT WENT ALL AROUND THE WORLD?

New York is home to hundreds of bridges. Including one that can take you just about

anywhere. It's the bridge called American Airlines®. And over 220* times every business day it

stretches from the New York area to Los Angeles, Chicago, London and hundreds of other

cities around the world. Call your Travel Agent or American at 1-800-433-7300. Or book online

at **www.aa.com** today. Getting where you want

to go is easy. As long as you take the right bridge.

American Airlines
New York's Bridge To The World℠

member of oneworld

Tom Seaver
Hall of Fame Pitcher and
Chase Middle Market
Spokesperson

No matter how good you are... you need to know the team is behind you.

IN BASEBALL, BUSINESS AND BANKING, IT TAKES A TEAM TO REACH THE TOP.

More growing companies rely on Chase, the leading bank for business

Your Chase Relationship Manager heads a team of professionals dedicated exclusively to growing companies

As your guide and advocate, your Relationship Manager gives you access to credit, cash management, investments, leasing, merger and acquisition advice and financing, derivatives, international – a full range of products and services

We're the leading bank for business because, like you, we play hard. We play to win. And we love the game. Get the best team in banking for your business.

 CHASE

THE RIGHT RELATIONSHIP IS EVERYTHING.®

www.chase.com

©1999 The Chase Manhattan Corporation.

Panoramic photo of SHEA STADIUM, New York, photographed on Opening Day 1987, the day the 1986 World Champion flag was raised. The photo was taken with a rotating, Cirkut panoramic camera and shows 210 degrees angle of view.

had been traded to Cincinnati in exchange for promising outfielder Steve Henderson and a flock of lesser prospects. Now, as the revolving door swung again, it was Henderson who was sent out of town as the price for reacquiring Kingman. King Kong had recently reached a home run peak in Chicago, blasting a league-best 48 in 1979, but had fallen well off the pace in an injury-wrecked 1980 season. Back in New York, Kingman once more rebounded in the power department. After a strike-shortened 1981 campaign kept his numbers down, he again matched his Mets' record of 37 dingers in 1982. But it all meant little in terms of any impact on team fortunes, with the club finishing fifth and then sixth twice during his second tenure. By 1983, the unpredictable slugger had again slumped badly, with all-time lows in homers (13), RBIs (29), and runs scored (25). He was soon dealt to Oakland, where he hit more than 30 homers in each of his final three seasons and set a still-standing record for the most round trippers ever (35) in a final season of big-league play (1986).

1986—BILL BUCKNER'S OVERSIZED BOOT

Bill Buckner is a modern version of Fred Merkle. Merkle, in the end, could boast a lengthy and respectable career with the New York Giants, but that career was never enough to erase the indelible legacy that was left by a single infamous rookie-season blunder. Merkle thus played forever in the shadow of a mistake that was often distorted into something that it never actually was at the time. (In the famed play in which he left the field without touching second on a teammate's apparent game-winning base hit, Merkle was only following standard practice of his era; and Merkle's out was not, as reported, the single "boneheaded" maneuver that lost a pennant for the Giants, since New York found other ways to let the season slip away in the three September weeks after the notorious gaffe.) Buckner's fate, of course, was reversed. One excusable error at the end of a solid big-league career is now destined to haunt Bill Buckner's legacy forever in baseball's history books.

The actual fatal damage to the Boston championship cause was done both before and after Buckner's fateful boot in the 10th inning of World Series Game 6. Here again, Bill Buckner's fate was most similar to Merkle's.

Boston's Bill Buckner is a portrait of dejection moments after committing one of the most infamous and costly errors in World Series history. (AP/Wide World Photos)

Fred Merkle did not singlehandedly lose a pennant for the Giants. His team had several golden opportunities to rebound from adversity, including a makeup game with the rival Cubs; and the failure of the Giants to remain in first place was a true team effort spread across the season's final stretch run. By the same token, Buckner did not singlehandedly lose a World Series, either, no matter how enticing such simplistic analysis may seem. The Red Sox had already given away a two-run extra-inning lead on the very pitch before the ball that was hit straight to Buckner. (Had Billy Buck made the easy play, as expected, the game would have still been tied and headed to the 11th.) Equal blame falls on manager John McNamara for the Boston disasters at Shea Stadium. It was the manager who had brought on Bob Stanley in relief and who had also opted to leave a gimpy Bill Buckner in the defensive lineup with the season and the Series squarely on the line. And it was Stanley who carelessly and improbably wild-pitched in the crucial run that had kept New York hopes alive. And it is also true that the snakebitten Red Sox had blown an earlier, seemingly insurmountable Series advantage after winning the opening two games at Shea Stadium. It also must be remembered that the 1986 Red Sox, like the 1908 Giants, had their opportunities for redemption after the fateful play that first sent them reeling. Boston would lead again in Game 7 and yet once more could not keep the Mets at bay. Bill Buckner had plenty of help in the Red Sox self-destruction scenario. And yet such is the nature of collective memory that a single image of that elusive ball squirting between Buckner's legs is destined to haunt Boston fans until the end of time.

1998—ARRIVAL OF MIKE PIAZZA

Slugging catcher Mike Piazza entered Shea Stadium with as much hoopla as any player in team history. Piazza's New York arrival on May 23, 1998, marked the end of a whirlwind month for the highly sought-after superstar. In a matter of weeks, the former five-time Dodger All-Star had fallen from his perch as a golden boy in Los Angeles, then been peddled off to one of the league's most desolate outposts—the rebuilding Florida Marlins—then been resurrected as a franchise hope by one of the circuit's most popular emerging contenders. Perhaps Mike Piazza had now found a home where he could concentrate on winning ball games and not on discussing his salary demands in a public forum. Yet for the remainder of his first New York summer, instability would continue to shadow one of baseball's biggest celebrities. Inspired by his arrival, the ball club surged into a wild-card race but nonetheless collapsed in the season's final days, blowing a golden playoff opportunity. Piazza, who was in the league's top 10, as usual, in both batting and slugging, nonetheless posted only 76 RBIs as a Met and was claimed by more curmudgeonly fans to have disappointed by not coming up quite big enough for the stretch run. Often the curse of such runaway expectations descends on even the most consistently productive diamond heroes.

So far, Mike Piazza has paid big dividends for the Mets. En route to becoming the only big leaguer to hit over .300 with 100 RBIs in each of the previous four seasons, Piazza's was the loudest bat in a slugging 1999 lineup that did succeed, finally, in lifting the New Yorkers into a long-absent playoff slot. His presence had con-

Mike Piazza arrived at Shea Stadium with more fanfare than anyone since Willie Mays. (Brace Photo)

tributed to the team's staying in the hunt throughout his first partial season in '98. With Piazza in the lineup for a full year in '99, the Mets unleashed one of the game's toughest batting orders. Piazza was at the heart of a New York offensive explosion in 1999 that produced three 100-RBI men and, more important, also produced 97 victories and a seat in the National League Championship Series.

Piazza's 2000 season again produced impressive statistical numbers, leading the Mets to the NL wild-card berth for a second consecutive season. His popularity spread well beyond the boundaries of New York City as he gathered a National League best 2,780,452 votes for the All-Star Game in Atlanta. Unfortunately, Big Mike wasn't able to participate due to his recovery from a Roger Clemens beaning on July 8. Piazza enjoyed several streaks during the 2000 campaign, including a 21-game hitting skein from June 7 through July 3 and at least one RBI in 15 straight contests from June 14 to July 2. For the year, he finished tied for 10th in the NL with his .324 batting average (including a league-best .377 average in road games), 10th with 38 home runs, 11th with 113 RBIs, and ninth with a .614 slugging percentage.

CHAPTER 5
A Dozen of the Mets'
Most Memorable Seasons

One huge loss caused by the modern baseball format featuring divisional play and multiple playoff qualifiers is that it has shifted focus away from the traditional notion of a season-long pennant race. For the first three-quarters of modern-era play, the baseball season was a true marathon haul across the slow-paced dog days of summer and into the ominous, life-squelching onset of early autumn—a single-winner chase that would leave only one league champion standing and all other clubs fallen by the wayside as moribund also-rans. Fans didn't seem to mind in the least when their own hometown favorite had already fallen hopelessly out of contention by the time school closed for the summer or Fourth of July celebrations were the bill of fare. This was simply the nature of an ordered baseball universe. Each morning, Cubs or Red Sox or Phillies or Tigers fans would peruse the newspaper box scores and league standings with breakfast coffee to see how much further the local favorites might have slipped behind the league-leading Yankees, Dodgers, or Cardinals. The season unfolded slowly, and the season was, after all, the thing. We marked our lives with the daily rituals of afternoon radio baseball and the heart-tugging ups and downs of the hometown nine. World Series play was but a brief ritual of closure—usually staged, it seemed, in New York and apparently for the benefit of Yankees, Giants, and Dodgers boosters—and not itself a second season of grinding marathon proportions.

That distant baseball universe has now been lost forever. Modern fans feed instead on a fragmented league in which numerous division races with small clusters of teams are designed to give a piece of the postseason pie to as many big-market cities as possible. It is a spectacle designed, in the end, to provide an elaborate, monthlong televised spectacle of postseason combat that has seemingly made much of the regular season warfare far less vital, if not entirely irrelevant. And yet the season—for all the tinkering with tradition—is still a recognized cornerstone of the baseball pageant. Baseball's championship campaign is much longer than those of other sports—in psychological dimension, if not by calendar count—and its ebbs and flows are much more carefully observed and noted than are the preliminaries to playoff action presented by the rival professional leagues in hockey, football, or basketball. In baseball, the season is still the organizing principle, even if that season no longer looks much like the one we once cherished. And if perhaps to some lesser extent in this hurried day and age at century's end, our baseball lives are still organized around its ancient, timeless rhythms. Basketball, hockey, and football still claim "second seasons," in which only a small handful of the year's combatants have departed. Baseball has only a true season and a postseason, and by the time the latter rolls around, most of the league's cities have already closed down operations, with hopes focused only toward a new opening day and a new springtime season of renewed possibilities looming on the distant horizon.

1962
A Year of Miraculous Firsts

The New York Mets ball club that trotted out onto the field to open the first National League expansion season of 1962 has been as

Bobby Thompson of the New York Giants hits his famous home run in the Polo Grounds against the Brooklyn Dodgers in the playoff game Oct. 3, 1951. Ralph Branca is the Dodger pitcher delivering his famous home run ball. (AP/Wide World Photos)

celebrated in press accounts and as rehashed in collective memory as any loser in American sports history. That so many books have been printed and so much ink expended on one of baseball's worst-ever teams might, at first glance, appear something of a paradox, despite widespread tolerance and even shameless glorification of heroic defeat throughout the baseball culture. (Professional baseball historians are so enamored of magnificent losers that the game's lore has now transformed the biggest decade-long winners of National League history into the snakebitten and tragedy-tinged Boys of Summer, simply because the '50s-era Dodgers suffered regular World Series defeats at the hands of the Dynasty Yankees.) Yet it doesn't take much in the way of close inspection to discover the true literary appeal of this original gang of big-league pretenders. The original expansion New York Mets were a fun team to watch—pure and simple—and they remain as colorful a collection of rascals and rogues as ever compiled in a single big-league clubhouse. They were also the object of one of modern baseball's greatest love stories. And they certainly didn't lack for stature when it came to a lasting impact on the baseball record book.

Foremost, this was a team of genuinely intriguing paradoxes. For starters, the Mets were led by one of baseball's most successful managers, a guaranteed Hall of Famer who had won pennants on the local scene for most of the past two decades at a rate unmatched anywhere in baseball's first century. And yet, once he cast his lot with the roster-thin Mets, loquacious Casey Stengel couldn't win his way out of a paper bag. Casey took the drastic switch in fortunes in full stride and even managed to convert daily disaster on the field into an ongoing morality play of the most entertaining sort. And his ballplaying charges were an entire lineup of such paradoxes. One top pitcher, Jay Hook, owned a university engineering degree and could elaborate for hours on the science of the curveball, even if he couldn't toss one very effectively against the opposition. There was, briefly, a most popular first baseman on the ball club who looked just like Mickey Mantle but often played more like an oversized Little League reject. There was a roster of floppy-armed catchers who couldn't catch, light-hitting infielders who couldn't field, and promising pitchers who couldn't win with only the mea-

ger offensive and defensive support they received nightly. The team regularly made a science out of either building promising leads and then finding countless ways to give them back, or falling hopelessly behind early, before always rallying, only to fall tantalizingly short of victory.

The club lost its maiden opener, which wasn't surprising, but then lost another eight straight, which was in a sport where even the worst teams manage victory in every third or fourth outing. The first-ever Mets game fell victim to a rainout, and when play did commence a day late, the very first opposition run was scored ignominiously when starter Roger Craig balked in the very first inning with a St. Louis runner on third. These events set the tone for an entire season of mishap and misadventure. Casey remarked more than once during the season's opening stretch that the team's initial losing was simply a case of bad timing, noting that a long losing streak in mid-year might go unnoticed, but one at the outset raised the possibility of losing all 162 games. Soon enough, there were also long losing streaks in the middle of the year and at the end of the year, and while all 162 games did not result in defeats, more of them did end that way than with any other big-league ball club before or since.

The inaugural Mets team set other memorable milestones for monstrous losing. The pitching staff gave up the most homers and made the most wild pitches on record. The staff's two 20-game losers were the first such pair since the sadsack Philadelphia Phillies outfit of 1936 had produced a similar feat. The club was eliminated from the pennant race on August 7, the earliest this had ever been accomplished. In winning 40 games, the club amazed its manager, who observed that he wasn't sure how his Amazin's won that many, since they regularly showed him ways to lose he didn't know even existed. There was another helpless expansion club in the league that same summer, but the Houston Colt .45s were 24 games better than the Mets and even beat out the long-toothed and tradition-draped Chicago Cubs for ninth place. It was about as embarrassing and forgettable a season as any ball club could ever experience. And yet for some inexplicable reason, no one has ever wanted to forget even the most horrific detail.

1964
Shea Stadium Debut

Today it seems as though new state-of-the-art ballparks are being opened somewhere every few months. Eight big-league clubs have changed ballparks in the past few years, and three new parks were unveiled in the opening week of the current season, with several more about to follow in the next two campaigns. With expansion teams unveiled in Colorado, Miami, St. Petersburg, and Phoenix, the number of ballpark openings in the past decade has stretched to more than ten. Back in 1964, however, the baseball world was still characterized by remarkable stability. A new ballpark opening was a rare event indeed, even at the outset of the modern expansion era. The fledgling Mets, Expos, Angels, Colt .45s (Astros), and Minnesota Twins all first played in renovated minor league ball yards or existing dilapidated big-league parks. When Shea Stadium opened its doors for action on April 17, 1964, it was only the fourth new big-league playing site of the previous half-dozen seasons. The new Flushing ballpark was indeed something truly special and something truly novel.

Marv Throneberry actually played more games in a Yankee uniform than he did with the Mets. (Brace Photo)

Shea Stadium's opening carried an added specialness since it coincided with the much-celebrated World's Fair taking place in Flushing Meadows that very spring. The history of the park's construction was itself a most interesting saga. When National League owners met in Chicago in 1960 to discuss league expansion, which seemingly had been forced by a Branch Rickey and William Shea plot to launch a third major league, the group made it known that New York might not be a favorable option without the promise of a new stadium to house the new Gotham ball club. In the face of these demands, Shea had extracted an 11th-hour pledge from Mayor Robert Wagner that a new park was in the offing. Ground was broken for the new playing site on October 28, 1961, only days after the big-league expansion draft had provided the new Mets team with its first roster of cast-offs and has-beens. The circular stadium was located on Grand Central Parkway adjacent to the site of the 1939-40 World's Fair, which was also now under construction, to house a new World's Fair scheduled for 1964-65. Originally, the facility was referred to only as Flushing Meadows Park, but by the time the first pitch was thrown in April 1964, the 55,300-seat five-tier structure had been appropriately renamed William A. Shea Municipal Stadium to honor the man who had played such a key role in returning National League baseball to its proper home in New York City.

When it opened for the 1964 season, the new $28.5 million ball yard in Queens boasted a number of architectural firsts when it came to the design of major league stadiums. This was the first sports stadium of such dimensions to provide an extensive escalator system designed to move patrons to seating on all levels; it was also the first that could be converted rapidly from a baseball configuration to a football gridiron by moving several motor-operated grandstands on underground rail tracks. Also for the first time, this ball park design featured all seats facing toward the center of the field, without a single column supporting upper-deck structures that would obstruct lower-level spectators' views.

Opening day on April 17 turned out to be a memorable occasion. Huge traffic snarls on the surrounding beltway and in the stadium parking lots delayed the arrival of many frustrated fans and left others parking their vehicles wherever they could find a roadside spot to abandon them. The game itself was another lost opener, this time at the hands of the Pittsburgh Pirates, 4-3. But the game, witnessed by a near-capacity throng of 48,736, was filled with memorable events. Pregame ceremonies featured such past greats as Bill Terry, Zack Wheat, Frankie Frisch, Red Faber, Luke Appling, and Burleigh Grimes. In the second inning, Pittsburgh's Willie Stargell belted the park's first home run, only the 12th of his young career. And because of an ongoing dispute between telephone and electrical workers, press facilities had not yet been completed, and game reports had to be transported by foot to the nearby World's Fair press center for electronic dispatching.

The remainder of the 1964 season was business as usual for a ball club that still had not escaped its expansion-era blues. Attendance was up from 1,080,108 for the final Polo Grounds season to 1,732,597 in the new park, but the victory count increased by only two games, and the team was a basement dweller for the third year running. There was some early-October pennant-race excitement for Mets fans to savor, even if it was of a rather second-hand nature. Casey Stengel's boys would be thrust into an unlikely spoiler's role on the season's final weekend in St. Louis. Winning the first pair of the season-ending series against the Cardinals, the Mets were suddenly a factor in the closest pennant race in NL history. A final Mets win on October 4 would have produced a three-way pennant tie between St. Louis, Philadelphia, and Cincinnati. When the New Yorkers dropped the game 11-5, the Cardinals clinched the pennant, but only after calling on ace Bob Gibson for four innings of emergency relief work. It was the first time a Mets ball club had ever lost a game that truly meant something, and also the first time that the Stengel bunch had ever earned so much genuine respect from the opposition.

1968
Gil Hodges and "The Year of the Pitcher"

The penultimate season of the tumultuous sixties was a most memorable campaign by almost any standard. For starters, it would be the last year of big-league baseball played in the two-league pennant-race format, as fans had always known it for nearly an entire century. It was also a year of exceptional pitching that almost seemed to hark back to the long-lost

dead-ball era. Earned run averages sank to microscopic levels in both leagues, with Bob Gibson pacing the senior circuit with a remarkable 1.12 and Cuban Luis Tiant nearly as effective in the junior circuit at 1.60. These were not one-man shows by any stretch: Five AL hurlers finished under the magical 2.00 standard, and unheralded Bobby Bolin of the Giants was runner-up to Gibson with a 1.99 ERA that cut in half the numbers he registered both a season earlier (4.88 in 1967) and a season later (4.44 in 1969). Don Drysdale of the Dodgers set a major league mark with 58.2 consecutive shutout innings, and Gibson nearly duplicated the feat with a string of his own that ran to 47.2 frames. Juan Marichal posted 26 wins (26-9) in the National League, while in the AL, Detroit's Denny McLain was the first 30-game winner (31–6) since Dizzy Dean 34 summers before and also the last of the entire century. And in New York, it was a year remembered for the return of Gil Hodges and for the first signs of true life from the beloved hometown Mets.

The nature of the upcoming season was perhaps already being foreshadowed when the Mets and Astros hooked up in the new Astrodome on the evening of April 15 for the longest night game in NL history. Second-year sensation Tom Seaver pitched 10 innings of scoreless, two-hit baseball, but benefited not the least from the silent bats emerging from his own dugout. Seaver was long gone by the time the Astros finally eked out an unearned tally in the 24th frame when an unmanicured infield led to a bad-hop grounder—a potential inning-ending double-play ball that shot through the legs of shortstop Al Weis was scored as an error and finally produced the game's lone marker. The two teams together managed a scant 11 hits, and the marathon affair also went on record as both the longest National League game ever played to completion and the longest scoreless game (the first 23 innings). No previous big-league contest had ever reached as many as 20 innings without a single run being scored. More significant perhaps, the exhausting encounter was the earliest sign that the season that was about to unfold was one in which pitchers in both leagues would maintain almost total dominance over suddenly impotent rival batters.

Gil Hodges had not yet turned the Mets into full-blown winners by the end of his first season at the helm. But he had made far more progress than any of his predecessors. The team

climbed to the impressive total of 73 victories, won its first home opener, climbed out of the basement for the second time in club history, and finished closer to the top spot (24 games out) than ever before. By Mets standards, this was true progress and something to feel giddy about. And in this "year of the pitcher," the Mets' own young mound corps had already become the talk of the entire baseball world. Seaver (16-12, 2.20 ERA) and rookie sensation Jerry Koosman (19-12, 2.08 ERA) anchored a rotation (also including Don Cardwell, Dick Selma, and Nolan Ryan) that trailed only the pennant-winning Cardinals (featuring Gibson) in shutouts (25) and also stood fourth in ERA. Seaver became the first Met to strike out 200 (205), and youngster Ryan rang up 133 Ks in only 134 innings. The Mets' sensational Kiddie Korps now had to play second fiddle to no one, and, at last, there was now legitimate reason for hope among the Shea Stadium faithful.

1969
Year of "The Miracle"

Everyone knew the previously hopeless Mets would be much improved in Gil Hodges's second year at the helm. And everyone from big-league insider to casual fan also knew that normal pennant races might take on a most unpredictable look under the new divisional format that was now being launched in the wake of further big-league expansion. But no one could have fully imagined just how much better the New York Mets would actually be in the last summer of the sixties, or how bizarrely the first experimental season of playoff baseball would ultimately play itself out.

The Mets' "miracle" season was played against the backdrop of a nation experiencing great upheaval and unprecedented transition. The war was still raging in Vietnam, and the Pentagon would announce in April that casualties had surpassed those of the Korean War. The riot at the Democratic National Convention in Chicago the previous August was still on people's minds. In midsummer, Apollo XI astronaut Neil Armstrong became the first man to set foot on the moon, as the nation's space program reached its ultimate hour of success. The following month, 500,000 gathered at Woodstock for the decade's most famous love-in. And a decade of war protests and civil rights demonstrations was finally grinding to its cha-

otic conclusion. It was fitting that the country should have the same kind of baseball season—one marked by a first-ever team in Canada, a strange new alignment of league opponents, the first-ever rainout of the All-Star Game, the arrival of Bowie Kuhn as commissioner, and a string of record performances, topped by Steve Carlton of the Cardinals, who struck out a record 19 New York Mets in a game he somehow managed to lose. And by summer's end in the nation's largest city, the same upstart Mets—a 100–1 pennant underdog—had united millions of miracle-starved fans with one of the most exciting sports stories in decades.

The Mets didn't emerge as a serious pennant challenger until much of the chaotic season had already run its course. Although there were early signs of a strengthened pitching staff in New York with Gary Gentry now joining earlier rookie phenoms Seaver and Koosman, the first indications of legitimacy came only with a club-record 11-game win streak in early June, followed by a key trade with Montreal for slugging first baseman Donn Clendenon. Yet despite a pair of successful showdown series in mid-July with the division-leading Chicago Cubs—which included a near-perfect game by Tom Seaver—the suddenly potent Mets were still trailing Chicago by seven games at the end of July and by five at the end of August. It was another early September face-off with the slumping Cubs at Shea that first alerted the baseball world to the increasing possibility that an upset of major proportions was looming on the baseball horizon. Pennant fever began to sweep the streets of New York as Durocher's embattled Cubbies showed their first signs of beginning to crack. A turning point came in the opener of the two-game showdown when Koosman not only struck out 13 in a close Mets win, but also decked Ron Santo in retaliation for an earlier beanball aimed at New York star Tommie Agee. A doubleheader sweep of the Expos two days later put the Mets in first place to stay. And 22 wins in the season's final 27 games salted away the biggest miracle finish since Durocher's own Giants caught Brooklyn at the wire two decades earlier.

The real story of the Mets' postseason run was, in the end, the story of some remarkable and unlikely playoff heroes. The first was Donn Clendenon, who had been snatched from the Expos in Montreal to platoon with Kranepool at first and add power to a pitching-rich but lum-

Tom "Terrific" Seaver celebrates victory number 25 in Philadelphia late in the 1969 championship season. (AP/Wide World Photos)

The 1969 New York Mets
Where They Are Now

Position	Residence	What They Are Doing Now
Pitchers		
Don Cardwell	Greensboro, North Carolina	Auto sales manager
Jack DiLauro	Malvern, Ohio	Sporting goods sales representative
Gary Gentry	Phoenix, Arizona	Troubleshooter for Frito-Lay food company
Cal Koonce	Deceased	
Jerry Koosman	Fort Myers, Florida	Markets his own ice-cream machine
Tug McGraw	Philadelphia, Pennsylvania	Sports and music promoter
Nolan Ryan	Alvin, Texas	Banker, rancher, minor league club owner
Tom Seaver	Northern California	Mets television announcer
Ron Taylor	Toronto, Canada	Blue Jays team physician
Catchers		
Duffy Dyer	Phoenix, Arizona	Minor league catching instructor
Jerry Grote	San Antonio, Texas	Owns a premium pen and pencil company
J.C. Martin	Greensboro, Texas	Retired
Infielders		
Ken Boswell	Austin, Texas	Antique auto sales and restoration
Ed Charles	New York, New York	Juvenile corrections counselor
Donn Clendenon	Sioux Falls, South Dakota	Lawyer
Wayne Garrett	Sarasota, Florida	Golf course manager
Bud Harrelson	Hauppauge, New York	Minor league club owner
Ed Kranepool	Old Westbury, New York	Retail display business
Bobby Pfeil	San Francisco, California	Real estate developer
Al Weis	Chicago, Illinois	Retired
Outfielders		
Tommie Agee	New York, New York	Real estate title search executive
Rod Gaspar	Orange County, California	Insurance broker
Cleon Jones	Mobile, Alabama	Parks and recreation
Art Shamsky	New York, New York	Entrepreneur
Ron Swoboda	New Orleans, Louisiana	Writer and broadcaster
Coaches		
Yogi Berra	Montclair, New Jersey	Corporate spokesperson
Joe Pignatano	New York, New York	Retired
Rube Walker	Deceased	
Eddie Yost	Wellesley, Massachusetts	Retired
Manager		
Gil Hodges	Deceased	

ber with a clutch hitting performance that was highlighted by a remarkable monthlong total of 26 RBIs and a pair of two-run homers that overcame Steve Carlton's record 19-strikeout performance in St. Louis. Swoboda, like Clendenon, also saved some of his year-end heroics for when they most counted—during World Series play. Swoboda endeared himself forever to the New York baseball scene with a memorable diving ninth-inning catch of a blast by Brooks Robinson, which saved an eventual extra-inning Game 4 Series victory. And a few other unsung and unlikely man-of-the-hour candidates also got into the act. Al Weis was another unheralded journeyman who played big in the limelight of the Fall Classic with a crucial game-tying homer in the deciding contest and a .455 Series batting average, which was an astounding .240 points above his more normal yearlong mark. Nolan Ryan never truly caught fire in New York but he did grab national attention for the first time ever with a seven-inning, seven-strikeout relief performance in the final NLCS game versus Atlanta. It has been said

ber-lean Mets attack. Clendenon did not disappoint, slugging a dozen homers down the stretch, some of them of the clutch variety. Two of Clendenon's homers came in the game that clinched the division title. But his biggest blast was the World Series Game 5 shot, which put New York back in the contest and would prove to be the championship decider. For his efforts in the Fall Classic, which included a .357 batting average, the previously unheralded Clendenon would walk off with World Series MVP honors. Another surprise star was Ron Swoboda, who burned up the league in Septem-

that this was a Mets team carried by a few great pitchers, with the rest of the lineup simply going along for the ride. But in the year's most crucial games, the entire New York roster seemed to get fully into the act.

1973
"The Miracle" Revisited

The Mets had made a truly stunning turnaround back in 1969, when they charged from their accustomed lowly position as baseball's laughingstock to overnight glory as a world

champion and the toast of the entire baseball universe. In fact, no team in recent memory had captured the entire nation's fancy quite the way the Amazin' Mets had done at the very moment of one of America's most riotous periods. The Mets were indeed far more than a mere sports-page headline item or insignificant leisure-time baseball success story. They were truly something of a feel-good cause that seemingly brought an entire dispirited nation together for a much-needed respite from the rigors of unpopular overseas warfare and rampant civil unrest on the home front. And in baseball terms alone, the Mets' 1969 resurgence was a titanic reversal of fortune that many immediately compared to the adventures of the 1914 "Miracle" Boston Braves and 1951 Bobby Thomson-led New York Giants. And yet the turnaround authored by the second Mets pennant winner only a handful of years later was, in reality, far more akin to those other two one-season reversals of 1914 and 1951. The 1973 Mets, for their own part, unleashed one of the most torrid late-season rallies on record, even though their own last-to-first accomplishment was now somewhat muted by a watered-down regular season and postseason chase that had resulted from the new format of divisional, rather than league, pennant races.

The untold story of the 1973 National League divisional pennant chase was, of course, the rather unexceptional nature of the several teams involved. The '73 Mets didn't overhaul quality ball clubs as the 1914 Braves and 1951 Giants had done by climbing past the John McGraw Polo Grounders or the Boys of Summer Brooklyn Dodgers. Instead, they played merely well enough to survive in a circuit crammed with other non-survivors. But there were reasons enough why the 1973 Mets played throughout much of the year just like the bunch of also-rans who surrounded them. The main culprit was the ongoing string of injury misfortunes that had plagued the club for two full seasons. The 1972 campaign had already seen its share of untimely visits to the disabled list. That year, which started out with the club reeling from the sudden death of beloved manager Gil Hodges, witnessed the team's fastest start in history with an early 11-game winning streak and a lofty 30-11 mark on June 1. The injury parade that followed knocked out regulars Staub, Jones, and Agee, plus pinch-hitting specialist Jim Beauchamp and role players Bud Harrelson

and Jim Fregosi over the summer's brief course and thus also knocked the club straight out of contention. The first half of 1973 was even more of a train wreck. Slugger John Milner was the first to fall, suffering a pulled hamstring before the end of April. Southpaw Jon Matlack suffered a concussion when hit by a line drive in early May; a pitched ball once more put Rusty Staub out of commission three days later. Willie Mays (sore shoulder) and backup catcher Jerry May (sprained wrist and pulled hamstring) also fell victim before June commenced. May had been acquired from Kansas City to replace an already-sidelined Jerry Grote, but lasted only a couple of weeks in the lineup. Bud Harrelson and Cleon Jones—along with rookie outfielder George Theodore—were other key players eventually sent to the sidelines by freak bounces and bad breaks. Eight Mets who visited the DL during the fate-marred stretch would eventually miss a total of 183 games. With the injuries mounting almost daily, the Mets slid in the standings throughout the summer, and a mediocre division composed of lackluster opponents was all that kept them from tumbling hopelessly off the pace. Only when the walking wounded began to heal during the final month of the season did the New Yorkers come back to life. Their lineup restored, Berra's forces almost immediately walked off with the division flag as the only team in the East capable of playing above .500 throughout September. Their delayed charge brought them from last to first in a mere three-week span, as they won 29 of the season's final 43 games.

But if the regular-season team that manager Berra had barely kept on a winning track was by most measures mediocre and injury-racked, the regrouped outfit that showed up in Mets flannels for postseason NLCS and World Series competition seemed to have undergone a rather stark transformation. The rejuvenated Mets were first able to brush aside one of the most talent-laden ball clubs of the entire decade, and they did so in most convincing fashion. The powerhouse Cincinnati lineup of Bench, Rose, Griffey, Pérez, Morgan, and company was only two seasons away from its own leap to the top as the vaunted Big Red Machine world champions. The Reds had won division titles in three of the past four seasons, captured 17 more games than New York during the current summer, and were defending NL champions. Yet the Mets prevailed this time out in a tense NLCS

Tug McGraw coined the famous Mets' battle cry of "Ya gotta believe!" (Brace Photo)

the home team that had all the odds stacked in its favor. Given a new life in Game 6 when Seaver admittedly didn't have his "good hard stuff" working, and again in Game 7 when Oakland home run bats awoke against a tired Jon Matlack, the Oakland A's suddenly came to life for a deadly two-game rally and thus put a huge exclamation point on the second of their own three straight World Series triumphs.

1979
Passing of the Old Guard

On the surface, at least, the final season of the seventies was hardly an exceptional or even noteworthy one in the Mets' camp. The ball club remained buried in the deep malaise that would characterize almost the entire five-year managerial reign of one-time NL MVP Joe Torre. Popular bobby sox idol Lee Mazzilli finally blossomed as a league All-Star and shone in the midsummer classic by socking a homer and knocking in the tying and winning runs. Mazzilli was also the New York team leader in both batting (.303) and RBIs (79), tying Richie Hebner in the latter category. Another notable youngster, Craig Swan, made an additional splash by emerging as the club's top starter with 14 victories and one less defeat. And an additional pair of promising hurlers, Skip Lockwood and Neil Allen, did admirable duty in the bullpen. Lockwood owned the club leadership in saves (9), though he didn't crack double figures and surpassed Allen by but one. The club again lost approximately 30 more games than it won for the third season running, not a measure of progress by any stretch. Not surprisingly, the once-proud Metropolitans suffered corresponding defeats at the ticket windows, where fewer ducats were sold than for any season since the team's first. And the last-place divisional finish was something that, unfortunately, seemed to be becoming rather old hat under Joe Torre's lingering reign on the bench.

What ultimately did make 1979 rather exceptional in the flow of Mets history was the string of changes that unfolded that year away from the field of play. Most significantly, club ownership would change by year's end for the first time in Mets annals, as the Payson family finally sold out their remaining control of ball club stock. Before relinquishing their control, however, Joan Payson's heirs stirred the increasingly troubled waters by first giving a pink slip

shootout, mainly on the strength of Tom Seaver, Jerry Koosman, Jon Matlack, and an overall edge in frontline pitching. It was a story reminiscent of four years earlier, when the strong New York arms were able to silence a team renowned for superior slugging. Yogi Berra, in the process, became only the second manager (after Joe McCarthy) to win pennants in both leagues. But the Mets' second miracle effort was not yet quite finished. Yogi had boasted earlier in the summer that "It ain't over till it's over!" And the aphorism was now ironically destined to be turned back upon its own author. As it turned out, there were no more miracles to be found in the Mets' bag of tricks this second time around, and the overachieving New Yorkers, matched against the defending world-champion Oakland A's, simply ran out of gas against their second power-packed foe of the month. They did manage to hold the Oakland sluggers silent for much of the World Series, not allowing a single home run in any of the first six divided games. With Oakland's offense stalled, the Mets again clawed their way back twice from early deficits for a 3-2 Series lead. But each decade can hold only so many miraculous comebacks. When the Series shifted back to Oakland for its final set of showdown games, it was suddenly to entrenched board chairman Donald Grant and replacing him with Payson's 48-year-old daughter Lorinda de Roulet. It was a landmark move that made the affable businesswoman the first female owner to be actively involved in daily hands-on operations of a big-league club. More than anything else, Payson's daughter seemed motivated by a desire to convince her less engaged father that the family should not unload the financially burdened team, but it was an effort clearly doomed to failure. The new owners who assumed control on January 24, 1980, after shelling out a seemingly outrageous $21.1 million, for their own part represented a partnership group headed by the Doubleday and Company publishing and media empire. Front men for the lucrative National League franchise would now be Nelson Doubleday, the established publishing tycoon, and partner Fred Wilpon, a savvy Long Island real estate investor. One immediate and crucial fallout of the deal was a fortuitous change that would also now take place in front-office leadership. Wilpon and Doubleday wasted little time in naming their choice for a new general manager,

Skip Lockwood anchored the bullpen in the late 1970s. (Brace Photo)

and he was Frank Cashen, the man who had recently held the reins in Baltimore during that team's own halcyon era of American League domination. This would, in the end, be a year that would strike a most promising path in the direction of true ball club rebirth.

1981
Infamous Year of "The Strike"

The second season of the eighties provided one of baseball's most usual topsy-turvy summers. Never before or since has there been any season that ended with a format of play that was not the one the summer had started out with. The early part of the year—in the National League at least—was dominated by a headline-grabbing spectacle of Fernandomania, a drama unfolding out on the west coast surrounding a previously unheralded young Mexican left-hander named Fernando Valenzuela. With four shutouts in his first five outings, the portly southpaw quickly captured the nation's attention and adoration, then proved he was no mere flash, when he became the first rookie ever to walk off with a Cy Young Award. And former Met icon Tom Seaver—who trailed Valenzuela at the Cy Young ballot box—also reached a new milestone in Cincinnati by recording his 3,000th career strikeout. But dark clouds fell early in the form of a bitter and irresolvable labor dispute separating players and management. On June 12 the ballparks suddenly fell silent, and the longest labor action to date in American sports history began. Before it was finally over two months later, 38 percent (706 games) of the year's schedule had been irretrievably lost. Against this backdrop, the Mets had quietly been undergoing a subtle front-office shifting of the guard, as GM Frank Cashen deftly filled the slots around his own with a number of his old sidekicks from his days as GM with the AL Baltimore Orioles. Cashen also attempted to restoke some gate interest in his sagging team by bringing back a pair of former crowd favorites. Rusty Staub was re-signed to a free-agent contract after six seasons on the road with Detroit, Texas, and Montreal. And a deal was worked out with the equally inefficient Chicago Cubs to return slugger Dave Kingman to the fold. Both veterans soon supplied some heavy-hitting entertainment during the shortened season, even if they didn't do much to bolster ball club performance.

Mookie Wilson and his slow roller will forever be linked to Bill Buckner. (Brace Photo)

Out on the field, the Mets struggled through the unusual interrupted campaign, still unable to make anything that looked like real progress under manager Joe Torre. The bizarre split-season format of division play caused by the mid-season strike gave every team two shots at postseason play. But for tailenders like the Mets, it wasn't much of a windfall. The commissioner's office had ruled that "winners" from both prestrike and poststrike halves of the season would meet in October to determine division playoff qualifiers. Torre's crew was swooning in fifth at 17–34 when the shutdown came; when play resumed on August 10, they seemed to show some improvement, but a 24-28 record down the stretch only moved the club up a single notch in the standings. Still, there were some subtle signs of positive change to be savored. The club would stand only two and a half strides behind the pacesetter with a mere dozen games remaining in the season's second half. Youngsters Mookie Wilson and Hubie Brooks both cracked the outfield lineup and made heavy contributions on both offense and defense. Neil Allen chalked up 18 saves and also seven relief wins in just 43 appearances for a most credible bullpen performance. And at year's end, yet another managerial shift—this one finally closing the door on Joe Torre's increasingly unproductive bench tenure—appeared to be the biggest step in a new and hopeful direction.

1984
Davey Johnson's Bold Surprise

Davey Johnson's arrival in New York was accompanied by a surprisingly pleasant summer of highly unanticipated success. Of course, it would have been hard for the Mets to go much of anywhere but straight up, given the painful string of half a dozen seasons with victory totals hovering in the sixties that had preceded Johnson's arrival. But a leap from the division basement to serious pennant contention was certainly beyond even the wildest dreams and expectations of most Mets faithful—front-office executives included. Johnson set the tone and the direction for the new season and new on-field leadership when he won a spring-training clash with GM Frank Cashen over promising rookie pitcher Dwight Gooden: Cashen wanted more seasoning for the 19-year-old phenom, and Johnson believed that 19 wins and 300 Ks at

Class A Lynchburg was evidence enough that Gooden could contribute immediately. The revamped club under rookie skipper Johnson's control sprinted out of the gate with a 12-8 April ledger and thus held a slim grip on first place in the division by the end of the first month. It was heady stuff for long-suffering Mets fans, but a full season still lay ahead. May proved that the honeymoon was already in jeopardy, with a slide that left the team teetering on the edge of a break-even record. It was at this point that Johnson again proved his mettle by cutting loose some of the deadwood with which he had been saddled. The first-year manager gave walking papers to a trio of veteran pitchers—Craig Swan, Dick Tidrow, and Mike Torrez—and installed his Tidewater youngsters from a year earlier—Wally Backman and Ron Gardenhire—in the infield. Backman, a scrappy hustler, was installed as the leadoff hitter, and fleet-footed but strikeout-prone Mookie Wilson was dropped to the bottom half of the order. These were bold moves that set the tone for the rest of the season, and from that point on, Johnson's ball club was headed in a different direction.

Much of Johnson's immediate success had to do with other contributors who arrived along with him. First and foremost among these reinforcements was the most exciting rookie impact pitcher baseball may have ever seen. The presence of 19-year-old Doc Gooden, as much as anything else, made the Mets into overnight contenders once the rookie flamethrower unleashed the most sensational debut effort of any pitcher in memory. The top 1982 draft pick exploded on the scene with the biggest strikeout onslaught of any first-year hurler on record. By year's end, Gooden was not only baseball's first-ever teenage strikeout king, but his full-season rate of mowing down batters had never before been equaled. And although Gooden was surely not invincible, as evidenced by his 17-9 record, he was the hands-down winner of top rookie honors in the senior circuit. But Gooden was hardly the only new face separating this Mets team from those of a few seasons past. Darryl Strawberry was now terrorizing pitchers regularly after his own Rookie of the Year splash a summer earlier. Strawberry would be the team's most effective power hitter for a second straight summer, with 26 homers and 97 RBIs, despite a rather mediocre .251 batting average. Keith Hernandez had also joined the team during Bamberger's last season and was now making his impact felt on both the offensive and defensive sides. In his first full year in Shea, Mex (a reference to Hernandez's Mexican heritage) hit .311 and drove home 94 runs. A fourth major addition to the Mets' improved lineup, and one that would render Doc Gooden even more effective, came at the end of the year with the off-season acquisition of All-Star catcher Gary Carter from the Montreal Expos. With such quality reinforcements to draw upon, it was not unexpected or even surprising that Davey Johnson himself enjoyed more rookie success than any Mets manager preceding him.

1986
Gift of a Second World Championship

No single season in Mets history can quite compare with the 1986 campaign. The '86 team—Davey Johnson's third—reached a Mets high-water mark for victories (108) and ran away with the league's divisional race by one of the largest margins ever. The big-lumber lineup set new club marks in numerous categories for of-

Howard Johnson, a prime-time, switch-hitting slugger. (Brace Photo)

fensive potency by batting and slugging more effectively than any Polo Grounds or Shea Stadium edition before it. Not surprisingly, the Mets drew the biggest season-long throngs that two-decade-old Shea Stadium had ever witnessed (2,762,417). The '86 Mets also barely hung on to capture an NLCS shootout with Houston's high-powered Astros that is still talked about by baseball purists as one of the most exciting playoff collisions of the modern big-league era. And for an encore, they came out on top in the most dramatic fashion imaginable in a World Series that must be viewed in hindsight as nothing short of truly classic.

The Bill Buckner moment, which sealed Boston's World Series fate, was destined to permanently overshadow much of the Mets' fine yearlong performance. But there were certainly other dramatic playoff moments almost as memorable and every bit as crucial to the final championship results. The entire World Series actually turned on New York's gutsy comeback performances in Game 3 and Game 4 in Boston's own backyard at Fenway Park. The Series-starved Red Sox had grabbed an early lead on the road, which seemed to drive a nail in the Mets' coffin. The Mets gave away the first game when Tim Teufel's error ruined an otherwise flawless mound effort by Ron Darling; Gooden was knocked all over the lot in the second match and seemed to have mysteriously lost his potent fastball. After Bob Ojeda became the first southpaw to handle the Bosox in postseason play in Fenway since 1918, and Darling rebounded with slugging support from Gary Carter, the affair was once more knotted at a pair of victories each.

The momentum promptly shifted back to Boston, with Gooden extending his string of postseason ineffectiveness and being slammed around once more by Boston's bats in the year's final game at historic Fenway. Even in the fateful Game 6 itself, Boston had seemingly found a handful of ways to self-destruct long before Mookie Wilson ever reached home plate in the 10th inning with a chance to author the latest chapter in the Red Sox's endless saga of playoff disasters. The Mets had come back twice in regulation innings to tie the affair, Clemens surrendering one lead in the fifth and Calvin Schiraldi failing to slam the door once Clemens left with a blister in the eighth. Buckner's misplay of Mookie's grounder was a memorable disaster, to be sure, but no bigger a blow than the ill-timed Bob Stanley wild pitch unleashed three tosses earlier. That inexcusably errant throw with Kevin Mitchell on third had allowed the Mets to knot the game and extend the Series, which only moments earlier seemed hopelessly lost for New York. When Boston was given one last chance at redemption in Game 7, it again failed to hold back the inevitable Mets victory tide, squandering an early three-run lead and pouring bullpen gas on the fires of a pair of late-inning New York rallies. Popular mythology is certain to long celebrate the smartly tailored and ironically satisfying tale suggesting that Boston's cursed Red Sox had again predictably snatched defeat from the jaws of victory. But the truth of the matter was that the inspired Mets were themselves good enough to repeatedly snatch improbable victory from the clutches of looming defeat whenever given even the slightest second chance to do so.

1988
Reaching the Century Mark

At the time it was slowly unfolding, the 1988 season looked like anything but the sudden end to an all-too-brief success story that had attached itself to Davey Johnson's tenure in the manager's chair. But that is what, of course, in short order it would surprisingly turn out to be. As it was playing itself out, however, the 1988 season looked more like a successful righting of the ship and an expected rebound from a surprising off year that had come on the heels of the club's second world championship. Not that the Mets had slid very far off the pace in 1987 or had a long way to rebound from the 92 wins and second-place finish that had marked their apparent skid a season earlier. The biggest key to the upswing seemed to be Dwight Gooden, who had tinkered with his delivery and now got out of the gate fast with four complete games in April. Gooden would never again be the terrorizing force he was in his first two seasons, but he had now rebounded enough to win eight in a row before tasting defeat. The solid Mets staff did have injury problems throughout the year, but they also looked like another of the same scary New York mound crews of the recent past. The club threw a league-high 17 shutouts and nine of them were rung up by the end of May. Ron Darling had finally mastered the art of control and flashed brilliance with seven complete games. But the true and surprising

Kevin McReynolds swung a hefty bat for Davey Johnson's 1988 bombers. (Brace Photo)

staff ace was David Cone; in his second New York season, Cone emerged overnight to win 20 games (20-3), post the league's top winning percentage at .870, and finish third behind Orel Hershiser (Los Angeles) and Danny Jackson (Cincinnati) in the year's NL Cy Young voting. The result of so much mound strength was a steady pace of winning that left the rest of the division rivals farther and farther behind as the summer progressed. One hundred victories were the prize at the end of the line, and the division title was finally clinched against the Phillies on September 21 in Shea Stadium.

Yet there were ominous storm clouds gathering on the horizon and disarming signs of disaster lurking not far down the road. Effective southpaw Bob Ojeda severely injured his pitching hand in a freak accident away from the ballpark, and this would greatly alter the dynamics of the postseason pennant series with the upstart LA Dodgers. Youngster Gregg Jefferies shone brilliantly at the plate in both the season's final month and in the playoffs, but Jefferies' sudden emergence was also ironically a potential threat to the harmony of an already solid infield corps. The Jefferies situation would worsen in the coming season when the glamorous rookie (who had not qualified for rookie honors with his brief '88 appearance) was moved into the keystone slot, and popular veteran Wally Backman was traded away to make room. The spring that followed a bitter NLCS defeat at the hands of the Dodgers indeed would be one of the most acrimonious the Mets family had ever experienced, and the controversy swirling around the soon-slumping Jefferies would only be the tip of the iceberg. Yet nothing in the fall of 1988 was more disarming or more galling than the way another potential pennant was allowed to slip away during the season's final game.

Except for one regrettable playoff inning, Johnson's 1988 club may well have duplicated the heady achievements of only two seasons earlier. Such are the twists and bounces on which the game of baseball irrevocably turns. There had been considerable optimism in the New York camp after a 100-win season, and that optimism focused on a potential showdown World Series with the glamorous Bash Brothers Oakland Athletics, featuring sluggers Mark McGwire and José Canseco. The intermediary step of winning a World Series berth by eliminating the surprising Tommy Lasorda Dodgers was a matter almost taken for granted. The Mets held their own against the Dodgers throughout six games of the NLCS despite better-than-anticipated pitching from LA's underestimated starting mound corps featuring Hershiser, Leary, Belcher, and Valenzuela. The Mets had finally put themselves in a position to win another World Series admissions ticket with a gutsy Game 6 performance in Dodger Stadium. With a two-run homer and a 4-for-4 assault on Tim Leary and a trio of LA relievers, Kevin McReynolds had inspired a series-evening 5-1 Mets rout. And then the roof fell in during a single inning against the pesky Lasorda outfit in the deciding game. Hershiser was handed an insurmountable early lead when Jefferies bungled one routine out at third, Backman kicked away an easy double-play ball at second, and five runs streaked home as a consequence. If only they had that inning back, Johnson's club might well have been able to boast two sets of championship rings. At least this was the inevitable conclusion for millions of Mets rooters when the charmed Dodgers depressingly moved on to experience surprisingly little difficulty in defending National League honors against a suddenly punchless outfit from Oakland.

1996
Broadway Muscle Power

The New York Mets rang up a record-setting offensive showing in 1996, and they did it with a surprising trio of heroes. It was an impressive summer of slugging in its own right, of course, but it could soon be viewed in retrospect as only the tame foreshadowing of some even more awesome lumber displays at decade's end.

The trio of unlikely heavy bangers was composed of emerging catching star Todd Hundley, normally light-hitting center-field import Lance Johnson, and another promising outfield newcomer, Bernard Gilkey. Gilkey had been acquired from the Cardinals in January for three minor leaguers after he had paced the St. Louis club in hitting with a .298 average. Gilkey paid immediate first-season dividends when he went on a second-half tear after June that produced a team record for doubles (44) and also equaled the Mets' club record with 117 RBIs (set by Howard Johnson in 1991). It was an added bonus that the righty-swinging outfielder also posted a league best (18) for outfield assists. The fleet-footed Johnson, a left-handed slap-hitting leadoff man, was fresh off a season in which he led the junior circuit in base hits during his final campaign with the Chicago White Sox. Johnson more than outdid his 1995 spree once he donned a Mets jersey, and his 221 safeties made him the first player ever to top both leagues in total hits. Johnson's career season was so outstanding, in fact, that he also paced the entire major leagues in triples (21), multi-hit games (75), and runs scored (117)—a truly rare display of versatile slugging by a normally unspectacular singles hitter. Hundley unleashed the most explosive attack of all when he nearly tripled his previous big-league high by smashing a record 41 round trippers. Hundley's power outburst represented not only a new team homer mark, but also the most homers ever hit in a single season by a big-league catcher. Together the triumvirate had accounted for 10 new team slugging records. And the overachieving trio's hefty lineup impact was

THE NEW YORK METS ENCYCLOPEDIA

Mets reliever John Franco is hugged by teammate Rico Brogna after recording career save #300 versus Montreal on April 29, 1996. (AP/Wide World Photos)

enough for overall club marks for hits (1,515), triples (44, thanks in large part to Lance Johnson), and team batting average (.270).

But for all the offensive fireworks, this was a disappointing season from start to finish and one that was perhaps most notable for still another drastic change in direction on the team's managerial front. The Mets won two more games than a season earlier, but that still meant 20 fewer wins than losses. The fourth slot in the NL East left them trailing 25 games behind the runaway Atlanta Braves and nine back of the fifth-year but third-place Florida Marlins. John Franco drew some early attention by becoming the first left-hander in baseball history to post 300 career saves when he rescued a 3-2 victory over the Expos at Shea on April 29. As the season unfolded, however, save opportunities were not very frequent for Franco, who did well to post as many as 28 against the backdrop of the club's dreadful starting pitching. Bobby Jones was the complete-games leader with only three, and the team would eventually manage only three shutouts (Jones, Pete Harnisch, and Jason Isringhausen) by year's end. Mark Clark was the big winner with a mediocre 14-11 ledger, while expected ace Bobby Jones struggled at 12-8 with a lofty 4.42 ERA. It was enough to

Rick Aguilera, one of five Mets double-figure winners in 1987. (Brace Photo)

keep ex-pitcher Dallas Green peering constantly over his shoulder, and it was not much of a surprise when Green was relieved of his duties in another bench shakeup during the traditional dog days of late August.

1997
Rebuilding the Winning Tradition

Bobby Valentine didn't waste much time getting the Mets organization moving back in a positive winning direction. The Mets' 11th manager (counting full-term skippers only, and not interims) engineered a 17-game improvement in the standings his first summer on the job; it was the ball club's first winning campaign since the final year under Davey Johnson seven seasons back. Part of the key to Valentine's success was a new winning attitude, which manifested itself in 47 come-from-behind victories—the most in the big leagues that year. The biggest of these uprisings came late in the year against Montreal when the Mets charged back from a 6-0 ninth-inning deficit to overhaul the Montreal Expos 9-6 in tense extra innings. Valentine seemed to create his magic largely by getting his players to believe in themselves. But he also did it with considerable help from an active front office. The addition of established stars like John Olerud, Robin Ventura, Mike Piazza, and Rickey Henderson over the first three years of Valentine's tenure would add a new luster to the Mets' recently sagging image, plus a healthy dose of potent run production to the day in, day out New York lineup.

The first year with Valentine at the helm resulted in one of the club's biggest turnarounds ever. The third-place divisional finish might not have seemed so exceptional when viewed from afar, but it took on quite a different complexion once it was noted that the Mets were now stuck in what was easily baseball's most competitive division. The two teams New York chased in the standings were the powerhouse, division-winning Atlanta Braves, proud winners of 100 games, and the eventual world-champion Florida Marlins, the league's wild-card front-runner with 92 victories. With their 88 triumphs for the season, Valentine's maiden club would have won the league's Central Division by a fair margin, or only been barely nipped out by the San Francisco Giants, had they played out in the West. This healthy advance in the National League standings came amidst a season full of

Randy Myers twice paced the club in saves at the end of the '80s. (Brace Photo)

Todd Hundley was the third Met to slug 30-plus homers in back-to-back seasons. (Brace Photo)

personal milestones. Catcher Todd Hundley slammed 30 homers to become only the third Met to slug that many in back-to-back seasons. The team's RBI leader, John Olerud, produced the first home club cycle at Shea Stadium since Tommie Agee had managed the feat more than 25 years earlier. Rey Ordoñez hit another milestone with his first Gold Glove, also the team's first since Ron Darling's way back in 1989. And the Mets' 11 pinch homers also were the highest total in the majors.

Perhaps the most notable event of the year was a novel regular-season showdown series with the crosstown New York Yankees, which highlighted the inaugural summer of baseball's latest bit of historical tweaking—interleague play. The Yanks and Mets had collided on numerous occasions over the years, in spring exhibitions as well as in a short-lived Mayor's Cup charity series back in the sixties, but this was the first time the games truly meant something and city-wide bragging rights were legitimately being put to the test. It was, in truth, perhaps the biggest thing in New York City baseball since the curtain rang down on the last-ever Dodgers-Yanks Subway Series in October of 1956. The Yankees were now once again riding the crest

of the baseball world and were headed for an eventual postseason wild-card slot. The first Mets-Yankees series opened to a blitz of media hoopla on June 16 at Yankee Stadium, with 56,188 crazed fans on hand for the emotion-charged event. The night's hero proved from the outset to be the Mets' often run-of-the-mill righty Dave Mlicki, who mesmerized the American Leaguers 6-0 with his first-ever shutout and also first-ever complete game. The Yankees would bounce back to take the final two games of the series, one win coming after extra innings. The first crosstown showdown had thus come about as close as possible to ending in a virtual draw when it came to deciding bragging rights among the city's rival fans. The excitement of the Mets' competitive series with their Bronx neighbors thus provided one of the earliest glimpses of a late-nineties resurgence that seemed again to raise hopes that the Mets themselves might also soon be standing proud near baseball's postseason summit.

Note: The 1999 season is described in detail in Chapter 1 (page 23) and coverage of the 2000 season appears at the front of this book (page 7).

CHAPTER 6
Postseason Heroics

It didn't take long for New York's popular new National League franchise to reach baseball's pinnacle. In reality, no fledgling modern ball club stocked with castoffs and retreads has ever managed to revamp its fortunes quite as quickly as the first-decade New York Mets. And once they had made it to the promised land of a World Series and thus tasted success, it took even less time for the club to work its way back to the winner's circle. Yet despite such a remarkably rapid start out of the blocks, overall, the Mets have been an infrequent visitor to postseason play. Only a single pennant in each of the club's first three decades have emerged as the high points for the massive Mets fandom. Small-market clubs like Pittsburgh and Cincinnati and Atlanta have done every bit as well or even far better over the course of the past quarter century. And until the 2000 season, there had been a 14-year hiatus since the last New York Mets visit to a World Series. Yet if much of the past 25 years have remained a stretch of rarely interrupted dry spells for the Mets franchise, the New York club has still enjoyed the widespread image of a proud winner. In large part, this may be credited to an all-pervasive New York media hype. Yet in no small part it has also resulted from the sensational headline-grabbing nature of each of the four Mets National League pennant triumphs.

Whenever the Mets have made a serious pennant challenge or launched a legitimate postseason run, they have done so with great doses of gripping on-field and off-field drama. In this respect, they are the true offspring of the two New York clubs they replaced—the Brooklyn Dodgers and New York Giants.

No World Series in the era of divisional play has been more filled with rags-to-riches surprises than the very first, which featured the "Miracle Mets" under Gil Hodges. And no moment of television-era Series drama across the past half century is more ingrained as a lasting image in the minds of millions of fans everywhere than the Mookie Wilson grounder that trickled through Bill Buckner's legs with such earthshaking results. The Mets haven't been to baseball's biggest dance very often. But when they have, the scene has always been highly explosive.

1969
Baseball's Most Improbable World Champions

No World Series has been packed with more entertaining unpredictability than the one featuring the upstart Mets and the Goliath-like Orioles staged at the close of the first season of divisional play. Only the new format, with both leagues split in two, could ever have permitted a team like the Mets to reach the grand stage of World Series play. The first year of postseason playoffs was, in fact, an immediate affirmation for all who doubted that baseball's new structure meant a whole new ball game when it came to choosing World Series qualifiers. The late-season momentum surrounding the Mets' shocking overnight success story had been building in slow stages all summer long. Despite the unlikely turnaround that had put the league's most hopeless losers more than 20 games over .500, New York was still five games off the pace at the end of August and still not a

Cleon Jones was a baseball rarity as a lefty-throwing and righty-batting outfielder. He also enjoyed his career year at exactly the right time. (Brace Photo)

New York Mets catcher Jerry Grote embraces pitcher Jerry Koosman as the Mets defeat the Baltimore Orioles in the fifth game to win the 1969 World Series at New York's Shea Stadium. The other ecstatic Met player is Ed Charles. (AP/Wide World Photos)

very sound bet for playoff contention. Even in early September, this still appeared to be the long-awaited atonement year for Chicago Cubs fans, a payback year in which the Cubs' postseason curse would finally be lifted and the Wrigley Field crew would taste their first World Series action in a full quarter century. Then came a dizzying dash to the finish by Gil Hodges' surprising team, which left fans in Chicago and New York and all points between reeling from the pure excitement and shocking implications of it all.

While the Mets' final 38-11 dash into the playoffs featured almost unbelievable moments of diamond drama—including 10 straight wins by Seaver and a most improbable defeat of the Cardinals in St. Louis despite a record 19 Ks by Steve Carlton—the inaugural NLCS offered very little to raise anyone's blood pressure, either in New York or in Atlanta or anywhere else around the nation. The Mets' final step toward their improbable pennant was anticlimactic, in the wake of the late-season charge by the New Yorkers, which had finally overhauled the fast-fading Chicago Cubs. The Braves were expected in most quarters to have too much heavy hitting (Hank Aaron, Felipe Alou, Orlando Cepeda, and Rico Carty) for the overachieving Mets, whose brilliant yearlong pitching and light-lumber lineup was not now seen as sufficient to carry the miracle-in-progress to any further illogical conclusion. But when the postseason bell rang, it was the Mets' hitting—the entire team slugging at a .327 pace for the three-game set—that suddenly ruled the day, and Atlanta went very quietly in a trio of uninspired pennant-deciding games.

The World Series that followed turned out to be a David-and-Goliath affair of epic proportions. The Orioles were universally acknowledged as the better club, and after the Atlanta sweep, it seemed as though the Mets' bottomless bag of season-long tricks certainly couldn't contain very many more miracles. Baltimore pitching (topped by Cy Young ace Mike Cuellar, 20-game winner Dave McNally, and AL winning-percentage leader Jim Palmer) was every bit as sound as New York's and probably the best around. And the Orioles had all the potent offensive weapons (including Frank Robinson, Brooks Robinson, Davey Johnson, Paul Blair, Don Buford, and Boog Powell in the heart of the

batting order) the New York club severely lacked. But the games still had to be played on the field, and each action-packed outing would prove to have its heart-stopping moments and its most surprising unsung heroes. The Series started out precisely according to form, with Baltimore pitching dominating in the opener: Cuellar went the distance and needed only some vacuum-cleaner fielding from Brooks Robinson at third to slam the door on New York scoring. But then the momentum took a sudden and telling swing in the second game. Jerry Koosman demonstrated that Mets pitchers could be equally stingy by allowing the Orioles only a single scratch run. Three consecutive two-out ninth-inning singles by the Mets handed New York the narrow 2-1 victory. From that point on, the Fall Classic was every bit as rapid and one-sided as expected, yet it was seemingly the wrong ball club that owned all of the on-field advantage. In the end, the Mets' 4-1 Series victory looked relatively easy. But every contest was a true war, and each was decided by a dra-

Crazed fans engulf Shea Stadium's playing field seconds after the hometown Mets defeat Baltimore to win the 1969 World Series. (AP/Wide World Photos)

THE NEW YORK METS ENCYCLOPEDIA

Tommie Agee connects for a first-inning homer off Orioles pitcher Jim Palmer during Shea Stadium World Series action on October 14, 1969. (AP/Wide World Photos)

matic event. In Game 2, Ed Charles imitated Brooks Robinson at third (ironically on a drive off Robinson's own bat) to record the game's final out with the tying and winning runs aboard. Game 3 turned on Tommie Agee's two impossible outfield catches, and Game 4 was rescued by a similar play by Swoboda. And Game 5 boasted the famous shoe-polish incident, which fortuitously put Cleon Jones on base ahead of a tide-turning homer off the bat of Donn Clendenon.

The Mets triumphed in October the same way they had won all season long. The true heroes were again the pitchers, as well as the unsung role players who always seemed to defy their scouting reports and exceed their abilities at precisely the moments when they were most needed. Seaver and Koosman were brilliant, as they would continue to be for much of the next decade. Seaver's incredible pitching effort during the 1969 regular season (25-7 and his first Cy Young trophy) continued in the postseason. While he suffered the club's only Series defeat

(Game 1, when he was outpitched by Mike Cuellar), Seaver also salted away a pair of crucial NLCS and Series wins; Koosman won both of his World Series outings and allowed only four earned runs in the process. Rookie Gary Gentry (13-12, 3.43) may well have proved the difference, however. During the summer campaign, the hot-and-cold righty led the team in losses, runs allowed, and earned runs allowed, though he did capture the division clincher versus the Cardinals in late September. Yet it was Gentry (assisted by fine relief from Nolan Ryan and two spectacular catches from center fielder Agee) who came to the fore with a peak performance in the third Series clash in which the momentum turned irreversibly in New York's favor. And it was Swoboda, Weis, and Clendenon, especially, who also overachieved and repeatedly saved the day. Swoboda, the erratic right fielder, rescued Game 4 with a tumbling grab of Brooks Robinson's ninth-inning liner and then smacked a double in the rally which gave the hometown heroes their final lead in the Series clincher. Light-hitting Al Weis also smacked his first Shea Stadium homer of the entire season to tie the year's final game in the seventh. And Series MVP Clendenon not only contributed adroit fielding at first base in Game 4, but also poked huge homers in each of the final three World Series contests. Seaver and Koosman may have been the most celebrated of the Mets' miracle workers, but the list of surprise heroes and true saviors seemed almost endless.

1973
Unlikely National League Champions Once More

No World Series participant ever seemed so unworthy of being there as the 1973 National League champions. The Mets had barely played break-even baseball all summer and yet had managed to remain in a pennant chase, thanks to baseball's much-maligned new system of divisional competition. It was a race that five teams all seemed intent on throwing away if they possibly could. In the end, the Mets came out on top in a race (often seeming more like a crawl) to the wire that was seemingly won by mere attrition. The Mets were left standing in

first place on October 1 with an anemic 82-79 ledger and a 1 1/2-game lead over the second-place Cardinals, who sat squarely at .500. No team had ever entered the playoffs with such a mediocre record. Such was the sad legacy of the new divisional format for pennant competition.

If the Mets seemed an unworthy playoff team to most, they certainly did their best in a hurry to prove that they actually did belong. An NLCS slugfest with the high-powered Cincinnati Reds quickly proved to be one of the best in postseason history. Cincinnati had been on a tear for several seasons, winning three divisional titles in four years, posting 95 wins or more in each of those outings, and peaking with 102 victories and a World Series visit in 1970. This year they had been every bit as dominant in the West as New York had been lackluster in the East. Yet the acrimonious games and see-saw series that followed were a pleasant surprise sufficient to suddenly enliven October baseball. The spirited play between the two teams was nonetheless nearly overshadowed by the first of two distasteful playoff incidents (one of which occurred in the World Series) that would grab most of the headlines. An on-field flare-up between Pete Rose and Bud Harrelson cast an ugly pall over the pivotal third game at Shea Stadium. Rose's hard slide into the New York shortstop incited a bench-clearing melee and a frightening shower of debris from the stands, which nearly resulted in a home-team forfeit. In the end, the focus returned to baseball, and the Mets simply outplayed and especially outpitched the suddenly mesmerized Reds.

World Series action perhaps couldn't be anything other than anticlimactic after such an emotion-charged NLCS showdown as the one just staged by New York and Cincinnati. And the ALCS had been a wild shootout of almost the same raw intensity. Oakland had gotten by a pitching-rich Baltimore club only by pulling out a hard-fought deciding fifth game on the strength of a masterful five-hitter from Catfish Hunter. The A's and Mets did battle all the way to the limit, but the Series never seemed all that engaging for all the nip-and-tuck contests it featured. If there was drama attached to the seven-game showdown, it mostly came off the field. Oakland owner Charlie Finley nearly ruined the whole affair when he threatened to banish his second baseman, Mike Andrews, in midstream as punishment for a pair of unfortunate errors that handed an extra-inning Game 2 victory to the Mets. Commissioner Bowie Kuhn had to intervene to block Finley's heavy-handed and unpopular reaction. Once that matter (the second black eye of the postseason) was put to rest, the Series resumed without any signs of either the vaunted Mets' pitching or the heralded Oakland bats ever taking command. Until the final game, at least, when Oakland's hefty lumber company finally came to life and two-run homers by Bert Campaneris and Reggie Jackson off Jon Matlack salted away the deciding victory, 5-2.

1986
World Champions, Thanks to the Bambino's Curse

No Mets team ever performed better from wire to wire than the one put on the field in 1986 by fiery third-year manager Davey Johnson. And perhaps no other Mets team was quite as talent laden from top to bottom and from bench to bullpen in all aspects of the game. The Mets would dominate the National League pennant race that season as few teams had done before and few have done since. The invincible New York club moved into first place in late April (shooting past the defending NL-champion Cardinals in the season's third week) and by September had made a shambles of the race. By September 7, they had clinched—the earliest clinching since the league format had provided division races—and three days later, they also owned the biggest lead in divisional history. Johnson's deep lineup never lost more than four in a row. Club records were set for wins (108), home wins, road wins, home runs (148), team batting average (.263), and home attendance. Only eight previous teams in modern history had won as many as 108 games.

That the Mets were a charmed as well as dominant team was also quickly evidenced during the NLCS matchup with Houston's potent NL West winners. The Astros had a true ace up their sleeve in Cy Young winner Mike Scott. And Scott was just dominant enough to throw a true scare into the team that appeared such a runaway choice to win everything. Scott had enjoyed a stellar season himself (2.22 ERA with 306 Ks) and had capped it off by throwing a rare no-hitter at the Giants in the late-September game that wrapped up the NL West title. The big righty was also, like his teammate Nolan Ryan, one of those slow-developing mound

phenoms the Mets had parted with a few seasons earlier. And there was a further edge to this series, since it matched New York with its expansion rivals, who had often given them fits over the years. This was also the first NLCS to be played in a best-of-seven format, and that fact turned out to be the best of fortunes for the favored New Yorkers. Mainly on the strength of Scott's pitching in Games 1 and 4, the Astros surprisingly managed to keep the series knotted through four. Gary Carter's clutch extra-inning, game-winning hit in Game 5 finally put the Mets back in the driver's seat. But Game 6 was also essential for New York in order to avoid facing Scott yet again, this time with the pennant squarely on the line. And that Game 6 tussle soon turned out to be one of the most exciting playoff matches of all time. Some later commentators would even overenthusiastically label it the best single baseball game ever played.

Crucial Game 6 action opened in the Astrodome, with the Astros jumping on Bob Ojeda for three runs in the initial frame. A pitching duel of classic proportions then followed and stretched on until the ninth, when the Mets pulled off one of their more memorable come-

Ray Knight was the Mets' brightest 1986 postseason hero. (Brace Photo)

Bob Ojeda logged two key World Series starts in 1986.
(Brace Photo)

backs. Further heroics fell on the Houston side with a dramatic extra-inning homer by Billy Hatcher. But the Mets on this day had what it takes to salt away a pennant. The final inning set off another delirious pennant celebration back in New York. The Mets had prevailed as expected, but not at all in quite the cakewalk manner anticipated.

The stage was now set for the unfolding of a baseball miracle almost as stunning as the one from 1969 World Series play. This time the "miracle" did not consist simply of the Mets being contenders in the first place. The Mets were instead the overwhelming Series favorites, despite their taxing struggles with Houston. The miracle now came instead in the form of an exotic bailout after a superior New York team had all but handed the World Series rings to Boston's long-overdue Red Sox. Boston had seemed for decades to be a team cursed in postseason play. The Red Sox had not won a world title since trading a star southpaw pitcher named Babe Ruth to the Yankees, and the October dry spell had taken on legendary trappings

as the reputed "Curse of the Bambino." Boston fans had plenty of reason to suspect a genuine curse. In 1949, the Red Sox had seen an expected World Series appearance fade on the final weekend in head-to-head combat with the dreaded Yankees. A season earlier, they had folded in a one-game pennant playoff with Cleveland. A couple of seasons before that they had lost a World Series on a memorable fielding lapse by Johnny Pesky and a daring sprint to home plate by Enos Slaughter. Now they seemed about to turn it all around, taking an early 2-0 lead in the Series, letting the Mets come back to life, but then rebounding to stand within a handful of outs of putting away their first Series title since 1918.

Bill Buckner's infamous error is likely to remain etched forever in the pages of World Series lore. It was also perhaps the most memorable single instant-replay moment of New York Mets history—and likely also of Boston Red Sox history. Nowhere is baseball's tragic element more adequately illustrated than with Buckner's moment in the shadows, one that equaled and surpassed similar debacles for Fred Snodgrass, Fred Merkle, and Mickey Owen. The events surrounding Buckner's boot unfolded in the late innings of Game 6, with the Mets struggling to avoid certain defeat. Boston had appeared to put the game and the title away in the 10th inning and now was but three outs from the sweetest of all victories. Backman and Hernandez were quickly retired on fly balls, and the door was all but closed on lingering New York hopes. And then the unlikely miracle of miracles began. Fans were already heading for the exits in droves when first Gary Carter and then Kevin Mitchell singled to keep the Mets barely alive. Knight battled gamely against a tiring Calvin Schiraldi and finally also singled. Then came the fateful at-bat of Mookie Wilson, the most storied plate appearance in New York Mets history.

Everything unraveled for Boston in the Mookie Wilson at-bat, and if there was ever irrefutable evidence for a Bambino's Curse, it now emerged in spades. Bob Stanley marched to the mound from the bullpen and promptly uncorked a wild pitch. Before Boston fans could fully sense the horror descending around them, Wilson rolled the next pitch toward Buckner at first, and the ball's elusive passage straight through Buckner's legs seemed to freeze time on every television screen in the land. The game

THE NEW YORK METS ENCYCLOPEDIA

was lost in a heartbeat, and the reputed curse had once more been renewed. Boston still had its chances, of course. The Bosox even held the lead for a while two nights later in the true deciding game. But the Mets climbed over one hill with a crucial two-run single by Keith Hernandez in the sixth and finally seized a three-run lead by the eighth. The Shea Stadium air was filled with irrepressible expectation from the earliest innings of Game 7 that Boston simply could not recover from so fateful a blow as the Buckner mishap. And the Mets were ruthlessly efficient in putting the final nails into the Boston coffin, winning the deciding contest by a score of 8-5.

1988
Underachieving National League East Champions

Like their ancestors of the early seventies, the Mets' 1988 East Division champions were a ball club with much to prove. This was a veteran group of players bent on demonstrating to themselves and league rivals that the championship they had won two years earlier had not been a complete fluke. It was also a club that felt pressure to erase some of the stark disappointments of an unanticipated slide in the standings a year earlier, one that had disappointed so many close to the club in the wake of an exciting 1986 World Series showing. The 1988 team, managed by Davey Johnson, was thus mired in almost exactly the same rut that the Yogi Berra team had found itself stuck in a couple of disappointing seasons after the amazing 1969 Mets' performance. But there were admittedly also considerable differences. Johnson still had substantially the same team on hand in 1988 that he had won with in '86, and the 1987 slide to second behind the Cardinals had really not been all that severe a collapse. The '87 team finished only a couple of games off the postseason pace, had the fourth-best record in the entire majors, and was only sabotaged down the stretch by a string of debilitating injuries that had disarmed a still-potent pitching staff. Ray Knight's departure represented the only serious lineup change for the defending champions; Kevin Mitchell's departure was more than compensated for by Kevin McReynolds, who replaced him in an eight-player exchange with San Diego. This was still a Mets team that had been one of baseball's biggest winners for several years running.

But if the motivations were clearly there in 1988, the necessary performance level never was. Johnson's second postseason entry simply didn't execute when the chips were down. During the regular season, the team had raced to an expected division title in a cakewalk. There had been very little pressure on the Mets all season as they rang up 100 victories and put 15 games between themselves and division runner-up Pittsburgh. Most of baseball's often-near-sighted pundits expected a similar New York waltz in the postseason encounter with Los Angeles. The Mets had, after all, manhandled the Dodgers all season by winning 10 of 11 regular-season meetings. The Dodgers, for their part, had been somewhat surprise winners in their own division by outlasting Cincinnati and San Diego on the strength of superior starting pitching, usually barely supported by an anemic offense. Lasorda's outfit was an unbalanced team that one writer described as "a sterling pitching staff supported by a three-legged table of a lineup." Most attention around the Mets camp therefore seemed focused on a looming dream World Series rematch with Roger "Rocket" Clemens and the Boston Red Sox, or perhaps a high-powered showdown with José Canseco and the high-octane Oakland Athletics. But the Dodgers, of course, had very different plans regarding the championship party. The NLCS showdown turned out to be a seesaw affair for six entertaining games. Neither team could pull away by bunching a string of victories, and a final tiebreaker seemed to be in the cards as the series slowly wound to its conclusion.

The final game of the truncated postseason was an embarrassing disaster, which is unmatched anywhere in team annals. It was almost as if Bill Buckner had now exacted revenge by putting on a New York Mets uniform and joining the Gotham infield. The true villain was not actually Buckner's ghost, of course, but a flesh-and-blood Mets infield that simply couldn't execute when the marbles were on the table. Rookie Gregg Jefferies at third opened the door with a second-inning misplay of a harmless bases-loaded roller off the bat of Orel Hershiser that had double play (or at least force at the plate) written all over it. A few batters later, everything came apart when usually reliable Wally Backman at second misplayed another tailor-made double-play ball. After the dreadful second inning, Hershiser unleashed his mastery over Mets bats. The night and game clearly belonged to the Dodgers' ace, who had not only brought home the opening run with his bat, but then proceeded to twirl a complete-game five-hitter. It is likely that New York could not have done anything with Hershiser, even if the giveaway inning had not occurred. But the fact remained that the Mets had made it altogether easy on the opposition by gift-wrapping the final game for the Dodgers before they were out of the fateful second frame. No Mets season ever came to an abrupt end on a more sour note.

1999
Overachieving National League Wild-Card Winners

Easily the most dramatic postseason contest for the New York Mets' last edition of the 20th century may well have been the unscheduled game at Cincinnati's Cinergy Field on October 4 that got them into playoff action in the first place. A year earlier, the Mets had hung in the race for an NL wild-card slot throughout an exciting month of August and a tense month of September. Then in the closing days, Bobby Valentine's outfit had folded up like a circus road show and let the Chicago Cubs overtake them for the final postseason spot. The collapse was especially painful, coming as it did during a closing weekend series with arch division rival Atlanta—a team that had already clinched a playoff trip and had little at stake—and a previous Shea Stadium two-game set with the weak-sister Montreal Expos. A year later, the team battled through several bouts with adversity, which included June and August tailspins, the demotion of Valentine's entire coaching staff, a couple of trade-related roster shake-ups, and a spate of injuries limiting the effectiveness of starting pitchers Bobby Jones and Rick Reed. The June slump had cost Bobby Valentine three of his trusted coaches and confidants, when Bob Apodaca (pitching coach), Randy Niemann (bullpen coach), and Tom Robson (batting coach) were all reassigned to minor league posts. But the manager had survived, with his underlings paying the price for lackluster team performance. Then in late season, the ball club looked ready to once more collapse, kicking away seven straight games as the season entered its final two weeks and thus blowing an opportunity to put distance between themselves and wild-card rival Cincinnati. The Mets did re-

verse this stall at the wire with a season-closing sweep of Pittsburgh, and this time they also got help from the opposition. Cincinnati underwent its own swoon, and the wild-card chase ended up in a dead heat at the final wire.

The one-game playoff in Cincinnati was thus a true highlight of the season. With their backs to the wall, the Mets came through in grand fashion when they had to. The season-saving hero was staff ace Al Leiter, a 13-game winner who had struggled early in the season but rebounded down the stretch after a confi-

---

New York Mets Postseason Playoff Results*

1969 NLCS (New York Mets 3, Atlanta Braves 0)
Mets 9, BRAVES 5 (WP-Tom Seaver, LP-Phil Niekro)
Mets 11, BRAVES 6 (WP-Ron Taylor, LP-Ron Reed)
METS 7, Braves 4 (WP-Nolan Ryan, LP-Pat Jarvis)

1973 NLCS (New York Mets 3, Cincinnati Reds 2)
REDS 2, Mets 1 (WP-Pedro Borbon, LP-Tom Seaver)
Mets 5, REDS 0 (WP-Jon Matlack, LP-Don Gullett)
METS 9, Reds 2 (WP-Jerry Koosman, LP-Ross Grimsley)
Reds 2, METS 1 (12) (WP-Clay Carroll, LP-Harry Parker)
METS 7, Reds 2 (WP-Tom Seaver, LP-Jack Billingham)

1986 NLCS (New York Mets 3, Houston Astros 2)
ASTROS 1, Mets 0 (WP-Mike Scott, LP-Doc Gooden)
Mets 5, ASTROS 1 (WP-Bob Ojeda, LP-Nolan Ryan)
METS 6, Astros 5 (WP-Jesse Orosco, LP-Dave Smith)
Astros 3, METS 1 (WP-Mike Scott, LP-Sid Fernandez)
METS 2, Astros 1 (12) (WP-Jesse Orosco, LP-Charlie Kerfeld)
Mets 7, ASTROS 6 (16) (WP-Jesse Orosco, LP-Aurelio Lopez)

1988 NLCS (Los Angeles Dodgers 4, New York Mets 3)
Mets 3, DODGERS 2 (WP-Randy Myers, LP-Jay Howell)
DODGERS 6, Mets 3 (WP-Tim Belcher, LP-David Cone)
METS 8, Dodgers 4 (WP-Randy Myers, LP-Alejandro Peña)
Dodgers 5, METS 4 (12) (WP-Alejandro Peña, LP-Roger McDowell)
Dodgers 7, METS 4 (WP-Tim Belcher, LP-Sid Fernandez)
METS 5, Dodgers 1 (WP-David Cone, LP-Tim Leary)
DODGERS 6, Mets 0 (WP-Orel Hershiser, LP-Ron Darling)

1999 Division Series (New York Mets 3, Arizona Diamondbacks 1)
Mets 8, DIAMONDBACKS 4 (WP-Turk Wendell, LP-Randy Johnson)
DIAMONDBACKS 7, Mets 1 (WP-Todd Stottlemyre, LP-Kenny Rogers)
METS 9, Diamondbacks 2 (WP-Rick Reed, LP-Omar Daal)
METS 4, Diamondbacks 3 (10) (WP-John Franco, LP-Mark Mantei)

1999 NLCS (Atlanta Braves 4, New York Mets 2)
BRAVES 4, Mets 2 (WP-Greg Maddux, LP-Masato Yoshii)
BRAVES 4, Mets 3 (WP-Kevin Millwood, LP-Kenny Rogers)
Braves 1, METS 0 (WP-Tom Glavine, LP-Al Leiter)
METS 3, Braves 2 (WP-Turk Wendell, LP-Mike Remlinger)
METS 4, Braves 3 (15) (WP-Octavio Dotel, LP-Kevin McGlinchy)
BRAVES 10, Mets 9 (11) (WP-Russ Springer, LP-Kenny Rogers)

*Home team indicated in all caps

Bobby Jones sat out the 1999 NLCS due to nagging injuries, a factor that may have tipped the Series outcome in Atlanta's favor. (Brace Photo)

ear with the most rapid expansion-era success story imaginable. In only their second go-around in the league, the novice team had won an amazing 100 games and outpaced every veteran franchise but two—the AL Yankees and the NL Braves, dual contenders for the title "Team of the Nineties." But the question had to be raised as to whether the feats of this recent overachieving newcomer were anything comparable to the most famous rags-to-riches expansion story—that of the Mets themselves. This was a far different baseball world than the one the Mets had been born into four decades earlier, one in which contending ball clubs for the first time could now be built almost overnight in an era of rampant free agency and diluted big-league talent. At any rate, the Mets would have the chance themselves to dull some of the luster of this latest Horatio Alger entrant. They could make certain that Arizona did not walk off with either a league pennant or a World Series trophy, as the original Shea Stadium tenants of the late sixties had once done.

Once play opened between the wild-card Mets and the West-champion Diamondbacks, the more venerable New York club proved in a

dence-building June victory against the world-champion New York Yankees in interleague play. Leiter had saved his most brilliant outing of the year, however, for the most clutch game of the season and perhaps of the decade. The lefty completely shut down a powerhouse Reds lineup with a complete-game two-hit masterpiece that benefited from home run support by Edgardo Alfonzo and Rickey Henderson. With their inspired "backs-against-the-wall" win in Cincinnati, the Mets were now in the postseason fray for the first time in a dozen years. But the prospects for going very far toward a World Series date—perhaps with the crosstown Yankees—still didn't look very bright. Both scheduled NL opponents (Arizona in the division series and either Atlanta or Houston in the NLCS) had tons of quality pitching on their division-winning rosters, and both the D-Backs and the Braves were runaway division champs with 100-plus wins to show for their relentless summer-long efforts.

That the Mets would now open the "official" round of the 1999 playoffs with the upstart expansion Arizona Diamondbacks was quite fitting from a historical perspective. The second-year D-Backs had set the entire league on its

John Franco finally enjoyed a taste of postseason glory in October 1999. (Brace Photo)

Edgardo Alfonzo bashed two clutch homers to pace a victory over the Arizona Diamondbacks in the Mets' opening 1999 playoff game. (Brace Photo)

hurry that franchise experience indeed counted for something. The New Yorkers first ganged up on Arizona's best hope, baseball's most intimidating strikeout ace, Randy Johnson. The Mets pounded Johnson early in Bank One Ballpark and rode a pair of Alfonzo homers to a comfortable 8-4 lid lifter. Arizona rebounded to even the series when a three-run third-inning uprising against New York starter Kenny Rogers was enough to seal a 7-1 victory. But then everything went the Mets' way back in New York. The fourth and final game featured a disastrous play that turned the tide against Arizona's luckless bullpen corps. Tony Womack's dropping of a routine outfield fly ball allowed New York to climb back into a tie in the eighth and prevented Arizona from bringing the series back to Phoenix and into the hands of Randy Johnson. It was a highlight moment of pressure-packed misadventure that could not help but recall Bill Buckner's misplay of Mookie Wilson's fateful grounder in 1986. Then Piazza understudy, Todd Pratt, stepped forth as an unlikely playoff hero cut from a traditional Mets postseason mold. Pratt's game-ending homer in the bottom of the 10th off Arizona closer Matt Mantei was only the fourth circuit blow in baseball history to end a sudden-death postseason series.

The NLCS that opened in Atlanta quickly proved one final time that the Mets were still a long way from catching up with the Braves' level of talent or matching their stellar pitching arsenal. Atlanta ace Greg Maddux shut the Mets down completely in the opener on a five-hit effort spread over seven innings. Two similar outings by Kevin Millwood and Tom Glavine followed, and it looked like the New York playoff ride would now come to a rapid halt. But the team had bounced back for Valentine all sea-son long, and there was seemingly one more miraculous comeback yet in order. Two victories at Shea Stadium temporarily pulled the Mets out of the fire. And the final game of the series, an extra-inning battle, also came tantalizingly close to sending the two teams into a final Game 7 tie-breaker matching Glavine and Rick Reed in a game in which anything might well have happened. In the end, the Braves had won by a seemingly comfortable margin of four games to two and had thus seemed to dominate much of the series. But the showdown, in truth, had been a much closer battle than almost anyone had anticipated. Only once was the margin of Atlanta victory more than a single run. The final run count was 24 to 21, and the two teams were evenly matched in nearly every statistical category.

One game stood out in this entertaining string of postseason action. It was a game that capsulized an entire season of seemingly endless gutsy comebacks by an overachieving New York Mets team. Game 5 at Shea Stadium was a marathon affair that was destined to be one of the most bizarre in postseason annals. The final twist came after 15 innings and nearly six hours of seesaw play, when Robin Ventura smacked one of the most unusual game-ending homers in playoff history. Ventura's apparent grand slam in the bottom of the 15th was scored as a game-winning single when the Mets hero was overrun by celebrating teammates after rounding first and thus never completed his full, celebratory trek around the base paths. It was a final highlight for a team that had been one of the most courageous Mets outfits in many years. And the kind of excitement that this edition of the Mets had brought to Gotham fans indeed boded well for a new season that would open an exciting new baseball millennium.

CHAPTER 7
The Mets Managers

Managers were once upon a time—back in the ancient dead-ball days of "scientific play"—baseball's most colorful center-stage protagonists. John McGraw, for three decades, loomed larger than any of his often legendary players. Connie Mack was the sum and substance of the Philadelphia Athletics franchise throughout a full half century. If the Yankees, in their various dynasty eras, always had lineups stuffed with next-generation Hall of Famers like Ruth, Gehrig, DiMaggio, Mantle, and Berra, they also boasted gigantic figures at the end of the bench named Miller Huggins, Joe McCarthy, and Casey Stengel, a trio of Cooperstown legends almost as lofty in importance as those of their lineup heroes. Today's managers have mostly fallen out of the limelight; they are, in fact, often (along with umpires) the most underrated, overlooked, and maligned tangential figures in the game. There is one universal truth about a big-league managerial career: almost, without exception, it ends with a firing. When it comes to New York Mets history, however, the dozen men who have held the club's reins on regular assignment provide an important and colorful chapter in the team's four-decade storybook saga.

CASEY STENGEL
(1962-65) Mets Managerial Record:
175 wins, 404 losses, .302 winning percentage

For a full dozen seasons, Casey Stengel couldn't seem to lose while wearing the pinstripes of the New York Yankees. The sometimes-clownish Stengel won five straight pennants and five straight World Series at the out-set of his Yankees tenure, a record likely never to be equaled by any brand-new manager on the job. The Ol' Perfessor continued his remarkable string with 10 pennants in 12 seasons and only once (in 1959) finished as low as third place. His other non-champion, in 1954, ironically produced his top tally of 103 victories and was outdistanced in the standings only by the winningest team (Cleveland, with 111 wins) in the first nine decades of American League competition. But once he inherited the Mets job at the tender age of 72, Casey Stengel constructed a far more charming image as baseball's all-time-losingest skipper. His first Mets club lost an all-time record 120 games. His next two editions continued the streak with three straight seasons buried out of sight, in 10th place, in an expanded National League. A fourth Stengel team was well on its way to another 10th-place slot and another 100 losses, when a serious fall and resulting hip injury ended Casey's legendary tenure on the eve of his 75th birthday.

Stengel's losing legacy with the Mets was not the first time in his career that baseball's most colorful manager was buried at the bottom rung of the ladder. His four-decade career on the bench had begun in the thirties and forties with three seasons in Brooklyn and another six with the wartime Boston Braves that never saw Stengel-led ball clubs climb any higher than fifth place (seventh in an eight-team league was his usual home); only once did he manage a team (the 1938 Braves, at 77-75) that lifted its head above water. In all, the lengthy managerial career of Charles Dillon Stengel—with its mediocre and even horrid results with the old Dodgers and Braves and the new Mets, and then

Casey Stengel (Brace Photo)

its unmatched triumphs with the Yankees—is baseball's prima facie evidence that great teams make great managers and not vice versa.

Like Berra and Hodges after him on the New York Mets bench, Stengel was a manager whose mixed successes where only icing on the cake of a playing career that already either merited or at least paralleled Hall of Fame stature. Stengel was a longtime outfield star in New York, first with the Dodgers and later with the Giants, whose solid playing career was almost as overshadowed as his managerial tenure was by a reputation for colorful and pranksterish behavior. As a player, he once pulled a live bird from his cap at home plate; as a manager, he donned raincoats to coax rain delays, napped on the far end of the bench, and always entertained writers, if not his ballplayers, with his unfathomable, twisted argot.

No matter how much Stengel remains respected for his '50s-era Yankees achievements, it was his late-career Mets tenure that ultimately endeared him to baseball fans and reporters. No one ever made a bigger splash in the baseball headlines or retained favor quite so long simply by losing; he even made losing tolerable and sometimes even fun. It was Stengel's witty observations, as much as anything, that made the Mets of the early sixties the beloved

enterprise they always were. When the new club drafted a washed-up catcher with few tools as its first prize in the 1962 expansion draft, the sage Casey entertained an eager press corps with his observation that "you gotta have a catcher or you'll have all passed balls." After sitting in the dugout one long afternoon of the inaugural season and watching his outfielders misplay several routine fly balls, Casey responded to a postgame report that astronaut John Glenn had just entered an orbit around earth by quipping: "That's just what we need on this club—someone in position to catch a fly ball." He defended his decision to keep bonus baby Ed Kranepool glued to the bench by explaining: "Look, he may be only 17, but he runs like he's 30." During a spring-training game preceding the 1962 season, Stengel left rookie pitcher Jay Hook on the mound to suffer through an entire single-inning 17-hit onslaught and then deflected criticism from beat writers by grousing: "There were two outs. How'd I know he couldn't get the third one? He had good control. He didn't knock anybody down, did he?" And once during an exhausting road trip, he told the team's PR director to hold off the Houston press; "Tell them I'm being embalmed!" was Casey's caustic instruction. Throughout the losingest season in baseball history, the manager's endless and classic utterances in his memorable Stengelese were, more often than not, the morning's or evening's biggest sports headlines.

The 1962 Mets lost a record total of games and fittingly hit into a triple play in their last pitiful game of the season. They put on the field perhaps the worst daily lineup in baseball history and owned a pitching staff that managed to set just about every known record for losing. But, as was frequently observed at the time, they were still destined to be best remembered by future generations for having "the slickest manager" baseball had ever known. An article in *The Sporting News* at season's end best summed up Stengel's charm as manager of baseball's most legendary losers: "He won in the Stadium [with the Yankees] with gusto, and he lost at the Polo Grounds [with the Mets] with spirit, sportsmanship and realism. He never entered excuses when no excuses were permissible. He took his trouncings like a man, and it was not easy to follow up his bright years with the Bombers with his dour season with perhaps the worst peacetime club in the last 40 years."

WES WESTRUM
(1965-67) Mets Managerial Record:
142 wins, 237 losses, .375 winning percentage

In the grand scheme of things, Wes Westrum remains largely a footnote to New York Mets history. The club's second manager was pressed into duty accidentally, after Stengel was felled by his career-ending hip injury 95 games into the 1965 season. He never measured up to the colorful Ol' Perfessor who preceded him, or the more popular and more successful Gil Hodges, who would be next in line for the job. It was not an easy task to follow the pixie-like Casey Stengel; and to make matters worse, Westrum was handed a team that still wasn't anywhere near ready for serious big-league competition. And it certainly didn't bode well for one's place in history to be followed onto the Mets bench by a universally beloved figure the stature of Gil Hodges.

Even as a ballplayer, Westrum was never a headliner, though he did enjoy a 10-year career with the Giants in which he made considerable accomplishments. As a part-time major leaguer and minor leaguer in 1949, the solidly built but lead-footed catcher set an International League record by slugging five grand slams in only 51

AAA games that summer. As the Giants' full-time receiver the following year, he banged 23 homers (a career best) and proved his defensive skills with a yearlong .999 fielding average, which half a century later, still remains the best ever in National League annals. He was also a league leader that year among catchers in both assists and double plays. And he caught every game for the Giants during both 1951 (against the Yankees) and 1954 (versus Cleveland) World Series action. But by the '54 Series, Westrum was already on the downside of his career, and he would lose his starting slot behind the plate the very next spring to unheralded Ray Katt.

Westrum coached with San Francisco's version of the Giants during its first summer on the west coast, and a few years later, he arrived with the Mets as part of the only straight-up trade of coaches in major league history. The bizarre deal in the 1963-64 off-season sent Cookie Lavagetto to San Francisco and brought Westrum to Shea Stadium to handle the Mets' underachieving and usually shell-shocked, patchwork pitching staff. Westrum was halfway through his second season of bench duties in New York when he got the sudden and unexpected call to take over for the incapacitated Stengel in the thankless job of directing an expansion ball club bound for its fourth straight basement finish and its fourth straight 100-loss season.

Westrum did achieve nothing short of a minor miracle his first full season on the job as Mets skipper when he led the club out of the National League cellar for the first time in its short history and also stopped the bleeding by finally keeping the loss-column total under triple digits. An improved pitching corps was certainly one key to these small steps forward, and two of Westrum's hurlers (Bob Shaw, 11-10, and Dennis Ribant, 11-9) actually produced winning ledgers. And a year later, the early-season progress produced more light at the end of the tunnel with the arrival of the team's first genuine star prospect, Tom Seaver. But the 1967 season was one of turmoil from the start, and Westrum rode on shaky ground for most of the summer. Bing Devine had inherited the club presidency from George Weiss, and Trader Bing had swung into action with nonstop dealing that led to the Mets using a record 54 players (including 27 pitchers) before the season was out.

Wes Westrum (NY Mets)

Don Bosch failed immediately that summer as the touted center fielder of the future, and young Bud Harrelson was also a major disappointment when he took over at shortstop.

But the clubhouse turmoil centered mostly on manager Westrum's worsening relations with many of his disgruntled ballplayers. There were publicized incidents involving promising outfielder Cleon Jones and catcher Jerry Grote. The unhappy skipper fined Grote in LA for allowing himself to get booted from a game with no other available catcher on the bench; he kept the talented but often lackluster Jones on the sidelines; and he even belittled first baseman Ed Kranepool as "the oldest 22-year-old player in the majors." Knowing that he probably would not be invited back for another season of bickering and lackluster performances, Westrum stepped down with 11 games remaining on the docket. On the eve of the club's final 1967 road trip, he told the New York press the extent of his frustrations: "I just don't want to manage this club anymore. I was not fired. I'm leaving on my own." It was a mutually agreed-upon and somewhat overdue divorce that pleased just about everyone inside the Mets organization.

SALTY PARKER
(1967) Mets Managerial Record:
4 wins, 7 losses, .364 winning percentage

The man who replaced Wes Westrum on the Mets' bench enjoyed his proverbial 15 minutes of fame. Francis James "Salty" Parker was accustomed to demitasse cups of coffee in his big-league career, having experienced a playing tenure that lasted only 11 games and 25 at-bats as a fill-in shortstop for the 1936 Detroit Tigers. His coaching tenure in the big time was, thankfully, much more extensive and included stints with half a dozen clubs, including the Giants (1958-61), Indians (1962), Angels (1964-66 and 1973-74), and Astros (1968-72). But it was during his one summer with the Mets that opportunity suddenly knocked and Parker was handed the managerial reins for a brief two-week span after Westrum's late-September resignation. Taking over a dispirited ball club torn apart by dissension, buried in the league basement, and on course for yet another 100-loss season, Parker desperately pushed the buttons for 11 games and managed to maintain the team's normal lackluster performance by winning a mere third of them. When Gil Hodges

Salty Parker (Brace Photo)

took command later that winter, with the announced charge of revamping the entire Mets operation, he found no spot on his coaching staff for the undistinguished and easily forgotten Salty Parker.

GIL HODGES
(1968-71) Mets Managerial Record:
339 wins, 309 losses, .523 winning percentage

Davey Johnson won more games in Mets flannels than Hodges, won more games in his best season (108 to 100), and also managed to surpass Gil's postseason ledger with a second trip to the NLCS as an encore to his 1986 World Series victory. And Johnson owned the better overall managerial record, winning 90-plus games in five straight seasons, while Hodges posted a losing mark in six of his nine campaigns with Washington of the AL and the Mets. But neither Johnson nor anyone else ever won as many hearts as the beloved and stoic skipper who earned respect everywhere for his quiet strength and his most surprising and renowned "miracle" championship season.

Gil Hodges was a much-beloved figure in New York City baseball long before the New York Mets ever came into existence. Hodges' glorious playing career adequately reflects the aura that surrounded this most popular of the Boys of Summer Brooklyn Dodgers. He was more beloved by Flatbush fans than even Jackie Robinson, Duke Snider, or Pee Wee Reese. In the midst of a 1952 World Series defeat at the hands of the crosstown rival Yankees, the powerful, slugging first baseman was mired in a dreadful 0-for-21 slump; yet the response by the die-hard Brooklyn faithful was an outpouring of support for their local hero that included prayers in churches all throughout the borough. So great was the universal respect for Hodges's steady efforts that during this and other career slumps, the eight-time All-Star first baseman was never booed by partisans in Ebbets Field, a phenomenon that never befell any of the other Dodger stalwarts—especially not Snider, Campanella, or Robinson. But, then, Hodges rarely ever slumped: a remarkably steady slugger, he collected over 100 RBIs seven straight seasons and better than 20 homers 11 years running. On August 31, 1950, he belted four Ebbets Field round trippers in a single game versus the Boston Braves. And in response to his horrid 1952 Series performance, Hodges rebounded to hit a team-best .364 during the following year's Fall Classic.

When the fledgling Mets plucked Hodges in the expansion draft on the eve of their maiden campaign, they scored one of several important public relations coups in early team history. Others included the hiring of Casey Stengel as manager; the signing of several other New York City greats, such as Duke Snider, Yogi Berra, and Willie Mays, to spice interest in the new National League club; and token appearances in Mets uniforms of such popular stars of the previous decade as Warren Spahn, Richie Ashburn, Jimmy Piersall, Gene Woodling, and Ken Boyer. But none of these moves was as celebrated or fortuitous as the recruitment of the beloved gentle giant from Brooklyn, and Hodges responded with a few last heroics (like smacking the first homer in Mets history), even though he was already well beyond his glory days as a front-line ballplayer. It was indeed a sad day for Mets partisans, but a great career break for Gil Hodges personally, when the once-powerful first sacker left the Polo Grounds on May 23, 1963, en route to the expansion Washington Senators in exchange for colorful veteran outfielder Jim Piersall. Hodges never played a single game with Washington, but was immediately tabbed to take over as manager for the struggling ball club.

Mets management calculated that it had scored a similar coup when it was able to get Hodges back as New York's field manager five seasons later, and the hunch proved to be squarely on the mark. From the start of his managerial tenure in Washington, Hodges had commanded respect in the clubhouse as a wise and fair team leader and had also inspired his run-of-the-mill ballplayers to overachieve on the field. In one brief season, he lifted an understaffed Senators roster out of the AL basement; and in his fifth campaign, he won a remarkable 76 games, pulled his club into a tie for sixth, and collected numerous Manager of the Year ballots. But his solid Washington stint was only a start. Blessed on his return to New York with a more talented group of ballplayers—especially sensational rookie pitcher Jerry Koosman and equally promising second-year hurler Tom Seaver—Hodges worked a seeming miracle his first summer on the job by simply guiding the NL's laughingstock team out of the basement for the second time in its seven-year history. The following year brought one of the biggest turnarounds in baseball history, as Gil Hodges's second Mets contingent improved 27 games in the won-lost columns and truly shocked the baseball world by pulling off one of the most unlikely pennant upsets and improbable World

Gil Hodges (NY Mets)

Series triumphs found anywhere in baseball annals. The surprising rise of the 1969 New York Mets was fueled by several Hodges managerial moves that bordered on true genius: He handed Tug McGraw a final and fortuitous opportunity to anchor his bullpen; he successfully platooned in right field (Ron Swoboda and Art Shamsky), at second base (Ken Boswell and Al Weis), and at third base (Wayne Garrett and Ed Charles); and he obtained eventual World Series MVP Donn Clendenon to platoon with Ed Kranepool at first.

The only handicaps to Hodges's tenure as manager in New York were his ongoing health problems, which had plagued the chain-smoking athlete for years. The Mets received a major shock when Gil suffered his first heart attack late in the 1968 season. That disturbing development, which came in Atlanta on September 24 and forced coach Rube Walker to finish out the season at the helm, was too soon dismissed as a false alarm, and Hodges was hard at work winning a pennant the following summer. In the spring of 1972—after two final seasons of identical third-place finishes and carbon-copy 83-79 records—48-year-old Gil Hodges was felled again by a second—and this time fatal—coronary. The numbing and tragic event occurred in Florida on April 2, during suspended spring training and on the eve of the first strike-delayed season in major league history. To date, his death is the darkest single moment in New York Mets history.

YOGI BERRA
(1972-75) Mets Managerial Record:
292 wins, 296 losses, .497 winning percentage

A Hall of Fame catcher considered by some the best of all time, Berra is likely to be best remembered for his halcyon playing days in the Bronx and not for his less impressive managerial sojourns in New York with either the Yankees or the Mets. Nonetheless, Berra was able to boast of some rather lofty managerial achievements with both New York teams. In one brief season as Ralph Houk's replacement on the bench with the invincible Mantle-Maris-Ford Yankees (1964), he extended the Stengel-Houk domination over American League rivals with one final pennant to cap the Yankees' dynasty era. He was then promptly fired after the Yankees lost to Johnny Keane's St. Louis Cardinals in a tense seven-game World Series. Joining the Mets the following year as a player-coach, he again eventually ascended to the manager's slot after the tragic death of Gil Hodges. Berra's managerial debut was not quite so dramatic the second time around, yet after one third-place finish in 1972, his 1973 "You Gotta Believe" edition rose from the ashes of last place in the final month to capture both a division title and an NL pennant despite the worst winning percentage (.509) of any league champion in history. The second banner also made him one of an exceedingly small fraternity of managers (Joe McCarthy was the only other at the time) who had directed clubs from both leagues to pennants.

The downside of Berra's limited and mixed managerial career was that early pennant successes were always followed by quick dismissals, usually amid charges that he had lost both control and the respect of his ballplayers. Nor were his pennants ever capped by the ultimate prize of a World Series ring. The charge that he ran a chaotic clubhouse was particularly strong in 1974, when Berra's Mets crashed and burned immediately after their surprising 1973 pennant, finishing 20 games under and in fifth place in the division. They again struggled around .500 for most of the following campaign, and Berra finally lost his job in early August. Berra's second demise came about amidst constant complaints from his players, culminating in a front-office meeting during which Tom Seaver reported to board chairman Donald Grant that the laid-back Berra had absolutely no respect left in the clubhouse. The entire season had been a troubled one both on and off the field for the sinking franchise, and an acrimonious early-season run-in between chairman Grant and moody outfielder Cleon Jones did not help Berra's cause with his ballplayers.

Berra had one more shot at managing in New York a decade later—this time with George Steinbrenner's Yankees—but that tenure was even more plagued by upheaval and controversy than either of his first sessions on the bench. After the Yankees limped home in third place in 1984, Berra quickly went the way of most of Steinbrenner's handpicked managers when he was fired only 16 games into the following season. Yogi was so disgusted with this blunt vote of no confidence from The Boss that he steadfastly refused to attend Old-Timers' events in Yankee Stadium for the next decade and a half.

THE NEW YORK METS ENCYCLOPEDIA

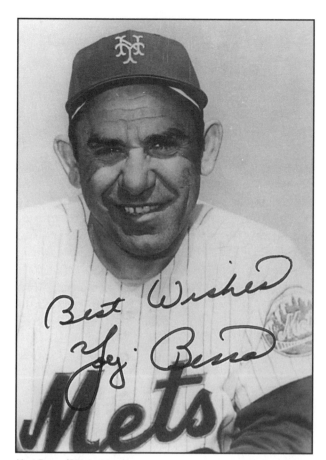

Yogi Berra (SPI Archives)

Cooperstown, and it is understandable why any managerial accomplishments would always get second billing to Yogi Berra's major league playing feats.

ROY MCMILLAN
(1975) Mets Managerial Record:
26 wins, 27 losses, .491 winning percentage

Roy McMillan's brief tenure as a fill-in on the Mets' bench came during one of the darkest periods in club history. The season in which he briefly served was one marred by yearlong on-field and off-field disappointment and tragedy—a pall that stretched from early spring-training sessions all the way to the September collapse that left New York frustrated on the postseason sidelines. Coming off the disastrous sub-.500 season that had followed the 1973 NL championship, the Mets were spiraling downward, and manager Yogi Berra seemed on thin ice from the start of the campaign. Joe Torre had been purchased from St. Louis to solve the ongoing third-base woes, but only at the considerable cost of bullpen ace Ray Sadecki. New GM, "Trader Joe" McDonald, had performed a small coup by acquiring heavy hitter Dave Kingman from San Francisco, but the club remained more noted for dependable bench players than frontline stars. After ugly bickering with star outfielder Cleon Jones in mid-season, manager Berra seemed to be losing all control over team harmony in the clubhouse. In early August, Berra was finally fired by team president Donald Grant with the Mets still barely clinging to a .500 record but also still eight games off the first-place pace set by Pittsburgh.

Roy McMillan was elevated from his coaching slot to replace Berra with 53 games remaining and the front office still suffering from delusions of a late-season pennant charge. McMillan had been a dependable glove man at shortstop in the team's early years, after establishing his reputation as one of the league's best defensive infielders with the Cincinnati Reds in the early and mid-fifties. He had already served one interim-manager's stint with Atlanta in 1972. It was now hoped in New York that he would prove an inspirational club leader cut in the "strong, silent type" mold of Gil Hodges. But this was an overestimation of McMillan and his personality by the Mets' front office, and broadcaster Ralph Kiner would later sum up the miscalculation by noting that McMillan was indeed

That Berra's managerial record didn't measure up to his playing achievements is hardly surprising—no matter how many pennants he did or didn't win as a bench boss—since his championship record as a ballplayer is almost unmatched. Despite a reputation for clownish malapropisms rivaling those of mentor Casey Stengel, Berra maintained his stature as one of the game's top two or three catchers of all time. In fact, he was named to Major League Baseball's recent All-Century Team. And as a winner in regular and postseason play, he had almost no equal. He played on 14 pennant winners (a record) and 10 world champions (also a record) during his 19-year career and was also selected to 15 consecutive AL All-Star squads. He also once played 148 straight games and handled 950 fielding chances without committing an error. He caught the only no-hitter (Larsen's perfect game) in World Series history, and his postseason presence was so regular throughout the late forties and fifties and early sixties that he holds Series records for base hits (71), doubles (10), at-bats (259), and games played (75). Add to that three awards as the American League MVP and a spot in the Hall of Fame in

Roy McMillan (Brace Photo)

silent, but little more. Under their new skipper, the team did enjoy some strong individual performances that enabled them to hang in the pennant race as late as the first week of September. On September 2, they were only four games behind the struggling first-place Pirates. But down the stretch, individual heroics were never transformed by McMillan into team harmony, and the club dropped 16 of its last 26 to slide quietly into a final third-place tie with the Cardinals. Overall, McMillan had produced a record that was only a single game under .500. But that was not good enough for a perceived contender, and over the winter, Joe Frazier was hired to manage the ball club, while Roy McMillan was hastily demoted to his original, less visible coaching assignment.

JOE FRAZIER
(1976-77) Mets Managerial Record:
101 wins, 106 losses, .488 winning percentage

Of the seven men who have filled in as Mets managers for less than two full seasons, Joe Frazier is the only one of the lot to boast 100 career victories for his efforts. Yet that is about the only thing in Frazier's tenure worth bragging about. He came on the scene as a com-

plete unknown to the baseball world at large, since his sideline apprenticeship had been served not in the majors but down on the farm, where he had won three straight minor league pennants for the Mets organization, including the AAA International League crown with the 1975 Tidewater Tides. At the time, Mets honchos appeared to cling to a vague hope that a mystery manager might duplicate recent successes of minor league-trained skippers such as Walter Alston with the LA Dodgers, Earl Weaver in Baltimore, and George "Sparky" Anderson, the latter of whom was currently constructing a powerhouse over in Cincinnati. The point was driven home to the local press and fans in a media release that emphasized that "Joe Frazier's got all the qualifications you could want. He wins." The same announcement, handed to the press the day Frazier was introduced at Shea Stadium as the new skipper, seemed to beg the question, however, by further stressing that "the game is played the same way up here as it is down there."

Obviously, managing in the National League would turn out to be a more mine-filled job than filling out lineup cards in Tidewater. Known as "Smokin' Joe" for his fiery personality, Frazier was able to inspire his charges to a quick bolt out of the gate in April 1976 with 18 wins in their first 27 outings and a solid early-season grip on first place. But from that point on, Joe Frazier never proved as big a winner in the big time as he had in the bushes. After the heady first month, his club began to fade rapidly, with losses in 22 of their next 30 contests. The team did hang on for a winning season and a third-place finish, thanks largely to heavy hitting by Kingman and Torre, and Koosman's and Seaver's brilliant pitching. Kingman launched an all-out assault on Ruth, Maris, and Hack Wilson in the first half and, despite missing six weeks in the second half, bested the club home run mark with 37. Koosman won 20 for the first time, and Seaver fanned 200-plus for a record ninth straight season. When the pitching sagged the following April, however, and the clubhouse was poisoned by the continuing circus surrounding Seaver's acrimonious contract negotiations, the club's fortunes dipped drastically, and so did Frazier's fortunes on the bench. On May 31 of Frazier's second season, a week after he had won his 100th career game and in the midst of a six-game tailspin, he was unceremoniously dumped, and utility infielder Joe Torre was handed the top job. Frazier's only consolation by year's end might have been that the team didn't perform any better in his absence, sliding to its first last-place finish in a decade.

JOE TORRE
(1977-81) Mets Managerial Record:
286 wins, 420 losses, .405 winning percentage

At the end of baseball's first full century, Joe Torre ranks as one of the game's most successful managers and seems almost a sure bet for Cooperstown enshrinement on managerial achievements alone. His five seasons of losing baseball in New York with the Mets of the late seventies and early eighties were followed by three seasons of immediate success in Atlanta and a string of solid achievements in St. Louis, where he had once starred as a good-hitting catcher-infielder and one-time NL MVP. Torre's Atlanta tenure got off to the fastest possible start, with a modern major league record of 12 victories to open the 1982 season. His first Atlanta ball club won a West Division title, and his other two editions both finished second. In St. Louis, his teams had winning records in three of five full seasons (he was fired partway into the sixth) despite failing to win a single first-place banner. And upon arriving back in New York with the Yankees in 1996, Joe Torre shot straight to the top of the managerial heap. He would win 90 games three times and a record 114 in a fourth campaign; his 1998 team was widely considered the most invincible one-season outfit in major league history; and three American League championships would be further validated by three World Series rings. The World Series appearances were especially noteworthy for Torre, as they put an end to a record string of 4,272 major league games as both player and manager without ever having participated in the sport's Fall Classic.

Torre's sudden successes in the 1980s and 1990s were a stark turnaround from his early efforts at big-league managing. When he completed his first bench job with the New York Mets two decades ago, there would have been few, if any, who might have predicted such heights for the former NL All-Star catcher. The most noteworthy aspect of Torre's managerial stint in Shea Stadium probably was the oddity that it began with the distinction of his being the first NL player-manager in nearly two full decades. Beyond that piece of oddball trivia,

there was only a string of four black-and-blue campaigns with 90 or more losses—the first of which he was responsible for only 70 percent of the carnage, having taken over for Joe Frazier at the end of May, with 30 defeats already on the books. And his last year in New York as a National Leaguer might also have reached that total, if not for a truncated summer caused by a season-wrecking midyear players' strike.

Torre's playing career was also one of the most noteworthy ever for a man who would later ascend to such grand managerial stature. A hot-hitting minor league third-base prospect with the Milwaukee Braves in the late fifties, Torre had to be converted to catcher because of the presence of Hall of Fame shoo-in Eddie Mathews on the parent club. Joe's brother Frank was playing with the big club at the same time as a reserve first baseman. Breaking in himself with Milwaukee as a full-timer in 1961, Torre quickly earned a permanent big-league job with his hefty bat and twice hit over .300 for the Braves (once in Milwaukee and once in Atlanta), five times earning a spot on the National League All-Star roster. Swapped to St. Louis between seasons in 1969 for future Hall of Famer Orlando Cepeda, the versatile infielder-catcher continued his All-Star play (four more appearances in the Midsummer Classic) and enjoyed a career MVP season in 1971, when he was the league batting champion (.363) and also topped the circuit in hits and RBIs. With the Mets during his final three active seasons, Torre unfortunately disappointed, becoming yet another unsuccessful attempt at solving the club's perennial third-base problem. He did, nevertheless, pace the club in hitting (.306 in 114 games) in his last full big-league season. But when Joe Torre finally removed himself from the active playing roster only two weeks after taking over the managerial reins from the ousted Joe Frazier, it was (unbeknownst at the time) more of a career beginning than any semblance of a career conclusion. Joe Torre's best years in baseball still lay ahead.

GEORGE BAMBERGER
(1982-83) Mets Managerial Record:
81 wins, 127 losses, .389 winning percentage

George Bamberger's shining moments as a manager came in Milwaukee with the Brewers and not in New York. Yet with the Mets, he also enjoyed a few memorable moments and

Joe Torre served briefly as a playing skipper at the outset of his managerial career, the first since Solly Hemus of the Cardinals back in 1959. (Brace Photo)

George Bamberger (Brace Photo)

in the second half and clunked into the division basement by year's end, there were signs of hope on a team that lost 97 games but featured a bullpen of Neil Allen and Jesse Orosco. Dave Kingman provided instant offense and tied the club mark of 37 homers; George Foster was acquired from the Reds and thus provided another heavy bat; Allen (19 saves) and Jesse Orosco (2.72 ERA) promised ongoing improvement in the bullpen; Craig Swan recovered from rotator cuff surgery and was the team's big winner (but with only 11 victories); and rookie Terry Leach signaled further mound strength by throwing a one-hitter during the season's final week. The following spring, however, the entire house-of-cards pitching staff collapsed—Neil Allen proved the biggest failure, as he lost confidence on the mound and became an agitator in the clubhouse—and Bamberger avoided another decline in his personal health by bailing out when the season was barely two months old.

FRANK HOWARD
(1983) Mets Managerial Record:
52 wins, 64 losses, .448 winning percentage

There have been precious few hitters who have ever looked more imposing with a Louisville Slugger in their hands than Frank Howard. He was bigger than Dave Kingman (two inches taller and 40 pounds heavier), he swung a more intelligent bat than Kingman (hitting 40 points higher and having 400 fewer strikeouts over the same 16-year career), and he hit the ball every bit as far—even though his 382 career round trippers fell a good deal short of King Kong's 442. And the slugger Ted Williams once called the strongest man ever to play big-league baseball (and Williams played with Jimmie Foxx) was also much more of a team player and fierce competitor during his productive seasons with the Dodgers, Senators, Rangers, and Tigers. But as a big-league manager, Howard was a more gentle giant, and the results were thus never all that imposing once he took up a post at the end of the bench. He enjoyed one full season on the job with the last-place San Diego Padres in the strike-split season of 1981 (sandwiched between Jerry Coleman in 1980 and Dick Williams in 1982) before getting a second shot for only a partial season two years later as George Bamberger's interim replacement with the Mets. The 1983 campaign had started off well

achievements. As a longtime minor league hurler, he won over 200 games in the bushes, yet only tasted a 10-game cup of coffee in the big time, which resulted in a single save and no victories. Yet Bamberger's knowledge of the pitching art was turned to good advantage when he served a nine-year tenure as pitching coach in Baltimore (under Earl Weaver) and handled pitching staffs that produced three Cy Young winners and 18 individual 20-win performances. Moving into the managerial ranks with the Milwaukee Brewers in 1978, he continued to perform admirably by elevating a heretofore lackluster outfit to a pair of 90-win campaigns and an eventual second-place finish. The Milwaukee tenure ended in personal tragedy for Bamberger, however, when he suffered a mid-season heart attack during his best campaign and then resigned at season's end to spend time with his family in hopes of rebuilding his sagging health. When Bamberger felt well enough to tackle a second big-time managing assignment, this time with the Mets, it quickly became clear that "Bambi's Bandits" in New York would never duplicate the successes of "Bambi's Bangers" in Milwaukee. The 1982 club he inherited in Shea Stadium started fast enough and found itself only three games off the NL East pace in late June; although the team slumped

Frank Howard (Brace Photo)

No matter what yardstick one chooses to use, the same conclusion is quite inevitable. Davey Johnson was the most successful manager in New York Mets franchise history. He won more games in a single season (108 in 1986) than any other Mets skipper. His 595 career victories come close to doubling the 339 recorded by runner-up Gil Hodges. His .588 winning percentage was challenged only by Bobby Valentine's .557 by the end of the 2000 season. He is one of only two Mets managers with two postseason appearances and the only one with two 100-win seasons. And his 1986 world champions may have fallen a bit short of the glamor and thrills of the 1969 Miracle Mets piloted by Hodges, but the Johnson-led winners were almost, without argument, the strongest team ever put on the field in blue and orange New York Mets colors. The final proof is provided by Johnson's successful string between 1984 and 1988, which saw the former infielder become the first big-league skipper in major league history to claim 90-plus victories for five seasons running.

It was ironic, to say the least, that the man who was destined to loom so large during the Mets' most recent championship successes would also contribute a small footnote to the team's first championship. When the Mets rang up the final out in the shocking 1969 World Series upset of the Baltimore Orioles, it was none other than Davey Johnson who banged out the history-making fly ball. Johnson slapped the final line drive of Game 5 straight at Cleon Jones in left field to set off a wild celebration in Shea Stadium and send Jones scampering toward the bullpen gate to escape the frenzied crowd rushing across the field. That fly ball was a small footnote not only to Mets history, but also to Johnson's own successful playing career. During his best seasons with Baltimore, he earned three Gold Gloves as a double-play partner of future Hall of Famer Luis Aparicio; during a short stint with the Atlanta Braves, he showed surprising overnight power in 1973 by blasting 43 homers, more than double his previous best. Johnson's one-season power surge with the Braves earned him two entries in the baseball record book—one for the most homers ever hit by a second baseman (overhauling Rogers

enough in New York, bolstered by the return of franchise hero Tom Seaver the previous December; but the ambitious plan hatched by Bamberger and front-office boss Frank Cashen to clean house (unloading veterans Mike Scott, Pat Zachry, Charlie Puleo, and Randy Jones) and rely upon a collection of promising young pitchers from the farm system (Tim Leary, Jeff Bittiger, Rick Ownbey, and Scott Holman) quickly went awry. Bamberger bailed out in total frustration on June 3, after his ineffective mound crew had already helped to send the team tumbling to 16-30 for a solid hold on last place. Over the season's final 116 games, Howard could do little with the cards he was dealt to right the sinking ship or pull the ball club out of last place in the NL East race. Two important developments did transpire during Frank Howard's partial-season tenure: rookie phenom Darryl Strawberry would solidify his spot in the starting lineup en route to an NL Rookie of the Year performance, and Cashen pulled the trigger on a deal with St. Louis that also put Keith Hernandez in a Mets uniform. But the dividends paid by those roster changes would not mature until well into the 1984 season, when Frank Howard was back on the coaching sidelines and Davey Johnson had come on board to launch one of the most successful managerial tenures in club history.

Hornsby's mark of 42) and the other as part of baseball's first trio (with Hank Aaron and Darrell Evans) of 40-homer teammates.

The highlight seasons for Davey Johnson in New York were the championship years of 1986 and 1988, without debate; but his entire six-year reign was somewhat magical. Few managers have been on the job for as many as half a dozen seasons and yet managed to avoid anything approaching a truly bad year. Stengel did it with the Yankees in the fifties, as did Joe McCarthy earlier with the same club in the thirties. John McGraw and Connie Mack had their stretches during the dead-ball era. But Stengel was also a relentless loser for years before inheriting the right club stocked with players named DiMaggio, Mantle, Berra, Ford, and Rizzuto. McGraw, Mack, and even McCarthy all experienced occasional dry spells. Perhaps Al Lopez in Cleveland (Indians) and Chicago (White Sox) during the fifties (nine straight seasons either first or second) would offer a closer parallel. Yet despite Johnson's successes, he was inevitably given the ax the first time his team slumped, even for the short haul. Such is the eventual fate of all managers. And such is the fate of managing any team in New York City.

Davey Johnson (Brace Photo)

One final irony of Davey Johnson's managerial sojourn was that he actually won more divisional titles in a shorter time span in Cincinnati (two in three years) and Baltimore (one in his two seasons) after leaving his first managing job in New York. The invincibility was restored after only a single off-season with the Reds; that was the year his first Cincinnati club came home a dozen games under .500 and in fifth place. But out in Los Angeles, where he took over in 1999 for the latest chapter of his big-league tenure (and where he was fired after the 2000 season), Johnson proved that any manager's abilities, in the end, seem only to reflect the quality of the team that is put around him. For all the ups and downs in other National League cities, it is unlikely that Davey Johnson will be better remembered for any single achievement than for the half dozen years of relentless glory with the 1980s New York Mets.

BUD HARRELSON
(1990-91) Mets Managerial Record:
145 wins, 129 losses, .529 winning percentage

Bud Harrelson is the only Mets skipper to serve in two different seasons and yet never finish out an entire single campaign as the team's bench boss. Yet if he didn't succeed in sticking around for very long during his ill-fated tenure sandwiched between Davey Johnson and Jeff Torborg, he did manage to post a winning career record, something only three other Mets skippers (Johnson, Hodges, and Valentine) have so far been able to accomplish.

It should be pointed out that all of Harrelson's successes came in one partial season, when he took over for the fired Davey Johnson and managed somehow to keep a balanced and potent club on even keel just long enough to extend Johnson's string of first- or second-place division finishes to seven. But when Darryl Strawberry departed via free agency before the start of the 1991 season and the Mets got off to a weak-hitting start in Harrelson's second time around the circuit, the once-popular shortstop wasted little time in proving that he was emotionally ill-equipped for handling the pressures of managing in New York City. The sagging season was increasingly scarred over the summer months by Harrelson's squabbling with the press about roster choices (especially those involving infield lineups and

Bud Harrelson (Brace Photo)

outing (featuring an NL-record-tying 19 Ks in Philadelphia on the final day of the disappointing season) came only after Harrelson's late-season departure. For all the individual heroics, however, the Mets played with visibly little enthusiasm under Harrelson, and the Mets' record of 77-84 (74-80 under Harrelson) was the team's worst showing in eight seasons. The fighting spirit and aggressive attitude that once had made Bud Harrelson so popular with both fans and management during his playing days would produce nothing but negative results once he had achieved his life's dream of managing the New York Mets.

MIKE CUBBAGE
(1991) Mets Managerial Record:
3 wins, 4 losses, .429 winning percentage

Mike Cubbage owns the dubious distinction of posting the shortest tenure among four Mets interim managers. Cubbage brings up the absolute rear on the Mets' managerial list, and his paltry achievements on the bench were restricted to record low totals of seven games and a mere three victories, all recorded in the final week of the tailspinning 1991 NL season. Only an effort at exhaustive completeness justifies even passing mention of Cubbage's brief time spent on the New York bench. As a ballplayer, Mike Cubbage was certainly more distinguished than the Mets' original interim skipper, Salty Parker, though not nearly the equal of the other temporary fill-ins, Frank Howard and Roy McMillan. Cubbage did log eight seasons as a big-league infielder, passing through Texas and Minnesota before ending up with the Mets for a single 1981 season of reserve third-base and pinch-hitting duties. After being traded by the Rangers to the Twins for likely Hall of Famer Bert Blyleven in 1976, the bespectacled Cubbage enjoyed a career year in 1978 when he set a Twins fielding record at the hot corner, batted a lifetime-best .282, and even managed to hit for the cycle. His swan song with the Mets in 1981 made him that season's most often used and most successful pinch hitter, picking up 12 base knocks in 44 pinch at-bats (almost half his year's total plate appearances). But chronic back pain ended his career that same season, and he would next serve as a minor league manager for several summers in the Mets' highly respected and prosperous farm system. During the second of six subsequent seasons as the

the manager's seemingly unbending support for increasingly unpopular second baseman Gregg Jefferies), grumbling in the clubhouse, dispirited play by key members of the team, and a much-celebrated public blowup between the manager and his ace pitcher, David Cone. Enthusiasm on the field and in the grandstands ebbed at Shea Stadium by late summer, and Bud Harrelson was finally fired only a week before the end of the disastrous season.

Harrelson's second season at the helm was, nonetheless, filled with numerous individual performances of high merit. Howard Johnson, who was shuffled between third (104 games), the outfield (30 games), and shortstop (28 games), was the big offensive star, setting a team record for RBIs (117) and leading the NL in home runs (38), extra-base hits (76), and sacrifice flies (15). HoJo's career season at the plate was so impressive that he also tied a club record with his 108 runs scored (second in the league behind LA's Brett Butler) and became only the second major leaguer, after Bobby Bonds, to post 30-30 numbers in steals and homers more than twice. Unsung Mark Carreon also established a new team milestone that summer for career pinch-hit homers. And mound ace Cone paced the senior circuit in strikeouts for the second year running, even though Cone's strongest

Mike Cubbage (Brace Photo)

Mets' third-base coach, Cubbage got the unexpected call for seven days of managing when Bud Harrelson finally suffered the ax from outgoing GM Frank Cashen, who had already announced his own decision to leave the organization and was doing some extensive housecleaning on his way out the door. As the disinterested Mets played out the string in fifth place, the lame duck substitute skipper fell one victory short of posting a winning record during his single, brief fling with the job.

JEFF TORBORG
(1992-93) Mets Managerial Record:
85 wins, 115 losses, .425 winning percentage

Jeff Torborg was one of the Mets' biggest disappointments on the managerial front and his two-year tenure (one full season and one partial campaign) accomplished little beyond symbolizing one of the most frustrating epochs of team history. Torborg's lackluster Mets squads never could seem to get very far off the ground. On the heels of his failed three-year tenure with the Cleveland Indians in the late seventies and a slightly more successful three-year stint with the White Sox a decade later (his team was AL West Division runner-up in both

'90 and '91), the former Dodgers and Angels catcher was tabbed by Mets management in 1992 after earning AL Manager of the Year plaudits in Chicago. It was hoped that the one-time Dodger $100,000 bonus baby could reverse the ominous 1991 single-season slide under Bud Harrelson that had snapped a seven-year streak of first- or second-place finishes. Unfortunately, Torborg only managed to pour gasoline on the brush fires of the previous summer at Shea Stadium, quickly turning them into a raging inferno.

In fairness, the total collapse of Torborg's first Mets team, which lost 90 games and remained buried in fifth, was not entirely the new manager's fault. The 1992 season was an injury-riddled affair for the Shea Stadium crew, with the carnage lasting from early April through late September, and with the club adding names to the disabled list a record 18 times (the previous record was only 11) and placing 14 different players on the DL over the course of the long, painful season—eight at one time in the crucial month of August. Veteran first baseman Eddie Murray, already in the twilight of a Hall of Fame career, was the team's only reliable offensive weapon and paced the club in most offensive categories, including RBIs (93) and BA (.261).

Jeff Torborg (Brace Photo)

Nobody in Mets pinstripes banged as many as 20 homers (Bobby Bonilla collected 19) and no pitcher could win 15 games (Sid Fernandez led with 14). This was not much artillery for a manager to work with, especially a manager not particularly noted for his abilities to win with mirrors alone. When fortunes didn't improve much over the first month of the following campaign, Mets management realized that it had likely miscalculated Torborg's abilities as a take-charge guy capable of lighting fires under the toes of a roster of underachievers. Dallas Green replaced Torborg on May 19, but the fateful die had already been cast for another lead-balloon season. The Torborg-and-Green-led squad of 1993 was destined to become the first Mets outfit since 1983 to finish dead last and also the first since the sixties to lose an embarrassing 100-plus times.

DALLAS GREEN
(1993-96) Mets Managerial Record:
229 wins, 283 losses, .447 winning percentage

Dallas Green had little to offer as a big-league pitcher, and many will also question his contributions on the bench and in the front office as a baseball architect. As a big-league hurler, he won 20 but lost 22 in six seasons with the Phillies, tossed a handful of games for the replacement Senators and expansion Mets without a single decision, and perhaps is best remembered only as the pitcher who gave up the Shea Stadium homer that Jimmy Piersall ran out by trotting around the bases backwards.

As a manager, Green debuted in spectacular fashion with a world championship in Philadelphia, but quickly proved a consistent loser over five New York seasons with the Yankees and Mets. And while there may have been some noteworthy achievements on the management front—producing the Phillies' first-ever World Series title as a manager, and lifting the Cubs to their first postseason appearance in four decades as a GM—none of these came with the New York Mets. Hired to stop the bleeding that started under Jeff Torborg in 1993, Green was of little help in reversing the fortunes of a team that lost 103 games and looked disturbingly like the early "lovable losers" of the Stengel-Westrum epoch. In the strike-disrupted summers of 1994 and 1995, Green's New York clubs were able to reach third and then second in the division, yet never climbed over .500 for the season. His fi-

nal team was headed back in the direction of record losing—at 59-72 and 20-plus games off the pace—when he was finally sacked by Mets management in late August in favor of Bobby Valentine.

Green's mediocre managing performances with the Mets were not that different from his brief tenure on the bench with Steinbrenner's Yankees, where he was also quickly canned for failure to reverse the team's losing and also for second-guessing The Boss's meddling into everyday operations. His firing by the Yankees came 120 games into his first season and resulted when he made the fatal mistake of ridiculing his boss in the press as "Manager George." Green had, however, enjoyed much greater success in his first two managerial roles. Hired late in 1979 by the Philadelphia Phillies—the team he had once toiled for as a part-time starter and bullpen hand in the first five seasons of the 1960s—Green, after one year on the job, led the "Futile Phils" to their first World Series appearance in 30 years and also their first world championship ever. He then quit after only one additional season, largely because of his team's failure to repeat in the division playoff series with Montreal. Taking over immediately as the Cubs' GM, he also enjoyed a string of triumphs in Chicago, shrewdly acquiring future franchise

Dallas Green (Brace Photo)

star Ryne Sandberg from his old employers in Philadelphia and also building a 1984 team that gave the Cubs their first postseason appearance since 1945. But his tenure in Chicago was also short lived, and he had already moved on in the wake of disagreements with corporate ownership before the team he had built around Sandberg and company won another division title five years later.

BOBBY VALENTINE
(1996–) Mets Managerial Record:
379 wins, 301 losses, .557
winning percentage

Bobby Valentine has seemingly thrived on his ongoing stormy relationship with his employers in the Mets organization. This is hardly surprising, since most of Valentine's big- league playing and managing career has been characterized, above all else, by both charisma and controversy. A recent typical incident came in late July of 1999, when the outspoken Mets manager suffered a public relations debacle by publicly moaning about the decision of Mets management to stage a celebration for the large local Dominican community at Shea Stadium by honoring the home run exploits of visiting Chicago Cubs player Sammy Sosa. Despite such occasional crossfire between Valentine and his boss, GM Steve Phillips, the current Mets skipper has shown an amazing resilience and a gritty ability not only to survive but also to win. In the process, he has been rapidly working his way up the list among the ball club's all-time most successful managers, now trailing only Davey Johnson in victories, after passing Yogi Berra, Joe Torre, and Gil Hodges in total victories during the 2000 season.

Valentine's ability to outlast adversity was capsulized by the 1999 wild-card season, when he survived one losing skid in June that threatened his job (and cost him two of his coaches) and then bounced back a second time in late September after another seven-game losing string in the season's final two weeks appeared to sabotage a shot at a National League wild-card slot for the second year in a row. But the

Mets had help down the stretch from the Central Division runner-up Cincinnati Reds, who also faded late under pressure and allowed Valentine's club to tie them for the final playoff opening, then dropped a one-game playoff to New York to settle the wild-card issue. A postseason berth came only on the strength of a brilliant two-hit shutout by staff ace Al Leiter, a somewhat ironic twist, since inconsistent pitching is what has most often sunk skipper Valentine's ship in both Texas and New York.

As a manager, Valentine has always coached contending teams, but has never won the universal praise that comes with winning expected postseason honors. His teams in Texas were among the league's most potent, and yet they could never get over the hump in the American League West, usually because mediocre pitching could not carry his team's heavy hitting. His solid job directing the 1986 Texas club (a second-place finish during his second season) garnered the postseason UPI Manager of the Year award. But after seven years total and three straight seasons lodged in third place in the low-voltage AL West, patience finally wore thin in the Rangers' front office, and Valentine was fired at the 1992 midway point. Not surprisingly, the Texas Rangers have stayed about the same—contenders, but never really more than pretenders—under his successors,

New York Mets All-Time Managers List*

Manager	Years	Wins	Losses	Pct.	Postseason
Davey Johnson	1984-90 (6+)	595	417	.588	1986 WS Winner 1988 NLCS
Bobby Valentine (active)	1996-00 (4+)	379	301	.557	2000 NL Winner 1999 NLCS
Gil Hodges	1968-71 (4)	339	309	.523	1969 WS Winner
Yogi Berra	1972-75 (3+)	292	296	.497	1973 NL Winner
Joe Torre	1977-81 (4+)	286	420	.405	None
Dallas Green	1993-96 (2+)	229	283	.447	None
Casey Stengel	1962-65 (3+)	175	404	.302	None
Bud Harrelson	1990-91 (-2)	145	129	.529	None
Wes Westrum	1965-67 (2+)	142	237	.375	None
Joe Frazier	1976-77 (1+)	101	106	.488	None
Jeff Torborg	1992-93 (1+)	85	115	.425	None
George Bamberger	1982-83 (1+)	81	127	.389	None
Frank Howard	1983 (-1)	52	64	.448	None
Roy McMillan	1975 (-1)	26	27	.491	None
Salty Parker	1967 (-1)	4	7	.364	None
Mike Cubbage	1991 (-1)	3	4	.429	None

*Ranked according to total victories with the New York Mets
Key: (-) equals less than one season; (+) indicates additional partial season

Kevin Kennedy for two seasons and Johnny Oates for six.

But any frustrations at not reaching the top rung in Texas were certainly not new to a career baseball man who has dealt with severe disappointment and tantalizing near misses his entire career. As a ballplayer, Bobby Valentine was something close to a modern version of Pete Reiser. Few have come on the big-league scene with a larger and more damning tag of "unlimited potential" or a more hopelessly unreachable set of overblown expectations. An outstanding Connecticut high school football and baseball star, Valentine was plucked in the first round of the June 1968 free agent draft by the Los Angeles Dodgers and immediately flashed brilliance by leading the 1970 Pacific Coast League with a hefty .340 average. But, as was the case with Brooklyn's Pete Reiser back in the '40s, a deadly combination of injury and aggressive play would soon cut off all the promise far short of its prime. During his 1970 PCL Player-of-the-Year season, the hard-hitting young outfielder fractured his cheekbone during postseason playoffs. After two eye-catching seasons in the big time with the parent Dodgers, the hot prospect was traded to the California Angels and promptly broke his leg in two places by (à la Reiser) running into an outfield wall. He was batting over .300 at the time and seemed finally

Bobby Valentine (NY Mets)

on his way to everyday stardom. Rebounding from the May 1973 leg injury, which almost prematurely ended his promising career, Valentine returned the next year but separated his shoulder. Brief big-league trials followed with both the Padres and the Mets, but the now-fragile outfielder was never again the same hard-hit-

---

New York Mets All-Time Coaches Roster*

Bob Apodaca (1996-2000)	Vern Hoscheit (1984-87)	Bill Robinson (1984-89)
Bruce Benedict (1997-2000)	**Frank Howard (1982-84, 1994-96)**	Sheriff Robinson (1964-67, 1972)
Yogi Berra (1965-71)	Darrell Johnson (1993)	Tom Robson (1997-99)
Tom Burgess (1977)	Deron Johnson (1981)	Red Ruffing (1962)
Chuck Cottier (1987-91)	Red Kress (1962)	Cookie Rojas (1997-2000)
Mike Cubbage (1990-96)	Dave LaRoche (1992-93)	Dick Sisler (1979-80)
Gene Dusan (1983)	Cookie Lavagetto (1962-63)	Dennis Sommers (1977-78)
Doc Edwards (1990-91)	Dal Maxvill (1978)	Warren Spahn (1965)
Barry Foote (1992-93)	Willie Mays (1974-79)	Tom Spencer (1991)
Jim Frey (1982-83)	Tom McCraw (1992-96)	Rusty Staub (1982++)
Bob Gibson (1981)	Clyde McCullough (1963)	Mel Stottlemyre (1984-93)
Harvey Haddix (1966-67)	**Roy McMillan (1973-76)**	Steve Swisher (1994-96)
Mel Harder (1964)	Bill Monbouquette (1982-83)	**Bobby Valentine (1983-85)**
Bud Harrelson (1982, 1985-90)	John Murphy (1967)	Rube Walker (1968-81)
Don Heffner (1964-65)	Randy Niemann (1997-99)	**Wes Westrum (1964-65)**
Solly Hemus (1962-63)	**Salty Parker (1967)**	Ernie White (1963)
Whitey Herzog (1966)	Greg Pavlick (1985-86, 1988-91, 1994)	Mookie Wilson (1997-2000)
Chuck Hiller (1990)	Sam Perlozzo (1987-89)	Bobby Wine (1993-96)
Rogers Hornsby (1962)	Joe Pignatano (1968-81)	Ed Yost (1968-75)

*Boldface indicates coaches who served as managers or interim managers; ++indicates player-coach

---

ting speedster he had once been and was finally forced by his reduced abilities to retire in 1979 after 10 disappointing seasons, only three of which saw him play 100-plus games.

Reviving his managerial career with the Mets as a late-season replacement for Dallas Green in 1996, Bobby Valentine has remained on the winning side of the ledger in all but his first partial season. His clubs have slowly climbed in a positive direction, finishing third in the NL East in 1997, climbing to second in 1988 with a second straight year of 88 victories, and repeating the second-place performance with 97 wins in 1999, his third full season on the job. For all the successes of the past few campaigns, however, there has also been more than the normal spate of team disharmony and unfulfilled expectation to balance out the ledger. The 1998 Mets team, riding the enthusiasm of the mid-season acquisition of Mike Piazza, collapsed in the final week of September and thus lost a postseason wild-card berth to the Chicago Cubs on the season's final day. The potent 1999 ball club—boasting an infield of Ventura, Ordoñez, Alfonzo, and Olerud, which many thought might be the best defense in big-league history—fell tantalizingly close to the century mark in victories, yet nonetheless trailed division rival Atlanta by seven full lengths. Clinching the wild-card berth this time around, Valentine's crew eliminated the NL West-cham-

pion Arizona Diamondbacks and also battled gamely against the pitching-rich Atlanta Braves in the NLCS before falling in six. The final pennant-deciding series was much closer than the two-game margin might suggest, since all but one game was decided by a single run. Valentine had finally silenced some of his critics in October 1999 by ending a frustrating skein of 1,704 games as a big-league manager without a single playoff appearance—the longest such string since divisional play began back in 1969. But the feisty manager still received less than rave reviews from some critics who faulted his team for lack of cohesiveness in the postseason after a celebrated incident in which disgruntled veterans Rickey Henderson and Bobby Bonilla played cards in the team clubhouse during the final innings of the last postseason game of the year.

Valentine's 2000 Mets club won 97 games, the fifth-highest victory total in club history. More important, his New Yorkers earned a wild-card berth in the playoffs for the second consecutive season. The Mets dispatched the San Francisco Giants in the Division Series, then beat the Cardinals in the NLCS, earning a spot in the World Series versus the crosstown Yankees.

Through the 2000 season, Valentine ranks eighth among active major league managers with 960 career victories.

CHAPTER 8
Legendary Front-Office Personalities and Memorable Broadcast Voices

Colorful characters in the New York Mets family have never been restricted to the oversized ballplaying heroes and colorful cup-of-coffee clowns who have manned the playing field, or even to the revolving cast of field managers who have directed team fortunes from the far end of the bench. No owner has been more beloved than Mrs. Joan Payson, and no broadcasters more engaging than Lindsey Nelson or Ralph Kiner. When it comes to general managers calling the shots, sealing club fortunes, and making the headline-grabbing blockbuster deals from the front office, the Mets also boast a notable tradition which begins with George Weiss and includes some of the most daring wheelers and dealers of baseball's past four decades.

GEORGE WEISS

The most farsighted single personnel maneuver of early Mets history was undoubtedly the hiring of Casey Stengel as the team's initial field manager. Not far behind, however, ranks the earlier landing of Stengel's old Yankees cohort George Weiss to run the club's front-office operations. Weiss, like Stengel, had been dumped by the Yankees in a premature house-cleaning that would eventually come back to haunt the venerable Bronx Bombers only a few years down the road. The man who had started as farm director for Col. Jacob Ruppert in the early '30s became GM at Yankee Stadium in 1948 and promptly hired Stengel to hold the reins of the greatest Yankee dynasty ever, but had been nonetheless forced into unwanted retirement immediately after the 1960 World Series. With both Weiss and Stengel gone, and with the Yanks' farm system no longer producing constant renewals, as it once did, the Yankees would soon be headed for a free fall into the cellar of the American League. But thankfully for New York ball fans, the Mets would—at precisely the same time—rise from their early ashes and emerge at the top of the National League heap.

A portrait of George Weiss, the new general manager of the New York Yankees, October 8, 1947. (AP/Wide World Photos)

Both developments had a lot to do, directly and indirectly, with George Weiss.

Weiss had not at first been earmarked for the top job with New York's expansion National League franchise. It was a shrewd move on the part of Joan Payson's chosen spokesperson, Donald Grant, however, that changed the direction of front-office operations before the ball club was ever truly out of the starting gate. Grant had wanted William Shea's original Continental League "co-conspirator," Branch Rickey, to be the front-office architect of the spanking new club. But Rickey immediately raised impossible demands that closed the door on his own candidacy. The man who had invented farm systems, integrated baseball with Jackie Robinson, and brought Roberto Clemente to the majors with the Pirates now wanted a $5 million operating budget and complete control of club operations. It was more than Grant could offer, and thus Weiss seemed to be a logical second choice. The architect of the Yankees' greatest era and four-time baseball executive of the year had been set adrift by Yankee owners Dan Topping and Del Webb, who now thought Weiss too old for the job, but for Weiss—for whom baseball was life's beginning, middle, and end—the prospect of leaving the game altogether was not easily accepted. Nor, apparently, was it an attractive prospect for Mrs. George Weiss, who greeted his Yankee dismissal with a famous caustic rejoinder: "I married him for better or for worse, but not for lunch."

Weiss was clearly not ready to retire, and although the Yankees' termination agreement with the 65-year-old executive banned him from serving in the GM capacity with some other club, Grant quickly saw his way around that obstacle by designating his new de facto GM as official club president. Weiss brought the Mets an unmatchable track record of success that some would argue had already proven him to be the most astute front-office operative in baseball history. And, of course, the revenge motive might also have had a hand in enhancing Weiss's value to a team whose first task was to compete at the ticket windows with the cross-town AL ball club. Whatever his own motivations, George Weiss wasted little time in putting the necessary pieces together to build a salable product at the box office and a competitive roster on the field. Of course, the former task was much easier than the latter. Weiss's method of operation on both fronts was to rely upon familiar names and faces—especially those with a National League flavor—that would hopefully attract the necessary fan base. The strategy produced few on-field results, with former heroes Duke Snider, Charlie Neal, Roger Craig, Gil Hodges, Don Zimmer, Warren Spahn, Richie Ashburn, and Yogi Berra cycling through the makeshift Mets lineup. There were some much larger dividends to be gained by bringing Willie Mays back to Gotham in a Mets uniform, since Mays actually had some hits left in his magic bat when he was acquired from the Giants in 1972. But the Mays deal came half a dozen years after Weiss had once more retired in 1966. Fortunately for the Mets' future, Weiss was also busy, during his four years on the job, rapidly shaping a farm system capable of producing a new generation of stars. Much of that work also received an able assist from Bing Devine, who was brought on board as Weiss's assistant and heir apparent in 1965, and Eddie Stanky, who came over from St. Louis with Devine to head up player development. (Stanky would remain only one year, before departing to manage the White Sox, and Devine would last only two, before returning to his old post with the Cardinals.) If there was a criticism of Weiss's short reign with the Mets, in the end, it would have to be his strategy of building at the start with journeymen and castoffs who offered nothing but a stopgap solution. But this was a tactic that would quickly be reversed—and for the better—by Weiss's immediate successors.

BING DEVINE

Bing Devine served only a pair of seasons in the Mets' front office—one as Weiss's assistant and the other as his successor—but it was a most memorable if brief tenure, during which many of the seeds were sown for the ball club's imminent rise to prominence. Devine's distinguished career as a baseball executive stretched far beyond his short stay in New York. As a talented front office operative with the St. Louis Cardinals both before and after his short New York adventure, Devine proved to be a remarkably innovative administrator. He had been chief architect of the 1964 St. Louis world-championship team that had finally ended the Yankees' dynasty. In his early '60s stint in the Cardinals' front office, he was most likely the first GM ever to employ the new technology of a telephone answering machine to receive daily farm-system updates. He also moved Whitey Herzog from his third-base coaching assignment into a front-office slot, a move that paid huge dividends down the road for the Mets when Herzog later directed the New York farm system boom of the late sixties and early seventies. And when Devine came on board with the Mets, he immediately saw that the club's future would have to rest upon a substantial youth movement of a type that had so far stalled under the tactics of his predecessor, George Weiss.

Surprisingly, for all his achievements, it was the one year in command in New York that may have been the true highlight of Devine's ever-active career of wheeling and dealing. That year also marked a reversal of fortune for the still-stumbling NL expansion club, launching the Mets toward their exciting future as a legitimate pennant contender. Much of the credit for that marvelous transformation goes directly to Bing Devine, the man known everywhere around the National League simply as Trader Bing. An expansion club on the verge of a breakout was, of course, the ideal spot for a notorious big-time deal-maker to be turned loose. If the Mets team of 1966 had been the most popular yet, with 66 wins and a first step out of the NL cellar, it was still an outfit that featured old-timers such as Ken Boyer and Roy McMillan in the everyday lineup. Devine immediately sensed that the club's future hinged on youngsters such as Ron Swoboda and Jerry Grote and not veterans such as Jim Hickman and Ron Hunt. He thus immediately set to work dismantling and reconstructing the team's lackluster roster. By opening day of 1967, half the roster included new faces, and a whopping 19 players had turned over since the opener a season earlier. His first week on the job, Devine traded All-Star second baseman Hunt and the last original Met, Hickman, to the LA Dodgers in exchange for outfielder Tommy Davis, who was coming off a .313 season and had twice paced the senior circuit in batting. A less successful deal—the one perhaps best remembered and most cursed from the brief Devine era—shipped the club's first winning pitcher, Dennis Ribant, to the Pirates for veteran hurler Don Cardwell and a hot outfield prospect named Don Bosch. Bosch was reputed to be a center fielder reminiscent of Willie Mays with his glove, if not his bat. But saddled with unrealistic expectations, Bosch would quickly prove a complete bust in New York. Despite Bosch's immediate failure (he was back in the

Bing Devine (St. Louis Cardinals Photo)

minors in June), Trader Bing was hardly discouraged about his reclamation project and continued dealing and tinkering at a pace that produced a record 54 players in Mets uniforms before the season was out. The 27 Mets hurlers on board that summer established a new NL mark and also tied the existing American League record. While fans were first baffled by the constant roster shuffling and attendance slid in the face of a stumble back into the basement, it was a season in which a corner had been turned. The club's future was now in the hands of its youngsters, and the most important youngster, Tom Seaver, made his rookie splash that very season. Devine was gone before another season opened: He returned to St. Louis after Stan Musial decided he really didn't want a career as a general manager. But the seeds had already been planted for a very different Mets team—one that would be making monumental waves before another pair of seasons had run their full course.

JOHN MURPHY

Other than the tragic death of Gil Hodges on the eve of the 1972 season, no sudden demise has shocked the Mets family more deeply than the unexpected loss of general manager

Johnny Murphy in the aftermath of the team's first exciting World Series victory. Murphy had been on the job as GM only two years, and those years had indisputably been the two most miraculous years of franchise history. Three decades later, the 1968 and 1969 campaigns may still well claim that distinction. Today John Murphy's memory is perpetually honored by an annual trophy presented to the top Mets rookie in spring training camp. Masato Yoshii and Melvin Mora have been the most recent winners of the prestigious John J. Murphy Award. Murphy's impact on the Mets family was brief but lasting: For a four-year span at the end of the first franchise decade, he served in a variety of capacities with the upstart New York National League team, including the roles of chief scout, vice president, and finally, general manager. And it was as the team's third general manager that his presence is likely never to be forgotten.

In his own ballplaying career, Murphy also owned quite a remarkable set of credentials as one of the most versatile pitchers of the 1930s and following war years. The durable righty, known enigmatically as "Grandma Murphy," began with the Joe McCarthy-managed Yankees as a starter in an era that did not yet feature bullpen specialization. But before his dozen Yankee seasons had played out, he had transformed himself into one of the leading relief specialists of his age and had set records for bullpen work that stood until the modern age completely altered the nature of pitching rotations: Murphy posted 12 relief wins in both 1937 and 1943 and had 107 career saves and 73 career relief wins. The World Series was his most successful venue, however, and in six Series with the Bronx Bombers, he compiled a remarkably stingy 1.10 ERA. At the conclusion of a playing career that ended in Boston in 1947, Murphy remained with the Red Sox as farm-club director, a post he was not dismissed from until 1961, during an overall shakeup of that club's top administrative staff. But in the end, Murphy will likely most be remembered as the chief architect of the improbable Miracle Mets. And no accomplishment of

that miraculous building task was more noteworthy than his role in bringing Gil Hodges to New York to manage the destiny-blessed Mets. Hodges had been an early choice to replace Stengel in 1965 and had been rumored to be headed back to New York several times during his successful five-year managerial stint devoted to legitimizing another expansion club—the new Washington Senators. But the move only came as the joint effort of two former Yankees teammates, Mets VP Murphy (still weeks away from replacing Devine as GM) and Senators GM George Selkirk, who worked out a deal in Boston during the 1967 World Series. Manager Hodges was traded to New York for pitcher Bill Denehy and $100,000 cash. As soon as Murphy formally replaced Devine, he pulled the trigger on a second major deal (largely at Hodges's urging), acquiring center fielder Tommie Agee and utility man Al Weis from the White Sox. Both would be major World Series heroes at the end of their second New York season. Murphy's final front-office maneuver, which solidified the Mets' miracle season, was the acquisition of Donn Clendenon from Montreal a third of the way into the championship 1969 campaign. The Hodges, Agee, and Clendenon transactions were the building blocks of a most surprising Mets pennant before 1969 was out. The tragedy of it all was that Murphy lived barely long enough to see the fruits of his labor, and he never truly got to savor the impact of all that he had accomplished.

BOB SCHEFFING

Bob Scheffing made his lasting, if not head-turning, mark on baseball history at each of its available career levels. As a ballplayer, he was a solid defensive catcher who also managed to hit .300 with the postwar Chicago Cubs in 1948. The Missouri native logged eight big-league seasons and rarely hit with much power, but did manage to post a one-year batting mark nearly 40 points above his career average with the 1948 edition of the Chicago North Siders. As a successful short-term field manager, he had the rare distinction

---

New York Mets Retired Numbers

42—Retired by MLB in honor of Jackie Robinson on April 15, 1997 (retired by all major league teams)

41—Retired in honor of Tom Seaver on July 24, 1988, making Seaver the only Mets player to have his number retired

37—Retired in honor of the first Mets field manager, Casey Stengel

14—Retired in honor of popular Mets field manager Gil Hodges

Bob Scheffing inks Tom Seaver to a contract in February 1970, one that would make Tom Terrific the highest paid player in baseball. (Daily News photo by Gene Kappock)

of winning 101 games with the 1961 Detroit Tigers and still finishing second to the Maris and Mantle-powered, homer-happy New York Yankees under Casey Stengel. And as a front office-executive, he played a vital role as Mets general manager in one of the most crucial six-year spans in club history. It was Scheffing who oversaw the New York club at the time of Gil Hodges's shocking death during the strike-torn preseason of 1972. It was also Scheffing who promptly hired Yogi Berra to replace Hodges and who thus also enjoyed the fruits of the team's second NL pennant. Scheffing himself was gone from the scene before Berra's eventual firing two seasons later, but it was nonetheless Scheffing who left perhaps the blackest mark on the Hodges-Berra era of Mets history when he traded Nolan Ryan to the California Angels in one of the worst deals in all of baseball history.

It was that Nolan Ryan trade that forever put Scheffing in the doghouse with New York Mets fans and earned him the scorn of revisionist baseball historians. At the time, however, the deal didn't appear to be such a bad one, given the club's desperate need to fill a perennial hole at the hot-corner slot (Jim Fregosi seemed as good a bet to help out there as anyone else who

might have been available), and also given Ryan's inconsistent performances over his first five seasons (he had only one winning season to date and walked nearly as many as he struck out) and his reported distaste for New York City life. The Mets would be in the hunt for a pennant in the upcoming 1972 season, with a little defensive tinkering, and there was every reason to believe that Fregosi was an outstanding defensive shortstop who could make the transition to third. Of course, Fregosi's failure to adjust to Shea Stadium, and Ryan's eventual Cooperstown credentials, later cast the whole matter in a different light. Years later, Scheffing would give his own explanation of the ill-fated deal to Jack Lang of the *New York Daily News*, stating that "Ryan told me after the 1971 season that he didn't want to spend another year in New York and hoped I would trade him. I don't think he would have walked away from baseball, but I couldn't take that chance." The three players the Mets added to the deal for Fregosi were never the source of grumblings from the Shea Stadium faithful: Leroy Stanton, Don Rose, and Francisco Estrada never became household names with the Angels. In hindsight, the transaction thus seems understandable enough. Unless, of course, you are a New York Mets fan.

JOAN PAYSON

Baseball has known few more beloved or successful team owners than Joan Payson, or few that have loved the game any more deeply than did the original owner of the New York Mets. But it also helped Mrs. Payson's impact on the game she loved so immeasurably that she was as deep in the pocketbook as she was long on enthusiasm. Few modern baseball owners have ever managed a healthier supply of ready cash, allowing them to successfully underwrite such an intense baseball passion. Joan Whitney Payson descended from a heritage well anchored in the nation's history. One of her grandfathers—John Hay—was a private secretary to Abraham Lincoln and secretary of state under William McKinley and Teddy Roosevelt; her other grandfather—William Collins Whitney—was Grover Cleveland's secretary of the navy. And throughout her life, she was almost as active and influential in the world of art (her personal collection included several Van Goghs) and horse racing (owning Greentree Stables, which produced a long line of thoroughbred champions) as she was in the world of baseball. Such "hobbies" were underwritten by a personal fortune estimated in the late fifties to be worth between $100 million and $200 million.

But it was baseball that was always Joan Payson's overriding passion, and it remained so throughout her 14-year association with the Mets' often roller-coaster operations. The love affair began as a child, when she attended New York Giants games in the Polo Grounds during the John McGraw era. Eventually, she would come to own 10 percent of the team she had rooted for as a child, and Mrs. Payson would be the only stockholder to oppose that team's flight in 1958 from New York City to the greener pastures of San Francisco. Payson was back in the baseball business only a few short years later when she grabbed a 30 percent share of New York's newly awarded expansion club from Mrs. Dorothy Killiam, a one-time Dodgers fan. It was enough to set her up as majority owner; and by the time of her death in 1975, she controlled more than 80 percent of the Mets' franchise value. Once she became the majority stockholder in the fledgling Mets ball club, the affluent sportswoman finally was in a position to place her indelible stamp upon the game she loved. And that stamp came in several distinct forms. Perhaps Payson's most enduring legacy will be that of the ball club's naming. It was Payson who picked out the moniker that would remain the foremost symbol of team identity, when she personally settled on "Mets" after her handpicked naming committee had narrowed the field to such enticing choices as Skyliners, Jets, Skyscrapers, and Burros. Other hands-on Joan Payson activities destined to affect club fortunes were her naming of Donald Grant as her personal representative and decision maker on team policy matters, her lobby-

Joan Whitney Payson celebrates a first world championship for her beloved Mets. (Daily News photo by James Garrett)

New York Mets General Managers	
George Weiss (1962-66)	Oversaw the five-year expansion epoch
Bing Devine (1967)	Hired Gil Hodges as Mets manager
Johnny Murphy (1968-69)	Died in office of sudden heart atttack
Bob Scheffing (1970-74)	Traded Nolan Ryan to California Angels
Joe McDonald (1975-79)	Traded Tom Seaver to Cincinnati Reds
Frank Cashen (1980-91)	Claimed Darryl Strawberry and Dwight Gooden in June amateur drafts
Al Harazin (1992-93)	Hired Jeff Torborg as Mets manager
Joe McIlvaine (1993-97)	Oversaw rebuilding under Dallas Green
Steve Phillips (1997-)	Rebuilt team under Bobby Valentine

ing to secure personal favorite Gil Hodges for the original Mets roster, and her convincing Casey Stengel that he should unretire to take on duties as the team's first field manager. But Payson, for all her ballpark passion, was a hands-off owner, leaving Grant in charge of every business detail and saving her own energies for rabid rooting (which often included hexing opposing players) from her strategic box seat behind home plate.

Upon Joan Payson's death in 1975, the club fell under the control of her husband, Charles Shipman Payson, who displayed little interest in its operations (or fortunes) and first delegated further power to Donald Grant before finally granting operating control to his daughter Lorinda de Roulet. Miss de Roulet made a futile short-term effort to resurrect the then-sagging fortunes of her mother's beloved ball club during the 1979 season, but the family finally abandoned ship that year and sold out to a group headed by Nelson Doubleday and Fred Wilpon on the eve of the 1980 National League season. Replacement owner Doubleday was a great-nephew of baseball's mythic founder, Abner Doubleday; and partner Fred Wilpon's own baseball roots stretched back to his schoolboy days, when he once pitched batting practice for the Brooklyn Dodgers in cozy Ebbets Field. But neither figurehead of the Mets' second ownership family could ever match Joan Payson when it came to a ball club mogul savoring the very heart and soul of the national game.

FRANK CASHEN

The New York Mets were built up, brick by brick, as a serious National League competitor on three separate occasions. The first construction project stretched across the woeful expansion seasons of the early and mid-sixties and was a front-office team effort. George Weiss had launched the slow birthing process with his patient oversight of the construction of a new ballpark home in Flushing Meadows and with the step-by-step acquisition of the first scattered pieces of a legitimate big-league playing roster. Bing Devine played a lesser but nonetheless significant role in his one brief year on the job as Weiss's replacement. And Johnny Murphy made the final, crucial adjustments before he was struck down tragically by a heart attack. It was ex-big-leaguer Murphy who arranged for Gil Hodges to rejoin the ball club as field manager,

Frank Cashen (NY Mets)

a move that solidified the Mets' progress toward overnight legitimacy. The second occasion for major construction—in truth, reconstruction—came with the rebuilding efforts after the "Miracle Mets" 1969 championship season. Bob Scheffing was the chief architect this time around, even if he had to suffer the onerous responsibility of trading away future Hall of Famer Nolan Ryan. Scheffing is unfairly remembered far more vividly for letting Ryan escape from New York than he is for a second trade—the one involving Felix Millan and southpaw hurler George Stone—which proved to have far greater impact on team fortunes at the time. The third, and by far most difficult, franchise reconstruction project involved the complete overhauling of the ball club engineered by Frank Cashen during the darkest franchise years. In the end, Cashen perhaps left a far more measurable mark on the Mets' future fortunes than any of his predecessors.

Most of the votes in any mythical poll to select the most successful New York Mets general manager would undoubtedly be cast for Frank Cashen, the sixth executive in club history to hold the title and also the longest-surviving operative in the top front-office position. Before joining the Mets in 1980 as chief operating officer (a job he held jointly with his GM post through 1991), Cashen had already rung up impressive credentials in a similar position with the AL Baltimore Orioles. Overall, teams under his direction would appear in five World Series (one for the Mets) and walk off with three

world-championship rings (again one for New York). And the dozen years he served at Shea Stadium saw some of the boldest feats of wheeling and dealing in the entire four-decade existence of the team.

Cashen came on board with the club still struggling badly both on the field and at the gate in the throes of the final years of Payson family ownership. Under manager Joe Torre in the late '70s, the Mets had dipped back to levels that were all too reminiscent of the dreadful teams of the very first expansion years. Only this time around, there were no lovable Casey Stengels or laughable Marv Throneberrys to distract patrons and provide guaranteed fun at the park. There was no forgiving honeymoon aura surrounding the Metropolitans ball club now. The Mets had already been big-time winners twice, and no longer would butcherous play; inept performers; or endless, yearlong losing be tolerated. The club had recently been further devastated by the forced trade of franchise icon Tom Seaver, who was now working magic for the rival and highly successful ball club in Cincinnati. And the rest of a once-vaunted Mets pitching staff had also collapsed by the end of the seventies. Koosman resurrected his career with 20 victories in 1979, but did so with Minnesota; Gary Gentry was out of baseball altogether; the Mets had recently been relying on hurlers with names like Nino Espinosa, Skip Lockwood, and Craig Swan, and this was a big comedown from a tandem like Seaver and Koosman. Once the best pitching staff in baseball for nearly a decade, the Mets' mound corps was now nearly worthless and altogether short on entertainment value. No Mets hurler had cracked 15 victories since 1976, and neither Swan nor Espinosa struck terror in the hearts of opponents as a staff ace. The team thus suffered its worst years at the gate (not even drawing a million in 1979, for the first time since the inaugural year), and the franchise was in a deep depression from the corporate office to the clubhouse when Cashen was handed the unlikely savior's role. It was a daunting task indeed that faced the new, yet experienced, general manager.

Few men in recent baseball history have more readily met such a front-office challenge head-on, or reversed a club's sagging fortunes any more swiftly. There was immediate progress during the 1980 season, when it came to re-creating interest among the local fandom, even if it did not mean escaping the league basement. Attendance began to climb for the first time in half a dozen seasons, first jumping back over the million mark in 1980 and then moving steadily in the direction of two million over the next five campaigns. A hopeful experiment with Cashen's old Baltimore pitching coach George Bamberger as field manager didn't prove very successful and was perhaps the only real black spot of the brief era. (Another was the accidental loss of Tom Seaver for a second time when GM Cashen left the veteran hurler unprotected in the 1984 free-agent-compensation draft pool.) The roster pieces were simply not yet there for Bamby to have much hope of winning consistently or leaping up in the NL East standings; if there was a fresh face on the end of the bench, there were few fresh arms in the shellshocked New York bullpen. But there were definite signs of clear progress in the early eighties, and two of them were the astute draft choices spent on high schoolers Darryl Strawberry and Dwight Gooden. The pair were destined to become two of the decade's biggest NL stars and also two of the grandest heroes in any period of Mets history. A final, important move orchestrated by Cashen was the promotion from Tidewater of manager Davey Johnson. (An equally important move was Johnson's insertion of rookies Gooden and Darling in the starting pitching rotation, a maneuver at first opposed by Cashen.) With Johnson at the helm and Strawberry and Gooden breaking into the lineup, the revamped Mets were suddenly the toast of the senior circuit. Other important elements had also been put in place by Cashen's front office to adequately supplement the new cast of showcase stars and efficient manager. As a result, the final few years of Cashen's reign would boast some of the brightest achievements in Mets history.

LINDSEY NELSON

Lindsey Nelson was one of the giants of baseball broadcasting whose nearly two decades behind the Mets' microphone established a legend that rests comfortably alongside those of Mel Allen, Red Barber, Ernie Harwell, Bob Prince, Bob Elson, Vin Scully, and Harry Caray. Nelson's tenure with the Mets, which began with the ball club's maiden season and lasted through 1978, was the final chapter in a celebrated broadcasting career that earned Nelson

the 1988 Ford C. Frick Award and thus a plaque on the walls of Cooperstown among baseball's immortals and indelible legends.

Lindsey Nelson's career began in another baseball era in the shadows of World War II. A native Tennessean, Nelson got his start in sports journalism as a teenage reporter for his hometown paper in Columbia. But he first made his mark on the broader regional scene by describing minor league action in Knoxville, then sprang on the national scene almost overnight when the new Liberty Broadcasting System chose him to re-create the then-popular major league radio game of the day. When night games became standard big-league fare in the late '40s, Nelson re-created 62 different games during one hectic stretch of one month. By 1952, the meteoric rise of the young broadcasting whiz had landed him the job of sports director for the National Broadcasting Company, even though he was still only 33 at the time. Other duties in the fifties and sixties included airing a National Basketball Association game of the week for six winter seasons and NCAA Saturday-afternoon college football for a lengthy span of 14 years. He also worked Saturday-afternoon Notre Dame football for a number of seasons, and NFL football for one network on Sundays and another on Monday nights. To top it all off, Nelson was also the radio voice of the New Year's Day Cotton Bowl in Dallas for a full quarter of a century.

It was in the wake of this whirlwind career as a household name in national sports broadcasting that Lindsey Nelson surprised many observers by leaving his comfortable network niche and signing on with the new expansion National League team in New York. For Nelson, it was a chance to enjoy the regular, if still hectic, schedule that a daily baseball assignment represented, and also a home base with his family in New York; for the Mets, it was another coup of early franchise history that ranked up there alongside the hiring of general manager George Weiss and field manager Casey Stengel. If the Mets were not to be immediately legitimate on the field, they would certainly be big league in the broadcast booth from day one, with Nelson manning the mike alongside experienced Bob Murphy (coming off nine seasons with the Red Sox and Orioles) and National League home run star Ralph Kiner, another household baseball name, if not yet a polished play-by-play man. Nelson was the big catch, hav-

Lindsey Nelson (SPI Archives)

ing just served the previous five summers as Lou Durocher's partner on popular NBC "Game of the Week" Saturday baseball telecasts. And Nelson quickly became a broadcast legend during early Mets seasons in New York, most renowned for his low-key descriptions of the earliest stumblebum editions of the expansion ball club, and also for his colorful checkered sports jackets, which became his personal trademark in front of the Mets' television cameras.

BOB MURPHY

When it comes to Mets baseball, Bob Murphy has pretty much seen it all. In fact, no man or woman alive has seen quite as much, except perhaps for original broadcast sidekick Ralph Kiner. Murphy joined the Mets' on-air team for the inaugural Polo Grounds season and has been a part of that airwaves team every season since—39 seasons and counting. While Kiner has, over the years, been the mainstay of the television booth, Murphy has played the same role on the radio side of Mets broadcasts.

Bob Murphy has worked alongside Ralph Kiner in the Mets' broadcast booth for all 39 seasons of ballclub history. (NY Mets)

In recent years, his long and faithful service has reaped some of the top awards in the profession, culminating with the prestigious Ford C. Frick trophy in 1994 and his corresponding induction into the writers' and broadcasters' wing of the National Baseball Hall of Fame. In February of 2000, Murphy added to his growing trophy case with the William J. Slocum Long and Meritorious Service Award from the New York chapter of the Baseball Writers Association of America.

Murphy's career did not begin at the Polo Grounds in 1962, nor has it been restricted to exclusive work describing action in the diamond sport. His big-league broadcast days were launched in 1954 with the Boston Red Sox at Fenway Park, and his play-by-play efforts have also included numerous college football broadcasts (including six Orange Bowls and five Gator Bowls) down through the years. There was also a short stint in the booth with the Baltimore Orioles at the outset of the sixties. And Bob Murphy also boasts a special family lineage when it comes to baseball journalism. He is the younger brother of renowned San Diego colum-

nist Jack Murphy, for whom that city's current major league ballpark was originally named.

RALPH KINER

Ralph Kiner qualified for 1975 Hall of Fame induction in Cooperstown by the slimmest of margins (by one vote in his final year of eligibility), but that near miss had only to do with the brevity of his eye-catching career and absolutely nothing to do with his on-field credentials or lasting record book entries. Playing only the minimum 10 years required for Cooperstown election, Ralph Kiner nonetheless amassed some of the most impressive slugging credentials found anywhere in baseball annals.

Over his full 10-year span with three lackluster ball clubs Kiner's total numbers for home run hitting dwarf those of many noteworthy sluggers who played almost 10 more years than Kiner and yet accomplished little more. His single-season marks are the ones by which he will be best remembered, and most of those came in his first few seasons on the scene in Pittsburgh with the lowly, loss-ridden Pirates. Debuting as the Pittsburgh left fielder in the aftermath of World War II, the muscular righty was immediately responsible for a surge in Steel City attendance when he became the club's first home run king since 1906, even though his total of 23 homers (1946) was the lowest figure to lead the circuit since the dawn of the Babe Ruth "big stick" era in 1921. When the Pirates acquired fading slugger Hank Greenberg in 1947, they also shortened their outfield fences to accommodate their two behemoth sluggers; Kiner's total soared to 51, enough to tie New York Giants fence-buster Johnny Mize for another league crown. Kiner and Mize shared the lead again in 1948 (with 40), but for the four seasons after that, Ralph Kiner reigned as the National League's supreme slugger. Among baseball's pantheon of great slugging threats—from Ruth to Aaron to McGwire—none before or since has duplicated Kiner's feat of winning or sharing the home run crown in each of his first seven seasons in the big leagues.

The Pirates dealt their slugging star to the Chicago Cubs early in the 1953 season after

Ralph Kiner has described Mets games since their inaugural season in 1962. (Brace Photo)

deciding that they were as likely to finish in the league's basement with him as they would be without him. By then, Kiner was clearly near the end of his short road in the big time, and a worsening back condition limited his home run output to mere human dimensions in a handful of disappointing final seasons with the Cubs and the Cleveland Indians. Although he was on the downslide at career's end, Kiner hung up his spikes still able to boast of a home run every 14.1 trips to the plate, a ratio of home runs to at-bats still surpassed half a century later only by McGwire and Ruth. After his chronic sciatica brought a premature end to Kiner's playing days, he established his mark for an equally brief time as a minor league executive, serving the PCL's San Diego Padres as GM in the late fifties. He then entered the broadcast booth of the Chicago White Sox and thus embarked on a baseball-related career that has been anything but short in its tenure. Joining the newborn Mets in time for their inaugural season in the Polo Grounds, Kiner has been a mainstay in the team's radio and television broadcast booths ever since. The uninterrupted tenure has been marked by a colorful penchant for uttering some of baseball's most outrageous and endearing malapropisms. These "Kinerisms" have included such gems as "We'll be back right after this word from our sponsor, Manufacturer's Hangover" and others even less fit to print. But this is only part of the colorful personality which—along with a melodious voice and sage interpretations of baseball strategy—has helped to make Ralph Kiner one of baseball's heaviest-hitting radio and television commentators.

TIM McCARVER

Tim McCarver has fused a colorful 16-year baseball broadcasting career onto a memorable major league playing career that lasted a remarkable 21 seasons. McCarver's durability as a player takes on special significance since, as a catcher, he manned one of the sport's most physically taxing lineup slots. Debuting with the St. Louis Cardinals in 1959, the savvy and dependable catcher didn't finally hang up his spikes with the Philadelphia Phillies until after the 1980 season. Sandwiched between his eight-game '59 St. Louis cup of coffee as a mere 17-year-old and his six-game swan song with Philly at age 38 were two full decades as one of the

top all-around defensive catchers of his era. His durability made McCarver one of only seven modern-era ballplayers—and the only catcher—to appear on a big-league field in four distinct decades.

As a two-time All-Star Game starter, McCarver also played in three World Series with the Cardinals and even managed to turn the 1964 Fall Classic into something of his own personal center-stage encore. During the seven-game set, which drove the final nail in the coffin of the Mantle-Berra-Stengel-era dynasty Yankees, McCarver took on a major offensive role, winning Game 5 single-handedly with a 10th-inning three-run homer and posting a Series-best .478 batting average. Two years later, he would earn another distinction for offensive proficiency, becoming the only catcher ever to lead a league in triples. The lefty swinger also earned special fame as something of a personal catcher both in St. Louis and Philadelphia for Hall of Fame southpaw Steve Carlton, one of baseball's top strikeout pitchers. But even before his association with one of the era's top lefties, McCarver also played a key role in handling and developing another Cooperstown-bound legend in St. Louis when he aided the early-sixties emergence of hard-throwing Bob Gibson. McCarver's other moment of stardom with the St. Louis Cardinals came in 1968, when he finished second in World Series MVP balloting to teammate Orlando Cepeda. One of the two no-hitters he caught in the course of his lengthy diamond career was the one Montreal's Bill Stoneman threw at the Mets on the final day of the 1972 season.

After his playing days were over, the popular ex-catcher enjoyed 16 seasons in the Mets' radio and television booths before his surprise release on the eve of the 1999 season. The replacement of McCarver by one-time franchise hero Tom Seaver marked the end of a tenure in the Mets booth that was sometimes stormy during its final several seasons. The outspoken McCarver was never one to mince words when it came to expounding on the home club's shortcomings, a trait which didn't always endear him to the New York ballplayers or his front-office bosses. His sometimes curmudgeonly attitude in the broadcast booth was always accompanied and redeemed by a folksy homespun style characterized by his famed quip that when he and Steve Carlton (the All-Star he caught regularly

in his later playing days with the Phillies) both passed on, they would most likely be buried exactly sixty feet and six inches apart.

But McCarver's broadcasting career has not been limited exclusively to the Mets over the past dozen-plus years. During the early 1990s, he was part of the CBS-TV top team of broadcasters for "Game of the Week" coverage, as well as for All-Star Game and postseason broadcasts. In 1994 and 1995, he continued in a similar role with the ABC baseball broadcast team. And for the past couple of seasons, he has joined forces with Arizona Diamondbacks play-by-play voice Thom Brennaman on nationally aired Fox Network MLB broadcasts. Thus, even after his Mets tenure, Tim McCarver remains a visible presence on the national baseball broadcasting scene. And at the rate it's going, his broadcast career, in the not-too-distant future, will probably have proved just about as durable as his ballplaying career.

Juan Alicea (NY Mets Photo)

BILLY BERROA AND JUAN ALICEA

Spanish-language radio broadcasts have now become a staple of many big-league clubs, especially those in sun-belt locations, such as the Texas Rangers, Florida Marlins, San Diego Padres, and Los Angeles Dodgers, who draw on large local Hispanic populations for crucial fan support. The Mets have turned increasingly in this direction in recent years and are now in a fourth season of regular play-by-play Spanish-language coverage on their WADO (1280 AM) flagship station. During the 1999 season, Billy Berroa and Juan Alicea sent action out over the airwaves for 94 contests, 69 at Shea Stadium and 25 on the road. A complete lineup of spring-training games was also added to the mix for the 2000 season.

A Dominican native of baseball-crazy San Pedro de Macoris, affable Billy Berroa has been broadcasting major league baseball in one venue or another since 1963—nearly the entire span of New York Mets franchise history. Berroa has been with the Mets (this is his second tour of duty with the club) for the past four seasons of WADO radio coverage. During an earlier tenure with the club, Berroa also handled sporadic Spanish-language game broadcasts for seven years, beginning in 1987. But Berroa's seat in the big-league play-by-play booth represents just a part of his major-league broadcasting experience. He has also been Major League Baseball's official Spanish-language voice for both postseason and All-Star Game coverage in each of the past 14 seasons. Outside of big-league venues, the popular Dominican has toiled for 43 seasons behind the microphone in the winter leagues back home, and he has also covered Car-

Billy Berroa (NY Mets Photo)

ibbean Series action, Olympic baseball tournaments, and professional boxing. Amidst these prolific broadcast duties, Berroa somehow also finds time to author a pair of popular baseball columns, one for the New York Spanish daily *Hoy,* and the other for the daily *Listin Diario,* the most widely circulated Dominican newspaper. In October 1998, Billy Berroa's lengthy sports broadcasting career was fittingly capped by his induction into the Dominican Republic's prestigious Sports Hall of Fame.

Berroa's sidekick for four seasons running has been Juan Alicea, a longtime team employee who has occupied a vari-

Gary Cohen (NY Mets Photo)

ety of community relations and scouting posts dating all the way back to the 1969 Miracle Mets season. Alicea has worked with the Mets' Spanish radio network since the early 1980s and today wears the official title of coordinator for broadcast production and Hispanic relations. He also worked as part of the International Spanish Network broadcast team, which carried Mets postseason games throughout Latin America in both 1986 and 1988. With Alicea handling the color work and Berroa delivering the snappy play-by-play, the Mets today boast a Spanish broadcasting duo that is second to none in the major leagues.

Fran Healy (NY Mets Photo)

Gary Thorne (NY Mets Photo)

New York Mets Radio/TV Broadcast Voices

Years	Venue	Announcers
1962-78	Radio/TV	Ralph Kiner, Bob Murphy, Lindsey Nelson
1979	Radio/TV	Ralph Kiner, Bob Murphy, Steve Albert
1980	Radio/TV	Ralph Kiner, Bob Murphy, Steve Albert
	Cable TV	Art Shamsky, Bob Goldsholl
1981	Radio	Ralph Kiner, Bob Murphy, Steve Albert, Art Shamsky
	TV	Ralph Kiner, Bob Murphy, Steve Albert
1982	Radio	Bob Murphy, Steve LaMar
	TV/Cable TV	Ralph Kiner, Lorn Brown
1983	Radio	Bob Murphy, Steve LaMar
	TV	Ralph Kiner, Tim McCarver, Steve Zabriskie
	Cable TV	Ralph Kiner, Tim McCarver, Bud Harrelson
1984	Radio	Bob Murphy, Steve LaMar
	TV	Ralph Kiner, Tim McCarver, Steve Zabriskie
	Cable TV	Ralph Kiner, Tim McCarver, Fran Healy
1985	Radio	Bob Murphy, Gary Thorne
	TV	Ralph Kiner, Tim McCarver, Steve Zabriskie
	Cable TV	Ralph Kiner, Tim McCarver, Fran Healy
1986-87	Radio	Bob Murphy, Gary Thorne
	TV	Ralph Kiner, Tim McCarver, Steve Zabriskie, Rusty Staub
	Cable TV	Ralph Kiner, Tim McCarver, Rusty Staub, Fran Healy
1988	Radio	Bob Murphy, Gary Thorne
	TV	Ralph Kiner, Tim McCarver, Steve Zabriskie, Rusty Staub
	Cable TV	Ralph Kiner, Tim McCarver, Fran Healy
1989	Radio	Bob Murphy, Gary Cohen
	TV	Ralph Kiner, Tim McCarver, Steve Zabriskie
	Cable TV	Ralph Kiner, Fran Healy, Rusty Staub
1990-91	Radio	Bob Murphy, Gary Cohen
	TV	Ralph Kiner, Tim McCarver
	Cable TV	Ralph Kiner, Fran Healy, Rusty Staub
1992-93	Radio	Bob Murphy, Gary Cohen, Todd Kalas
	TV	Ralph Kiner, Tim McCarver
	Cable TV	Ralph Kiner, Fran Healy, Rusty Staub
1994-95	Radio	Bob Murphy, Gary Cohen, Howie Rose
	TV	Ralph Kiner, Tim McCarver, Gary Thorne
	Cable TV	Ralph Kiner, Fran Healy, Rusty Staub
1996-98	Radio	Bob Murphy, Gary Cohen, Ed Coleman
	TV	Ralph Kiner, Tim McCarver, Gary Thorne
	Cable TV	Ralph Kiner, Howie Rose, Fran Healy, Matt Loughlin
	Spanish Radio	Billy Berroa, Juan Alicea
1999-present	Radio	Bob Murphy, Gary Cohen, Ed Coleman
	TV	Tom Seaver, Gary Thorne
	Cable TV	Ralph Kiner, Howie Rose, Fran Healy, Matt Loughlin
	Spanish Radio	Billy Berroa, Juan Alicea

Ed Coleman (NY Mets Photo)

Matt Loughlin (NY Mets Photo)

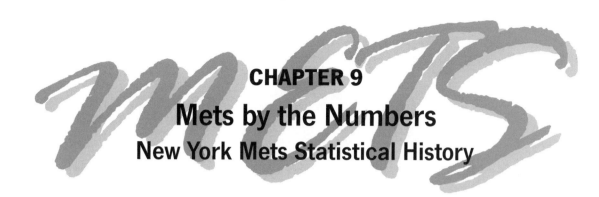

CHAPTER 9
Mets by the Numbers
New York Mets Statistical History

ALL-TIME CAREER STATISTICS

Below are career major league statistics for all players appearing in at least one game with the New York Mets through the 2000 campaign. This all-time Mets roster is arranged according to position players (batters) and pitchers, and all ballplayers in both categories are further arranged alphabetically. The source here for big-league statistics is John Thorn's and Pete Palmer's *Total Baseball*, Sixth Edition (1999, Total Sports), everywhere considered the "official" Major League Baseball encyclopedia, as well as *USA Today Baseball Weekly 2000 Almanac* (2000, Total Sports), the guideline for updated 1999 season statistics.

METS BATTERS

Player (Position)	Mets Seasons	MLB Years	G	H	2B	3B	HR	RBI	BA-SLG
Abbott, Kurt (IF)	00	93-00	696	521	109	23	62	242	**.256**-.424
Other Teams: Oakland (AL); Colorado, Florida (NL)									
Nationality: USA (Zanesville, Ohio)									
Agbayani, Benny (OF)	98-00	98-00	231	182	37	4	29	102	**.284**-.490
Other Teams: None									
Nationality: USA (Honolulu, Hawaii)									
Agee, Tommie (OF)	68-72	62-73	1129	999	170	27	130	433	**.255**-.412
Other Teams: Chicago, Cleveland (AL); Houston, St. Louis (NL)									
Nationality: USA (Magnolia, Alabama)									
Alexander, Manny (IF)	97	92-00	541	280	46	11	15	108	**.234**-.328
Other Teams: Baltimore, Boston (AL); Chicago (NL)									
Nationality: Dominican Republic									
Alfonzo, Edgardo (IF)	95-00	95-00	827	874	164	14	87	433	**.296**-.450
Other Teams: None									
Nationality: Venezuela									
Allensworth, Jermaine (OF)	98	96-99	342	268	49	8	15	114	**.260**-.367
Other Teams: Boston, Kansas City (AL); Pittsburgh (NL)									
Nationality: USA (Anderson, Indiana)									
Almon, Bill (IF)	80, 87	74-88	1236	846	138	25	36	296	**.254**-.343
Other Teams: Chicago, Oakland (AL); Montreal, Philadelphia, Pittsburgh, San Diego (NL)									
Nationality: USA (Providence, Rhode Island)									
Alomar, Sandy (SS)	67	64-78	1481	1168	126	19	13	282	**.245**-.288
Other Teams: California, Chicago, New York, Texas (AL); Atlanta, Milwaukee (NL)									
Nationality: Puerto Rico (father of Roberto Alomar and Sandy Alomar, Jr.)									

Player (Position)	Mets Seasons	MLB Years	G	H	2B	3B	HR	RBI	BA-SLG
Alou, Jesus (OF)	75	63-79	1380	1216	170	26	32	377	**.280**-.353

Other Teams: Oakland (AL); Houston, San Francisco (NL)
Nationality: Dominican Republic (brother of Felipe Alou and Matty Alou)

Altman, George (OF)	64	59-67	991	832	132	34	101	403	**.269**-.432

Other Teams: Chicago, St. Louis (NL)
Nationality: USA (Goldsboro, North Carolina)

Alvarado, Luis (2B)	77	68-77	463	248	43	4	5	84	**.214**-.271

Other Teams: Boston, Chicago, Cleveland, Detroit (AL); St. Louis (NL)
Nationality: Puerto Rico

Ashburn, Richie (OF)	62	48-62	2189	2574	317	109	29	586	**.308**-.382

Other Teams: Chicago, Philadelphia (NL)
Nationality: USA (Tilden, Nebraska)

Ashford, Tucker (IF)	83	76-84	222	111	31	1	6	55	**.218**-.318

Other Teams: Kansas City, New York, Texas (AL); San Diego (NL)
Nationality: USA (Memphis, Tennessee)

Aspromonte, Bob (IF)	71	56-71	1324	1103	135	26	60	457	**.252**-.336

Other Teams: Atlanta, Brooklyn, Houston, Los Angeles (NL)
Nationality: USA (Brooklyn, New York) (brother of Ken Aspromonte)

Ayala, Benny (OF)	74-76	74-85	425	217	42	1	38	145	**.251**-.434

Other Teams: Baltimore, Cleveland (AL); St. Louis (NL)
Nationality: Puerto Rico

Backman, Wally (IF)	80-88	80-93	1102	893	138	19	10	240	**.275**-.339

Other Teams: Minnesota, Seattle (AL); Philadelphia, Pittsburgh (NL)
Nationality: USA (Hillsboro, Oregon)

Baerga, Carlos (IF)	96-98	90-99	1280	1400	246	17	124	686	**.291**-.427

Other Teams: Cleveland, Tampa Bay (AL); Cincinnati (NL)
Nationality: Puerto Rico

Baez, Kevin (IF)	90, 92-93	90-93	63	27	10	0	0	7	**.179**-.245

Other Teams: None
Nationality: USA (Brooklyn, New York)

Bailor, Bob (IF)	80-83	75-85	955	775	107	23	9	222	**.264**-.325

Other Teams: Baltimore, Toronto (AL); Los Angeles (NL)
Nationality: USA (Connellsville, Pennsylvania)

Baldwin, Billy (OF)	76	75-76	39	27	4	1	5	13	**.231**-.410

Other Teams: Detroit (AL)
Nationality: USA (Tazewell, Virginia)

Barnes, Lute (IF)	72-73	72-73	27	18	2	2	0	7	**.243**-.324

Other Teams: None
Nationality: USA (Forest City, Iowa)

Barry, Jeff (OF)	95	95-99	104	53	18	0	5	28	**.244**-.396

Other Teams: Colorado (NL)
Nationality: USA (Medford, Oregon)

Bass, Kevin (OF)	92	82-95	1571	1308	248	40	118	611	**.270**-.411

Other Teams: Baltimore, Milwaukee (AL); Houston, San Francisco (NL)
Nationality: USA (Redwood City, California)

Beane, Billy (OF)	84-85	84-89	148	66	14	0	3	29	**.219**-.296

Other Teams: Detroit, Minnesota, Oakland (AL)
Nationality: USA (Orlando, Florida)

Beauchamp, Jim (1B)	72-73	63-73	393	153	18	4	14	90	**.231**-.334

Other Teams: Atlanta, Cincinnati, Houston, Milwaukee, St. Louis (NL)
Nationality: USA (Vinita, Oklahoma)

Becker, Rich (OF)	98	93-00	789	570	100	12	45	243	**.253**-.372

Other Teams: Baltimore, Detroit, Milwaukee, Minnesota, Oakland (AL)
Nationality: USA (Aurora, Illinois)

Player (Position)	Mets Seasons	MLB Years	G	H	2B	3B	HR	RBI	BA-SLG
Bell, Derrick (OF)	00	91-00	1164	1235	229	15	129	655	**.279**-.419

Other Teams: Toronto (AL); Houston, San Diego (NL)
Nationality: USA (Tampa, Florida)

Bell, Gus (OF)	62	50-64	1741	1823	311	66	206	942	**.281**-.445

Other Teams: Cincinnati, Milwaukee, Pittsburgh (NL)
Nationality: USA (Louisville, Kentucky) (father of Buddy Bell and grandfather of David Bell)

Benton, Butch (C)	78-80	78-85	51	16	4	0	0	10	**.162**-.202

Other Teams: Cleveland (AL); Chicago (NL)
Nationality: USA (Tampa, Florida)

Berra, Yogi (Lawrence) (C)	65	46-65	2120	2150	321	49	358	1430	**.285**-.482

Other Teams: New York (AL)
Nationality: USA (St. Louis, Missouri) (father of Dale Berra)

Bieser, Steve (OF)	97	97-98	60	20	4	0	0	5	**.250**-.300

Other Teams: Pittsburgh (NL)
Nationality: USA (Perryville, Missouri)

Bishop, Mike (C)	83	83	3	1	1	0	0	0	**.125**-.250

Other Teams: None
Nationality: USA (Santa Maria, California)

Blocker, Terry (OF)	85	85-89	110	50	5	2	2	11	**.205**-.266

Other Teams: Atlanta (NL)
Nationality: USA (Columbia, South Carolina)

Bochy, Bruce (C)	82	78-87	358	192	37	2	26	93	**.239**-.388

Other Teams: Houston, San Diego (NL)
Nationality: France

Bogar, Tim (IF)	93-96	93-00	689	340	67	9	22	159	**.227**-.327

Other Teams: Houston (NL)
Nationality: USA (Indianapolis, Indiana)

Boisclair, Bruce (OF)	74, 76-79	74-79	410	241	47	6	10	77	**.263**-.360

Other Teams: None
Nationality: USA (Putnam, Connecticut)

Bonilla, Bobby (IF)	92-95, 99	86-00	2020	1973	401	61	282	1152	**.280**-.475

Other Teams: Baltimore, Chicago (AL); Florida, Los Angeles, Pittsburgh (NL)
Nationality: USA (Bronx, New York)

Bordick, Mike (IF)	00	90-00	1443	1264	207	25	71	506	**.262**-.359

Other Teams: Baltimore, Oakland (AL)
Nationality: USA (Marquette, Michigan)

Bosch, Don (OF)	67-68	66-69	146	52	6	1	4	13	**.164**-.226

Other Teams: Montreal, Pittsburgh (NL)
Nationality: USA (San Francisco, California)

Boston, Daryl (OF)	90-92	84-94	1058	655	131	22	83	278	**.249**-.410

Other Teams: Chicago, New York (AL); Colorado (NL)
Nationality: USA (Cincinnati, Ohio)

Boswell, Ken (2B)	67-74	67-77	930	625	91	19	31	244	**.248**-.337

Other Teams: Houston (NL)
Nationality: USA (Austin, Texas)

Bouchee, Ed (1B)	62	56-62	670	583	114	21	61	290	**.265**-.419

Other Teams: Chicago, Philadelphia (NL)
Nationality: USA (Livingston, Montana)

Bowa, Larry (SS)	85	70-85	2247	2191	262	99	15	525	**.260**-.320

Other Teams: Chicago, Philadelphia (NL)
Nationality: USA (Sacramento, California)

Boyer, Ken (3B)	66-67	55-69	2034	2143	318	68	282	1141	**.287**-.462

Other Teams: Chicago (AL); Los Angeles, St. Louis (NL)
Nationality: USA (Liberty, Missouri) (brother of Clete Boyer and Cloyd Boyer)

Player (Position)	Mets Seasons	MLB Years	G	H	2B	3B	HR	RBI	BA-SLG
Bradley, Mark (OF)	83	81-83	90	23	5	0	3	5	.204-.327

Other Teams: Los Angeles (NL)
Nationality: USA (Elizabethtown, Kentucky)

Bressoud, Eddie (SS)	66	56-67	1186	925	184	40	94	365	.252-.401

Other Teams: Boston (AL); New York Giants, St. Louis, San Francisco (NL)
Nationality: USA (Los Angeles, California)

Brogna, Rico (1B)	94-96	92-00	776	744	167	13	103	437	.270-.453

Other Teams: Boston, Detroit (AL); Philadelphia (NL)
Nationality: USA (Turners Falls, Massachusetts)

Brooks, Hubie (IF)	80-84, 91	80-94	1645	1608	290	31	149	824	.269-.403

Other Teams: California, Kansas City (AL); Los Angeles, Montreal (NL)
Nationality: USA (Los Angeles, California)

Brown, Leon (OF)	76	76	64	15	3	0	0	2	.214-.257

Other Teams: None
Nationality: USA (Sacramento, California)

Buchek, Jerry (2B)	67-68	61-68	421	259	35	11	22	108	.220-.325

Other Teams: St. Louis (NL)
Nationality: USA (St. Louis, Missouri)

Buford, Damon (OF)	95	93-00	664	433	84	9	51	210	.245-.389

Other Teams: Baltimore, Boston, Texas (AL); Chicago (NL)
Nationality: USA (Baltimore, Maryland) (son of Don Buford)

Burnitz, Jeromy (OF)	93-94	93-00	839	711	156	19	154	504	.259-.498

Other Teams: Cleveland, Milwaukee (AL), Milwaukee (NL)
Nationality: USA (Westminster, California)

Burright, Larry (IF)	63-64	62-64	159	73	8	6	4	33	.205-.295

Other Teams: Los Angeles (NL)
Nationality: USA (Roseville, Illinois)

Butler, Brett (OF)	95	81-97	2213	2375	277	131	54	578	.290-.376

Other Teams: Cleveland (AL); Atlanta, Los Angeles, San Francisco (NL)
Nationality: USA (Los Angeles, California)

Cangelosi, John (OF)	94	85-99	1038	501	73	15	12	134	.250-.319

Other Teams: Chicago, Texas (AL); Colorado, Florida, Houston, Pittsburgh (NL)
Nationality: USA (Brooklyn, New York)

Cannizzaro, Chris (C)	62-65	60-74	740	458	66	12	18	169	.235-.309

Other Teams: Chicago, Los Angeles, Pittsburgh, St. Louis, San Diego (NL)
Nationality: USA (Oakland, California)

Cardenal, José (OF)	79-80	63-80	2017	1913	333	46	138	775	.275-.395

Other Teams: California, Cleveland, Kansas City, Milwaukee (AL); Chicago, Philadelphia, St. Louis, San Francisco (NL)
Nationality: Cuba

Carmel, Duke (1B)	63	59-65	124	48	7	3	4	23	.211-.322

Other Teams: New York (AL); St. Louis (NL)
Nationality: USA (New York, New York)

Carr, Chuck (OF)	90-91	90-97	507	435	81	7	13	123	.254-.332

Other Teams: Florida, Milwaukee (AL); Houston, St. Louis (NL)
Nationality: USA (San Bernadino, California)

Carreon, Mark (OF)	87-91	87-96	738	557	108	5	69	289	.277-.438

Other Teams: Cleveland, Detroit (AL); San Francisco (NL)
Nationality: USA (Chicago, Illinois)

Carter, Gary (C)	85-89	74-92	2296	2092	371	31	324	1225	.262-.439

Other Teams: Los Angeles, Montreal, San Francisco (NL)
Nationality: USA (Culver City, California)

Castillo, Alberto (C)	95-98	95-00	251	142	20	0	7	61	.228-.294

Other Teams: Toronto (AL); St. Louis (NL)
Nationality: Dominican Republic

Player (Position)	Mets Seasons	MLB Years	G	H	2B	3B	HR	RBI	BA-SLG
Cedeño, Roger (OF)	99	95-00	540	388	59	13	17	117	**.277**-.375
Other Teams: Houston, Los Angeles (NL)									
Nationality: Venezuela									
Cerone, Rick (C)	91	75-92	1329	998	190	15	59	436	**.245**-.343
Other Teams: Boston, Cleveland, Milwaukee, New York, Toronto (AL); Atlanta, Montreal (NL)									
Nationality: USA (Newark, New Jersey)									
Chacón, Elio (IF)	62	60-62	228	143	15	5	4	39	**.232**-.292
Other Teams: Cincinnati (NL)									
Nationality: Venezuela									
Chapman, Kelvin (IF)	79, 84-85	79-85	172	94	17	2	3	34	**.223**-.295
Other Teams: None									
Nationality: USA (Willits, California)									
Charles, Ed (3B)	67-69	62-69	1005	917	147	30	86	421	**.263**-.397
Other Teams: Kansas City (AL)									
Nationality: USA (Daytona Beach, Florida)									
Chiles, Rich (OF)	73	71-78	284	157	37	2	6	76	**.254**-.350
Other Teams: Minnesota (AL); Houston (NL)									
Nationality: USA (Sacramento, California)									
Chiti, Harry (C)	62	50-62	502	356	49	9	41	179	**.238**-.365
Other Teams: Detroit, Kansas City (AL); Chicago (NL)									
Nationality: USA (Kincaid, Illinois)									
Christensen, John (OF)	84-85	84-88	132	66	16	2	5	33	**.224**-.344
Other Teams: Minnesota, Seattle (AL)									
Nationality: USA (Downey, California)									
Christopher, Joe (OF)	62-65	59-66	638	434	68	17	29	173	**.260**-.374
Other Teams: Boston (AL); Pittsburgh (NL)									
Nationality: Virgin Islands									
Clendenon, Donn (1B)	69-71	61-72	1362	1273	192	57	159	682	**.274**-.442
Other Teams: Montreal, Pittsburgh, St. Louis (NL)									
Nationality: USA (Neosho, Missouri)									
Clines, Gene (OF)	75	70-79	870	645	85	24	5	187	**.277**-.341
Other Teams: Texas (AL); Chicago, Pittsburgh (NL)									
Nationality: USA (San Pablo, California)									
Coleman, Choo Choo (C)	62-63, 66	61-66	201	91	8	2	9	30	**.197**-.281
Other Teams: Philadelphia (NL)									
Nationality: USA (Orlando, Florida)									
Coleman, Vince (OF)	91-93	85-97	1371	1425	176	89	28	346	**.264**-.345
Other Teams: Detroit, Kansas City, Seattle (AL); Cincinnati, St. Louis (NL)									
Nationality: USA (Jacksonville, Florida)									
Collins, Kevin (IF)	65, 67-69	65-71	201	81	17	4	6	34	**.209**-.320
Other Teams: Detroit (AL); Montreal (NL)									
Nationality: USA (Springfield, Massachusetts)									
Cook, Cliff (OF)	62-63	59-63	163	80	17	3	7	35	**.201**-.312
Other Teams: Cincinnati (NL)									
Nationality: USA (Dallas, Texas)									
Corcoran, Tim (1B)	86	77-86	509	283	46	4	12	128	**.270**-.355
Other Teams: Detroit, Minnesota (AL); Philadelphia (NL)									
Nationality: USA (Glendale, California)									
Cowan, Billy (OF)	65	63-72	493	281	44	8	40	125	**.236**-.387
Other Teams: California, New York (AL); Chicago, Milwaukee, Philadelphia (NL)									
Nationality: USA (Calhoun City, Mississippi)									
Cubbage, Mike (IF)	81	74-81	703	503	74	20	34	251	**.258**-.369
Other Teams: Minnesota, Texas (AL)									
Nationality: USA (Charlottesville, Virginia)									

Player (Position)	Mets Seasons	MLB Years	G	H	2B	3B	HR	RBI	BA-SLG
Davis, Tommy (OF)	67	59-76	1999	2121	272	35	153	1052	**.294**-.405

Other Teams: Baltimore, California, Chicago, Kansas City, Oakland, Seattle (AL); Chicago, Houston, Los Angeles (NL)
Nationality: USA (Brooklyn, New York)

DeMerit, John (OF)	62	57-62	93	23	3	0	3	7	**.174**-.265

Other Teams: Milwaukee (NL)
Nationality: USA (West Bend, Wisconsin)

Diaz, Mario (IF)	90	87-95	374	198	31	4	5	84	**.256**-.326

Other Teams: Seattle, Texas (AL); Florida (NL)
Nationality: Puerto Rico

Donnels, Chris (IF)	91-92	91-95	283	142	27	4	7	53	**.238**-.332

Other Teams: Boston (AL); Houston (NL)
Nationality: USA (Los Angeles, California)

Dozier, D.J. (OF)	92	92	25	9	2	0	0	2	**.191**-.234

Other Teams: None
Nationality: USA (Norfolk, Virginia)

Drake, Sammy (2B)	62	60-62	53	11	0	0	0	7	**.153**-.153

Other Teams: Chicago (NL)
Nationality: USA (Little Rock, Arkansas) (brother of Solly Drake)

Dunston, Shawon (OF-IF)	99	85-00	1654	1511	277	59	140	634	**.270**-.416

Other Teams: Cleveland (AL); Chicago, Pittsburgh, St. Louis, San Francisco (NL)
Nationality: USA (Brooklyn, New York)

Dwyer, Jim (OF)	76	73-90	1328	719	115	17	77	349	**.260**-.398

Other Teams: Baltimore, Boston, Minnesota (AL); Montreal, St. Louis, San Francisco (NL)
Nationality: USA (Evergreen Park, Illinois)

Dyer, Duffy (C)	68-74	68-81	722	441	74	11	30	173	**.221**-.315

Other Teams: Detroit (AL); Montreal, Pittsburgh (NL)
Nationality: USA (Dayton, Ohio)

Dykstra, Lenny (OF)	85-89	85-96	1278	1298	281	43	81	404	**.285**-.419

Other Teams: Philadelphia (NL)
Nationality: USA (Santa Ana, California)

Elliot, Larry (OF)	64, 66	62-66	157	103	22	2	15	56	**.236**-.398

Other Teams: Pittsburgh (NL)
Nationality: USA (San Diego, California)

Elster, Kevin (SS)	86-92	86-98, 00	940	648	136	12	88	376	**.228**-.377

Other Teams: New York, Texas (AL); Los Angeles, Philadelphia, Pittsburgh (NL)
Nationality: USA (San Pedro, California)

Espinoza, Alvaro (IF)	96	84-97	942	630	105	9	22	201	**.254**-.331

Other Teams: Cleveland, Minnesota, New York, Seattle (AL)
Nationality: Venezuela

Estrada, Francisco (C)	71	71	1	1	0	0	0	0	**.500**-.500

Other Teams: None
Nationality: Mexico

Everett, Carl (OF)	95-97	93-00	742	682	149	16	103	425	**.282**-.484

Other Teams: Boston (AL); Florida, Houston (NL)
Nationality: USA (Tampa, Florida)

Fabregas, Jorge (C)	98	94-99	485	340	44	3	15	156	**.246**-.315

Other Teams: Anaheim, California, Chicago (AL); Arizona, Atlanta (NL)
Nationality: USA (Miami, Florida)

Fernández, Chico (SS)	63	56-63	856	666	91	19	40	259	**.240**-.329

Other Teams: Detroit (AL); Brooklyn, Philadelphia (NL)
Nationality: Cuba

Fernández, Tony (IF)	93	83-99	2082	2240	410	92	92	829	**.288**-.399

Other Teams: Cleveland, New York, Toronto (AL); Cincinnati, San Diego (NL)
Nationality: Dominican Republic

Player (Position)	Mets Seasons	MLB Years	G	H	2B	3B	HR	RBI	BA-SLG
Ferrer, Sergio (IF)	78-79	74-79	125	43	3	4	0	3	.242-.303

Other Teams: Minnesota (AL)
Nationality: Puerto Rico

| **Fitzgerald, Mike** (C) | 83-84 | 83-92 | 848 | 545 | 95 | 9 | 48 | 293 | .235-.346 |

Other Teams: California (AL); Montreal (NL)
Nationality: USA (Long Beach, California)

| **Fitzmaurice, Shaun** (OF) | 66 | 66 | 9 | 2 | 0 | 0 | 0 | 0 | .154-.154 |

Other Teams: None
Nationality: USA (Worcester, Massachusetts)

| **Flores, Gil** (OF) | 78-79 | 77-79 | 185 | 121 | 20 | 6 | 2 | 37 | .261-.343 |

Other Teams: California (AL)
Nationality: Puerto Rico

| **Flynn, Doug** (IF) | 77-81 | 75-85 | 1308 | 918 | 115 | 39 | 7 | 284 | .238-.294 |

Other Teams: Detroit, Texas (AL); Cincinnati, Montreal (NL)
Nationality: USA (Lexington, Kentucky)

| **Foli, Tim** (IF) | 70-71, 78-79 | 70-85 | 1696 | 1515 | 241 | 20 | 25 | 501 | .251-.309 |

Other Teams: California, New York (AL); Montreal, Pittsburgh, San Francisco (NL)
Nationality: USA (Culver City, California)

| **Fordyce, Brook** (C) | 95 | 95-00 | 310 | 250 | 59 | 2 | 27 | 121 | .282-.445 |

Other Teams: Baltimore, Chicago (AL); Cincinnati (NL)
Nationality: USA (New London, Connecticut)

| **Foster, George** (OF) | 82-86 | 69-86 | 1977 | 1925 | 307 | 47 | 348 | 1239 | .274-.480 |

Other Teams: Chicago (AL); Cincinnati, San Francisco (NL)
Nationality: USA (Tuscaloosa, Alabama)

| **Foster, Leo** (IF) | 76-77 | 71-77 | 144 | 52 | 8 | 0 | 2 | 26 | .198-.252 |

Other Teams: Atlanta (NL)
Nationality: USA (Covington, Kentucky)

| **Foy, Joe** (3B) | 70 | 66-71 | 716 | 615 | 102 | 16 | 58 | 291 | .248-.372 |

Other Teams: Boston, Kansas City, Washington (AL)
Nationality: USA (Bronx, New York)

| **Franco, Matt** (IF) | 96-00 | 95-00 | 468 | 163 | 23 | 2 | 13 | 72 | .255-.359 |

Other Teams: Chicago (NL)
Nationality: USA (Santa Monica, California)

| **Fregosi, Jim** (3B) | 72-73 | 61-78 | 1902 | 1726 | 264 | 78 | 151 | 706 | .265-.398 |

Other Teams: California, Texas (AL); Los Angeles, Pittsburgh (NL)
Nationality: USA (San Francisco, California)

| **Gallagher, Bob** (OF) | 75 | 72-75 | 213 | 56 | 6 | 1 | 2 | 13 | .220-.275 |

Other Teams: Boston (AL), Houston (NL)
Nationality: USA (Newton, Massachusetts)

| **Gallagher, Dave** (OF) | 92-93 | 87-95 | 794 | 564 | 100 | 10 | 17 | 190 | .271-.353 |

Other Teams: Baltimore, California, Chicago, Cleveland (AL); Atlanta, Philadelphia (NL)
Nationality: USA (Trenton, New Jersey)

| **Gardenhire, Ron** (SS) | 81-85 | 81-85 | 285 | 165 | 27 | 3 | 4 | 49 | .232-.296 |

Other Teams: None
Nationality: Germany

| **Gardner, Jeff** (IF) | 91 | 91-94 | 186 | 121 | 21 | 8 | 1 | 26 | .246-.327 |

Other Teams: Montreal, San Diego (NL)
Nationality: USA (Newport Beach, California)

| **Garrett, Wayne** (3B) | 69-76 | 69-78 | 1092 | 786 | 107 | 22 | 61 | 340 | .239-.341 |

Other Teams: Montreal, St. Louis (NL)
Nationality: USA (Brooksville, Florida) (brother of Adrian Garrett)

| **Gaspar, Rod** (OF) | 69-70 | 69-74 | 178 | 54 | 6 | 1 | 1 | 17 | .208-.250 |

Other Teams: San Diego (NL)
Nationality: USA (Long Beach, California)

Player (Position)	Mets Seasons	MLB Years	G	H	2B	3B	HR	RBI	BA-SLG
Gibbons, John (C)	84, 86	84, 86	18	11	4	0	1	2	.220-.360
Other Teams: None									
Nationality: USA (Great Falls, Montana)									
Gilbert, Shawn (IF)	97-98	97-00	51	7	1	0	2	4	.149-.298
Other Teams: Los Angeles, St. Louis (NL)									
Nationality: USA (Camden, New Jersey)									
Giles, Brian (IF)	81-83	81-90	287	162	27	0	10	50	.228-.309
Other Teams: Chicago, Milwaukee, Seattle (AL)									
Nationality: USA (Manhattan, Kansas)									
Gilkey, Bernard (OF)	96-98	90-00	1170	1086	238	24	116	532	.275-.435
Other Teams: Boston (AL); Arizona, St. Louis (NL)									
Nationality: USA (St. Louis, Missouri)									
Ginsberg, Joe (C)	62	48-62	695	419	59	8	20	182	.241-.320
Other Teams: Baltimore, Boston, Chicago, Cleveland, Detroit, Kansas City (AL)									
Nationality: USA (New York, New York)									
Gonder, Jesse (C)	63-65	60-67	395	220	28	2	26	94	.251-.377
Other Teams: New York (AL); Cincinnati, Milwaukee, Pittsburgh (NL)									
Nationality: USA (Monticello, Arkansas)									
Goossen, Greg (C)	65-68	65-70	193	111	24	1	13	44	.241-.383
Other Teams: Milwaukee, Seattle, Washington (AL)									
Nationality: USA (Los Angeles, California)									
Gosger, Jim (OF)	69, 73-74	63-74	705	411	67	16	30	177	.226-.331
Other Teams: Boston, Kansas City, Oakland, Seattle (AL); Montreal (NL)									
Nationality: USA (Port Huron, Michigan)									
Graham, Wayne (3B)	64	63-64	30	7	1	0	0	0	.127-.145
Other Teams: Philadelphia (NL)									
Nationality: USA (Yoakum, Texas)									
Green, Pumpsie (3B)	63	59-63	344	196	31	12	13	74	.246-.364
Other Teams: Boston (AL)									
Nationality: USA (Oakland, California)									
Greene, Charlie (C)	96	96-00	55	13	2	0	0	2	.173-.200
Other Teams: Baltimore, Toronto (AL); Milwaukee (NL)									
Nationality: USA (Miami, Florida)									
Grieve, Tom (OF)	78	70-79	670	474	76	10	65	254	.249-.401
Other Teams: Texas, Washington (AL); St. Louis (NL)									
Nationality: USA (Pittsfield, Massachusetts) (father of Ben Grieve)									
Grote, Jerry (C)	66-77	63-81	1421	1092	160	22	39	404	.252-.326
Other Teams: Kansas City (AL); Houston, Los Angeles (NL)									
Nationality: USA (San Antonio, Texas)									
Hahn, Don (OF)	71-74	69-75	454	235	38	4	7	74	.236-.303
Other Teams: Montreal, Philadelphia, St. Louis, San Diego (NL)									
Nationality: USA (San Francisco, California)									
Halter, Shane (SS)	99	97-00	272	41	29	3	7	50	.249-.349
Other Teams: Detroit, Kansas City (AL)									
Nationality: USA (LaPlata, Maryland)									
Hamilton, Darryl (OF)	99-00	88-00	1276	1306	197	36	50	449	.293-.388
Other Teams: Milwaukee, Texas (AL); Colorado, San Francisco (NL)									
Nationality: USA (Baton Rouge, Louisiana)									
Hampton, Ike (C)	74	74-79	113	28	4	1	4	18	.207-.341
Other Teams: California (AL)									
Nationality: USA (Camden, South Carolina)									
Haney, Todd (IF)	98	92-98	101	50	10	0	3	12	.244-.337
Other Teams: Chicago, Montreal (NL)									
Nationality: USA (Waco, Texas)									

Player (Position)	Mets Seasons	MLB Years	G	H	2B	3B	HR	RBI	BA-SLG
Hardtke, Jason (IF)	96-97	96-98	67	31	7	0	2	16	.231-.328

Other Teams: Chicago (NL)
Nationality: USA (Milwaukee, Wisconsin)

Hare, Shawn (OF)	94	91-95	64	19	4	1	0	9	.174-.229

Other Teams: Detroit, Texas (AL)
Nationality: USA (St. Louis, Missouri)

Harkness, Tim (1B)	63-64	61-64	259	132	18	4	14	61	.235-.356

Other Teams: Los Angeles (NL)
Nationality: Canada

Harrelson, Bud (SS)	65-77	65-80	1533	1120	136	45	7	267	.236-.288

Other Teams: Texas (AL); Philadelphia (NL)
Nationality: USA (Niles, California)

Harris, Lenny (IF-OF)	98, 00	88-00	1421	895	136	18	31	305	.273-.353

Other Teams: Arizona, Cincinnati, Colorado, Los Angeles (NL)
Nationality: USA (Miami, Florida)

Harts, Greg (PH)	73	73	3	1	0	0	0	0	.500-.500

Other Teams: None
Nationality: USA (Atlanta, Georgia)

Hearn, Ed (C)	86	86-88	62	45	9	0	4	14	.263-.386

Other Teams: Kansas City (AL)
Nationality: USA (Stuart, Florida)

Hebner, Richie (3B)	79	68-85	1908	1694	273	57	203	890	.276-.438

Other Teams: Detroit (AL); Chicago, Philadelphia, Pittsburgh (NL)
Nationality: USA (Boston, Massachusetts)

Heep, Danny (OF)	83-86	79-91	883	503	96	6	30	229	.257-.357

Other Teams: Boston (AL); Atlanta, Houston, Los Angeles (NL)
Nationality: USA (San Antonio, Texas)

Heidemann, Jack (IF)	75-76	69-77	426	231	27	4	9	75	.211-.268

Other Teams: Cleveland, Milwaukee (AL); St. Louis (NL)
Nationality: USA (Brenham, Texas)

Heise, Bob (IF)	67-69	67-77	499	283	43	3	1	86	.247-.293

Other Teams: Boston, California, Kansas City, Milwaukee (AL); St. Louis, San Francisco (NL)
Nationality: USA (San Antonio, Texas)

Henderson, Ken (OF)	78	65-80	1444	1168	216	26	122	576	.257-.396

Other Teams: Chicago, Texas (AL); Atlanta, Chicago, Cincinnati, San Francisco (NL)
Nationality: USA (Carroll, Iowa)

Henderson, Rickey (OF)	99-00	79-00	2856	2914	486	62	282	1052	.282-.423

Other Teams: Anaheim, New York, Oakland, Seattle, Toronto (AL); San Diego (NL)
Nationality: USA (Chicago, Illinois)

Henderson, Steve (OF)	77-80	77-88	1085	976	162	49	68	428	.280-.413

Other Teams: Oakland, Seattle (AL); Chicago, Houston (NL)
Nationality: USA (Houston, Texas)

Hernandez, Keith (1B)	83-89	74-90	2088	2182	426	60	162	1071	.296-.436

Other Teams: Cleveland (AL); St. Louis (NL)
Nationality: USA (San Francisco, California)

Herr, Tom (2B)	90-91	79-91	1514	1450	254	41	28	574	.271-.350

Other Teams: Minnesota (AL); Philadelphia, St. Louis, San Francisco (NL)
Nationality: USA (Lancaster, Pennsylvania)

Herrscher, Rick (IF)	62	62	35	11	3	0	1	6	.220-.340

Other Teams: None
Nationality: USA (St. Louis, Missouri)

Hickman, Jim (OF)	62-66	62-74	1421	1002	163	25	159	560	.252-.426

Other Teams: Chicago, Los Angeles, St. Louis (NL)
Nationality: USA (Henning, Tennessee)

Player (Position)	Mets Seasons	MLB Years	G	H	2B	3B	HR	RBI	BA-SLG
Hicks, Joe (OF)	63	59-63	212	92	11	3	12	39	.221-.349

Other Teams: Chicago, Washington (AL)
Nationality: USA (Ivy, Virginia)

Hiller, Chuck (IF)	65-67	61-68	704	516	76	9	20	152	.243-.316

Other Teams: Philadelphia, Pittsburgh, San Francisco (NL)
Nationality: USA (Johnsburg, Illinois)

Hodges, Gil (1B)	62-63	43-63	2071	1921	295	48	370	1274	.273-.487

Other Teams: Brooklyn, Los Angeles (NL)
Nationality: USA (Princeton, Indiana) (father of Ron Hodges)

Hodges, Ron (C)	73-84	73-84	666	342	56	2	19	147	.240-.322

Other Teams: None
Nationality: USA (Rocky Mount, Virginia) (son of Gil Hodges)

Housie, Wayne (OF)	93	91, 93	29	5	2	0	0	1	.208-.292

Other Teams: Boston (AL)
Nationality: USA (Hampton, Virginia)

Howard, Mike (OF)	81-83	81-83	48	12	1	0	1	7	.182-.242

Other Teams: None
Nationality: USA (Seattle, Washington)

Howell, Pat (OF)	92	92	31	14	1	0	0	1	.187-.200

Other Teams: None
Nationality: USA (Mobile, Alabama)

Hughes, Keith (OF)	90	87-93	93	41	6	2	2	24	.204-.284

Other Teams: Baltimore (AL); Cincinnati, Philadelphia (NL)
Nationality: USA (Bryn Mawr, Pennsylvania)

Hundley, Todd (C)	90-98	90-00	1033	775	148	7	172	522	.240-.451

Other Teams: Los Angeles (NL)
Nationality: USA (Martinsville, Virginia) (son of Randy Hundley)

Hunt, Ron (2B)	63-66	63-74	1483	1429	223	23	39	370	.273-.347

Other Teams: Los Angeles, Montreal, St. Louis, San Francisco (NL)
Nationality: USA (St. Louis, Missouri)

Hurdle, Clint (C)	83, 85, 87	77-87	515	360	81	12	32	193	.259-.403

Other Teams: Kansas City (AL); Cincinnati, St. Louis (NL)
Nationality: USA (Big Rapids, Michigan)

Huskey, Butch (OF)	93, 95-98	93-00	597	523	90	4	82	318	.263-.437

Other Teams: Boston, Minnesota, Seattle (AL)
Nationality: USA (Anadarko, Oklahoma)

Jackson, Darrin (OF)	93	85-99	960	676	114	15	80	317	.257-.403

Other Teams: Chicago, Minnesota, Toronto (AL); Chicago, Milwaukee, San Diego (NL)
Nationality: USA (Los Angeles, California)

Jefferies, Gregg (IF)	87-91	87-00	1465	1593	300	27	126	663	.289-.421

Other Teams: Anaheim, Detroit, Kansas City (AL); Philadelphia, St. Louis (NL)
Nationality: USA (Burlingame, California)

Jefferson, Stanley (OF)	86	86-91	296	180	25	9	16	67	.216-.326

Other Teams: Baltimore, Cleveland, New York (AL); Cincinnati, San Diego (NL)
Nationality: USA (New York, New York)

Jelic, Chris (C)	90	90	4	1	0	0	1	1	.091-.364

Other Teams: None
Nationality: USA (Bethlehem, Pennsylvania)

Johnson, Bob (IF)	67	60-70	874	628	88	11	44	230	.272-.377

Other Teams: Baltimore, Kansas City, Oakland, Washington (AL); Atlanta, Cincinnati, St. Louis (NL)
Nationality: USA (Omaha, Nebraska)

Johnson, Howard (3B-OF)	85-93	82-95	1531	1229	247	22	228	760	.249-.446

Other Teams: Detroit (AL); Chicago, Colorado (NL)
Nationality: USA (Clearwater, Florida)

Player (Position)	Mets Seasons	MLB Years	G	H	2B	3B	HR	RBI	BA-SLG
Johnson, Lance (OF)	96-97	87-99	1430	1556	174	117	34	484	.291-.386

Other Teams: Chicago (AL); Chicago, St. Louis (NL)
Nationality: USA (Cincinnati, Ohio)

Johnson, Mark (IF/OF)	00	95-98, 00	315	192	40	1	31	110	.233-.399

Other Teams: Anaheim (AL); Pittsburgh (NL)
Nationality: USA (Worchester, Massachusettes)

Jones, Chris (OF)	95-96	91-98	536	254	41	11	30	130	.253-.405

Other Teams: Arizona, Cincinnati, Colorado, Houston, San Diego, San Francisco (NL)
Nationality: USA (Utica, New York)

Jones, Cleon (OF)	63, 65-75	63-76	1213	1196	183	33	93	524	.281-.404

Other Teams: Chicago (AL)
Nationality: USA (Plateau, Alabama)

Jones, Ross (SS)	84	84-87	67	32	5	2	0	11	.221-.283

Other Teams: Kansas City, Seattle (AL)
Nationality: USA (Miami, Florida)

Jorgensen, Mike (1B)	68-83	68-85	1633	833	132	13	95	426	.243-.373

Other Teams: Oakland, Texas (AL); Atlanta, Montreal, St. Louis (NL)
Nationality: USA (Passaic, New Jersey)

Kanehl, Rod (IF)	62-64	62-64	340	192	23	3	6	47	.241-.300

Other Teams: None
Nationality: USA (Wichita, Kansas)

Kent, Jeff (IF)	92-96	92-00	1191	1228	274	25	194	793	.284-.493

Other Teams: Cleveland, Toronto (AL); San Francisco (NL)
Nationality: USA (Bellflower, California)

Kingman, Dave (OF-IF)	75-83	71-86	1941	1575	240	25	442	1210	.236-.305

Other Teams: California, New York, Oakland (AL); Chicago, San Diego, San Francisco (NL)
Nationality: USA (Pendleton, Oregon)

Kinkade, Mike (IF)	98	98-00	33	9	2	1	2	6	.188-.396

Other Teams: None
Nationality: USA (Livonia, Michigan)

Kirby, Wayne (OF)	98	91-98	516	302	51	9	14	119	.252-.345

Other Teams: Cleveland (AL); Los Angeles (NL)
Nationality: USA (Williamsburg, Virginia)

Klaus, Bobby (IF)	64-65	64-65	215	123	25	4	6	29	.208-.295

Other Teams: Cincinnati (NL)
Nationality: USA (Spring Grove, Illinois) (brother of Billy Klaus)

Kleven, Jay (C)	76	76	2	1	0	0	0	2	.200-.200

Other Teams: None
Nationality: USA (Oakland, California)

Klimchock, Lou (PH)	66	58-70	318	155	21	3	13	69	.232-.330

Other Teams: Cleveland, Kansas City, Washington (AL); Milwaukee (NL)
Nationality: USA (Hostetter, Pennsylvania)

Knight, Ray (3B)	84-86	74-88	1495	1311	266	27	84	595	.271-.390

Other Teams: Baltimore, Detroit (AL); Cincinnati, Houston (NL)
Nationality: USA (Albany, Georgia)

Kolb, Gary (OF)	65	60-69	293	94	9	6	6	29	.209-.296

Other Teams: Milwaukee, Pittsburgh, St. Louis (NL)
Nationality: USA (Rock Falls, Illinois)

Kranepool, Ed (1B)	62-79	62-79	1853	1418	225	25	118	614	.261-.377

Other Teams: None
Nationality: USA (New York, New York)

Lamb, David (IF)	00	99-00	62	29	5	1	1	13	.225-.302

Other Teams: Tampa Bay (AL)
Nationality: USA (West Hills, California)

Player (Position)	Mets Seasons	MLB Years	G	H	2B	3B	HR	RBI	BA-SLG
Landrith, Hobie (C)	62	50-63	772	450	69	5	34	203	**.233**-.327

Other Teams: Baltimore, Washington (AL); Chicago, Cincinnati, St. Louis, San Francisco (NL)
Nationality: USA (Decatur, Illinois)

Player (Position)	Mets Seasons	MLB Years	G	H	2B	3B	HR	RBI	BA-SLG
Landum, Ced (OF)	93	91, 93	78	25	3	1	0	7	**.238**-.286

Other Teams: Chicago (NL)
Nationality: USA (Butler, Alabama)

Player (Position)	Mets Seasons	MLB Years	G	H	2B	3B	HR	RBI	BA-SLG
Ledesma, Aaron (IF)	95	95-00	284	223	38	4	2	76	**.296**-.365

Other Teams: Baltimore, Tampa Bay (AL); Colorado (NL)
Nationality: USA (Union City, California)

Player (Position)	Mets Seasons	MLB Years	G	H	2B	3B	HR	RBI	BA-SLG
Lewis, Johnny (OF)	65-67	64-67	266	175	24	6	22	74	**.227**-.359

Other Teams: St. Louis (NL)
Nationality: USA (Greenville, Alabama)

Player (Position)	Mets Seasons	MLB Years	G	H	2B	3B	HR	RBI	BA-SLG
Liddell, Dave (C)	90	90	1	1	0	0	0	0	**1.000**-1.000

Other Teams: None
Nationality: USA (Los Angeles, California)

Player (Position)	Mets Seasons	MLB Years	G	H	2B	3B	HR	RBI	BA-SLG
Lindeman, Jim (OF-1B)	94	86-94	351	165	34	1	21	89	**.244**-.391

Other Teams: Detroit (AL); Houston, Philadelphia, St. Louis (NL)
Nationality: USA (Evanston, Illinois)

Player (Position)	Mets Seasons	MLB Years	G	H	2B	3B	HR	RBI	BA-SLG
Linz, Phil (2B)	67-68	62-68	519	322	64	4	11	96	**.235**-.311

Other Teams: New York (AL); Philadelphia (NL)
Nationality: USA (Baltimore, Maryland)

Player (Position)	Mets Seasons	MLB Years	G	H	2B	3B	HR	RBI	BA-SLG
Lombardi, Phil (C)	89-90	86-89	43	22	4	0	3	9	**.239**-.380

Other Teams: New York (AL)
Nationality: USA (Abilene, Texas)

Player (Position)	Mets Seasons	MLB Years	G	H	2B	3B	HR	RBI	BA-SLG
López, Luis (IF)	97-99	93-00	498	285	63	4	15	113	**.244**-.344

Other Teams: Milwaukee, San Diego (NL)
Nationality: Puerto Rico

Player (Position)	Mets Seasons	MLB Years	G	H	2B	3B	HR	RBI	BA-SLG
Luplow, Al (OF)	66-67	61-67	481	292	34	6	33	125	**.235**-.352

Other Teams: Cleveland (AL); Pittsburgh (NL)
Nationality: USA (Saginaw, Michigan)

Player (Position)	Mets Seasons	MLB Years	G	H	2B	3B	HR	RBI	BA-SLG
Lyons, Barry (C)	86-90	86-95	253	150	26	2	15	89	**.239**-.358

Other Teams: California, Chicago (AL); Los Angeles (NL)
Nationality: USA (Biloxi, Mississippi)

Player (Position)	Mets Seasons	MLB Years	G	H	2B	3B	HR	RBI	BA-SLG
Maddox, Elliott (OF)	78-80	70-80	1029	742	121	16	18	234	**.261**-.334

Other Teams: Baltimore, Detroit, New York, Texas, Washington (AL)
Nationality: USA (East Orange, New Jersey)

Player (Position)	Mets Seasons	MLB Years	G	H	2B	3B	HR	RBI	BA-SLG
Magadan, Dave (1B-3B)	86-92	86-00	1491	1165	211	13	41	483	**.289**-.378

Other Teams: Oakland, Seattle (AL); Chicago, Florida, Houston, San Diego (NL)
Nationality: USA (Tampa, Florida)

Player (Position)	Mets Seasons	MLB Years	G	H	2B	3B	HR	RBI	BA-SLG
Mangual, Pepe (OF)	76-77	72-77	319	235	35	6	16	83	**.242**-.340

Other Teams: Montreal (NL)
Nationality: Puerto Rico

Player (Position)	Mets Seasons	MLB Years	G	H	2B	3B	HR	RBI	BA-SLG
Mankowski, Phil (3B)	80-82	76-82	269	195	23	4	8	64	**.264**-.338

Other Teams: Detroit (AL)
Nationality: USA (Buffalo, New York)

Player (Position)	Mets Seasons	MLB Years	G	H	2B	3B	HR	RBI	BA-SLG
Mantilla, Felix (IF)	62	56-66	969	707	97	10	89	330	**.261**-.403

Other Teams: Boston (AL); Milwaukee, Houston (NL)
Nationality: Puerto Rico

Player (Position)	Mets Seasons	MLB Years	G	H	2B	3B	HR	RBI	BA-SLG
Marshall, Dave (OF)	70-72	67-73	490	258	41	4	16	114	**.246**-.338

Other Teams: San Francisco, San Diego (NL)
Nationality: USA (Artesia, California)

Player (Position)	Mets Seasons	MLB Years	G	H	2B	3B	HR	RBI	BA-SLG
Marshall, Jim (1B)	62	58-62	410	206	24	7	29	106	**.242**-.388

Other Teams: Baltimore (AL); Chicago, Pittsburgh, San Francisco (NL)
Nationality: USA (Danville, Illinois)

Player (Position)	Mets Seasons	MLB Years	G	H	2B	3B	HR	RBI	BA-SLG
Marshall, Mike (OF)	90	81-91	1035	971	173	8	148	530	**.270**-.446
Other Teams: Boston, California (AL); Los Angeles (NL)									
Nationality: USA (Libertyville, Illinois)									
Martin, J.C. (C)	68-69	59-72	908	487	82	12	32	230	**.222**-.315
Other Teams: Chicago (AL), Chicago (NL)									
Nationality: USA (Axton, Virginia)									
Martin, Jerry (OF)	84	74-84	1018	666	130	17	85	345	**.251**-.409
Other Teams: Kansas City (AL); Chicago, Philadelphia, San Francisco (NL)									
Nationality: USA (Columbia, South Carolina)									
Martinez, Teddy (IF)	70-74	70-79	657	355	50	16	7	108	**.240**-.271
Other Teams: Oakland (AL); Los Angeles, St. Louis (NL)									
Nationality: Dominican Republic									
May, Jerry (C)	73	64-73	556	357	63	10	15	130	**.234**-.318
Other Teams: Kansas City (AL); Pittsburgh (NL)									
Nationality: USA (Swoope, Virginia)									
Mayne, Brent (C)	96	90-00	882	648	136	3	26	282	**.270**-.362
Other Teams: Kansas City, Oakland (AL); Colorado, San Francisco (NL)									
Nationality: USA (Loma Linda, California)									
Mays, Willie (OF)	72-73	51-73	2992	3283	523	140	660	1903	**.302**-.557
Other Teams: New York Giants, San Francisco (NL)									
Nationality: USA (Westfield, Alabama)									
Mazzilli, Lee (OF)	76-81, 86-89	76-89	1475	1068	191	24	93	460	**.259**-.385
Other Teams: New York, Texas, Toronto (AL); Pittsburgh (NL)									
Nationality: USA (New York, New York)									
McCray, Rodney (OF)	92	90-92	67	3	0	0	0	1	**.214**-.214
Other Teams: Chicago (AL)									
Nationality: USA (Detroit, Michigan)									
McDaniel, Terry (OF)	91	91	23	6	1	0	0	2	**.207**-.241
Other Teams: None									
Nationality: USA (Kansas City, Missouri)									
McEwing, Joe (IF/OF)	00	98-00	249	179	43	5	11	64	**.261**-.386
Other Teams: St. Louis (NL)									
Nationality: USA (Bristol, Pennsylvania)									
McGuire, Ryan (IF/OF)	00	97-00	303	121	31	4	6	45	**.220**-.323
Other Teams: Montreal (NL)									
Nationality: USA (Bellflower, California)									
McKnight, Jeff (IF)	89, 92-94	89-94	218	94	10	2	5	34	**.233**-.304
Other Teams: Baltimore (AL)									
Nationality: USA (Conway, Arkansas) (son of Jim McKnight)									
McMillan, Roy (IF)	64-66	51-66	2093	1639	253	35	68	594	**.243**-.321
Other Teams: Cincinnati, Milwaukee (NL)									
Nationality: USA (Bonham, Texas)									
McRae, Brian (OF)	97-99	90-99	1354	1336	264	58	103	532	**.261**-.396
Other Teams: Kansas City, Toronto (AL); Chicago, Colorado (NL)									
Nationality: USA (Bradenton, Florida) (son of Hal McRae)									
McReynolds, Kevin (OF)	87-91	83-94	1502	1439	284	35	211	807	**.265**-.447
Other Teams: Kansas City (AL); San Diego (NL)									
Nationality: USA (Little Rock, Arkansas)									
Mendoza, Carlos (OF)	97	97	15	3	0	0	0	1	**.250**-.250
Other Teams: None									
Nationality: Venezuela									
Mercado, Orlando (C)	90	82-90	253	112	17	4	7	45	**.199**-.281
Other Teams: Detroit, Minnesota, Oakland, Seattle, Texas (AL); Los Angeles, Montreal (NL)									
Nationality: Puerto Rico									

Player (Position)	Mets Seasons	MLB Years	G	H	2B	3B	HR	RBI	BA-SLG
Millan, Felix (2B)	73-77	66-77	1480	1617	229	38	22	403	.279-.343
Other Teams: Atlanta (NL)									
Nationality: Puerto Rico									
Miller, Keith (IF-OF)	87-91	87-95	465	347	67	8	12	92	.262-.351
Other Teams: Kansas City (AL)									
Nationality: USA (Midland, Michigan)									
Milliard, Ralph (IF)	98	96-98	42	16	2	0	0	3	.172-.194
Other Teams: Florida (NL)									
Nationality: Curacao									
Milligan, Randy (OF)	87	87-94	703	553	106	10	70	284	.261-.420
Other Teams: Baltimore, Cleveland (AL); Cincinnati, Montreal, Pittsburgh (NL)									
Nationality: USA (San Diego, California)									
Milner, John (OF)	71-77	71-82	1215	855	140	16	131	498	.249-.413
Other Teams: Montreal, Pittsburgh (NL)									
Nationality: USA (Atlanta, Georgia)									
Mitchell, Kevin (OF)	84, 86	84-98	1223	1173	224	25	234	760	.284-.520
Other Teams: Boston, Cleveland, Oakland, Seattle (AL); Cincinnati, San Diego, San Francisco (NL)									
Nationality: USA (San Diego, California)									
Montañez, Willie (1B)	78-79	66-82	1632	1604	279	25	139	802	.275-.402
Other Teams: California, Texas (AL); Atlanta, Montreal, Philadelphia, Pittsburgh, San Diego, San Francisco (NL)									
Nationality: Puerto Rico									
Moock, Joe (3B)	67	67	13	9	2	0	0	5	.225-.275
Other Teams: None									
Nationality: USA (Plaquemine, Louisiana)									
Mora, Melvin (OF)	99-00	99-00	198	119	22	5	8	48	.267-.393
Other Teams: Baltimore (AL)									
Nationality: Venezuela									
Morales, Jerry (OF)	80	69-83	1441	1173	199	36	95	570	.259-.382
Other Teams: Detroit (AL); Chicago, St. Louis, San Diego (NL)									
Nationality: Puerto Rico									
Moran, Al (IF)	63-64	63-64	135	69	5	2	1	27	.195-.229
Other Teams: None									
Nationality: USA (Detroit, Michigan)									
Moreno, José (IF)	80	80-82	82	20	4	1	2	15	.206-.330
Other Teams: California (AL); San Diego (NL)									
Nationality: Dominican Republic									
Morgan, Kevin (IF)	97	97	1	0	0	0	0	0	.000-.000
Other Teams: None									
Nationality: USA (Lafayette, Louisiana)									
Murphy, Billy (OF)	66	66	84	31	4	1	3	13	.230-.341
Other Teams: None									
Nationality: USA (Pineville, Louisiana)									
Murray, Eddie (1B)	92-93	77-97	3026	3255	560	35	504	1917	.287-.476
Other Teams: Anaheim, Baltimore, Cleveland (AL); Los Angeles (NL)									
Nationality: USA (Los Angeles, California)									
Napoleon, Dan (OF)	65-66	65-66	80	21	3	1	0	7	.162-.200
Other Teams: None									
Nationality: USA (Claysburg, Pennsylvania)									
Navarro, Tito (IF)	93	93	12	1	0	0	0	1	.059-.059
Other Teams: None									
Nationality: Puerto Rico									
Neal, Charlie (IF)	62-63	56-63	970	858	113	38	87	391	.259-.394
Other Teams: Brooklyn, Cincinnati, Los Angeles (NL)									
Nationality: USA (Longview, Texas)									

Player (Position)	Mets Seasons	MLB Years	G	H	2B	3B	HR	RBI	BA-SLG
Noboa, Junior (IF)	92	84-94	317	118	13	4	1	33	**.239**-.288

Other Teams: Cleveland, Oakland (AL); Montreal, Pittsburgh (NL)
Nationality: Dominican Republic

Nolan, Joe (C)	72	72-85	621	382	66	10	27	178	**.263**-.378

Other Teams: Baltimore (AL); Atlanta, Cincinnati (NL)
Nationality: USA (St. Louis, Missouri)

Norman, Dan (OF)	77-80	77-82	192	79	8	3	11	37	**.227**-.362

Other Teams: Montreal (NL)
Nationality: USA (Los Angeles, California)

O'Brien, Charlie (C)	90-93	85-00	800	493	119	4	56	261	**.221**-.353

Other Teams: Anaheim, Chicago, Milwaukee, Oakland, Toronto (AL); Atlanta, Montreal (NL)
Nationality: USA (Tulsa, Oklahoma)

Ochoa, Alex (OF)	95-97	95-00	537	376	85	12	30	178	**.283**-.433

Other Teams: Milwaukee, Minnesota (AL); Cincinnati (NL)
Nationality: USA (Miami Lakes, Florida)

Olerud, John (1B)	97-99	89-00	1555	1595	367	11	186	865	**.299**-.477

Other Teams: Seattle, Toronto (AL)
Nationality: USA (Seattle, Washington)

O'Malley, Tom (IF)	89-90	82-90	466	310	54	5	13	131	**.256**-.340

Other Teams: Chicago, Baltimore, Texas (AL); Montreal, San Francisco (NL)
Nationality: USA (Orange, New Jersey)

Oquendo, José (IF)	83-84	83-95	1190	821	104	24	14	254	**.256**-.317

Other Teams: St. Louis (NL)
Nationality: Puerto Rico

Ordoñez, Rey (SS)	96-00	96-00	623	489	66	11	4	174	**.243**-.292

Other Teams: None
Nationality: Cuba

Orsulak, Joe (OF)	93-95	83-97	1494	1173	186	37	57	405	**.273**-.374

Other Teams: Baltimore (AL); Florida, Montreal, Pittsburgh (NL)
Nationality: USA (Glen Ridge, New Jersey)

Ortiz, Junior (C)	81-83	82-94	749	484	71	4	5	186	**.256**-.305

Other Teams: Cleveland, Minnesota, Texas (AL); Pittsburgh (NL)
Nationality: Puerto Rico

Ostrosser, Brian (SS)	73	73	4	0	0	0	0	0	**.000**-.000

Other Teams: None
Nationality: Canada

Otero, Ricky (OF)	95	95-97	189	157	19	9	2	36	**.256**-.326

Other Teams: Philadelphia (NL)
Nationality: Puerto Rico

Otis, Amos (OF)	67, 69	67-84	1998	2020	374	66	193	1007	**.277**-.425

Other Teams: Kansas City (AL); Pittsburgh (NL)
Nationality: USA (Mobile, Alabama)

Paciorek, Tom (OF)	85	70-87	1392	1162	232	30	86	503	**.282**-.415

Other Teams: Chicago, Seattle, Texas (AL); Atlanta, Los Angeles (NL)
Nationality: USA (Detroit, Michigan) (brother of John Paciorek)

Paquette, Craig (IF)	98	93-00	608	470	97	9	80	293	**.239**-.420

Other Teams: Kansas City, Oakland (AL); St. Louis (NL)
Nationality: USA (Long Beach, California)

Parker, Rick (OF)	94	90-96	163	55	9	0	2	24	**.244**-.311

Other Teams: Houston, Los Angeles, San Francisco (NL)
Nationality: USA (Kansas City, Missouri)

Payton, Jay (OF)	98-00	98-00	177	151	25	1	17	63	**.292**-.442

Other Teams: None
Nationality: USA (Zanesville, Ohio)

Player (Position)	Mets Seasons	MLB Years	G	H	2B	3B	HR	RBI	BA-SLG
Pecota, Bill (IF)	92	86-94	698	380	72	11	22	148	**.249**-.354
Other Teams: Kansas City (AL); Atlanta (NL)									
Nationality: USA (Redwood City, California)									
Pedrique, Al (IF)	87	87-89	174	111	18	1	1	36	**.247**-.298
Other Teams: Detroit (AL); Pittsburgh (NL)									
Nationality: Venezuela									
Pemberton, Brock (1B)	74-75	74-75	13	4	0	0	0	1	**.167**-.167
Other Teams: None									
Nationality: USA (Tulsa, Oklahoma)									
Petagine, Roberto (1B)	96-97	94-98	193	69	13	1	10	43	**.225**-.371
Other Teams: Cincinnati, Houston, San Diego (NL)									
Nationality: Venezuela									
Pérez, Timoniel (OF)	00	00	24	14	4	1	1	3	**.286**-.469
Other Teams: None									
Nationality: Dominican Republic									
Pfeil, Bob (3B)	69	69, 71	106	68	12	0	2	19	**.242**-.469
Other Teams: Philadelphia (NL)									
Nationality: USA (Passaic, New Jersey)									
Phillips, Mike (IF)	75-77	73-83	712	412	46	26	11	145	**.240**-.314
Other Teams: Montreal, St. Louis, San Diego, San Francisco (NL)									
Nationality: USA (Beaumont, Texas)									
Phillips, Tony (OF)	98	82-99	2161	2023	360	50	160	819	**.266**-.389
Other Teams: Anaheim, California, Chicago, Detroit, Oakland, Toronto (AL)									
Nationality: USA (Atlanta, Georgia)									
Piazza, Mike (C)	98-00	92-00	1117	1356	199	4	278	881	**.328**-.580
Other Teams: Florida, Los Angeles (NL)									
Nationality: USA (Norristown, Pennsylvania)									
Piersall, Jim (OF)	63	50-67	1734	1604	256	52	104	591	**.272**-.386
Other Teams: Boston, California, Cleveland, Washington (AL); Los Angeles (NL)									
Nationality: USA (Waterbury, Connecticut)									
Pignatano, Joe (C)	62	57-62	307	161	25	4	16	62	**.234**-.351
Other Teams: Kansas City (AL); Brooklyn, Los Angeles, San Francisco (NL)									
Nationality: USA (Brooklyn, New York)									
Pratt, Todd (C)	97-00	92-00	333	200	40	2	24	119	**.260**-.410
Other Teams: Chicago, Philadelphia (NL)									
Nationality: USA (Bellevue, Nebraska)									
Puig, Rich (IF)	74	74	4	0	0	0	0	0	**.000**-.000
Other Teams: None									
Nationality: USA (Tampa, Florida)									
Rajsich, Gary (1B)	82-83	82-85	149	70	17	3	3	27	**.236**-.345
Other Teams: St. Louis, San Francisco (NL)									
Nationality: USA (Youngstown, Ohio)									
Ramirez, Mario (IF)	80	80-85	184	55	8	3	4	28	**.192**-.283
Other Teams: San Diego (NL)									
Nationality: Puerto Rico									
Randle, Lenny (IF)	77-78	71-82	1138	1016	145	40	27	322	**.257**-.335
Other Teams: New York, Seattle, Texas, Washington (AL); Chicago (NL)									
Nationality: USA (Long Beach, California)									
Randolph, Willie (IF)	92	75-92	2202	2210	316	65	54	687	**.276**-.351
Other Teams: Milwaukee, New York, Oakland (AL); Los Angeles, Pittsburgh (NL)									
Nationality: USA (Holly Hill, South Carolina)									
Reed, Darren (OF)	90	90, 92	82	28	8	1	6	16	**.183**-.366
Other Teams: Minnesota (AL); Montreal (NL)									
Nationality: USA (Ojai, California)									

Player (Position)	Mets Seasons	MLB Years	G	H	2B	3B	HR	RBI	BA-SLG
Reynolds, Ronn (C)	82-83, 85	82-90	143	67	12	0	4	21	.188-.256

Other Teams: Houston, Philadelphia, San Diego (NL)
Nationality: USA (Wichita, Kansas)

Reynolds, Tommie (OF)	67	63-72	513	265	35	5	12	87	.226-.296

Other Teams: None
Nationality: USA (Arizona, Louisiana)

Rivera, Luis (IF)	94	86-98	781	516	114	12	28	209	.233-.333

Other Teams: Boston, Kansas City (AL); Houston, Montreal (NL)
Nationality: Puerto Rico

Roberson, Kevin (OF)	96	93-96	165	61	10	1	20	51	.197-.430

Other Teams: Chicago (NL)
Nationality: USA (Decatur, Illinois)

Rosado, Luis (1B)	77, 80	77, 80	11	5	1	0	0	3	.179-.214

Other Teams: None
Nationality: Puerto Rico

Samuel, Amado (IF)	64	62-64	144	79	18	0	3	25	.215-.288

Other Teams: Milwaukee (NL)
Nationality: Dominican Republic

Samuel, Juan (OF)	89	83-98	1720	1578	287	102	161	703	.259-.420

Other Teams: Detroit, Kansas City, Toronto (AL); Cincinnati, Los Angeles, Philadelphia (NL)
Nationality: Dominican Republic

Santana, Rafael (SS)	84-87	83-90	668	497	74	5	13	156	.246-.307

Other Teams: Cleveland, New York (AL); St. Louis (NL)
Nationality: Dominican Republic

Sasser, Mackey (C)	88-92	87-95	534	317	69	7	16	156	.267-.377

Other Teams: Seattle (AL); Pittsburgh, San Francisco (NL)
Nationality: USA (Fort Gaines, Georgia)

Saunders, Doug (IF)	93	93	28	14	2	0	0	0	.209-.239

Other Teams: None
Nationality: USA (Yorba Linda, California)

Schaffer, Jimmie (C)	65	61-68	304	128	28	3	11	56	.223-.340

Other Teams: Chicago (AL); Chicago, Cincinnati, Philadelphia, St. Louis (NL)
Nationality: USA (Limeport, Pennsylvania)

Schneck, Dave (OF)	72-74	72-74	143	82	14	4	8	35	.199-.310

Other Teams: None
Nationality: USA (Allentown, Pennsylvania)

Schofield, Dick (SS)	92	83-96	1368	989	137	32	56	353	.230-.316

Other Teams: California, Toronto (AL); Los Angeles (NL)
Nationality: USA (Springfield, Illinois) (son of Dick Schofield)

Schreiber, Ted (IF)	63	63	39	8	0	0	0	2	.160-.160

Other Teams: None
Nationality: USA (Brooklyn, New York)

Segui, David (1B)	94-95	90-00	1263	1220	249	14	121	590	.292-.445

Other Teams: Baltimore, Cleveland, Seattle, Texas, Toronto (AL); Montreal (NL)
Nationality: USA (Kansas City, Kansas) (son of Diego Segui of Cuba)

Shamsky, Art (OF)	68-71	65-72	665	426	60	15	68	233	.253-.427

Other Teams: Oakland (AL); Chicago, Cincinnati (NL)
Nationality: USA (St. Louis, Missouri)

Sherry, Norm (C)	63	59-63	194	107	9	1	18	69	.215-.346

Other Teams: Los Angeles (NL)
Nationality: USA (New York, New York) (brother of Larry Sherry)

Shipley, Craig (IF)	89	86-98	582	364	63	6	20	138	.271-.371

Other Teams: Anaheim (AL); Houston, Los Angeles, San Diego (NL)
Nationality: Australia

Player (Position)	Mets Seasons	MLB Years	G	H	2B	3B	HR	RBI	BA-SLG
Shirley, Bart (2B)	67	64-68	75	33	4	1	0	11	.204-.241
Other Teams: Los Angeles (NL)									
Nationality: USA (Corpus Christi, Texas)									
Singleton, Ken (OF)	70-71	70-84	2082	2029	317	25	246	1065	.282-.436
Other Teams: Baltimore (AL); Montreal (NL)									
Nationality: USA (New York, New York)									
Smith, Bobby Gene (OF)	62	57-65	476	234	35	5	13	96	.243-.331
Other Teams: California (AL); Chicago, Philadelphia, St. Louis (NL)									
Nationality: USA (Hood River, Oregon)									
Smith, Charley (3B)	64-65	60-69	771	594	83	18	69	281	.239-.370
Other Teams: Chicago, New York (AL); Chicago, Los Angeles, Philadelphia, St. Louis (NL)									
Nationality: USA (Charleston, South Carolina)									
Smith, Dick (OF)	63-64	63-65	76	31	6	2	0	7	.218-.289
Other Teams: Los Angeles (NL)									
Nationality: USA (Lebanon, Oregon)									
Snider, Duke (OF)	63	47-64	2143	2116	358	85	407	1333	.295-.540
Other Teams: Brooklyn, Los Angeles, San Francisco (NL)									
Nationality: USA (Los Angeles, California)									
Spehr, Tim (C)	98	91-99	363	110	31	1	19	72	.198-.360
Other Teams: Kansas City (AL); Atlanta, Montreal (NL)									
Nationality: USA (Excelsior Springs, Missouri)									
Spiers, Bill (IF)	95	89-00	1248	921	158	35	37	388	.270-.370
Other Teams: Milwaukee (AL); Houston (NL)									
Nationality: USA (Orangeburg, South Carolina)									
Springer, Steve (IF)	92	90, 92	8	4	1	0	0	1	.235-.294
Other Teams: Cleveland (AL)									
Nationality: USA (Long Beach, California)									
Stahl, Larry (OF)	67-68	64-73	730	400	58	19	36	163	.232-.351
Other Teams: Kansas City (AL); Cincinnati, San Diego (NL)									
Nationality: USA (Belleville, Illinois)									
Staiger, Roy (3B)	75-77	75-79	152	104	19	1	4	38	.228-.300
Other Teams: New York (AL)									
Nationality: USA (Tulsa, Oklahoma)									
Stanton, Leroy (OF)	70-71	70-78	829	628	114	13	77	358	.244-.388
Other Teams: California, Seattle (AL)									
Nationality: USA (Latta, South Carolina)									
Staub, Rusty (OF)	72-75, 81-85	63-85	2951	2716	499	47	292	1466	.279-.431
Other Teams: Detroit, Texas (AL); Houston, Montreal (NL)									
Nationality: USA (New Orleans, Louisiana)									
Stearns, John (C)	75-84	74-84	810	696	152	10	46	312	.260-.375
Other Teams: Philadelphia (NL)									
Nationality: USA (Denver, Colorado)									
Stephenson, John (C)	64-66	64-73	451	214	37	3	12	93	.216-.296
Other Teams: California (AL); Chicago, San Francisco (NL)									
Nationality: USA (South Portsmouth, Kentucky)									
Stinnett, Kelly (C)	94-95	94-00	424	281	52	4	39	140	.233-.380
Other Teams: Milwaukee (AL); Arizona (NL)									
Nationality: USA (Lawton, Oklahoma)									
Strawberry, Darryl (OF)	83-90	83-99	1583	1401	256	38	335	1000	.259-.505
Other Teams: New York (AL); Los Angeles, San Francisco (NL)									
Nationality: USA (Los Angeles, California)									
Stuart, Dick (1B)	66	58-69	1112	1055	157	30	228	743	.264-.489
Other Teams: Boston, California (AL); Los Angeles, Philadelphia, Pittsburgh (NL)									
Nationality: USA (San Francisco, California)									

Player (Position)	Mets Seasons	MLB Years	G	H	2B	3B	HR	RBI	BA-SLG
Sudakis, Bill (C)	72	68-75	530	362	56	7	59	214	**.234**-.393

Other Teams: California, Cleveland, New York, Texas (AL); Los Angeles (NL)
Nationality: USA (Joliet, Illinois)

Sullivan, John (C)	67	63-68	116	59	5	0	2	18	**.228**-.270

Other Teams: Detroit (AL); Philadelphia (NL)
Nationality: USA (Somerville, New Jersey)

Sweet, Rick (C)	82	78-83	272	172	23	1	6	57	**.234**-.292

Other Teams: Seattle (AL); San Diego (NL)
Nationality: USA (Longview, Washington)

Swoboda, Ron (OF)	65-70	65-73	928	624	87	24	73	344	**.242**-.379

Other Teams: New York (AL); Montreal (NL)
Nationality: USA (Baltimore, Maryland)

Tabler, Pat (OF)	90	81-92	1202	1101	190	25	47	512	**.282**-.379

Other Teams: Cleveland, Kansas City, Toronto (AL); Chicago (NL)
Nationality: USA (Hamilton, Ohio)

Tatum, Jim (OF)	98	92-98	173	39	7	3	3	29	**.194**-.303

Other Teams: Boston, Milwaukee (AL); Colorado, San Diego (NL)
Nationality: USA (Grossmont, California)

Taveras, Frank (SS)	79-81	71-82	1150	1029	144	44	2	214	**.255**-.302

Other Teams: Montreal, Pittsburgh (NL)
Nationality: Dominican Republic

Taylor, Bob (Hawk) (C)	64-67	57-70	394	159	25	0	16	82	**.218**-.319

Other Teams: California, Kansas City (AL); Milwaukee (NL)
Nationality: USA (Metropolis, Illinois)

Taylor, Sammy (C)	62-63	58-63	473	309	47	9	33	147	**.245**-.375

Other Teams: Cleveland (AL); Chicago, Cincinnati (NL)
Nationality: USA (Woodruff, South Carolina)

Templeton, Garry (SS)	91	76-91	2079	2096	329	106	70	728	**.271**-.369

Other Teams: St. Louis, San Diego (NL)
Nationality: USA (Lockney, Texas)

Teufel, Tim (IF)	86-91	83-93	1073	789	185	12	86	379	**.254**-.404

Other Teams: Minnesota (AL); San Diego (NL)
Nationality: USA (Greenwich, Connecticut)

Theodore, George (OF)	73-74	73-74	105	42	5	0	2	16	**.219**-.276

Other Teams: None
Nationality: USA (Salt Lake City, Utah)

Thomas, Frank (OF)	62-64	51-66	1766	1671	262	31	286	962	**.266**-.454

Other Teams: Chicago, Cincinnati, Houston, Milwaukee, Philadelphia, Pittsburgh (NL)
Nationality: USA (Pittsburgh, Pennsylvania)

Thompson, Ryan (OF)	92-96	92-96	291	245	53	4	40	131	**.240**-.418

Other Teams: Cleveland (AL)
Nationality: USA (Chestertown, Maryland)

Thornton, Lou (OF)	89-90	85-90	95	22	2	1	1	9	**.247**-.326

Other Teams: Toronto (AL)
Nationality: USA (Montgomery, Alabama)

Throneberry, Marv (1B)	62-63	55-63	480	281	37	8	53	170	**.237**-.416

Other Teams: Baltimore, Kansas City, New York (AL)
Nationality: USA (Collierville, Tennessee)

Thurman, Gary (OF)	97	87-97	424	194	27	6	2	64	**.243**-.299

Other Teams: Detroit, Kansas City, Seattle (AL)
Nationality: USA (Indianapolis, Indiana)

Tillman, Rusty (OF)	82	82-88	38	13	2	0	2	9	**.232**-.375

Other Teams: Oakland (AL); San Francisco (NL)
Nationality: USA (Jacksonville, Florida)

Player (Position)	Mets Seasons	MLB Years	G	H	2B	3B	HR	RBI	BA-SLG
Toca, Jorge (1B-OF)	99-00	99-00	12	4	1	0	0	4	.400-.500

Other Teams: None
Nationality: Cuba

Tomberlin, Andy (OF)	96-97	93-98	192	71	6	2	11	38	.233-.374

Other Teams: Boston, Detroit, Oakland (AL); Pittsburgh (NL)
Nationality: USA (Monroe, North Carolina)

Torre, Joe (IF)	75-77	60-77	2209	2342	344	59	252	1185	.297-.452

Other Teams: Atlanta, Milwaukee, St. Louis (NL)
Nationality: USA (Brooklyn, New York)

Torve, Kelvin (1B)	90-91	88-91	42	14	4	0	1	4	.226-.339

Other Teams: Minnesota (AL)
Nationality: USA (Rapid City, South Dakota)

Trammell, Bubba (OF)	00	97-00	287	232	55	3	40	132	.273-.486

Other Teams: Detroit, Tampa Bay (AL)
Nationality: USA (Knoxville, Tennessee)

Treviño, Alex (C)	78-81, 90	78-90	939	604	117	10	23	244	.249-.333

Other Teams: Atlanta, Cincinnati, Houston, Los Angeles, San Francisco (NL)
Nationality: Mexico

Tyner, Jason (OF)	00	00	13	8	2	0	0	5	.195-.244

Other Teams: None
Nationality: USA (Beaumont, Texas)

Unser, Del (OF)	75-76	68-82	1799	1344	179	42	87	481	.258-.358

Other Teams: Cleveland, Washington (AL); Montreal, Philadelphia (NL)
Nationality: USA (Decatur, Illinois)

Vail, Mike (OF)	75-77	75-84	665	447	71	11	34	219	.279-.400

Other Teams: Cleveland (AL); Chicago, Cincinnati, Los Angeles, Montreal, San Francisco (NL)
Nationality: USA (San Francisco, California)

Valentine, Bobby (IF-OF)	77-78	69-79	639	441	59	9	12	157	.260-.326

Other Teams: California, Seattle (AL); Los Angeles, San Diego (NL)
Nationality: USA (Stamford, Connecticut)

Valentine, Ellis (OF)	81-82	75-85	894	881	169	15	123	474	.278-.458

Other Teams: California, Texas (AL); Montreal (NL)
Nationality: USA (Helena, Arkansas)

Velandia, Jorge (IF)	00	97-00	118	16	4	0	0	4	.136-.179

Other Teams: Oakland (AL); San Diego (NL)
Nationality: Venezuela

Ventura, Robin (IF)	99-00	89-00	1556	1530	270	13	227	945	.273-.450

Other Teams: Chicago (AL)
Nationality: USA (Santa Maria, California)

Veryzer, Tom (SS)	82	73-84	996	687	84	12	14	231	.241-.294

Other Teams: Cleveland, Detroit (AL); Chicago (NL)
Nationality: USA (Port Jefferson, New York)

Vina, Fernando (IF-OF)	94	93-00	754	746	116	32	26	203	.285-.384

Other Teams: Milwaukee, Seattle (AL); Milwaukee, St. Louis (NL)
Nationality: USA (Sacramento, California)

Vizcaino, José (IF)	94-96	89-00	1181	1035	133	34	21	339	.269-.338

Other Teams: Cleveland, New York (AL); Chicago, Los Angeles, San Francisco (NL)
Nationality: Dominican Republic

Walker, Chico (IF-OF)	92-93	80-93	526	299	37	7	17	116	.246-.329

Other Teams: Boston, California (AL); Chicago (NL)
Nationality: USA (Jackson, Mississippi)

Player (Position)	Mets Seasons	MLB Years	G	H	2B	3B	HR	RBI	BA-SLG
Washington, Claudell (OF)	80	74-90	1912	1884	334	69	164	824	**.278**-.420

Other Teams: California, Chicago, New York, Oakland, Texas (AL); Atlanta (NL)
Nationality: USA (Los Angeles, California)

Weis, Al (IF)	68-71	62-71	800	346	45	11	7	115	**.219**-.275

Other Teams: Chicago (AL)
Nationality: USA (Franklin Square, New York)

Wilkins, Rick (C)	98	91-00	708	511	94	7	80	267	**.242**-.411

Other Teams: Seattle (AL); Chicago, Houston, Los Angeles, St. Louis, San Francisco (NL)
Nationality: USA (Jacksonville, Florida)

Wilson, Mookie (OF)	80-89	80-91	1403	1397	227	71	67	438	**.274**-.386

Other Teams: Toronto (AL)
Nationality: USA (Bamberg, South Carolina) (father of Preston Wilson)

Wilson, Preston (OF)	98	98-00	332	303	58	7	58	195	**.266**-.482

Other Teams: Florida (NL)
Nationality: USA (Bamberg, South Carolina) (son of Mookie Wilson)

Wilson, Vance (C)	99-00	99-00	5	0	0	0	0	0	**.000**-.000

Other Teams: None
Nationality: USA (Mesa, Arizona)

Winningham, Herm (OF)	84	84-92	868	452	69	26	19	147	**.239**-.334

Other Teams: Boston (AL); Cincinnati, Montreal (NL)
Nationality: USA (Orangeburg, South Carolina)

Woodling, Gene (OF)	62	43-62	1796	1585	257	63	147	830	**.284**-.431

Other Teams: Baltimore, Cleveland, New York, Washington (AL); Pittsburgh
Nationality: USA (Akron, Ohio)

Youngblood, Joel (OF)	77-82	76-89	1408	969	180	23	80	422	**.265**-.392

Other Teams: Cincinnati, Montreal, St. Louis, San Francisco (NL)
Nationality: USA (Houston, Texas)

Zeile, Todd (IF)	00	89-00	1626	1576	323	20	205	884	**.268**-.434

Other Teams: Baltimore, Texas (AL); Chicago, Florida, Los Angeles, Philadelphia, St. Louis (NL)
Nationality: USA (Van Nuys, California)

Zimmer, Don (3B)	62	54-65	1095	773	130	22	91	352	**.235**-.372

Other Teams: Washington (AL); Brooklyn, Chicago, Cincinnati, Los Angeles (NL)
Nationality: USA (Cincinnati, Ohio)

METS PITCHERS

Player (Position)	Mets Seasons	MLB Years	W-L	Pct.	ERA	IP	ShO	Saves	SO-BB
Aase, Don (RHP)	89	77-90	66-60	.524	3.80	1109.1	5	82	641-457

Other Teams: Baltimore, Boston, California (AL); Los Angeles (NL)
Nationality: USA (Orange, California)

Acevedo, Juan (RHP)	97	95-00	24-25	.490	4.61	397.0	0	19	232-150

Other Teams: Colorado, Milwaukee, St. Louis (NL)
Nationality: Mexico

Aguilera, Rick (RHP)	85-89	85-00	86-81	.515	3.52	1291.2	0	318	1030-351

Other Teams: Boston, Minnesota (AL); Chicago (NL)
Nationality: USA (San Gabriel, California)

Aker, Jack (RHP)	74	64-74	47-45	.511	3.28	746.0	0	123	404-274

Other Teams: Kansas City, New York, Oakland, Seattle (AL); Atlanta, Chicago (NL)
Nationality: USA (Tulare, California)

Allen, Neil (RHP)	79-83	79-89	58-70	.453	3.88	988.1	6	75	611-417

Other Teams: Chicago, Cleveland, New York (AL); New York, St. Louis (NL)
Nationality: USA (Kansas City, Kansas)

Anderson, Craig (RHP)	62-64	61-64	7-23	.233	5.10	192.1	0	5	94-81

Other Teams: St. Louis (NL)
Nationality: USA (Washington, DC)

Anderson, Rick (RHP)	86	86-88	4-4	.500	4.75	96.2	0	1	42-29

Other Teams: Kansas City (AL)
Nationality: USA (Everett, Washington)

Apodaca, Bob (RHP)	73-77	73-77	16-25	.390	2.86	361.1	0	26	197-131

Other Teams: None
Nationality: USA (Los Angeles, California)

Arrigo, Gerry (LHP)	66	61-70	35-40	.467	4.14	620.0	3	4	433-291

Other Teams: Chicago, Minnesota (AL); Cincinnati (NL)
Nationality: USA (Chicago, Illinois)

Baldwin, Rick (RHP)	75-77	75-77	4-7	.364	3.60	182.2	0	7	86-75

Other Teams: None
Nationality: USA (Fresno, California)

Bauta, Ed (RHP)	63-64	60-64	6-6	.500	4.35	149.0	0	11	89-70

Other Teams: St. Louis (NL)
Nationality: Cuba

Bearnarth, Larry (RHP)	63-66	63-71	13-21	.382	4.13	322.2	0	8	124-135

Other Teams: Milwaukee (AL)
Nationality: USA (New York, New York)

Beatty, Blaine (LHP)	89, 91	89-91	0-0	.000	2.30	15.2	0	0	10-6

Other Teams: None
Nationality: USA (Victoria, Texas)

Beltran, Rigo (LHP)	98	97-00	2-3	.400	3.88	105.1	0	1	106-43

Other Teams: Colorado, St. Louis (NL)
Nationality: Mexico

Benitez, Armando (RHP)	99-00	94-00	19-23	.452	3.04	367.2	0	100	517-208

Other Teams: Baltimore (AL)
Nationality: Dominican Republic

Bennett, Dennis (LHP)	67	62-68	43-47	.478	3.69	863.0	6	6	572-281

Other Teams: Boston, California (AL); Philadelphia (NL)
Nationality: USA (Oakland, California)

Berenguer, Juan (RHP)	78-80	78-92	67-62	.519	3.90	1205.1	2	32	975-604

Other Teams: Detroit, Kansas City, Minnesota, Toronto (AL); Atlanta, San Francisco (NL)
Nationality: Panama

Player (Position)	Mets Seasons	MLB Years	W-L	Pct.	ERA	IP	ShO	Saves	SO-BB
Berenyi, Bruce (RHP)	84-86	80-86	44-55	.444	4.03	781.2	5	0	607-425
Other Teams: Cincinnati (NL)									
Nationality: USA (Bryan, Ohio)									
Bernard, Dwight (RHP)	78-79	78-82	4-8	.333	4.14	176.0	0	6	92-86
Other Teams: Milwaukee (AL)									
Nationality: USA (Mount Vernon, Illinois)									
Bethke, Jim (RHP)	65	1965	2-0	1.000	4.27	40.0	0	0	19-22
Other Teams: None									
Nationality: USA (Falls City, Nebraska)									
Birkbeck, Mike (RHP)	95	86-95	12-19	.387	4.86	270.1	0	0	149-93
Other Teams: Milwaukee (AL)									
Nationality: USA (Orrville, Ohio)									
Bohanon, Brian (LHP)	97-98	90-00	49-52	.485	5.07	1019.0	0	2	624-442
Other Teams: Detroit, Texas, Toronto (AL); Colorado, Los Angeles (NL)									
Nationality: USA (Denton, Texas)									
Boitano, Dan (RHP)	81	78-82	2-2	.500	5.68	71.1	0	0	52-28
Other Teams: Milwaukee, Texas (AL); Philadelphia (NL)									
Nationality: USA (Sacramento, California)									
Bomback, Mark (RHP)	80	78-82	16-18	.471	4.47	314.1	1	0	124-110
Other Teams: Milwaukee, Toronto (AL)									
Nationality: USA (Portsmouth, Virginia)									
Borland, Toby (RHP)	97	94-98	9-7	.563	4.01	224.2	0	8	178-120
Other Teams: Boston (AL); Philadelphia (NL)									
Nationality: USA (Ruston, Louisiana)									
Bross, Terry (RHP)	91	91-93	0-0	.000	3.00	12.0	0	0	6-4
Other Teams: San Francisco (NL)									
Nationality: USA (El Paso, Texas)									
Brown, Kevin (LHP)	90	90-92	3-5	.375	4.82	89.2	0	0	44-45
Other Teams: Milwaukee, Seattle (AL)									
Nationality: USA (Oroville, California)									
Bruhert, Mike (RHP)	78	1978	4-11	.267	4.78	133.2	1	0	56-34
Other Teams: None									
Nationality: USA (Jamaica, New York)									
Burke, Tim (RHP)	91-92	85-92	49-33	.598	2.72	699.1	0	102	444-219
Other Teams: New York (AL); Montreal (NL)									
Nationality: USA (Omaha, Nebraska)									
Burris, Ray (RHP)	79-80	73-87	108-134	.446	4.17	2188.1	10	4	1065-764
Other Teams: Milwaukee, New York, Oakland (AL); Chicago, Montreal, St. Louis (NL)									
Nationality: USA (Idabel, Oklahoma)									
Byrd, Paul (RHP)	95-96	95-00	29-28	.509	4.21	461.1	1	0	292-179
Other Teams: Atlanta, Philadelphia (NL)									
Nationality: USA (Louisville, Kentucky)									
Cammack, Eric (RHP)	00	00	0-0	.000	6.30	10.0	0	0	9-10
Other Teams: None									
Nationality: USA (Nederland, Texas)									
Candelaria, John (LHP)	87	75-93	177-122	.592	3.33	2525.2	13	29	1673-592
Other Teams: California, Minnesota, New York, Toronto (AL); Los Angeles, Montreal, Pittsburgh (NL)									
Nationality: USA (New York, New York)									
Capra, Buzz (RHP)	71-73	71-77	31-37	.456	3.87	544.1	5	5	362-258
Other Teams: Atlanta (NL)									
Nationality: USA (Chicago, Illinois)									

Player (Position)	Mets Seasons	MLB Years	W-L	Pct.	ERA	IP	ShO	Saves	SO-BB
Cardwell, Don (RHP)	67-70	57-70	102-138	.425	3.92	2122.2	17	7	1211-671

Other Teams: Atlanta, Chicago, Philadelphia, Pittsburgh (NL)
Nationality: USA (Winston-Salem, North Carolina)

Castillo, Juan (RHP)	94	1994	0-0	.000	6.94	11.2	0	0	1-5

Other Teams: None
Nationality: Venezuela

Castillo, Tony (LHP)	91	88-98	28-23	.549	3.93	526.2	0	22	333-179

Other Teams: Chicago, Toronto (AL); Atlanta (NL)
Nationality: Venezuela

Chance, Dean (RHP)	70	61-71	128-115	.527	2.92	2147.1	33	23	1534-739

Other Teams: California, Cleveland, Detroit, Minnesota (AL); Los Angeles (NL)
Nationality: USA (Plain Township, Ohio)

Cisco, Galen (RHP)	62-65	61-69	25-56	.309	4.56	659.0	3	2	325-281

Other Teams: Boston, Kansas City (AL)
Nationality: USA (St. Mary's, Ohio)

Clark, Mark (RHP)	96-97	91-00	74-71	.510	4.48	1246.1	3	0	728-367

Other Teams: Cleveland, Texas (AL); Chicago, St. Louis (NL)
Nationality: USA (Bath, Illinois)

Clontz, Brad (RHP)	98	95-00	22-8	.733	4.32	277.2	0	8	210-120

Other Teams: Arizona, Atlanta, Los Angeles, Pittsburgh (NL)
Nationality: USA (Stuart, Virginia)

Cone, David (RHP)	87-92	86-00	184-116	.600	3.19	2745.0	22	1	2540-1067

Other Teams: Kansas City, New York, Toronto (AL)
Nationality: USA (Kansas City, Missouri)

Connors, Bill (RHP)	67-68	66-68	0-2	.000	7.53	43.0	0	0	24-19

Other Teams: Chicago (NL)
Nationality: USA (Schenectady, New York)

Cook, Dennis (LHP)	98-00	88-00	62-44	.585	3.90	942.0	3	9	741-366

Other Teams: Cleveland, Texas (AL); Florida, Los Angeles, Philadelphia, San Francisco (NL)
Nationality: USA (LaMarque, Texas)

Cornejo, Mardie (RHP)	78	1978	4-2	.667	2.45	36.2	0	3	17-14

Other Teams: None
Nationality: USA (Wellington, Kansas)

Cornelius, Reid (RHP)	95	1995	3-7	.300	5.54	66.2	0	0	39-30

Other Teams: Montreal (NL)
Nationality: USA (Thomasville, Georgia)

Craig, Roger (RHP)	62-63	55-66	74-98	.430	3.83	1536.1	7	19	803-522

Other Teams: Brooklyn, Cincinnati, Los Angeles, Philadelphia, St. Louis (NL)
Nationality: USA (Durham, North Carolina)

Cram, Jerry (RHP)	74-75	69-76	0-3	.000	2.98	48.1	0	0	22-13

Other Teams: Kansas City (AL)
Nationality: USA (Los Angeles, California)

Crawford, Joe (LHP)	97	1997	4-3	.571	3.30	46.1	0	0	25-13

Other Teams: None
Nationality: USA (Gainesville, Florida)

Darling, Ron (RHP)	83-91	83-95	136-116	.540	3.87	2360.1	13	0	1590-906

Other Teams: Oakland (AL); Montreal (NL)
Nationality: USA (Honolulu, Hawaii)

Daviault, Ray (RHP)	62	1962	1-5	.167	6.22	81.0	0	0	51-48

Other Teams: None
Nationality: Canada

Denehy, Bill (RHP)	67	67-71	1-10	.091	4.56	104.2	0	1	63-61

Other Teams: Detroit, Washington (AL)
Nationality: USA (Middletown, Connecticut)

Player (Position)	Mets Seasons	MLB Years	W-L	Pct.	ERA	IP	ShO	Saves	SO-BB
Dewey, Mark (RHP)	92	90-96	12-7	.632	3.65	249.0	0	8	168-102

Other Teams: Pittsburgh, San Francisco (NL)
Nationality: USA (Grand Rapids, Michigan)

Diaz, Carlos (LHP)	82-83	82-86	13-6	.684	3.21	258.0	0	4	207-97

Other Teams: Atlanta, Los Angeles (NL)
Nationality: USA (Kaneohe, Hawaii)

DiLauro, Jack (LHP)	69	69, 72	2-7	.222	3.05	97.1	0	4	50-35

Other Teams: Houston (NL)
Nationality: USA (Akron, Ohio)

Dillon, Steve (LHP)	63-64	63-64	0-0	.000	9.64	4.2	0	0	3-2

Other Teams: None
Nationality: USA (Yonkers, New York)

Dipoto, Jerry (RHP)	95-96	93-99	27-24	.529	4.05	481.2	0	49	343-216

Other Teams: Cleveland (AL); Colorado (NL)
Nationality: USA (Jersey City, New Jersey)

Dotel, Octavio (RHP)	99	99-00	11-10	.524	4.59	274.1	0	16	281-151

Other Teams: Houston (NL)
Nationality: Dominican Republic

Draper, Mike (RHP)	93	1993	1-1	.500	4.25	42.1	0	0	16-14

Other Teams: None
Nationality: USA (Hagerstown, Maryland)

Edens, Tom (RHP)	87	87-95	19-12	.613	3.86	312.1	0	6	182-123

Other Teams: Milwaukee, Minnesota (AL); Chicago, Houston, Philadelphia (NL)
Nationality: USA (Ontario, Oregon)

Eilers, Dave (RHP)	65-66	64-67	8-6	.571	4.45	123.1	0	3	52-29

Other Teams: Houston, Milwaukee (NL)
Nationality: USA (Oldenburg, Texas)

Ellis, Dock (RHP)	79	68-79	138-119	.537	3.46	2127.2	14	1	1136-674

Other Teams: New York, Oakland, Texas (AL); Pittsburgh (NL)
Nationality: USA (Los Angeles, California)

Espinosa, Nino (RHP)	74-78	74-81	44-55	.444	4.17	820.1	5	0	338-252

Other Teams: Toronto (AL); Philadelphia (NL)
Nationality: Dominican Republic

Estrada, Chuck (RHP)	67	60-67	50-44	.532	4.07	764.1	2	2	535-416

Other Teams: Baltimore (AL); Chicago (NL)
Nationality: USA (San Luis Obispo, California)

Falcone, Pete (LHP)	79-82	75-84	70-90	.438	4.07	1435.1	7	7	865-671

Other Teams: Atlanta, St. Louis, San Francisco (NL)
Nationality: USA (Brooklyn, New York)

Fernandez, Sid (LHP)	84-93	83-97	114-96	.543	3.36	1866.2	9	1	1743-715

Other Teams: Baltimore (AL); Houston, Los Angeles, Philadelphia (NL)
Nationality: USA (Honolulu, Hawaii)

Filer, Tom (RHP)	92	82-92	22-17	.564	4.25	307.1	1	0	115-107

Other Teams: Milwaukee, Toronto (AL); Chicago (NL)
Nationality: USA (Philadelphia, Pennsylvania)

Fisher, Jack (RHP)	64-67	59-69	86-139	.382	4.06	1975.2	9	9	1017-605

Other Teams: Baltimore, Chicago (AL); Cincinnati, San Francisco (NL)
Nationality: USA (Frostburg, Maryland)

Florence, Don (LHP)	95	1995	3-0	1.000	1.50	12.0	0	0	5-6

Other Teams: None
Nationality: USA (Manchester, New Hampshire)

Player (Position)	Mets Seasons	MLB Years	W-L	Pct.	ERA	IP	ShO	Saves	SO-BB
Folkers, Rich (LHP)	70	70-77	19-23	.452	4.11	423.0	0	7	242-170
Other Teams: Milwaukee (AL); St. Louis, San Diego (NL)									
Nationality: USA (Waterloo, Iowa)									
Foss, Larry (RHP)	62	61-62	1-2	.333	5.33	27.0	0	0	12-18
Other Teams: Pittsburgh (NL)									
Nationality: USA (Castleton, Kansas)									
Franco, John (LHP)	90-00	84-00	82-74	.526	2.68	1097.0	0	420	857-430
Other Teams: Cincinnati (NL)									
Nationality: USA (Brooklyn, New York)									
Friend, Bob (RHP)	66	51-66	197-230	.461	3.58	3611.0	36	11	1734-894
Other Teams: New York (AL); Pittsburgh (NL)									
Nationality: USA (Lafayette, Indiana)									
Frisella, Danny (RHP)	67-72	67-76	34-40	.459	3.32	609.1	0	57	471-286
Other Teams: Milwaukee (AL); Atlanta, St. Louis, San Diego (NL)									
Nationality: USA (San Francisco, California)									
Fyhrie, Mike (RHP)	96	1996	0-1	.000	15.43	2.1	0	0	0-3
Other Teams: None									
Nationality: USA (Long Beach, California)									
Gaff, Brent (RHP)	82-84	82-84	4-5	.444	4.06	126.1	0	1	60-47
Other Teams: None									
Nationality: USA (Fort Wayne, Indiana)									
Gardner, Rob (LHP)	65-66	65-73	14-18	.438	4.35	331.0	0	2	193-133
Other Teams: Cleveland, Milwaukee, New York, Oakland, (AL); Chicago (NL)									
Nationality: USA (Binghamton, New York)									
Gardner, Wes (RHP)	84-85	84-91	18-30	.375	4.90	466.1	0	14	358-218
Other Teams: Boston, Kansas City (AL); San Diego (NL)									
Nationality: USA (Benton, Arkansas)									
Gentry, Gary (RHP)	69-72	69-75	46-49	.484	3.56	902.2	8	2	615-369
Other Teams: Atlanta (NL)									
Nationality: USA (Phoenix, Arizona)									
Gibson, Bob (RHP)	87	83-87	12-18	.400	4.24	269.2	1	13	166-166
Other Teams: Milwaukee (AL)									
Nationality: USA (Philadelphia, Pennsylvania)									
Gibson, Paul (LHP)	92-93	88-96	22-24	.478	4.07	556.2	0	11	345-236
Other Teams: Detroit, New York (AL)									
Nationality: USA (Southampton, New York)									
Glynn, Ed (LHP)	79-80	75-85	12-17	.414	4.25	264.2	0	12	184-151
Other Teams: Cleveland, Detroit (AL); Montreal (NL)									
Nationality: USA (Flushing, New York)									
Gooden, Dwight (RHP)	84-94	84-00	194-112	.637	3.46	2796.2	24	3	2292-951
Other Teams: Cleveland, New York, Tampa Bay (AL)									
Nationality: USA (Tampa, Florida)									
Gorman, Tom (LHP)	82-85	81-87	12-10	.545	4.34	213.2	0	0	144-66
Other Teams: Montreal, Philadelphia, San Diego (NL)									
Nationality: USA (Portland, Oregon)									
Gozzo, Mauro (RHP)	93-94	89-94	7-7	.500	5.30	124.0	0	1	55-51
Other Teams: Cleveland, Minnesota, Toronto (AL)									
Nationality: USA (New Britain, Connecticut)									
Graham, Bill (RHP)	67	66-67	1-2	.333	2.45	29.1	0	0	16-11
Other Teams: Detroit (AL)									
Nationality: USA (Flemingsburg, Kentucky)									

Player (Position)	Mets Seasons	MLB Years	W-L	Pct.	ERA	IP	ShO	Saves	SO-BB
Green, Dallas (RHP)	66	60-67	20-22	.476	4.26	562.1	2	4	268-197
Other Teams: Washington (AL); Philadelphia (NL)									
Nationality: USA (Newport, Delaware)									
Greer, Kenny (RHP)	93	93, 95	1-2	.333	4.85	13.0	0	0	9-5
Other Teams: San Francisco (NL)									
Nationality: USA (Boston, Massachusetts)									
Grzenda, Joe (LHP)	67	61-72	14-13	.519	4.00	308.0	0	14	173-120
Other Teams: Detroit, Kansas City, Minnesota, Washington (AL); St. Louis (NL)									
Nationality: USA (Scranton, Pennsylvania)									
Guetterman, Lee (LHP)	92	84-96	38-36	.514	4.33	658.1	1	25	287-222
Other Teams: New York, Seattle (AL); St. Louis (NL)									
Nationality: USA (Chattanooga, Tennessee)									
Gunderson, Eric (LHP)	94-95	90-00	8-11	.421	4.89	228.2	0	2	137-84
Other Teams: Boston, Seattle, Texas, Toronto (AL); San Francisco (NL)									
Nationality: USA (Portland, Oregon)									
Hall, Tom (LHP)	75-76	68-77	52-33	.612	3.27	852.2	3	32	797-382
Other Teams: Kansas City, Minnesota (AL); Cincinnati (NL)									
Nationality: USA (Thomasville, North Carolina)									
Hamilton, Jack (RHP)	66-67	62-69	32-40	.444	4.53	611.2	2	20	357-348
Other Teams: California, Chicago, Cleveland, Detroit (AL); Philadelphia (NL)									
Nationality: USA (Burlington, Iowa)									
Hampton, Mike (LHP)	00	93-00	85-53	.616	3.44	1260.2	7	1	852-489
Other Teams: Seattle (AL); Houston (NL)									
Nationality: USA (Brooksville, Florida)									
Harnisch, Pete (RHP)	95-97	88-00	110-100	.524	3.78	1923.2	8	0	1351-699
Other Teams: Baltimore, Milwaukee (AL); Cincinnati, Houston (NL)									
Nationality: USA (Commack, New York)									
Harris, Greg (RHP)	81	81-95	74-90	.451	3.69	1467.0	0	54	1141-652
Other Teams: Boston, New York, Texas (AL); Cincinnati, Montreal, Philadelphia, San Diego (NL)									
Nationality: USA (Lynwood, California)									
Hassler, Andy (LHP)	79	71-85	44-71	.383	3.83	1123.1	5	29	630-520
Other Teams: Boston, California, Kansas City (AL); Pittsburgh, St. Louis (NL)									
Nationality: USA (Texas City, Texas)									
Hausman, Tom (RHP)	78-82	75-82	15-23	.395	3.80	441.0	0	3	180-121
Other Teams: Milwaukee (AL); Atlanta (NL)									
Nationality: USA (Mobridge, South Dakota)									
Hendley, Bob (LHP)	67	61-67	48-52	.480	3.97	879.1	6	12	522-329
Other Teams: Chicago, Milwaukee, San Francisco (NL)									
Nationality: USA (Macon, Georgia)									
Hennigan, Phil (RHP)	73	69-73	17-14	.548	4.26	280.2	0	25	188-133
Other Teams: Cleveland (AL)									
Nationality: USA (Jasper, Texas)									
Henry, Doug (RHP)	95-96	91-00	29-39	.426	3.98	511.2	0	82	468-275
Other Teams: Milwaukee (AL); Houston, San Francisco (NL)									
Nationality: USA (Sacramento, California)									
Hepler, Bill (LHP)	66	1966	3-3	.500	3.52	69.0	0	0	25-51
Other Teams: None									
Nationality: USA (Covington, Virginia)									
Herbel, Ron (RHP)	70	63-71	42-37	.532	3.83	894.0	3	16	447-285
Other Teams: Atlanta, San Diego, San Francisco (NL)									
Nationality: USA (Denver, Colorado)									

Player (Position)	Mets Seasons	MLB Years	W-L	Pct.	ERA	IP	ShO	Saves	SO-BB
Hernández, Manny (RHP)	89	86-89	2-7	.222	4.47	50.1	0	0	22-17

Other Teams: Houston (NL)
Nationality: Dominican Republic

Hershiser, Orel (RHP)	99	83-00	204-150	.576	3.41	3105.2	0	5	2014-1007

Other Teams: Cleveland (AL); Los Angeles, San Francisco (NL)
Nationality: USA (Buffalo, New York)

Hillman, Dave (RHP)	62	55-62	21-37	.362	3.87	624.0	1	3	296-185

Other Teams: Boston (AL); Chicago, Cincinnati (NL)
Nationality: USA (Dungannon, Virginia)

Hillman, Eric (LHP)	92-94	92-94	4-14	.222	4.85	232.0	1	0	96-45

Other Teams: None
Nationality: USA (Gary, Indiana)

Hinsley, Jerry (RHP)	64, 67	64, 67	0-2	.000	7.08	20.1	0	0	14-11

Other Teams: None
Nationality: USA (Hugo, Oklahoma)

Holman, Scott (RHP)	80, 82-83	80-83	3-8	.273	3.34	134.2	0	0	58-60

Other Teams: None
Nationality: USA (Santa Paula, California)

Hook, Jay (RHP)	62-64	57-64	29-62	.319	5.23	752.2	2	1	394-275

Other Teams: Cincinnati (NL)
Nationality: USA (Waukegan, Illinois)

Hudek, John (RHP)	98	94-99	10-15	.400	4.43	201.1	0	29	206-123

Other Teams: Toronto (AL); Atlanta, Cincinnati, Houston (NL)
Nationality: USA (Tampa, Florida)

Hudson, Jesse (LHP)	69	1969	0-0	.000	4.50	2.0	0	0	3-2

Other Teams: None
Nationality: USA (Mansfield, Louisiana)

Hunter, Willard (LHP)	62, 64	62-64	4-9	.308	5.68	114.0	0	5	63-47

Other Teams: Los Angeles (NL)
Nationality: USA (Newark, New Jersey)

Hurst, Jonathan (RHP)	94	92, 94	1-2	.333	8.20	26.1	0	0	10-12

Other Teams: Montreal (NL)
Nationality: USA (New York, New York)

Innis, Jeff (RHP)	87-93	87-93	10-20	.333	3.05	360.0	0	5	192-121

Other Teams: None
Nationality: USA (Decatur, Illinois)

Isringhausen, Jason (RHP)	95-97	95-00	24-26	.480	4.49	428.0	1	42	302-192

Other Teams: Oakland (AL)
Nationality: USA (Brighton, Illinois)

Jackson, Al (LHP)	62-65, 68-69	59-69	67-99	.404	3.98	1389.1	14	10	738-407

Other Teams: Cincinnati, Pittsburgh, St. Louis (NL)
Nationality: USA (Waco, Texas)

Jackson, Roy Lee (RHP)	77-80	77-86	28-34	.452	3.77	559.0	0	34	351-203

Other Teams: Minnesota, Toronto (AL); San Diego (NL)
Nationality: USA (Opelika, Alabama)

Jacome, Jason (RHP)	94-95	94-98	10-18	.357	5.34	261.0	1	1	141-98

Other Teams: Cleveland, Kansas City (AL)
Nationality: USA (Tulsa, Oklahoma)

Johnson, Bob (RHP)	69	69-77	28-34	.452	3.48	692.1	2	12	507-269

Other Teams: Cleveland, Kansas City (AL); Atlanta, Pittsburgh (NL)
Nationality: USA (Aurora, Illinois)

Player (Position)	Mets Seasons	MLB Years	W-L	Pct.	ERA	IP	ShO	Saves	SO-BB
Jones, Barry (RHP)	92	86-93	33-33	.500	3.66	433.0	0	23	250-194
Other Teams: Chicago (AL); Montreal, Philadelphia, Pittsburgh (NL)									
Nationality: USA (Centerville, Indiana)									
Jones, Bobby J. (RHP)	93-00	93-00	74-56	.569	4.13	1215.2	4	0	714-353
Other Teams: None									
Nationality: USA (Fresno, California)									
Jones, Bobby M. (LHP)	00	97-00	14-20	.416	5.77	294.2	0	0	208-169
Other Teams: Colorado (NL)									
Nationality: USA (Fresno, California)									
Jones, Randy (LHP)	81-82	73-82	100-123	.448	3.42	1933.0	19	2	735-503
Other Teams: San Diego (NL)									
Nationality: USA (Fullerton, California)									
Jones, Sherman (RHP)	62	60-62	2-6	.250	4.73	110.1	0	3	53-46
Other Teams: Cincinnati, San Francisco (NL)									
Nationality: USA (Winton, North Carolina)									
Jordan, Ricardo (LHP)	97	95-98	5-4	.556	5.25	70.1	0	1	47-47
Other Teams: Toronto (AL); Cincinnati, Philadelphia (NL)									
Nationality: USA (Boynton Beach, Florida)									
Kaiser, Jeff (LHP)	93	85-93	0-2	.000	9.17	52.0	0	2	38-46
Other Teams: Cleveland, Detroit, Oakland (AL); Cincinnati (NL)									
Nationality: USA (Wyandotte, Michigan)									
Kashiwada, Takashi (LHP)	97	1997	3-1	.750	4.31	31.1	0	0	19-18
Other Teams: None									
Nationality: Japan									
Kobel, Kevin (LHP)	78-80	73-80	18-34	.346	3.88	476.0	3	0	205-152
Other Teams: Milwaukee (AL)									
Nationality: USA (Buffalo, New York)									
Koonce, Cal (RHP)	67-70	62-71	47-49	.490	3.78	971.1	3	24	504-368
Other Teams: Boston (AL); Chicago (NL)									
Nationality: USA (Fayetteville, North Carolina)									
Koosman, Jerry (LHP)	67-78	67-85	222-209	.515	3.36	3839.1	33	17	2556-1198
Other Teams: Chicago, Minnesota (AL); Philadelphia (NL)									
Nationality: USA (Appleton, Minnesota)									
Kroll, Gary (RHP)	64-65	64-69	6-7	.462	4.24	159.1	0	1	138-91
Other Teams: Cleveland (AL); Houston, Philadelphia (NL)									
Nationality: USA (Culver City, California)									
Labine, Clem (RHP)	62	50-62	77-56	.579	3.63	1079.2	2	96	551-396
Other Teams: Detroit (AL); Brooklyn, Los Angeles, Pittsburgh (NL)									
Nationality: USA (Lincoln, Rhode Island)									
Lamabe, Jack (RHP)	67	62-68	33-41	.446	4.24	711.2	3	15	434-238
Other Teams: Boston, Chicago (AL); Chicago, Houston, Pittsburgh, St. Louis (NL)									
Nationality: USA (Farmingdale, New York)									
Lary, Frank (RHP)	64-65	54-65	128-116	.525	3.49	2162.1	21	11	1099-616
Other Teams: Chicago, Detroit (AL); Milwaukee (NL)									
Nationality: USA (Northport, Alabama)									
Latham, Bill (LHP)	85	85-86	1-4	.200	5.35	38.2	0	0	18-13
Other Teams: Minnesota (AL)									
Nationality: USA (Birmingham, Alabama)									
Leach, Terry (RHP)	81-82, 85-89	81-93	38-27	.585	3.15	700.0	3	10	331-197
Other Teams: Chicago, Kansas City, Minnesota (AL)									
Nationality: USA (Selma, Alabama)									

Player (Position)	Mets Seasons	MLB Years	W-L	Pct.	ERA	IP	ShO	Saves	SO-BB
Leary, Tim (RHP)	81, 83-84	81-94	78-105	.426	4.36	1491.1	9	1	888-535

Other Teams: Milwaukee, New York, Seattle, Texas (AL); Cincinnati, Los Angeles (NL)
Nationality: USA (Santa Monica, California)

Leiter, Al (LHP)	98-00	87-00	106-79	.573	4.01	1502.2	7	2	1307-759

Other Teams: New York, Toronto (AL); Florida (NL)
Nationality: USA (Toms River, New Jersey) (brother of Mark Leiter)

Lidle, Cory (RHP)	97	97-00	12-8	.600	3.74	183.2	0	2	120-51

Other Teams: Tampa Bay (AL)
Nationality: USA (Hollywood, California)

Linton, Doug (RHP)	94	92-96	16-16	.500	5.84	237.1	0	0	168-96

Other Teams: California, Kansas City, Toronto (AL)
Nationality: USA (Santa Ana, California)

Locke, Ron (LHP)	64	1964	1-2	.333	3.48	41.1	0	0	17-22

Other Teams: None
Nationality: USA (Wakefield, Rhode Island)

Lockwood, Skip (RHP)	75-79	69-80	57-97	.370	3.55	1236.0	5	68	829-490

Other Teams: Boston, California, Milwaukee, Seattle (AL)
Nationality: USA (Boston, Massachusetts)

Lolich, Mickey (LHP)	76	63-79	217-191	.532	3.44	3638.1	41	11	2832-1099

Other Teams: Detroit (AL); San Diego (NL)
Nationality: USA (Portland, Oregon)

Lomon, Kevin (RHP)	95	95-96	0-1	.000	5.94	16.2	0	0	7-8

Other Teams: Atlanta (NL)
Nationality: USA (Fort Smith, Arkansas)

Lynch, Ed (RHP)	80-86	80-87	47-54	.465	4.00	940.1	2	8	396-229

Other Teams: Chicago (NL)
Nationality: USA (Brooklyn, New York)

MacDonald, Rob (LHP)	96	90-96	8-9	.471	4.34	234.1	0	3	142-107

Other Teams: Detroit, New York, Toronto (AL)
Nationality: USA (East Orange, New Jersey)

Machado, Julio (RHP)	89-90	89-91	7-5	.583	3.12	147.0	0	6	151-83

Other Teams: Milwaukee (AL)
Nationality: Venezuela

MacKenzie, Ken (LHP)	62-63	60-65	8-10	.444	4.80	208.1	0	5	142-63

Other Teams: Houston, Milwaukee, St. Louis, San Francisco (NL)
Nationality: Canada

Maddux, Mike (RHP)	93-94	86-00	39-37	.513	3.98	861.1	1	20	564-284

Other Teams: Boston, Seattle (AL); Houston, Los Angeles, Montreal, Philadelphia, Pittsburgh, San Diego (NL)
Nationality: USA (Dayton, Ohio) (brother of Greg Maddux)

Mahomes, Pat (RHP)	99-00	92-00	34-31	.523	5.55	546.2	0	5	355-308

Other Teams: Boston, Minnesota (AL)
Nationality: USA (Bryan, Texas)

Mann, Jim (RHP)	00	00	0-0	.000	10.13	2.2	0	0	0-1

Other Teams: None
Nationality: USA (Brockton, Massachussetts)

Manuel, Barry (RHP)	97	91-98	7-2	.778	3.87	149.0	0	0	109-60

Other Teams: Texas (AL); Arizona, Montreal (NL)
Nationality: USA (Mamou, Louisiana)

Manzanillo, Josias (RHP)	93-99	91-00	7-8	.467	4.81	206.2	0	3	177-103

Other Teams: Boston, Milwaukee, New York, Seattle (AL); Pittsburgh (NL)
Nationality: Dominican Republic

Player (Position)	Mets Seasons	MLB Years	W-L	Pct.	ERA	IP	ShO	Saves	SO-BB
Marshall, Mike (RHP)	81	67-81	97-112	.464	3.14	1386.2	1	188	880-514

Other Teams: Detroit, Minnesota, Seattle, Texas (AL); Atlanta, Houston, Los Angeles, Montreal (NL)
Nationality: USA (Adrian, Michigan)

Martínez, Pedro (LHP)	96	93-97	7-4	.636	3.97	142.2	0	3	114-93

Other Teams: Cincinnati, Houston, San Diego (NL)
Nationality: Dominican Republic

Mason, Roger (RHP)	94	84-94	22-35	.386	4.02	416.1	1	13	286-161

Other Teams: Detroit (AL); Houston, Philadelphia, Pittsburgh, San Diego, San Francisco (NL)
Nationality: USA (Bellaire, Michigan)

Matlack, Jon (LHP)	71-77	71-83	125-126	.498	3.18	2363.0	30	3	1516-638

Other Teams: Texas (AL)
Nationality: USA (West Chester, Pennsylvania)

McAndrew, Jim (RHP)	68-73	68-74	37-53	.411	3.65	771.1	6	4	424-213

Other Teams: San Diego (NL)
Nationality: USA (Lost Nation, Iowa)

McClure, Bob (LHP)	88	75-93	68-57	.544	3.81	1158.2	1	52	701-497

Other Teams: California, Kansas City, Milwaukee (AL); Florida, Montreal, St. Louis (NL)
Nationality: USA (Oakland, California)

McDowell, Roger (RHP)	85-89	85-96	70-70	.500	3.30	1050.0	0	159	524-410

Other Teams: Baltimore, Texas (AL); Los Angeles, Philadelphia (NL)
Nationality: USA (Cincinnati, Ohio)

McElroy, Chuck (LHP)	99	89-99	33-27	.550	3.64	601.0	0	17	507-282

Other Teams: Anaheim, California, Chicago (AL); Chicago, Cincinnati, Colorado, Philadelphia (NL)
Nationality: USA (Port Arthur, Texas)

McGraw, Tug (LHP)	65-74	65-84	96-92	.511	3.14	1514.2	1	180	1109-582

Other Teams: Philadelphia (NL)
Nationality: USA (Martinez, California)

McMichael, Greg (RHP)	97-99	93-00	31-29	.517	3.21	523.0	0	53	459-193

Other Teams: Oakland (AL); Atlanta, Los Angeles (NL)
Nationality: USA (Knoxville, Tennessee)

Medich, George (Doc) (RHP)	77	72-82	124-105	.541	3.78	1996.1	16	2	955-624

Other Teams: Milwaukee, New York, Oakland, Pittsburgh, Seattle, Texas (AL)
Nationality: USA (Aliquippa, Pennsylvania)

Metzger, Butch (RHP)	78	74-78	18-9	.667	3.74	293.1	0	23	175-140

Other Teams: St. Louis, San Diego, San Francisco (NL)
Nationality: USA (Lafayette, Indiana)

Miller, Bob G. (LHP)	62	53-62	6-8	.429	4.72	188.2	0	2	75-92

Other Teams: Detroit (AL); Cincinnati (NL)
Nationality: USA (Berwyn, Illinois)

Miller, Bob L. (RHP)	62, 73-74	57-74	69-81	.460	3.37	1551.1	0	51	895-608

Other Teams: Chicago, Cleveland, Detroit, Minnesota (AL); Chicago, Los Angeles, Pittsburgh, St. Louis, San Diego (NL)
Nationality: USA (St. Louis, Missouri)

Miller, Dyar (RHP)	80-81	75-81	23-17	.575	3.23	465.1	0	22	235-177

Other Teams: Baltimore, California, Toronto (AL)
Nationality: USA (Batesville, Indiana)

Miller, Larry (LHP)	65-66	64-66	5-14	.263	4.71	145.1	0	0	93-57

Other Teams: Los Angeles (NL)
Nationality: USA (Topeka, Kansas)

Minor, Blas (RHP)	95-96	92-97	13-10	.565	4.40	225.0	0	5	184-70

Other Teams: Seattle (AL); Houston, Pittsburgh (NL)
Nationality: USA (Merced, California)

Mitchell, John (RHP)	86-89	86-90	9-14	.391	4.35	240.0	0	0	107-93

Other Teams: Baltimore (AL)
Nationality: USA (Dickson, Tennessee)

Player (Position)	Mets Seasons	MLB Years	W-L	Pct.	ERA	IP	ShO	Saves	SO-BB
Mizell, Wilmer (LHP)	62	52-62	90-88	.506	3.85	1528.2	15	0	918-680

Other Teams: Pittsburgh, St. Louis (NL)
Nationality: USA (Leakesville, Mississippi)

Mlicki, Dave (RHP)	95-98	92-00	51-59	.464	4.25	978.2	2	1	680-364

Other Teams: Cleveland, Detroit (AL); Los Angeles (NL)
Nationality: USA (Cleveland, Ohio)

Moford, Herb (RHP)	62	55-62	5-13	.278	5.03	157.1	0	3	78-64

Other Teams: Boston, Detroit, (AL); St. Louis (NL)
Nationality: USA (Brooksville, Kentucky)

Moore, Tommy (RHP)	72-73	72-77	2-4	.333	5.40	88.1	0	0	40-49

Other Teams: Seattle, Texas (AL); St. Louis (NL)
Nationality: USA (Lynwood, California)

Moorhead, Bob (RHP)	62, 65	62, 65	0-3	.000	4.51	119.2.0	0	0	68-47

Other Teams: None
Nationality: USA (Chambersburg, Pennsylvania)

Murray, Dale (RHP)	78-79	74-85	53-50	.515	3.85	902.1	0	60	400-329

Other Teams: New York, Texas, Toronto (AL); Cincinnati, Montreal (NL)
Nationality: USA (Cuero, Texas)

Musgraves, Dennis (RHP)	65	1965	0-0	.000	0.56	16.0	0	0	11-7

Other Teams: None
Nationality: USA (Indianapolis, Indiana)

Musselman, Jeff (LHP)	89-90	86-90	23-15	.605	4.31	248.2	0	3	125-123

Other Teams: Toronto (AL)
Nationality: USA (Doylestown, Pennsylvania)

Myers, Randy (LHP)	85-89	85-98, 00	44-63	.411	3.19	886.2	0	347	887-396

Other Teams: Baltimore, Toronto (AL); Chicago, Cincinnati, San Diego, (NL)
Nationality: USA (Vancouver, Washington)

Myrick, Bob (LHP)	76-78	76-78	3-6	.333	3.48	139.2	0	2	73-59

Other Teams: None
Nationality: USA (Hattiesburg, Mississippi)

Niemann, Randy (LHP)	85-86	79-87	7-8	.467	4.64	200.0	2	3	102-82

Other Teams: Chicago, Minnesota (AL); Houston, Pittsburgh (NL)
Nationality: USA (Scotia, California)

Nomo, Hideo (RHP)	98	95-00	69-61	.531	3.82	1150.2	5	0	1212-516

Other Teams: Los Angeles, Milwaukee (NL)
Nationality: Japan

Nuñez, Edwin (RHP)	88	82-94	28-36	.438	4.19	652.1	0	54	508-280

Other Teams: Detroit, Milwaukee, Oakland, Seattle, Texas (AL)
Nationality: Puerto Rico

Ojeda, Bob (LHP)	86-90	80-94	115-98	.540	3.65	1884.1	16	1	1128-676

Other Teams: Boston, Cleveland, New York (AL); Los Angeles (NL)
Nationality: USA (Los Angeles, California)

Orosco, Jesse (LHP)	79, 81-87	79-00	84-75	.528	3.03	1218.0	0	141	1106-542

Other Teams: Baltimore, Cleveland, Milwaukee (AL); Los Angeles, St. Louis (NL)
Nationality: USA (Santa Barbara, California)

Ownbey, Rick (RHP)	82-83	82-86	3-11	.214	4.11	146.2	0	0	83-91

Other Teams: St. Louis (NL)
Nationality: USA (Corona, California)

Pacella, John (RHP)	77, 79-80	77-86	4-10	.286	5.73	191.2	0	3	116-133

Other Teams: Baltimore, Detroit, Minnesota, New York (AL)
Nationality: USA (Brooklyn, New York)

Player (Position)	Mets Seasons	MLB Years	W-L	Pct.	ERA	IP	ShO	Saves	SO-BB
Parker, Harry (RHP)	73-75	70-76	15-21	.417	3.85	315.1	0	12	172-128
Other Teams: Cleveland (AL); St. Louis (NL)									
Nationality: USA (Highland, Illinois)									
Parsons, Tom (RHP)	64-65	63-65	2-13	.133	4.72	114.1	1	1	70-25
Other Teams: Pittsburgh (NL)									
Nationality: USA (Lakeville, Connecticut)									
Peña, Alejandro (RHP)	90-91	81-96	56-52	.519	3.11	1057.2	7	74	839-331
Other Teams: Boston (AL); Atlanta, Florida, Los Angeles, Pittsburgh (NL)									
Nationality: Dominican Republic									
Pérez, Yorkis (LHP)	97	91-00	14-15	.483	4.50	255.0	0	1	234-133
Other Teams: Chicago, Florida, Houston, Philadelphia (NL)									
Nationality: Dominican Republic									
Person, Robert (RHP)	95-96	95-00	32-30	.516	5.04	589.1	0	8	519-299
Other Teams: Toronto (AL); Philadelphia (NL)									
Nationality: USA (St. Louis, Missouri)									
Powell, Grover (LHP)	63	1963	1-1	.500	2.72	49.2	1	0	39-32
Other Teams: None									
Nationality: USA (Sayre, Pennsylvania)									
Puleo, Charlie (RHP)	81-82	81-89	29-39	.426	4.25	633.0	1	2	387-319
Other Teams: Atlanta, Cincinnati (NL)									
Nationality: USA (Glen Ridge, New Jersey)									
Pulsipher, Bill (LHP)	95, 98	95-99	13-17	.433	4.87	286.1	0	0	174-112
Other Teams: Milwaukee (NL)									
Nationality: USA (Benning, Georgia)									
Rauch, Bob (RHP)	72	1972	0-1	.000	5.00	27.0	0	1	23-21
Other Teams: None									
Nationality: USA (Brookings, South Dakota)									
Reardon, Jeff (RHP)	79-81	79-94	73-77	.487	3.16	1132.1	0	367	877-358
Other Teams: Boston, Minnesota, New York (AL); Atlanta, Cincinnati, Montreal (NL)									
Nationality: USA (Dalton, Massachusetts)									
Reed, Rick (RHP)	97-00	88-00	60-45	.571	3.94	1020.1	4	1	636-199
Other Teams: Kansas City, Texas (AL); Cincinnati, Pittsburgh (NL)									
Nationality: USA (Huntington, West Virginia)									
Remlinger, Mike (LHP)	94-95	91-00	34-35	.493	4.25	568.2	2	15	520-298
Other Teams: Atlanta, Cincinnati, San Francisco (NL)									
Nationality: USA (Middletown, New York)									
Reniff, Hal (RHP)	67	61-67	21-23	.477	3.27	471.1	0	45	314-242
Other Teams: New York (AL)									
Nationality: USA (Warren, Ohio)									
Reynoso, Armando (RHP)	97-98	91-00	67-58	.536	4.56	1031.2	1	1	537-362
Other Teams: Arizona, Atlanta, Colorado (NL)									
Nationality: Mexico									
Ribant, Dennis (RHP)	64-66	64-69	24-29	.453	3.87	518.2	2	9	241-126
Other Teams: Chicago, Detroit (AL); Cincinnati, Pittsburgh, St. Louis (NL)									
Nationality: USA (Detroit, Michigan)									
Richardson, Gordie (LHP)	65-66	64-74	6-6	.500	4.04	118.0	0	4	86-37
Other Teams: St. Louis (NL)									
Nationality: USA (Colquitt, Georgia)									
Riggan, Jerrod (RHP)	00	00	0-0	.000	0.00	2.0	0	0	1-0
Other Teams: None									
Nationality: USA (Brewster, Washington)									

Player (Position)	Mets Seasons	MLB Years	W-L	Pct.	ERA	IP	ShO	Saves	SO-BB
Roberts, Dave (LHP)	81	69-81	103-125	.452	3.78	2099.0	20	15	957-615

Other Teams: Detroit, Seattle (AL); Chicago, Houston, Pittsburgh, San Diego, San Francisco (NL)
Nationality: USA (Gallipolis, Ohio)

Roberts, Grant (RHP)	00	00	0-0	.000	11.57	7.0	0	0	6-4

Other Teams: None
Nationality: USA (El Cajon, California)

Rodriguez, Rich (RHP)	00	90-00	26-18	.591	3.75	581.1	0	7	350-232

Other Teams: Florida, St. Louis, San Diego, San Francisco (NL)
Nationality: USA (Downey, California)

Rogers, Kenny (LHP)	99	89-00	127-91	.583	4.05	1928.1	6	28	1241-729

Other Teams: New York, Oakland, Texas (AL)
Nationality: USA (Savannah, Georgia)

Rohr, Les (LHP)	67-69	67-69	2-3	.400	3.70	24.1	0	0	20-17

Other Teams: None
Nationality: England

Rojas, Mel (RHP)	97-98	90-99	34-31	.523	3.82	667.0	0	126	562-254

Other Teams: Detroit (AL); Chicago, Montreal (NL)
Nationality: Dominican Republic

Rose, Don (RHP)	71	71-74	1-4	.200	4.14	45.2	0	0	40-20

Other Teams: California (AL); San Francisco (NL)
Nationality: USA (Covina, California)

Rowe, Don (LHP)	63	1963	0-0	.000	4.28	54.2	0	0	27-21

Other Teams: None
Nationality: USA (Brawley, California)

Rusch, Glendon (RHP)	99-00	97-00	23-36	.390	5.13	521.2	1	1	371-149

Other Teams: Kansas City (AL)
Nationality: USA (Seattle, Washington)

Rusteck, Dick (RHP)	66	1966	1-2	.333	3.00	24.0	1	0	9-8

Other Teams: None
Nationality: USA (Chicago, Illinois)

Ryan, Nolan (RHP)	66, 68-71	66-93	324-292	.526	3.19	5386.0	61	3	5714-2795

Other Teams: California, Texas (AL); Houston (NL)
Nationality: USA (Refugio, Texas)

Saberhagen, Bret (RHP)	92-95	84-99	166-115	.591	3.33	2547.2	16	1	1705-471

Other Teams: Boston, Kansas City (AL); Colorado (NL)
Nationality: USA (Chicago Heights, Illinois)

Sadecki, Ray (LHP)	70-74, 77	60-77	135-131	.508	3.78	2500.2	20	7	1614-922

Other Teams: Kansas City, Milwaukee (AL); Atlanta, St. Louis, San Francisco (NL)
Nationality: USA (Kansas City, Kansas)

Sambito, Joe (LHP)	85	76-87	37-38	.493	3.03	629.0	1	84	489-195

Other Teams: Boston (AL); Houston (NL)
Nationality: USA (Brooklyn, New York)

Sanders, Ken (RHP)	75-76	64-76	29-45	.392	3.97	656.2	0	86	360-258

Other Teams: Boston, California, Cleveland, Kansas City, Milwaukee, Minnesota, Oakland (AL)
Nationality: USA (St. Louis, Missouri)

Sauveur, Rich (LHP)	91	86-96	0-1	.000	6.56	35.2	0	0	21-23

Other Teams: Chicago, Kansas City (AL); Pittsburgh, Montreal (NL)
Nationality: USA (Arlington, Virginia)

Scarce, Mac (LHP)	75	72-78	6-19	.240	3.69	209.2	0	21	164-117

Other Teams: Minnesota (AL); Philadelphia (NL)
Nationality: USA (Danville, Virginia)

Player (Position)	Mets Seasons	MLB Years	W-L	Pct.	ERA	IP	ShO	Saves	SO-BB
Schatzeder, Dan (LHP)	90	77-91	69-68	.504	3.74	1317.0	4	10	748-475

Other Teams: Cleveland, Detroit, Kansas City, Minnesota (AL); Houston, Montreal, Philadelphia, San Francisco (NL)
Nationality: USA (Elmhurst, Illinois)

Schiraldi, Calvin (RHP)	84-85	84-91	32-39	.451	4.28	553.1	1	21	471-267

Other Teams: Boston, Texas (AL); Chicago, San Diego (NL)
Nationality: USA (Houston, Texas)

Schmelz, Al (RHP)	67	1967	0-0	.000	3.00	3.0	0	0	2-1

Other Teams: None
Nationality: USA (Whittier, California)

Schourek, Pete (LHP)	91-94	91-00	65-72	.474	4.54	1118.1	1	2	793-405

Other Teams: Boston (AL); Cincinnati, Houston, Pittsburgh (NL)
Nationality: USA (Austin, Texas)

Schulze, Don (RHP)	87	83-89	15-25	.375	5.47	338.2	0	0	144-105

Other Teams: Cleveland, New York (AL); Chicago, San Diego (NL)
Nationality: USA (Roselle, Illinois)

Scott, Mike (RHP)	79-82	79-91	124-108	.534	3.54	2068.2	22	3	1469-627

Other Teams: Houston (NL)
Nationality: USA (Santa Monica, California)

Searage, Ray (LHP)	81	81-90	11-13	.458	3.50	287.2	0	11	193-137

Other Teams: Chicago, Milwaukee (AL); Los Angeles (NL)
Nationality: USA (Freeport, New York)

Seaver, Tom (RHP)	67-77, 83	67-86	311-205	.603	2.86	4782.2	61	1	3640-1390

Other Teams: Boston, Chicago (AL); Cincinnati (NL)
Nationality: USA (Fresno, California)

Selma, Dick (RHP)	65-68	65-74	42-54	.438	3.62	840.0	6	31	681-381

Other Teams: California, Milwaukee (AL); Chicago, Philadelphia, San Diego (NL)
Nationality: USA (Santa Ana, California)

Seminara, Frank (RHP)	94	92-94	12-9	.571	4.12	163.2	0	0	90-75

Other Teams: San Diego (NL)
Nationality: USA (Brooklyn, New York)

Shaw, Bob (RHP)	66-67	57-67	108-98	.524	3.52	1778.0	14	32	880-511

Other Teams: Chicago, Detroit, Kansas City, Milwaukee (AL); Chicago, San Francisco (NL)
Nationality: USA (Bronx, New York)

Shaw, Don (LHP)	67-68	67-72	13-14	.481	4.01	188.2	0	6	123-101

Other Teams: Oakland (AL); Montreal, St. Louis (NL)
Nationality: USA (Pittsburgh, Pennsylvania)

Short, Bill (LHP)	68	60-69	5-11	.313	4.70	132.0	1	2	71-64

Other Teams: Baltimore, Boston, New York (AL); Cincinnati, Pittsburgh (NL)
Nationality: USA (Kingston, New York)

Siebert, Paul (LHP)	77-78	74-78	3-8	.273	3.77	129.0	1	3	59-73

Other Teams: Houston, San Diego (NL)
Nationality: USA (Minneapolis, Minnesota)

Simons, Doug (LHP)	91	91-92	2-3	.400	6.68	66.0	0	1	44-21

Other Teams: Montreal (NL)
Nationality: USA (Bakersfield, California)

Sisk, Doug (RHP)	82-87	82-91	22-20	.524	3.27	523.1	0	33	195-267

Other Teams: Baltimore (AL); Atlanta (NL)
Nationality: USA (Renton, Washington)

Smith, Pete (RHP)	94	87-98	47-71	.398	4.55	1025.2	4	1	640-404

Other Teams: Baltimore (AL); Atlanta, Cincinnati, San Diego (NL)
Nationality: USA (Abington, Massachusetts)

Spahn, Warren (LHP)	65	42-65	363-245	.597	3.09	5243.2	63	29	2583-1434

Other Teams: Boston (AL), Milwaukee, San Francisco (NL)
Nationality: USA (Buffalo, New York)

Player (Position)	Mets Seasons	MLB Years	W-L	Pct.	ERA	IP	ShO	Saves	SO-BB
Stallard, Tracy (RHP)	63-64	60-66	30-57	.345	4.17	764.2	3	4	477-343
Other Teams: Boston (AL), St. Louis (NL)									
Nationality: USA (Coeburn, Virginia)									
Sterling, Randy (RHP)	74	1974	1-1	.500	21.60	5.0	0	0	2-3
Other Teams: None									
Nationality: USA (Key West, Florida)									
Stone, George (LHP)	73-76	67-75	60-57	.513	3.89	1020.2	5	5	590-270
Other Teams: Atlanta (NL)									
Nationality: USA (Ruston, Louisiana)									
Strohmayer, John (RHP)	73-74	70-74	11-9	.550	4.47	312.1	0	4	200-128
Other Teams: Montreal (NL)									
Nationality: USA (Belle Fourche, South Dakota)									
Strom, Brent (LHP)	72	72-77	22-39	.361	3.95	501.0	3	0	278-180
Other Teams: Cleveland (AL); San Diego (NL)									
Nationality: USA (San Diego, California)									
Sturdivant, Tom (RHP)	64	55-64	59-51	.536	3.74	1137.0	7	17	704-449
Other Teams: Boston, Detroit, Kansas City, New York, Washington (AL); Pittsburgh (NL)									
Nationality: USA (Gordon, Kansas)									
Sutherland, Darrell (RHP)	64-65	64-68	5-4	.556	4.78	122.1	0	1	50-58
Other Teams: Cleveland (AL)									
Nationality: USA (Glendale, California)									
Swan, Craig (RHP)	73-84	73-84	59-72	.450	3.74	1235.2	7	2	673-368
Other Teams: California (AL)									
Nationality: USA (Van Nuys, California)									
Tam, Jeff (RHP)	98-99	98-99	1-1	.500	5.88	26.0	0	0	16-8
Other Teams: None									
Nationality: USA (Fullerton, California)									
Tanana, Frank (LHP)	93	73-93	240-236	.504	3.66	4188.1	34	1	2773-1255
Other Teams: Boston, California, Detroit, New York, Texas (AL)									
Nationality: USA (Detroit, Michigan)									
Tapani, Kevin (RHP)	89	89-00	134-111	.547	4.27	2097.0	9	0	1333-514
Other Teams: Chicago, Minnesota (AL); Chicago, Los Angeles (NL)									
Nationality: USA (Des Moines, Iowa)									
Tate, Randy (RHP)	75	1975	5-13	.278	4.45	137.2	0	0	99-86
Other Teams: None									
Nationality: USA (Florence, Alabama)									
Taylor, Billy (RHP)	99	94-00	16-28	.364	4.02	323.0	0	100	304-133
Other Teams: Oakland, Tampa Bay (AL)									
Nationality: USA (Monticello, Florida)									
Taylor, Chuck (RHP)	72	69-76	28-20	.583	3.07	607.0	2	31	282-162
Other Teams: Milwaukee (AL); Montreal, St. Louis (NL)									
Nationality: USA (Murfreesboro, Tennessee)									
Taylor, Ron (RHP)	67-71	62-72	45-43	.511	3.93	800.0	0	72	464-209
Other Teams: Cleveland (AL); Houston, St. Louis, San Diego (NL)									
Nationality: Canada									
Telgheder, Dave (RHP)	93-95	93-98	15-19	.441	5.23	311.2	1	0	158-103
Other Teams: Oakland (AL)									
Nationality: USA (Middletown, New York)									
Terrell, Walt (RHP)	82-84	82-92	111-124	.472	4.22	1986.2	14	0	929-748
Other Teams: Detroit, New York (AL); Pittsburgh, San Diego (NL)									
Nationality: USA (Jeffersonville, Indiana)									

Player (Position)	Mets Seasons	MLB Years	W-L	Pct.	ERA	IP	ShO	Saves	SO-BB
Terry, Ralph (RHP)	66-67	56-67	107-99	.519	3.62	1849.1	20	11	1000-446

Other Teams: Cleveland, Kansas City, New York (AL)
Nationality: USA (Big Cabin, Oklahoma)

Tidrow, Dick (RHP)	84	72-84	100-94	.515	3.68	1746.2	5	55	975-579

Other Teams: Chicago, Cleveland, New York (AL), Chicago (NL)
Nationality: USA (San Francisco, California)

Todd, Jackson (RHP)	77	77-81	10-16	.385	4.40	286.2	0	0	138-88

Other Teams: Toronto (AL)
Nationality: USA (Tulsa, Oklahoma)

Torrez, Mike (RHP)	83-84	67-84	185-160	.536	3.96	3044.0	15	0	1404-1371

Other Teams: Baltimore, Boston, New York, Oakland (AL); Montreal, St. Louis (NL)
Nationality: USA (Topeka, Kansas)

Trlicek, Ricky (RHP)	96-98	92-97	5-8	.385	5.23	125.2	0	1	66-65

Other Teams: Boston, Toronto (AL); Los Angeles (NL)
Nationality: USA (Houston, Texas)

Twitchell, Wayne (RHP)	79	70-79	48-65	.425	3.98	1063.0	6	2	789-537

Other Teams: Milwaukee, Seattle (AL); Montreal, Philadelphia (NL)
Nationality: USA (Portland, Oregon)

Valera, Julio (RHP)	90-91	90-96	15-20	.429	4.85	317.1	2	5	179-117

Other Teams: California, Kansas City (AL)
Nationality: Puerto Rico

Viola, Frank (LHP)	89-91	82-96	176-150	.540	3.73	2836.1	16	0	1844-864

Other Teams: Boston, Minnesota, Toronto (AL); Cincinnati (NL)
Nationality: USA (Hempstead, New York)

Vitko, Joe (RHP)	92	1992	0-1	.000	13.50	4.2	0	0	6-1

Other Teams: None
Nationality: USA (Somerville, New Jersey)

Wakefield, Bill (RHP)	64	1964	3-5	.375	3.61	119.2	0	2	61-61

Other Teams: None
Nationality: USA (Kansas City, Missouri)

Walker, Pete (RHP)	95	95-96	1-0	1.000	4.42	18.1	0	0	6-8

Other Teams: San Diego (NL)
Nationality: USA (Beverly, Massachusetts)

Wallace, Derek (RHP)	1996	1996	2-3	.400	4.01	24.2	0	3	15-14

Other Teams: None
Nationality: USA (Van Nuys, California)

Walter, Gene (LHP)	87	85-88	4-7	.364	3.74	182.2	0	4	140-96

Other Teams: Seattle (AL); San Diego (NL)
Nationality: USA (Chicago, Illinois)

Webb, Hank (RHP)	72-76	72-77	7-9	.438	4.31	169.0	1	0	71-91

Other Teams: Los Angeles (NL)
Nationality: USA (Copiague, New York)

Wendell, Turk (RHP)	97-00	93-00	29-25	.537	3.83	498.0	0	31	421-250

Other Teams: Chicago (NL)
Nationality: USA (Pittsfield, Massachusetts)

West, Dave (LHP)	88-89	88-98	31-38	.449	4.66	569.1	0	3	437-311

Other Teams: Boston, Minnesota (AL); Philadelphia (NL)
Nationality: USA (Memphis, Tennessee)

Weston, Mickey (RHP)	93	89-93	1-2	.333	7.15	45.1	0	1	19-11

Other Teams: Baltimore, Toronto (AL); Philadelphia (NL)
Nationality: USA (Flint, Michigan)

Player (Position)	Mets Seasons	MLB Years	W-L	Pct.	ERA	IP	ShO	Saves	SO-BB
White, Rick (RHP)	00	94-95, 98-00	15-20	.429	3.94	335.0	0	7	207-108
Other Teams: Tampa Bay (AL); Pittsburgh (NL)									
Nationality: USA (Springfield, Ohio)									
Whitehurst, Wally (RHP)	89-92	89-96	20-37	.351	4.02	487.2	0	3	313-130
Other Teams: New York (AL); San Diego (NL)									
Nationality: USA (Springfield, Ohio)									
Willey, Carl (RHP)	63-65	58-65	38-58	.396	3.76	875.2	11	1	493-326
Other Teams: Milwaukee (NL)									
Nationality: USA (Cherryfield, Maine)									
Willhite, Nick (LHP)	67	63-67	6-12	.333	4.55	182.0	1	1	118-75
Other Teams: California, Washington (AL); Los Angeles (NL)									
Nationality: USA (Tulsa, Oklahoma)									
Williams, Charlie (RHP)	71	71-78	23-22	.511	3.97	573.1	0	4	257-275
Other Teams: San Francisco (NL)									
Nationality: USA (Flushing, New York)									
Wilson, Paul (RHP)	1996	1996	5-12	.294	5.38	149.0	0	0	109-71
Other Teams: None									
Nationality: USA (Orlando, Florida)									
Wynne, Billy (RHP)	67	67-71	8-11	.421	4.33	187.0	1	0	97-78
Other Teams: California, Chicago (AL)									
Nationality: USA (Williamston, North Carolina)									
Yoshii, Masato (RHP)	98-99	98-00	24-31	.436	4.17	512.2	0	0	310-164
Other Teams: Colorado (NL)									
Nationality: Japan									
Young, Anthony (RHP)	91-93	91-96	15-48	.238	3.89	460.0	0	20	245-167
Other Teams: Chicago, Houston (NL)									
Nationality: USA (Houston, Texas)									
Zachry, Pat (RHP)	77-82	76-85	69-67	.507	3.52	1177.1	7	3	669-495
Other Teams: Cincinnati, Los Angeles, Philadelphia (NL)									
Nationality: USA (Richmond, Texas)									

TEAM AND INDIVIDUAL RECORDS

METS' ALL-TIME CAREER BATTING LEADERS (1962-2000) (METS STATISTICS ONLY)	

BATTING AVERAGE (1,000 or more at-bats)

Mike Piazza (1998-present)	.323
John Olerud (1997-1999)	.315
Keith Hernandez (1983-1989)	.297
Edgardo Alfonzo (1995-present)	.296
Dave Magadan (1986-1992)	.292
Steve Henderson (1977-1980)	.287
Wally Backman (1980-1988)	.283
Ron Hunt (1963-1966)	.282
José Vizcaino (1994-1996)	.282
Cleon Jones (1963, 1965-1975)	.281
Jeff Kent (1992-1996)	.279

AT-BATS

Ed Kranepool (1962-1979)	5,436
Bud Harrelson (1965-1977)	4,390
Cleon Jones (1963, 1965-1975)	4,223
Mookie Wilson (1980-1989)	4,027
Howard Johnson (1985-1993)	3,968
Darryl Strawberry (1985-1993)	3,903
Jerry Grote (1966-1977)	3,881
Keith Hernandez (1983-1989)	3,164
Lee Mazzilli (1976-1981, 1986-1989)	3,013
Edgardo Alfonzo (1995-present)	2,950

BASE HITS

Ed Kranepool (1962-1979)	1,418
Cleon Jones (1963, 1965-1975)	1,188
Mookie Wilson (1980-1989)	1,112
Bud Harrelson (1965-1977)	1,029
Darryl Strawberry (1985-1993)	1,025
Howard Johnson (1985-1993)	997
Jerry Grote (1966-1977)	994
Keith Hernandez (1983-1989)	939
Edgardo Alfonzo (1995-present)	874
Lee Mazzilli (1976-1981, 1986-1989)	796

EXTRA-BASE HITS

Darryl Strawberry (1985-1993)	469
Howard Johnson (1985-1993)	424
Ed Kranepool (1962-1979)	368
Cleon Jones (1963, 1965-1975)	308
Mookie Wilson (1980-1989)	292
Kevin McReynolds (1987-1991, 1994)	289
Edgardo Alfonzo (1995-present)	265
Keith Hernandez (1983-1989)	249

Todd Hundley (1990-1998)	249
Lee Mazzilli (1976-1981, 1986-1989)	238

HOME RUNS

Darryl Strawberry (1985-1993)	252
Howard Johnson (1985-1993)	192
Dave Kingman (1975-1977, 1981-1983)	154
Todd Hundley (1990-1998)	124
Kevin McReynolds (1987-1991, 1994)	122
Ed Kranepool (1962-1979)	118
Mike Piazza (1998-present)	101
George Foster (1982-1986)	99
Bobby Bonilla (1992-1995, 1999)	95
John Milner (1971-1977)	94

DOUBLES

Ed Kranepool (1962-1979)	225
Howard Johnson (1985-1993)	214
Darryl Strawberry (1985-1993)	187
Cleon Jones (1963, 1965-1975)	182
Mookie Wilson (1980-1989)	170
Edgardo Alfonzo (1995-present)	164
Keith Hernandez (1983-1989)	159
Kevin McReynolds (1987-1991, 1994)	153
John Stearns (1975-1984)	152
Lee Mazzilli (1976-1981, 1986-1989)	148

TRIPLES

Mookie Wilson (1980-1989)	62
Bud Harrelson (1965-1977)	45
Cleon Jones (1963, 1965-1975)	33
Steve Henderson (1977-1980)	31
Darryl Strawberry (1985-1993)	30
Lance Johnson (1996-1997)	27
Doug Flynn (1977-1981)	26
Ed Kranepool (1962-1979)	25
Lee Mazzilli (1976-1981, 1986-1989)	22
Ron Swoboda (1965-1970)	20
Wayne Garrett (1969-1976)	20

TOTAL BASES

Ed Kranepool (1962-1979)	2,047
Darryl Strawberry (1985-1993)	2,028
Howard Johnson (1985-1993)	1,823
Cleon Jones (1963, 1965-1975)	1,715
Mookie Wilson (1980-1989)	1,586
Keith Hernandez (1983-1989)	1,358
Kevin McReynolds (1987-1991, 1994)	1,338
Edgardo Alfonzo (1995-present)	1,327
Jerry Grote (1966-1977)	1,278
Bud Harrelson (1965-1977)	1,260

RUNS BATTED IN

Darryl Strawberry (1983-1990)	733
Howard Johnson (1985-1993)	629
Ed Kranepool (1962-1979)	614
Cleon Jones (1963, 1965-1975)	521
Keith Hernandez (1983-1989)	468
Kevin McReynolds (1987-1991, 1994)	456
Edgardo Alfonzo (1995-present)	433
Rusty Staub (1972-1975, 1981-1985)	399
Todd Hundley (1990-1998)	397
Dave Kingman (1975-1977, 1981-1983)	389

STOLEN BASES

Mookie Wilson (1980-1989)	281
Howard Johnson (1985-1993)	202
Darryl Strawberry (1983-1990)	191
Lee Mazzilli (1976-1981, 1986-1989)	152
Len Dykstra (1985-1989)	116
Bud Harrelson (1965-1977)	115
Wally Backman (1980-1988)	106
Vince Coleman (1991-1993)	99
Tommie Agee (1968-1972)	92
Cleon Jones (1963, 1965-1975)	91
John Stearns (1975-1984)	91

RUNS SCORED

Darryl Strawberry (1983-1990)	662
Howard Johnson (1985-1993)	627
Mookie Wilson (1980-1989)	592
Cleon Jones (1963, 1965-1975)	563
Ed Kranepool (1962-1979)	536
Bud Harrelson (1965-1977)	490
Edgardo Alfonzo (1995-present)	472
Keith Hernandez (1983-1989)	455
Kevin McReynolds (1987-1991, 1994)	405
Lee Mazzilli (1976-1981, 1986-1989)	404

PINCH HITS

Ed Kranepool (1962-1979)	90
Rusty Staub (1972-1975, 1981-1985)	77
Gil Hodges (1962-1963)	48
Matt Franco (1996-Present)	48
Bruce Boisclair (1974, 1976-1979)	38
Lee Mazzilli (1976-1981, 1986-1989)	38
Mookie Wilson (1980-1989)	37
Mackey Sasser (1988-1992)	32
Mike Jorgensen (1968, 1970-71, 1980, 1983)	30
Danny Heep (1983-1986)	29

TIMES HIT BY PITCHER

Ron Hunt (1963-1966)	41
Cleon Jones (1963, 1965-1975)	39
Felix Millan (1973-1977)	36
Jeff Kent (1992-1996)	28
John Olerud (1997-1999)	28
Darryl Strawberry (1983-1990)	26
John Stearns (1975-1984)	25

Todd Hundley (1990-1998)	22
Jerry Grote (1966-1977)	21
Bud Harrelson (1965-1977)	21

GAMES PLAYED

Ed Kranepool (1962-1979)	1,853
Bud Harrelson (1965-1977)	1,322
Jerry Grote (1966-1977)	1,235
Cleon Jones (1963, 1965-1975)	1,201
Howard Johnson (1985-1993)	1,154
Mookie Wilson (1980-1989)	1,116
Darryl Strawberry (1983-1990)	1,109
Lee Mazzilli (1976-1981, 1986-1989)	979
Rusty Staub (1972-1975, 1981-1985)	942
Wayne Garrett (1969-1976)	883

METS' ALL-TIME CAREER PITCHING LEADERS (1962-2000) (METS STATISTICS ONLY)

MOST WINS

Tom Seaver (1967-1977, 1983)	198
Dwight Gooden (1984-1994)	157
Jerry Koosman (1967-1978)	140
Ron Darling (1983-1991)	99
Sid Fernandez (1984-1993)	98
Jon Matlack (1971-1977)	82
David Cone (1987-1992)	80
Bobby Jones (1993-Present)	74
Craig Swan (1973-1984)	59
Bob Ojeda (1986-1990)	51
Rick Reed (1997-present)	51

MOST LOSSES

Jerry Koosman (1967-1978)	137
Tom Seaver (1967-1977, 1983)	124
Dwight Gooden (1984-1994)	85
Jon Matlack (1971-1977)	81
Al Jackson (1962-1965, 1968-1969)	80
Sid Fernandez (1984-1993)	78
Jack Fisher (1964-1967)	73
Craig Swan (1973-1984)	71
Ron Darling (1983-1991)	70
Bobby Jones (1993-present)	56

BASE HITS ALLOWED

Tom Seaver (1967-1977, 1983)	2,431
Jerry Koosman (1967-1978)	2,281
Dwight Gooden (1984-1994)	1,898
Ron Darling (1983-1991)	1,473
Bobby Jones (1993-Present)	1,426
Jon Matlack (1971-1977)	1,312
Craig Swan (1973-1984)	1,191
Sid Fernandez (1984-1993)	1,167
Al Jackson (1962-1965, 1968-1969)	1,033
David Cone (1987-1992)	991

EARNED RUN AVERAGE (500 Innings Pitched)

Tom Seaver (1967-1977, 1983)	2.57
Jesse Orosco (1979, 1981-1987)	2.74
Jon Matlack (1971-1977)	3.03
David Cone (1987-1992)	3.08
Jerry Koosman (1967-1978)	3.09
Dwight Gooden (1984-1994)	3.10
Bob Ojeda (1986-1990)	3.12
Sid Fernandez (1984-1993)	3.14
Bret Saberhagen (1992-1995)	3.16
Tug McGraw (1965-1967, 1969-1974)	3.17

GAMES APPEARED

John Franco (1990-Present)	547
Tom Seaver (1967-1977, 1983)	401
Jerry Koosman (1967-1978)	376
Jesse Orosco (1979, 1981-1987)	372
Tug McGraw (1965-1967, 1969-1974)	361
Dwight Gooden (1984-1994)	305
Jeff Innis (1987-1993)	288
Roger McDowell (1985-1989)	280
Ron Taylor (1967-1971)	269
Doug Sisk (1982-1987)	263

COMPLETE GAMES

Tom Seaver (1967-1977, 1983)	171
Jerry Koosman (1967-1978)	108
Dwight Gooden (1984-1994)	67
Jon Matlack (1971-1977)	65
Al Jackson (1962-1965, 1968-1969)	41
Jack Fisher (1964-1967)	35
David Cone (1987-1992)	34
Roger Craig (1962-1963)	27
Ron Darling (1983-1991)	25
Craig Swan (1973-1984)	25

INNINGS PITCHED

Tom Seaver (1967-1977, 1983)	3,045.0
Jerry Koosman (1967-1978)	2,545.0
Dwight Gooden (1984-1994)	2,169.2
Ron Darling (1983-1991)	1,620.0
Sid Fernandez (1984-1993)	1,584.2
Jon Matlack (1971-1977)	1,448.0
Craid Swan (1973-1984)	1,229.1
Bobby Jones (1993-Present)	1,215.2
David Cone (1987-1992)	1,191.1
Al Jackson (1962-1965, 1968-1969)	980.0

STRIKEOUTS

Tom Seaver (1967-1977, 1983)	2,541
Dwight Gooden (1984-1994)	1,875
Jerry Koosman (1967-1978)	1,799
Sid Fernandez (1984-1993)	1,449
David Cone (1987-1992)	1,159

Ron Darling (1983-1991)	1,148
Jon Matlack (1971-1977)	1,023
Bobby Jones (1993-Present)	714
Craig Swan (1973-1984)	671
Tug McGraw (1965-1967, 1969-1974)	618

BASES ON BALLS ALLOWED

Tom Seaver (1967-1977, 1983)	847
Jerry Koosman (1967-1978)	820
Dwight Gooden (1984-1994)	651
Ron Darling (1983-1991)	614
Sid Fernandez (1984-1993)	596
Jon Matlack (1971-1977)	419
David Cone (1987-1992)	418
Craig Swan (1973-1984)	368
Bobby Jones (1993-present)	353
Tug McGraw (1965-1967, 1969-1974)	350

SHUTOUTS

Tom Seaver (1967-1977, 1983)	44
Jerry Koosman (1967-1978)	26
Jon Matlack (1971-1977)	26
Dwight Gooden (1984-1994)	23
David Cone (1987-1992)	15
Ron Darling (1983-1991)	10
Al Jackson (1962-1965, 1968-1969)	10
Sid Fernandez (1984-1993)	9
Bob Ojeda (1986-1990)	9
Gary Gentry (1969-1972)	8

SAVES

John Franco (1990-Present)	272
Jesse Orosco (1979, 1981-1987)	107
Tug McGraw (1965-1967, 1969-1974)	85
Roger McDowell (1985-1989)	84
Neil Allen (1979-1983)	69
Skip Lockwood (1975-1979)	65
Armando Benitez (1999-present)	63
Randy Myers (1985-1989)	56
Doug Sisk (1982-1987)	33
Ron Taylor (1967-1971)	28
Bob Apodaca (1973-1979)	26

GAMES STARTED

Tom Seaver (1967-1977, 1983)	395
Jerry Koosman (1967-1978)	346
Dwight Gooden (1984-1994)	303
Sid Fernandez (1984-1993)	250
Ron Darling (1983-1991)	241
Jon Matlack (1971-1977)	199
Bobby Jones (1993-Present)	190
Craig Swan (1973-1984)	184
David Cone (1987-1992)	165
Al Jackson (1962-1965, 1968-1969)	138

METS' ALL-TIME SINGLE-SEASON BATTING LEADERS (1962-2000)

BATTING AVERAGE

John Olerud	(1998)	.354
Cleon Jones	(1969)	.340
Lance Johnson	(1996)	.333
Dave Magadan	(1990)	.328
Edgardo Alfonso	(2000)	.324
Mike Piazza	(2000)	.324
Shawon Dunston	(1999)	.321
Cleon Jones	(1971)	.319
Bernard Gilkey	(1996)	.317
Edgardo Alfonzo	(1997)	.315
Rickey Henderson	(1999)	.315
Darryl Hamilton	(1999)	.315

AT-BATS

Lance Johnson	(1996)	682
Felix Millan	(1975)	676
Mookie Wilson	(1982)	639
Felix Millan	(1973)	638
Mookie Wilson	(1983)	638
Tommie Agee	(1970)	636
Frank Taveras	(1979)	635
Edgardo Alfonzo	(1999)	628
Eddie Murray	(1993)	610
Willie Montañez	(1978)	609

BASE HITS

Lance Johnson	(1996)	227
John Olerud	(1998)	197
Edgardo Alfonzo	(1999)	191
Felix Millan	(1975)	191
Felix Millan	(1973)	185
Keith Hernandez	(1985)	183
Tommie Agee	(1970)	182
Bernard Gilkey	(1996)	181
Lee Mazzilli	(1979)	181
Mookie Wilson	(1982)	178
Robin Ventura	(1999)	177
Edgardo Alfonzo	(2000)	176

EXTRA BASE HITS

Howard Johnson	(1989)	80
Bernard Gilkey	(1996)	77
Howard Johnson	(1991)	76
Darryl Strawberry	(1987)	76
Todd Hundley	(1996)	74
Robin Ventura	(1999)	70
Darryl Strawberry	(1988)	69
Edgardo Alfonzo	(1999)	68
Edgardo Alfonzo	(2000)	67
Kevin McReynolds	(1987)	66
Mike Piazza	(1999)	65

HOME RUNS

Todd Hundley	(1996)	41
Mike Piazza	(1999)	40
Darryl Strawberry	(1987)	39
Darryl Strawberry	(1988)	39
Mike Piazza	(2000)	38
Howard Johnson	(1991)	38
Dave Kingman	(1976)	37
Darryl Strawberry	(1990)	37
Dave Kingman	(1982)	37
Howard Johnson	(1989)	36
Dave Kingman	(1975)	36
Howard Johnson	(1987)	36

DOUBLES

Bernard Gilkey	(1996)	44
Howard Johnson	(1989)	41
Edgardo Alfonzo	(2000)	40
Gregg Jefferies	(1990)	40
John Olerud	(1999)	39
Robin Ventura	(1999)	38
Felix Millan	(1975)	37
Joel Youngblood	(1979)	37
Lenny Dykstra	(1987)	37
Howard Johnson	(1990)	37
Eddie Murray	(1992)	37
Todd Zeile	(2000)	36
Rusty Staub	(1973)	36
John Olerud	(1998)	36
Hal McCrae	(1998)	36

TRIPLES

Lance Johnson	(1996)	21
Mookie Wilson	(1984)	10
Charlie Neal	(1962)	9
Steve Henderson	(1978)	9
Frank Taveras	(1979)	9
Mookie Wilson	(1982)	9

SLUGGING AVERAGE

Mike Piazza	(2000)	.614
Darryl Strawberry	(1987)	.583
Mike Piazza	(1999)	.575
Bernard Gilkey	(1996)	.562
Howard Johnson	(1989)	.559
Todd Hundley	(1996)	.550
John Olerud	(1998)	.550
Todd Hundley	(1997)	.549
Edgardo Alfonso	(2000)	.542
Robin Ventura	(1999)	.529
Bobby Bonilla	(1993)	.522

TOTAL BASES

Lance Johnson	(1996)	327
Bernard Gilkey	(1996)	321
Howard Johnson	(1989)	319
Edgardo Alfonzo	(1999)	315
Darryl Strawberry	(1987)	310

Mike Piazza	(1999)	307
John Olerud	(1998)	307
Howard Johnson	(1991)	302
Tommie Agee	(1970)	298
Todd Hundley	(1996)	297
Darryl Strawberry	(1988)	296
Mike Piazza	(2000)	296

RUNS BATTED IN

Mike Piazza	(1999)	124
Bernard Gilkey	(1996)	117
Howard Johnson	(1991)	117
Mike Piazza	(2000)	113
Todd Hundley	(1996)	112
Edgardo Alfonzo	(1999)	108
Darryl Strawberry	(1990)	108
Rusty Staub	(1975)	105
Gary Carter	(1986)	105
Darryl Strawberry	(1987)	104
John Olerud	(1997)	102

RUNS SCORED

Edgardo Alfonzo	(1999)	123
Lance Johnson	(1996)	117
Edgardo Alfonzo	(2000)	109
Bernard Gilkey	(1996)	108
Darryl Strawberry	(1987)	108
Howard Johnson	(1991)	108
John Olerud	(1999)	107
Tommie Agee	(1970)	107
Howard Johnson	(1989)	104
Darryl Strawberry	(1988)	101
Mike Piazza	(1999)	100
Tommie Agee	(1969)	97
Gregg Jefferies	(1990)	96
Keith Hernandez	(1986)	94
Edgardo Alfonzo	(1998)	94

STOLEN BASES

Roger Cedeño	(1999)	66
Mookie Wilson	(1982)	58
Mookie Wilson	(1983)	54
Lance Johnson	(1996)	50
Mookie Wilson	(1984)	46
Frank Taveras	(1979)	42
Howard Johnson	(1989)	41
Lee Mazzilli	(1980)	41
Vince Coleman	(1993)	38
Vince Coleman	(1991)	37
Darryl Strawberry	(1987)	36

BASES ON BALLS

John Olerud	(1999)	125
Darryl Strawberry	(1987)	97
Keith Hernandez	(1984)	97
John Olerud	(1998)	95
Bud Harrelson	(1970)	95

Edgardo Alfonzo	(2000)	95
Keith Hernandez	(1986)	94
Lee Mazzilli	(1979)	93
Hal McCrae	(1998)	90
Wayne Garrett	(1974)	89
Howard Johnson	(1988)	86
Darryl Strawberry	(1988)	85
Edgardo Alfonzo	(1999)	85

GAMES PLAYED

John Olerud	(1999)	162
Felix Millan	(1975)	162
Robin Ventura	(1999)	161
John Olerud	(1998)	160
Hal McCrae	(1998)	159
Willie Montañez	(1978)	159
Lee Mazzilli	(1977)	159
Willie Montañez	(1978)	159
Mookie Wilson	(1982)	159
Edgardo Alfonzo	(1999)	158
Lee Mazzilli	(1979)	158
Joel Youngblood	(1979)	158
Keith Hernandez	(1985)	158

Bobby Bonilla (Brace Photo)

MOST WINS

Tom Seaver	(1969)	25
Dwight Gooden	(1985)	24
Tom Seaver	(1975)	22
Jerry Koosman	(1976)	21
Tom Seaver	(1972)	21
Tom Seaver	(1971)	20
David Cone	(1988)	20
Frank Viola	(1990)	20

MOST LOSSES

Roger Craig	(1962)	24
Jack Fisher	(1965)	24
Roger Craig	(1963)	22
Al Jackson	(1962)	20
Al Jackson	(1965)	20
Jerry Koosman	(1977)	20
Tracy Stallard	(1964)	20
Jay Hook	(1962)	19
Galen Cisco	(1964)	19
Jack Fisher	(1967)	18

EARNED RUNS ALLOWED

Roger Craig	(1962)	117
Jack Fisher	(1967)	115
Jay Hook	(1962)	115
Al Jackson	(1962)	113
Jack Fisher	(1965)	111
Mike Torrez	(1983)	108
Nino Espinosa	(1978)	107
Jack Fisher	(1964)	107
Frank Viola	(1991)	102
Al Jackson	(1964)	101

EARNED RUN AVERAGE

Dwight Gooden	(1985)	1.53
Tom Seaver	(1971)	1.76
Tom Seaver	(1973)	2.08
Jerry Koosman	(1968)	2.08
Tom Seaver	(1968)	2.20
Tom Seaver	(1969)	2.21
David Cone	(1988)	2.22
Jerry Koosman	(1969)	2.28
Jon Matlack	(1972)	2.32
Tom Seaver	(1975)	2.38

GAMES APPEARED

Turk Wendell	(1999)	80
Armando Benitez	(1999)	77
Turk Wendell	(2000)	77
Jeff Innis	(1992)	76
Armando Benitez	(2000)	76
Roger McDowell	(1986)	75
Greg McMichael	(1997)	73
Dennis Cook	(1998)	73
Dennis Cook	(1999)	71
Jeff Innis	(1991)	69
Dennis Cook	(2000)	68
Jeff Innis	(1993)	67
Doug Sisk	(1983)	67
Turk Wendell	(1998)	66
Randy Myers	(1989)	65
Skip Lockwood	(1977)	63

GAMES STARTED

Jack Fisher	(1965)	36
Tom Seaver	(1970)	36
Tom Seaver	(1973)	36
Tom Seaver	(1975)	36
Thirteen others tied with 35 starts in a single season		35

COMPLETE GAMES

Tom Seaver	(1971)	21
Tom Seaver	(1970)	19
Tom Seaver	(1967)	18
Tom Seaver	(1969)	18
Tom Seaver	(1973)	18
Jerry Koosman	(1976)	17
Jerry Koosman	(1968)	17
Dwight Gooden	(1985)	16
Jerry Koosman	(1969)	16
Jon Matlack	(1976)	16

INNINGS PITCHED

Tom Seaver	(1970)	291.0
Tom Seaver	(1973)	290.0
Tom Seaver	(1971)	286.0
Tom Seaver	(1975)	280.0
Tom Seaver	(1968)	278.0
Dwight Gooden	(1985)	276.2
Tom Seaver	(1969)	273.0
Tom Seaver	(1976)	271.0
Jon Matlack	(1974)	265.0
Jerry Koosman	(1974)	265.0

STRIKEOUTS

Tom Seaver	(1971)	289
Tom Seaver	(1970)	283
Dwight Gooden	(1984)	276
Dwight Gooden	(1985)	268
Tom Seaver	(1973)	251
Tom Seaver	(1972)	249
Tom Seaver	(1975)	243
David Cone	(1991)	241
Tom Seaver	(1976)	235
David Cone	(1990)	233

BASES ON BALLS ALLOWED

Nolan Ryan	(1971)	116
Ron Darling	(1985)	114
Mike Torrez	(1983)	113

Ron Darling	(1984)	104
Jon Matlack	(1973)	99
Mike Hampton	(2000)	99
Jerry Koosman	(1975)	98
Nolan Ryan	(1970)	97
Ron Darling	(1987)	96
Al Leiter	(1999)	93
Sid Fernandez	(1986)	91

HITS ALLOWED

Roger Craig	(1962)	261
Frank Viola	(1991)	259
Jerry Koosman	(1974)	258
Jack Fisher	(1964)	256
Jack Fisher	(1965)	252
Jack Fisher	(1967)	251
Roger Craig	(1963)	249
Al Jackson	(1962)	244
Dwight Gooden	(1988)	242
Craig Swan	(1979)	241

RUNS ALLOWED

Jay Hook	(1962)	137
Roger Craig	(1962)	133
Al Jackson	(1962)	132
Al Jackson	(1963)	128
Jack Fisher	(1964)	124
Jack Fisher	(1967)	121
Jack Fisher	(1965)	121
Mike Torrez	(1983)	120

Roger Craig	(1963)	117
Nino Espinosa	(1978)	117

SHUTOUTS

Dwight Gooden	(1985)	8
Jerry Koosman	(1968)	7
Jon Matlack	(1974)	7
Jerry Koosman	(1969)	6
Jpn Matlack	(1976)	6
Bob Ojeda	(1988)	5
Tom Seaver	(1974)	5
Tom Seaver	(1976)	5
Tom Seaver	(1969)	5
Tom Seaver	(1968)	5
David Cone	(1992)	5

SAVES

Armando Benitez	(2000)	41
John Franco	(1998)	38
John Franco	(1997)	36
John Franco	(1990)	33
Jesse Orosco	(1984)	31
John Franco	(1994)	30
John Franco	(1991)	30
John Franco	(1995)	29
John Franco	(1996)	28
Tug McGraw	(1972)	27
Randy Myers	(1988)	26
Billy Taylor	(1999)	26

METS' INDIVIDUAL BATTING RECORDS (1962-2000)

MOST AT-BATS

Game	Dave Schneck	11 (September 25, 1974, 25 Innings)
Season	Lance Johnson	682 (1996)
Rookie Season	Lee Mazzilli	537 (1977)
Career	Ed Kranepool	5436 (1962-1979)

MOST RUNS SCORED

Game	Bernard Gilkey	5 (April 19, 1998 at Cincinnati)
	Darryl Strawberry	5 (August 16, 1987 at Chicago)
	Lee Mazzilli	5 (August 14, 1979 at Atlanta)
	Lenny Randle	5 (May 18, 1978 versus Atlanta, 10 innings)
Season	Edgardo Alfonzo	123 (1999)
Rookie Season		
	Cleon Jones	74 (1966)
Career	Darryl Strawberry	662 (1983-1990)

MOST HITS

Game	Alex Ochoa	5* (July 3, 1996 at Philadelphia)
	*most recent (accomplished 24 times)	
Season	Lance Johnson	227 (1996)
Rookie Season		
	Ron Hunt	145 (1963
Career	Ed Kranepool	1418 (1962-1979)

HITTING STREAKS

Consecutive Games	Hubie Brooks	24 (1984)
Consecutive Games (LH)	John Olerud	23 (1998)
Consecutive Games (Rookie)	Mike Vail	23 (1975)

DOUBLES

Game	Edgardo Alfonzo	3* (April 18, 2000 vs. Milwaukee)
	*most recent (accomplished 17 times)	
Season	Bernard Gilkey	44 (1996)
Rookie Season		
	Gregg Jefferies	28 (1989)
	Ron Hunt	28 (1963)
Career	Ed Kranepool	225 (1962-1979)

TRIPLES

Game	Doug Flynn	3 (August 15, 1980 at Montreal)
Season	Lance Johnson	21 (1996)
Rookie Season		
	Mookie Wilson	8 (1981)
Career	Mookie Wilson	62 (1980-1989)

HOME RUNS

Game	Gary Carter	3 (September 3, 1995 at San Diego)
	Darryl Strawberry	3 (August 5, 1985 at Chicago)
	Claudell Washington	3 (June 22, 1980 at Los Angeles)
	Dave Kingman	3 (June 4, 1976 at Los Angeles)
	Jim Hickman	3 (September 3, 1965 at St. Louis)
Game, Pitcher		
	Walt Terrell	2 (August 6, 1983 at Chicago)
Two Consecutive Games		
	Gary Carter	5 (September 3-4, 1985)
Three Consecutive Games		
	Frank Thomas	6 (August 1-2-3, 1962)
First Major League At-Bat		
	Mike Fitzgerald	September 3, 1983 at Philadelphia
	Benny Ayala	August 27, 1974 versus Houston
Season (Switch Hitter)		
	Todd Hundley	41 (1996)
Season (RH)		
	Mike Piazza	40 (1999)
Season (LH)		
	Darryl Strawberry	39 (1987 and 1988)
Rookie Season		
	Darryl Strawberry	26 (1983)
Career	Darryl Strawberry	252 (1983-1990)
Career (RH)		
	Dave Kingman	154 (1975-1977, 1981-1983)
Career (Switch Hitter)		
	Howard Johnson	192 (1985-1993)
Consecutive Games		
	Bobby Bonilla	4 (August 19-23, 1992)
	Dave Kingman	4 (May 25-29, 1981)
	Lee Mazzilli	4 July 1-4, 1980
	Ron Swoboda	4 (April 19-21, 1968)
	Larry Elliot	4 (July 21-24, 1964)
Grand Slams, Season		
	John Milner	3 (1976)
Grand Slams, Career		
	Howard Johnson	5 (1985-1993)
	Kevin McReynolds	5 (1987-1991, 1994)
	John Milner	5 (1971-1977)

RUNS BATTED IN

Game	Dave Kingman	8 (June 4, 1976 at Los Angeles)
Consecutive Games		
	Bobby Bonilla	9 (May 20-29, 1994)
Season	Mike Piazza	124 (1999)
Season (LH)		
	Robin Ventura	120 (1999)
Rookie Season		
	Darryl Strawberry	74 (1983)
Career	Darryl Strawberry	773 (1983-1990)

MOST TOTAL BASES

Game	Darry Strawberry	13 (August 5, 1985 at Chicago)
	Claudell Washington	13 (June 22, 1980 at Los Angeles)
	Jim Hickman	13 (September 3, 1965 at St. Louis)
Season	Lance Johnson	327 (1996)
Season (RH)		
	Bernard Gilkey	321 (1996
Season (Switch Hitter)		
	Howard Johnson	319 (1989)
Career	Ed Kranepool	2047 (1962-1979)

MOST STOLEN BASES

Game	Vince Coleman	4 (June 23, 1993 versus St. Louis)
	Vince Coleman	4 (June 26, 1992 at St. Louis)
Season	Roger Cedeño	66 (1999)
Rookie Season		
	Mookie Wilson	24 (1981)
Career	Mookie Wilson	281 (1980-1989)

MOST CAUGHT STEALING

Season	Lenny Randle	21 (1977)
Career	Mookie Wilson	90 (1980-1989)

MOST SACRIFICE HITS

Game	Sid Fernandez	3 (July 24, 1987 versus Houston)
Season	Felix Millan	24 (1974)
Career	Dwight Gooden	85 (1984-1994)
	Jerry Koosman	85 (1967-1978)

MOST SACRIFICE FLIES

Season	Howard Johnson	15 (1991)
	Gary Carter	15 (1986)
Career	Ed Kranepool	58 (1962-1979)

STRIKEOUTS (BATTING)

Most, Game		
	Ryan Thompson	5 (September 29, 1993 versus St. Louis)
	Dave Kingman	5 (May 28, 1982 versus Houston)
	Frank Taveras	5 (May 1, 1979 versus San Diego)
	Ron Swoboda	5 (June 22, 1969 versus St. Louis)
Most, Season		
	Dave Kingman	156 (1982)
	Tommy Agee	156 (1970)
Most, Career		
	Darryl Strawberry	960 (1983-1990)
Fewest, Season		
	Felix Millan	14 (1974 with 585 plate appearances)

MOST BASES ON BALLS (BATTING)

Game		
	Vince Coleman	5 (August 10, 1992 versus Pittsburgh)
Game, Intentional		
	Todd Hundley	3 (June 28, 1997 at Pittsburgh)
Season		
	John Olerud	125 (1999)
Career		
	Darryl Strawberry	580 (1983-1990)

MOST HIT-BY-PITCHER (BATTING)

Season	Ron Hunt	13 (1963)
	John Olerud	13 (1997)
Career	Ron Hunt	41 (1963-1966)

GROUNDING INTO DOUBLE PLAYS

Most, Game		
	Joe Torre	4 (July 21, 1975 versus Houston)
Most, Season		
	Cleon Jones	26 (1970)
Fewest, Season		
	Howard Johnson	4 (1991)

BATTING AVERAGE

Season (LH)		
	John Olerud	.354 (1998)
Season (RH)		
	Cleon Jones	.340 (1969)
Season (Switch Hitter)		
	Lenny Randle	.304 (1977)
Rookie Season		
	Cleon Jones	.275 (1966)
Career (LH)		
	John Olerud	.315 (through 2000)
Career (RH)		
	Edgardo Alfonzo	.296 (through 2000)
Career (Switch Hitter)		
	Wally Backman	.283 (through 2000)

SLUGGING AVERAGE

Season		
	Darryl Strawberry	.583 (1987)
Season (RH)		
	Mike Piazza	.575 (1999)
Rookie Season		
	Darryl Strawberry	.512 (1983)
Career		
	Darryl Strawberry	.520 (1983-1990)

MOST EXTRA BASE HITS

Season		
	Howard Johnson	80 (1989)
Rookie Season		
	Darryl Strawberry	48 (1983)
Career		
	Darryl Strawberry	469 (1983-1990)

METS' INDIVIDUAL PITCHING RECORDS (1962-2000)

MOST GAMES APPEARED

Season	Turk Wendell	80 (1999)
Season (LH)		
	Dennis Cook	73 (1998)
Rookie Season		
	Doug Sisk	67 (1983)
Consecutive		
	Turk Wendell	9 (September 14-23, 1998)
Career	John Franco	547 (1990-Present)
Career (RH)		
	Tom Seaver	401 (1967-1977, 1983)

MOST STARTS

Season	Jack Fisher	36 (1965)
	Tom Seaver	36 (1970, 1973 and 1975)
Season (LH)		
	Frank Viola	35 (1990 and 1991)
	John Matlack	35 (1976)
	Jerry Koosman	35 (1973 and 1974)
Rookie Season		
	Gary Gentry	35 (1969)
Career	Tom Seaver	395 (1967-1977, 1983)
Career (LH)		
	Jerry Koosman	346 (1967-1978)

MOST COMPLETE GAMES

Season	Tom Seaver	21 (1971)
Season (LH)		
	Jerry Koosman	17 (1976 and 1968)
Rookie Season		
	Tom Seaver	18 (1967)
Career	Tom Seaver	171 (1967-1977, 1983)
Career (LH)		
	Jerry Koosman	108 (1967-1978)
Consecutive		
	Jerry Koosman	8 (1976)
	Tom Seaver	8 (1969)

MOST INNINGS PITCHED

Game	Rob Gardner	15 (October 2, 1965 versus Philadelphia)
	Al Jackson	15 (August 14, 1962 versus Philadelphia)
Season	Tom Seaver	290.0 (1970)
Season (LH)		
	Jon Matlack	265.0 (1974)
	Jerry Koosman	265.0 (1974)
Rookie Season		
	Jerry Koosman	264.0 (1967)
Career	Tom Seaver	3045.0 (1967-1977, 1983)
Career (LH)		
	Jerry Koosman	2545.0 (1967-1978)
Without Allowing a Run		
	Jerry Koosman	31.2 (August 19-September 7, 1973)

Without Allowing a Walk

Bret Saberhagen 47.2 (May 10-June 13, 1994)

MOST CONSECUTIVE BATTERS RETIRED

Game	Tom Seaver	25 (July 9, 1969 versus Chicago)

HITS ALLOWED

No Hitters

None in franchise history

Most, Season		
	Roger Craig	261 (1962)
Most, Rookie Season		
	Al Jackson	244 (1962)
Most, Career		
	Tom Seaver	2431 (1967-1977, 1983)

MOST RUNS ALLOWED

Season	Jay Hook	137 (1962)
Season (Earned)		
	Roger Craig	117 (1962)
Rookie Season		
	Al Jackson	132 (1962)
Career	Jerry Koosman	994 (1967-1978)

MOST HOME RUNS ALLOWED

Consecutive, Inning		
	Pete Harnish	3 (April 1, 1997 at San Diego)
Game	Roger Craig	5 (May 4, 1963)
Season	Roger Craig	35 (1962)
Rookie Season		
	Gary Gentry	24 (1969)
Career	Tom Seaver	212 (1967-1977, 1983)

MOST STRIKEOUTS (PITCHING)

Inning	Derek Wallace	4 (September 13, 1996 versus Atlanta)
Game	David Cone	19 (October 6, 1991 at Philadelphia)
	Tom Seaver	19 (April 22, 1970 versus San Diego)
Game (LH)		
	Sid Fernandez	16 (July 14, 1989 at Atlanta)
Game, Rookie		
	Dwight Gooden	16 (September 17, 1984 at Philadelphia)
	Dwight Gooden	16 (September 12, 1984 versus Pittsburgh)
Season	Tom Seaver	289 (1971)
Season (LH)		
	Jon Matlack	205 (1973)
Rookie Season		
	Dwight Gooden	276 (1984)

Consecutive

	Tom Seaver	10 (April 22, 1970 versus San Diego)
Career	Tom Seaver	2541 (1967-1977, 1983)

MOST BASES ON BALLS (PITCHING)

Game	Mike Torrez	10 (July 21, 1983 at Cincinnati)
Season	Nolan Ryan	116 (1971)
Season (LH)		
	Jon Matlack	99 (1973)
Rookie Season		
	Ron Darling	104 (1984)
Career	Tom Seaver	847 (1967-1977, 1983)

PITCHING WILDNESS

Most Hit Batsmen, Season		
	Nolan Ryan	15 (1971)
Most Wild Pitches, Season		
	Jack Hamilton	18 (1966)
Bases on Balls, Season		
	Nolan Ryan	116 (1971)

MOST WINS

Season	Tom Seaver	25 (1969)
Season (LH)		
	Jerry Koosman	21 (1976)
Rookie Season		
	Jerry Koosman	19 (1968)
Season, Reliever		
	Roger McDowell	14 (1986)
Consecutive		
	Dwight Gooden	14 (1985)
Consecutive Starts		
	Bobby Jones	8 (1997)
	David Cone	8 (1988)
	Tom Seaver	8 (1969)
Career	Tom Seaver	198 (1967-1977, 1983)
Career (LH)		
	Jerry Koosman	140 (1967-1978)
Percentage		
	David Cone	.870 (20-3 in 1988)

MOST LOSSES

Season	Roger Craig	24 (1962)
	Jack Fisher	24 (1965)
Season (LH)		
	Jerry Koosman	20 (1977)
	Al Jackson	20 (1962)
	Al Jackson	20 (1965)
Season (Reliever)		
	Skip Lockwood	13 (1978)

Rookie Season		
	Al Jackson	20 (1962)
Consecutive, Season		
	Roger Craig	18 (1963)
Consecutive, Two Seasons		
	Anthony Young	27 (1992-1993)
Career	Jerry Koosman	137 (1967-1978)
Career (RH)		
	Tom Seaver	124 (1967-1977, 1983)

MOST SHUTOUTS

Season	Dwight Gooden	8 (1985)
Season (LH)		
	Jon Matlack	7 (1974)
	Jerry Koosman	7 (1968)
Rookie Season		
	Jerry Koosman	7 (1968)
Career	Tom Seaver	44 (1967-1977, 1983)
Career (LH)		
	Jerry Koosman	26 (1967-1978)
	Jon Matlack	26 (1971-1977)

MOST SAVES

Consecutive Appearances		
	John Franco	9 (September 5-30, 1995)
	John Franco	9 (July 4-25, 1990)
	John Franco	9 (April 27-May 20, 1997)
Season	Armando Benitez	41 (2000)
Season (RH)		
	Roger McDowell	25 (1987)
Rookie Season		
	Roger McDowell	17 (1985)
Career	John Franco	272 (1990-Present)
Career (RH)		
	Roger McDowell	84 (1985-1989)

No-Hit Games Versus New York Mets

(1) June 30, 1962—Sandy Koufax (Los Angeles), 5-0

(2) June 21, 1964—Jim Bunning (Philadelphia), 6-0 (Perfect Game, First Game of Doubleheader)

(3) June 14, 1965—Jim Mahoney (Cincinnati), 10 innings (of no-hit ball but Mets won in 11th inning)

(4) September 20, 1969—Bob Moose (Pittsburgh), 4-0

(5) October 2, 1972—Bill Stoneman (Montreal), 7-0 (First Game of Doubleheader)

(6) August 24, 1975—Ed Halicki (San Francisco), 6-0 (Second Game of Doubleheader)

(7) September 8, 1993—Darryl Kile (Houston), 6-1

METS' SEASON-BY-SEASON SUMMARIES

1962

40-120, 60.5 GB, 10th in NL
Manager: Casey Stengel

Postseason Record: No postseason play
Important Firsts: Mets part of first NL expansion of century, along with Houston Colt .45s; Jay Hook is winning hurler in first franchise victory (April 23) in Pittsburgh
League Leaders: Roger Craig (24 losses)
Memorable Moments: First franchise game is 11-4 loss to St. Louis Cardinals; historic home opener at Polo Grounds (April 13) is 4-3 loss to Pittsburgh Pirates
Best Pitchers: Roger Craig (10-24) and Al Jackson (8-20)
Best Hitters: Frank Thomas (34 HRs, 94 RBIs) and Richie Ashburn (.306 BA)
Home Attendance: 922,530

Casey Stengel (AP/Wide World Photos)

1963

51-111, 48.5 GB, 10th in NL
Manager: Casey Stengel

Postseason Record: No postseason play

Important Firsts: Jim Hickman becomes first Met to hit for cycle (August 7); first Mets-Yankees Mayor's Trophy Game won by Mets 6-2 in Yankee Stadium (June 20)

League Leaders: None

Memorable Moments: Roger Craig endures club-record 18-game losing streak, broken on August 9 by Jim Hickman's grand slam in ninth for 7-3 win over Chicago Cubs; Mets set modern major league record with 22 straight road losses

Best Pitchers: Al Jackson (13-17) and Carl Willey (9-14, 3.10 ERA)

Best Hitter: Ron Hunt (.272 BA; Hunt finishes second to Pete Rose for NL Rookie of the Year honors)

Home Attendance: 1,080,108 (new record)

Duke Snider (AP/Wide World Photos)

1964

53-109, 40.0 GB, 10th in NL
Manager: Casey Stengel

Postseason Record: No postseason play
Important Firsts: Shea Stadium opened with 4-3 loss to Pittsburgh Pirates (April 17); Ron Hunt is first Mets starter in All-Star Game
League Leaders: None
Memorable Moments: Unforgettable individual games include 19-1 rout of Chicago Cubs (May 26); 26-inning doubleheader nightcap loss to San Francisco Giants (May 31); perfect game tossed by Phillies' Jim Bunning (June 21) at Shea Stadium
Best Pitcher: Al Jackson (11-16)
Best Hitters: Ron Hunt (.303 BA) and Charley Smith (20 HRs)
Home Attendance: 1,732,597 (new record)

Jim Bunning (SPI Archives)

1965

50-112, 47.0 GB, 10th in NL
Managers: Casey Stengel (31-64), Wes Westrum (19-48)

Postseason Record: No postseason play
Important Firsts: Jim Hickman first Met to homer three times in one game (September 3)
League Leaders: Jack Fisher (24 losses)
Memorable Moments: Future Hall of Famers Warren Spahn and Yogi Berra make brief appearances with club; managerial career of Casey Stengel ended (July 24) by fractured hip; Jim Maloney of Cincinnati no-hits Mets for 10 innings (June 14), but loses on Johnny Lewis's 11th-inning homer
Best Pitchers: Jack Fisher (8-24, 3.94 ERA) and Al Jackson (8-20)
Best Hitter: Ron Swoboda (19 HRs)
Home Attendance: 1,768,389 (new record)

Warren Spahn (AP/Wide World Photos)

1966

66-95, 28.5 GB, 9th in NL
Manager: Wes Westrum

Postseason Record: No postseason play
Important Firsts: Mets escape cellar for first time in club history
League Leaders: None
Memorable Moments: George Weiss retires and Bing Devine is named team's second GM (November 14)
Best Pitcher: Dennis Ribant (11-9, 3.21 ERA)
Best Hitters: Ken Boyer (61 RBIs) and Ed Kranepool (16 HRs)
Home Attendance: 1,932,693 (new record)

Mets mascot (SPI Archives)

1967

61-101, 40.5 GB, 10th in NL
Managers: Wes Westrum (57-94), Salty Parker (4-7)

Postseason Record: No postseason play

Important Firsts: Tom Seaver is first Mets player to win major postseason award as Rookie of the Year; Salty Parker is ball club's first-ever interim manager

League Leaders: None

Memorable Moments: Tommy Davis is acquired from Los Angeles Dodgers, and Tom Seaver debuts with club; Westrum resigns as manager (September 21), and Gil Hodges is named new skipper (October 11) after season ends

Awards: Tom Seaver (NL Rookie of the Year)

Best Pitcher: Tom Seaver (16-13, 2.76 ERA)

Best Hitter: Tommy Davis (.302 BA, 16 HRs, 73 RBIs)

Home Attendance: 1,565,492

Tom Seaver (AP/Wide World Photos)

1968

73-89, 24.0 GB, 9th in NL
Manager: Gil Hodges

Postseason Record: No postseason play
Important Firsts: Seaver, rookie hurler Jerry Koosman, and catcher Jerry Grote give Mets first multiple entries in All-Star Game; Mets win first-ever home opener (April 17) on Jerry Koosman's 3-0 shutout of San Francisco Giants
League Leaders: None
Memorable Moments: Young pitching sensations Seaver and Koosman anchor staff that is second in NL in shutouts (25) and fourth in ERA (2.72); Nolan Ryan fans 133 batters in 134 innings; Hodges suffers mild heart attack in Atlanta (September 24) but doctors give okay for 1969 return
Best Pitchers: Jerry Koosman (19-12, 2.08 ERA) and Tom Seaver (16-12, 2.20 ERA)
Best Hitter: Cleon Jones (.297 BA)
Home Attendance: 1,781,657

Nolan Ryan (NY Daily News)

1969

100-62, 8.0 GA, 1st in NL East, NL and WORLD CHAMPIONS
Manager: Gil Hodges

Postseason Record: Defeat Atlanta Braves (3-0) in NLCS; defeat Baltimore Orioles (4-1) in World Series

Important Firsts: In historic first season of divisional play, Mets stun baseball world with first-ever world championship and first-ever 100-win season

League Leaders: Tom Seaver (25 wins); Seaver (.781 winning pct.)

Memorable Moments: Seaver captures his first Cy Young Award and teams with Koosman and rookie Gary Gentry for majors' best staff; Donn Clendenon acquired from Montreal (June 15) in key trade; Mets clinch NL East title (September 24) with 6-0 win over St. Louis Cardinals

Awards: Tom Seaver (Cy Young); Seaver (*Sports Illustrated* Man of the Year); Al Weis (BBWAA World Series MVP)

Best Pitchers: Tom Seaver (25-7, 2.21 ERA) and Jerry Koosman (17-9, 2.28 ERA)

Best Hitters: Cleon Jones (.340 BA) and Tommie Agee (26 HRs, 76 RBIs)

Home Attendance: 2,175,373 (new record)

New York Mets' Tommie Agee is congratulated by a bat boy and applauded by fans after hitting a home run against the Chicago Cubs at Shea Stadium in New York, in this July 20, 1969 photo. (AP/Wide World Photos)

1970

83-79, 6.0 GB, 3rd in NL East
Manager: Gil Hodges

Postseason Record: No postseason play
Important Firsts: Tommie Agee is Mets' first-ever Gold Glove outfielder
League Leaders: Tom Seaver (283 Ks); Seaver (2.82 ERA); Ron Herbel (74 games pitched)
Memorable Moments: GM Johnny Murphy suffers fatal heart attack (January 14) and is replaced by Bob Scheffing; Seaver fans record 19 San Diego Padres (April 22) at Shea Stadium; Cleon Jones posts team-record 23-game hitting streak
Awards: Tommie Agee (OF Gold Glove)
Best Pitcher: Tom Seaver (18-12, 2.81 ERA)
Best Hitter: Tommie Agee (.286 BA, 24 HRs, 31 SBs)
Home Attendance: 2,697,479 (new record)

Karl Ehrhardt, Mets fan know as the Sign Man. (AP/Wide World Photos)

1971

83-79, 14.0 GB, 3rd (Tie) in NL East
Manager: Gil Hodges

Postseason Record: No postseason play

Important Firsts: None

League Leaders: Tom Seaver (289 Ks); Seaver (1.76 ERA)

Memorable Moments: Seaver enjoys perhaps his best year, notching 20 wins and a sub-2.00 ERA; Bud Harrelson wins Gold Glove at shortstop; Mets score club-record 20 runs in 20-6 rout of Atlanta Braves (August 7)

Awards: Bud Harrelson (SS Gold Glove)

Best Pitcher: Tom Seaver (20-10, 1.76 ERA)

Best Hitter: Cleon Jones (.319 BA, 69 RBIs)

Home Attendance: 2,266,680

Tom Seaver (AP/Wide World Photos)

1972

83-73, 13.5 GB, 3rd in NL East
Manager: Yogi Berra

Postseason Record: No postseason play
Important Firsts: Tug McGraw is Mets' first All-Star Game winning pitcher
League Leaders: None
Memorable Moments: Gil Hodges suffers fatal heart attack (April 2) and Yogi Berra is named manager; fastest start in club history with 11-game win streak and 30-11 June 1 record; Willie Mays homers in first game as Met (May 14)
Awards: Jon Matlack (NL Rookie of the Year)
Best Pitcher: Tom Seaver (21-12)
Best Hitter: Rusty Staub (.293 BA)
Home Attendance: 2,134,185

Roberto Clemente and Willie Mays (AP/Wide World Photos)

1973

82-79, 1.5 GA, 1st in NL East, NATIONAL LEAGUE CHAMPIONS
Manager: Yogi Berra

Postseason Record: Defeat Cincinnati Reds (3-2) in NLCS; lose to Oakland Athletics (3-4) in World Series
Important Firsts: None
League Leaders: Tom Seaver (18 complete games); Seaver (251 Ks); Seaver (2.08 ERA)
Memorable Moments: Seaver wins second Cy Young; Mets rally from last place on August 11 in one of most stunning turnarounds in league pennant-race history
Awards: Tom Seaver (Cy Young)
Best Pitcher: Tom Seaver (19-10, 2.08 ERA)
Best Hitters: John Milner (23 HRs) and Felix Millan (.290 BA)
Home Attendance: 1,912,390

New York Mets pitcher Tom Seaver. (AP/Wide World Photos)

1974

71-91, 17.0 GB, 5th in NL East
Manager: Yogi Berra

Postseason Record: No postseason play
Important Firsts: Benny Ayala becomes first Met to homer in first plate appearance (August 27)
League Leaders: Jon Matlack (7 shutouts)
Memorable Moments: Mets lose 25-inning marathon to St. Louis Cardinals at Shea Stadium (September 11); Joe McDonald named GM (October 1)
Best Pitchers: Jerry Koosman (15-11) and Jon Matlack (2.41 ERA)
Best Hitter: John Milner (20 HRs, 10 SBs)
Home Attendance: 1,722,209

Benny Ayala (Brace Photo)

1975

82-80, 10.5 GB, 3rd (Tie) in NL East
Managers: Yogi Berra (56-53), Roy McMillan (26-27)

Postseason Record: No postseason play
Important Firsts: Rusty Staub is first Met to top 100-RBI mark
League Leaders: Tom Seaver (22 wins); Seaver (243 Ks)
Memorable Moments: Seaver rebounds from poor 1974 season to capture third Cy Young; Joe Torre acquired from Cardinals, and Dave Kingman purchased from Giants; Berra fired as manager (August 6) and replaced by Roy McMillan; Casey Stengel and owner Joan Payson both pass away during off-season
Awards: Tom Seaver (Cy Young)
Best Pitcher: Tom Seaver (22-9, 2.38 ERA)
Best Hitters: Dave Kingman (36 HRs) and Rusty Staub (105 RBIs)
Home Attendance: 1,730,566

Tom Seaver (AP/Wide World Photos)

1976

86-76, 15.0 GB, 3rd in NL East
Manager: Joe Frazier

Postseason Record: No postseason play
Important Firsts: None
League Leaders: Tom Seaver (235 Ks)
Memorable Moments: Dave Kingman sets club record with 37 home runs; Jerry Koosman registers his first 20-win season; Seaver fans over 200 for record ninth straight year
Best Pitcher: Jerry Koosman (21-10)
Best Hitter: Dave Kingman (37 HRs, 86 RBIs)
Home Attendance: 1,468,754

Tom Seaver, Jerry Koosman and Jon Matlack (AP/Wide World Photos)

THE NEW YORK METS ENCYCLOPEDIA

1977

64-98, 37.0 GB, 6th in NL East
Managers: Joe Frazier (15-30), Joe Torre (49-68)

Postseason Record: No postseason play
Important Firsts: None
League Leaders: Tom Seaver (7 shutouts)
Memorable Moments: Joe Frazier fired (May 31) and Joe Torre named first player-manager in big leagues since Solly Hemus (St. Louis Cardinals in 1959); stunning trades of Tom Seaver to Cincinnati (June 15) and Dave Kingman to San Diego (for future manager Bobby Valentine)
Best Pitcher: Nino Espinosa (10-13, 3.42)
Best Hitter: Len Randle (.304 BA, 33 SBs)
Home Attendance: 1,066,825

Bobby Valentine (Brace Photo)

1978

66-96, 24.0 GB, 6th in NL East
Manager: Joe Torre

Postseason Record: No postseason play
Important Firsts: None
League Leaders: Craig Swan (2.43 ERA)
Memorable Moments: Nino Espinosa is team's winningest pitcher for second straight year; Koosman spends last season with Mets before trade to Minnesota
Best Pitcher: Craig Swan (2.43 ERA) and Nino Espinosa (11-15)
Best Hitter: Willie Montañez (17 HRs, 96 RBIs)
Home Attendance: 1,007,328

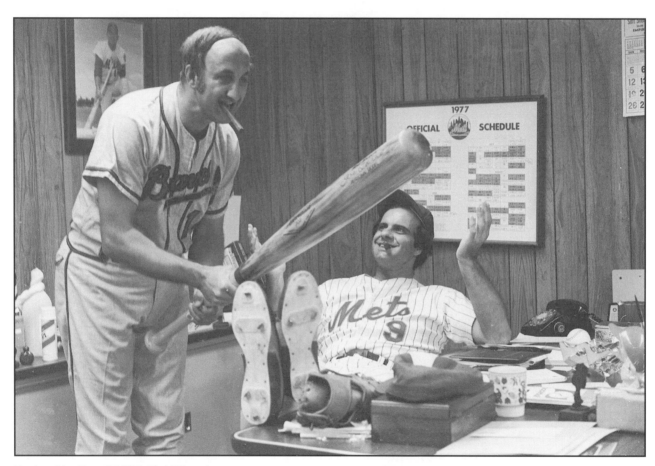

Frank and Joe Torre (AP/Wide World Photos)

1979

63-99, 35.0 GB, 6th in NL East
Manager: Joe Torre

Postseason Record: No postseason play
Important Firsts: None
League Leaders: None
Memorable Moments: Lee Mazzilli knocks in tying and winning runs in All-Star Game; Ed Kranepool retires after 18 seasons with Mets; club sold by Payson family to group headed by Doubleday & Company
Best Pitcher: Craig Swan (14-13, 3.30 ERA)
Best Hitter: Lee Mazzilli (.303 BA, 79 RBIs)
Home Attendance: 788,905 (current franchise record low)

Lee Mazzilli (AP/Wide World Photos)

1980

67-95, 24.0 GB, 5th in NL East
Manager: Joe Torre

Postseason Record: No postseason play

Important Firsts: None

League Leaders: None

Memorable Moments: Turnaround season, as club leaves cellar for first time since 1976 and enjoys first home attendance increase since 1975; Neil Allen emerges as one of NL's top firemen; Claudell Washington belts three homers in one game at Los Angeles (June 21); Shea Stadium undergoes extensive renovation

Awards: Doug Flynn (2B Gold Glove)

Best Pitcher: Neil Allen (22 saves)

Best Hitter: Lee Mazzilli (16 HRs, 76 RBIs, 41 SBs)

Home Attendance: 1,178,659

Neil Allen (Brace Photo)

1981

41-62, 18.5 GB, 5th in NL East
Manager: Joe Torre

Postseason Record: No postseason play

Important Firsts: First strike-induced split season in big-league history finds Mets in fifth for first half and fourth during second half

League Leaders: None

Memorable Moments: Dave Kingman reacquired in trade with Chicago Cubs; rookies Mookie Wilson and Hubie Brooks crack starting lineup; Rusty Staub reacquired as free agent; Torre announces departure as manager on final day of season

Best Pitcher: Neil Allen (18 saves)

Best Hitter: Dave Kingman (22 HRs, 59 RBIs)

Home Attendance: 701,910 (shortened season)

Mookie Wilson (AP/Wide World Photos)

1982

65-97, 27.0 GB, 6th in NL East
Manager: George Bamberger

Postseason Record: No postseason play
Important Firsts: Rookie Terry Leach throws first extra-inning one-hitter in Mets history, beating Philadelphia 1-0 in 10 innings (October 1)
League Leaders: Dave Kingman (37 HRs)
Memorable Moments: Kingman ties club home run record with 37 dingers; George Foster acquired from Cincinnati Reds; state-of-the-art Diamond Vision scoreboard installed at Shea Stadium; Mookie Wilson sets club record with 58 steals
Best Pitcher: Craig Swan (11-7, 3.35 ERA)
Best Hitter: Dave Kingman (37 HRs, 99 RBIs)
Home Attendance: 1,320,055

Craig Swan (Brace Photo)

1983

68-94, 22.0 GB, 6th in NL East
Managers: George Bamberger (16-30), Frank Howard (52-64)

Postseason Record: No postseason play

Important Firsts: Mike Fitzgerald becomes second Met to homer in first plate appearance

League Leaders: None

Memorable Moments: Keith Hernandez acquired from St. Louis Cardinals, hits .306 in Mets uniform, wins Gold Glove; Mets tie major league record with dozen pinch homers (Danny Heep leading NL with four); Rusty Staub has 24 pinch hits (one less than major league record) and 25 pinch RBIs (tying major league record); Darryl Strawberry cracks starting lineup as league's best rookie; early-season resignation of Bamberger followed by season-end naming of Davey Johnson as new manager

Awards: Darryl Strawberry (NL Rookie of the Year); Keith Hernandez (1B Gold Glove)

Best Pitcher: Jesse Orosco (13-7)

Best Hitter: George Foster (28 HRs, 90 RBIs)

Home Attendance: 1,103,808

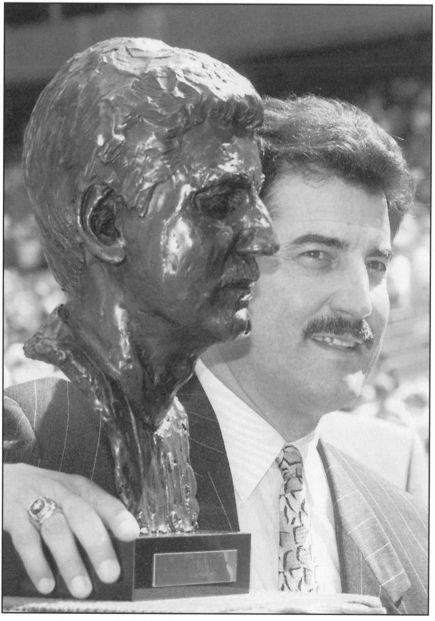

Keith Hernandez (AP/Wide World Photos)

1984

90-72, 6.5 GB, 2nd in NL East
Manager: Davey Johnson

Postseason Record: No postseason play

Important Firsts: Dwight Gooden is first teenage rookie ever to lead majors in strikeouts

League Leaders: Dwight Gooden (276 Ks)

Memorable Moments: Fireballing 19-year-old Gooden is Mets' second straight NL top rookie; Gooden sets major league mark, averaging 11.39 Ks per nine innings; Hernandez captures seventh straight Gold Glove at first base; Hubie Brooks has club-record 24-game hitting streak; Rusty Staub paces NL in pinch hits and pinch RBIs for second year in a row; Jesse Orosco claims club-record 31 saves

Awards: Dwight Gooden (NL Rookie of the Year); Keith Hernandez (1B Gold Glove)

Best Pitcher: Dwight Gooden (17-9, 2.60 ERA)

Best Hitters: Darryl Strawberry (26 HRs, 97 RBIs) and Keith Hernandez (.311 BA)

Home Attendance: 1,829,482

Darryl Strawberry (SPI Archives)

1985

98-64, 3.0 GB, 2nd in NL East
Manager: Davey Johnson

Postseason Record: No postseason play

Important Firsts: Dwight Gooden is youngest-ever NL Cy Young winner and youngest 20-game winner in modern major league history

League Leaders: Dwight Gooden (24 wins); Gooden (16 complete games); Gooden (276.2 innings pitched); Gooden (268 Ks); Gooden (1.53 ERA)

Memorable Moments: Mets again finish second with second-best win total in club history; newcomer Gary Carter (acquired from Montreal) paces club in power departments; Keith Hernandez sets major league mark with 24 game-winning RBIs; home attendance is best ever by a New York City big-league club

Awards: Dwight Gooden (Cy Young); Keith Hernandez (1B Gold Glove)

Best Pitcher: Dwight Gooden (24-4, 1.53 ERA)

Best Hitter: Gary Carter (32 HRs, 100 RBIs)

Home Attendance: 2,751,437 (new record)

Dwight Gooden (SPI Archives)

1986

108-54, 21.5 GA, 1st in NL East, NL and WORLD CHAMPIONS
Manager: Davey Johnson

Postseason Record: Defeat Houston Astros (4-2) in NLCS; Defeat Boston Red Sox (4-3) in World Series

Important Firsts: Dwight Gooden is first pitcher in major league history to fan 200-plus in each of first three seasons

League Leaders: Keith Hernandez (94 walks); Bob Ojeda (.783 winning pct.)

Memorable Moments: Mets capture second world title and post club records for wins, home and road wins, homers (148), batting average (.263), and attendance; Gary Carter ties club standard with 105 RBIs; Keith Hernandez captures ninth straight NL Gold Glove, and Ray Knight is World Series MVP; Bob Ojeda (acquired from Boston) is winningest Mets southpaw (18-5) in full decade; record five Mets (Carter, Hernandez, Strawberry, Gooden, Sid Fernandez) on NL All-Star roster; Mets stage last-gasp rally (on famed Bill Buckner play) when one out away from elimination in World Series Game 6

Awards: Ray Knight (BBWAA World Series MVP), Keith Hernandez (1B Gold Glove)

Best Pitcher: Bob Ojeda (18-5, 2.57 ERA)

Best Hitters: Keith Hernandez (.310 BA) and Gary Carter (105 RBIs)

Home Attendance: 2,762,417 (new record)

Gary Carter (AP/Wide World Photos)

1987

92-70, 3.0 GB, 2nd in NL East
Manager: Davey Johnson

Postseason Record: No postseason play

Important Firsts: Darryl Strawberry and Howard Johnson become first pair of 30-homer and 30-steal teammates in major league history; team tops three million in home attendance

League Leaders: Dwight Gooden (.682 winning pct.)

Memorable Moments: Davey Johnson becomes winningest manager (388-260) in Mets history; Darryl Strawberry breaks club marks in runs, home runs, extra-base hits, total bases, and slugging percentage and ties record with 97 walks; Keith Hernandez garners 10th consecutive Gold Glove and also surpasses 2,000 career base hits; Terry Leach begins season with club-record 10 straight victories

Awards: Keith Hernandez (1B Gold Glove)

Best Pitcher: Dwight Gooden (15-7, 3.21 ERA)

Best Hitter: Darryl Strawberry (39 HRs, 104 RBIs)

Home Attendance: 3,027,121 (new record)

Tom Seaver and Dwight Gooden (AP/Wide World Photos)

1988

100-60, 15.0 GA, 1st in NL East
Manager: Davey Johnson

Postseason Record: Lose to Los Angeles Dodgers (3-4) in NLCS
Important Firsts: Davey Johnson first manager in NL history to capture 90 or more victories in each of first five seasons
League Leaders: Darryl Strawberry (39 HRs, tie); Strawberry (.545 SA); David Cone (.870 winning pct.)
Memorable Moments: Mets capture fourth NL East banner with second-highest club winning percentage; Strawberry tops circuit in homers and ties club mark with 39; Strawberry becomes leading home run hitter in team history; Carter hits home run No. 300 and catches 100-plus games for 12th year in a row; Mets' pitching staff tops NL in ERA (2.91) and strikeouts (1,100)
Awards: Keith Hernandez (1B Gold Glove)
Best Pitcher: David Cone (20-3, 2.22 ERA)
Best Hitter: Darryl Strawberry (39 HRs, 101 RBIs)
Home Attendance: 3,047,742 (current franchise record)

Carter's 300th home run. (SPI Archives)

1989

87-75, 6.0 GB, 2nd in NL East
Manager: Davey Johnson

Postseason Record: No postseason play

Important Firsts: None

League Leaders: None

Memorable Moments: Mets complete 6 seasons under Davey Johnson, never finishing lower than second in NL East Division; Howard Johnson becomes only third player in big-league history to register 30 homers and 30 steals more than once; Kevin Elster sets major league mark with 88 consecutive errorless games at short; Mets are best homer-hitting team in NL with 147; Gooden becomes third-youngest pitcher in modern era to win 100-plus games

Awards: Ron Darling (RHP Gold Glove), Gary Carter (Roberto Clemente Award)

Best Pitcher: Sid Fernandez (14-5, 2.83 ERA)

Best Hitter: Howard Johnson (.287 BA, 36 HRs, 101 RBIs)

Home Attendance: 2,918,710

Howard Johnson (AP/Wide World Photos)

1990

91-71, 4.0 GB, 2nd in NL East
Managers: Davey Johnson (20-22), Bud Harrelson (71-49)

Postseason Record: No postseason play
Important Firsts: None
League Leaders: Gregg Jefferies (40 doubles); Dave Magadan (.425 OBP); David Cone (233 Ks); John Franco (33 saves); Frank Viola (249.2 innings pitched)
Memorable Moments: Bud Harrelson replaces Davey Johnson on May 29 in Cincinnati; John Franco leads NL with club-record 33 saves; Dave Magadan posts third-best Mets BA ever and finishes third in NL batting; Strawberry ends Mets career as club leader in career homers and career RBIs; David Cone leads the majors in strikeouts
Awards: John Franco (Rolaids Relief Man)
Best Pitchers: Frank Viola (20-12, 2.67 ERA) and John Franco (33 saves)
Best Hitter: Darryl Strawberry (37 HRs, 108 RBIs)
Home Attendance: 2,732,745

John Franco (AP/Wide World Photos)

1991

77-84, 20.5 GB, 5th in NL East
Managers: Bud Harrelson (74-80), Mike Cubbage (3-4)

Postseason Record: No postseason play
Important Firsts: None
League Leaders: Howard Johnson (38 HRs); Johnson (117 RBIs); David Cone (241 Ks)
Memorable Moments: Howard Johnson tops NL in power hitting and sets team record for RBIs; Johnson joins Bobby Bonds as only major leaguer to post 30 homers and 30 steals more than twice; David Cone ties NL and club record with 19 Ks in final game of season (October 6); off-season blockbuster trade acquires two-time Cy Young Award winner Bret Saberhagen
Best Pitcher: David Cone (14-14, 3.29 ERA, 241 Ks)
Best Hitter: Howard Johnson (38 HRs, 117 RBI)
Home Attendance: 2,284,484

David Cone (SPI Archives)

1992

72-90, 24.0 GB, 5th in NL East
Manager: Jeff Torborg

Postseason Record: No postseason play

Important Firsts: Dick Schofield is Mets' first NL fielding leader at shortstop

League Leaders: Dick Schofield (.988 fielding pct.)

Memorable Moments: David Cone falls single strikeout behind John Smoltz (Atlanta) for NL leadership; newcomer Eddie Murray leads club in most offensive categories; Murray passes milestones with career homer No. 400 (May 2) and career RBI No. 1,500 (May 23); Jeff Innis posts club record with 76 appearances out of bullpen

Best Pitcher: Sid Fernandez (14-11, 2.73 ERA)

Best Hitter: Eddie Murray (.261, 83 RBIs)

Home Attendance: 1,779,534

Jeff Torborg (AP/Wide World Photos)

1993

59-103, 38.0 GB, 7th in NL East
Managers: Jeff Torborg (13-25), Dallas Green (46-78)

Postseason Record: No postseason play
Important Firsts: Mets open season with 3-0 shutout of Colorado in Rockies' inaugural game
League Leaders: None
Memorable Moments: Sixth 100-loss season brings first last-place finish in 11 years; Dallas Green replaces Jeff Torborg as manager in mid-May; Bobby Bonilla slugs career-high 34 homers; Anthony Young sets major league record with 27 straight losses
Best Pitcher: Dwight Gooden (12-15, 3.45 ERA)
Best Hitter: Eddie Murray (.285 BA, 100 RBIs)
Home Attendance: 1,873,138

Bobby Bonilla (Joe Robbins Photos)

1994

55-58, 18.5 GB, 3rd in NL East
Manager: Dallas Green

Postseason Record: No postseason play (strike-shortened season)
Important Firsts: Three-game opening sweep of Chicago Cubs in Wrigley Field represents first time Mets start season with three wins on road
League Leaders: John Franco (30 saves); Bret Saberhagen (.778 winning percentage)
Memorable Moments: Improvement of 20.5 games in standings is third-best turnaround in club history; Bonilla sets club mark in late May, producing RBIs in nine straight games; John Franco leads NL in saves for third time in career (second as Met); Bret Saberhagen posts best walks-per-nine-innings ratio in modern big-league history
Best Pitchers: Bret Saberhagen (14-4, 2.74 ERA) and John Franco (30 saves)
Best Hitters: Jeff Kent (.292 BA) and Bobby Bonilla (20 HRs)
Home Attendance: 1,151,471 (shortened season)

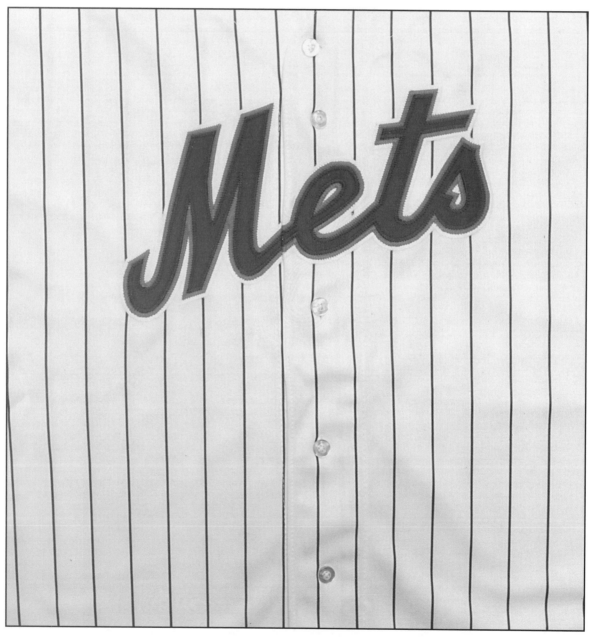

Mets uniform (SPI Archives)

1995

69-75, 21.0 GB, 2nd (Tie) in NL East
Manager: Dallas Green

Postseason Record: No postseason play
Important Firsts: None
League Leaders: Brett Butler (9 triples, partial season with Mets); Rico Brogna (1B fielding pct.)
Memorable Moments: Season ends with 11 straight home wins, tying a team record; team's .267 BA is second highest in Mets history; Todd Hundley hits two grand slams for NL lead in this category; Rico Brogna is best-fielding first sacker in NL; John Franco reaches 20-save plateau for eighth time in career
Best Pitcher: John Franco (29 saves)
Best Hitter: Rico Brogna (.289 BA, 22 HRs, 76 RBIs)
Home Attendance: 1,273,183 (shortened season)

Dallas Green (Joe Robbins Photos)

1996

71-91, 25.0 GB, 4th in NL East
Managers: Dallas Green (59-72), Bobby Valentine (12-19)

Postseason Record: No postseason play
Important Firsts: Lance Johnson becomes first player in baseball history to lead both NL (227, 1996) and AL (186, 1995) in hits; Derek Wallace first Mets pitcher (September 13) to strike out four batters in one inning
League Leaders: Lance Johnson (227 hits); Lance Johnson (21 triples)
Memorable Moments: Heavy hitting of Todd Hundley, Lance Johnson, and Bernard Gilkey pace team records for BA (.270), hits (1,515), and triples (47); Hundley posts major league record for homers by catcher (41); Alex Ochoa collects sixth cycle in Mets history (July 3) at Philadelphia; José Vizcaino sets club record with nine consecutive hits
Best Pitcher: John Franco (28 saves)
Best Hitter: Lance Johnson (.333 BA, 227 hits, 21 triples)
Home Attendance: 1,588,323

Lance Johnson (Joe Robbins Photos)

1997

88-74, 13.0 GB, 3rd in NL East
Manager: Bobby Valentine

Postseason Record: No postseason play
Important Firsts: Mets and Yankees clash in regular-season play with three-game June series at Yankee Stadium as MLB launches interleague play for first time ever
League Leaders: None
Memorable Moments: Mets tie Atlanta Braves for second-best home record (50-31) in all of baseball; team posts year's top total (47) of come-from-behind wins, including 9-6, 11-inning win over Montreal (September 13) after trailing 6-0 in ninth; Todd Hundley becomes third Met to post 30-plus homers in back-to-back seasons; Mets crack 11 pinch-hit homers to lead majors; John Franco becomes career NL saves king (359, for fourth on all-time list); Steve Phillips replaces Joe McIlvaine as GM at mid-season
Awards: Rey Ordoñez (SS Gold Glove)
Best Pitchers: Rick Reed (2.89 ERA) and John Franco (36 saves)
Best Hitter: Edgardo Alfonzo (.315 BA, 163 hits)
Home Attendance: 1,766,174

Rick Reed (Joe Robbins Photos)

1998

88-74, 18.0 GB, 2nd in NL East
Manager: Bobby Valentine

Postseason Record: No postseason play

Important Firsts: Mets face Yankees for first time in regular season at Shea Stadium during second season of MLB interleague play

League Leaders: None

Memorable Moments: Opening-day 14-inning victory over Phillies represents longest season opener in majors since 1919; Mets and Yankees both play home games at Shea on April 15 due to structural damage at Yankee Stadium; John Olerud posts highest single-season BA (.354) in franchise history; Mike Piazza acquired from Florida Marlins (May 22) in stunning trade; John Olerud posts 23-game hitting streak during July and August; John Franco moves into second place on all-time major league saves list; Turk Wendell's nine consecutive appearances out of the bullpen in late September sets team record; Mets fall single game shy of NL wild-card postseason berth

Awards: Rey Ordoñez (SS Gold Glove)

Best Pitchers: Al Leiter (17-6, 2.47 ERA) and John Franco (38 Saves)

Best Hitter: John Olerud (.354 BA, second in National League)

Home Attendance: 2,287,942

John Olerud (Joe Robbins Photos)

1999

97-66, 7.0 GB, NATIONAL LEAGUE WILD CARD
Manager: Bobby Valentine

Postseason Record: Defeat Arizona Diamondbacks (3-1) in NL Divisional Series; lose to Altanta Braves (2-4) in NLCS

Important Firsts: Mets earn their first National League wild-card postseason berth

League Leaders: None

Memorable Moments: Consecutive-game homers by Mike Piazza in mid-July spark two straight wins over crosstown rival Yankees; new single-season individual team offensive marks established in runs scored (Alfonzo); RBIs (Piazza), steals (Roger Cedeño), walks (Olerud), games played (Olerud); Mets win NL wild card in one-game playoff against Cincinnati Reds on Al Leiter's two-hit 5-0 whitewashing

Awards: Rey Ordoñez (SS Gold Glove); Robin Ventura (3B Gold Glove)

Best Pitcher: Al Leiter (13-12, 4.23 ERA)

Best Hitter: Roger Cedeño (.313 BA; 66 stolen bases, second in National League)

Home Attendance: 2,725,920

Roger Cedeño (Joe Robbins Photos)

Allen, Maury. *The Incredible Mets.* New York: Coronet Communications (Paperback Library), 1969.

Aronstein, Mark (Ed.). Daily News *Scrapbook History of the New York Mets' 1986 Season.* New York: *New York Daily News,* 1987.

Bock, Duncan, and John Jordan. *The Complete Year-by-Year N.Y. Mets Fan's Almanac.* New York: Crown Publishers, 1992.

Breslin, Jimmy (Introduction by Dick Schaap). *Can't Anybody Here Play This Game? The Hilarious Saga of the Amazin' Mets' First Season.* New York: Penguin Books (Penguin Sports Library), 1982 (originally published in 1963 by The Viking Press).

Cohen, Stanley. *A Magic Summer: The '69 Mets.* New York and London: Harcourt Brace Jovanovich, 1988.

Durso, Joseph. *Amazing: The Miracle of the Mets.* Boston: Houghton Mifflin Company Publishers, 1970.

Editors of the *New York Daily News. Amazing Mets: The Miracle of '69.* Champaign, Illinois: Sports Publishing, 1999.

Fox, Larry (Foreword by Lindsey Nelson). *Last to First: The Story of the Mets.* New York: Harper and Row Publishers, 1970.

Gutman, Bill. *Baseball's Great Dynasties: The Mets.* New York: W.H. Smith Publishers (Gallery Books) and Brompton Books, 1991.

Honig, Donald. *The New York Mets: The First Quarter Century (The Official 25th Anniversary Book).* New York: Crown Publishers, 1986.

Johnson, Davey (with Peter Golenbock). *Bats: The Man Behind the Miracle.* New York: G.P. Putnam's Sons, 1986 (New York: Bantam Books, 1987).

Jones, Cleon (with Ed Hershey). *The Life Story of the One and Only Cleon.* New York: Coward-McCann Publishers, 1970.

Kalinsky, George (with text by Jon Scher). *The New York Mets: A Photographic History.* New York: Macmillan Publishers, 1995.

Koppett, Leonard. *The New York Mets: The Whole Story.* New York and London: Collier-Macmillan, 1970.

Mitchell, Jerry (with cartoons by Willard Mullin). *The Amazing Mets.* New York: Grosset and Dunlap Publishers, 1970.

Oppenheimer, Joel. *The Wrong Season.* Indianapolis: The Bobbs-Merrill Company, 1973 (New York: Award Books, 1973).

Vecsey, George. *Joy in Mudville: Being a Complete Account of the Unparalleled History of the New York Mets from Their Most Perturbed Beginnings to Their Amazing Rise to Glory and Renown.* New York: The McCall Publishing Company, 1970.

Zimmerman, Paul D., and Dick Schaap. *The Year the Mets Lost Last Place.* New York and Cleveland: The World Publishing Company, 1969.

Zimmerman, Paul D., and Dick Schaap. *The Year the Mets Lost Last Place: The Most Amazing Year in the History of Baseball.* New York: The New American Library (Signet), 1969.